FROM PLANET EARTH
A CRY FOR JUSTICE
A CRY FOR PEACE

ALEX SALIBA, M.D.

Note for Librarians: A cataloguing record for this book is available from Library and Archives Canada at www.collectionscanada.ca/amicus/index-e.html
ISBN 1-4120-8973-5

Printed on paper with minimum 30% recycled fibre.
Trafford's print shop runs on "green energy" from solar, wind and other environmentally-friendly power sources.

TRAFFORD
PUBLISHING™
Offices in Canada, USA, Ireland and UK

Book sales for North America and international:
Trafford Publishing, 6E–2333 Government St.,
Victoria, BC V8T 4P4 CANADA
phone 250 383 6864 (toll-free 1 888 232 4444)
fax 250 383 6804; email to orders@trafford.com
Book sales in Europe:
Trafford Publishing (UK) Limited, 9 Park End Street, 2nd Floor
Oxford, UK OX1 1HH UNITED KINGDOM
phone 44 (0)1865 722 113 (local rate 0845 230 9601)
facsimile 44 (0)1865 722 868; info.uk@trafford.com
Order online at:
trafford.com/06-0729

10 9 8 7 6 5 4 3

REFLECTION

This is taken from material provided at a local church in Malta

It was late spring and the buds still refused to open
Lightly wrapped up in themselves, they were as hard as stones.
The wind shook them. The hail beat them.
The frost squeezed them in a fist of iron.
All three shouted: 'Open up, Open up'!
Instead of opening up, the buds reinforced their shells,
And retreated, even more deeply, into themselves.
Then along came the sun,
It issued no threats, and made no demands.
It just created a more, friendly, climate.
And what happened?
Almost overnight, the buds began to soften and expand.
Then their shells cracked, and they burst out.
If you love, you are gentle.
And there are certain tasks, which only gentleness, can accomplish.

Because we have all been a witness, to so much violence in wars, and other types of violence; because of so many abuses in our society, corruption in governments and corporations; neglect of hunger, and poverty, and rampant disease, amongst our brothers, and sisters; and there is so much destruction, of the environment. And, because we are now living, in an increasingly, troubled, world-----because of all this, as well as the potential for unfathomable beauty, all around us, it behooves our leaders, and all citizens on this planet, the mighty and the lowly, the rich and the poor, to take the above reflection to heart, to change the course of evil, for good, to change history---!

The above reflection suggests, that, we can achieve far greater results, with love, with gentleness, with thoughtfulness, with consideration and peace; that we need to put our words into actions, to truly nurture, and protect our environment; and, to look out for our brothers, and sisters, wherever they are, on this earth.

Acknowledgements

I wish to recognize a number of friends, who have offered me assistance, in one form, or another, in the preparation of this material. My deepest thanks go to the following:

To my dearest wife, Maureen, for, her continued, patience, and understanding, as I was going through numerous papers, magazine articles, etc.; and for her suggestions, as she reviewed these chapters. Without the support of, 'our other half', such projects are not, easily, accomplished.

To Dr. and Mrs. L. Pacini, of Florida, for their support, and in memory of Luigi, a close friend, who has since, died.

To Professor Frank Vella, of Canada, for encouragement, and other suggestions along the way; and material provided.

To Dr. Raphael Attard, of Great Britain, for his opinion, and comments, and materials provided.

To Mr. R. Weisenberger, of Switzerland, for his comments, and for bringing some important, reports, to my attention.

To Dr. Walter Delia, of Malta, for suggestions, and for providing material to be used, in this book.

To Rev. Fr. Frank Grech S.J., of Malta, for his encouragement, and for many comments he made during this process. Fr. Frank is our cousin, and is also a physician.

To our dear daughter, Theresa, for her artistic talents, in the composite paintings, as presented, on the front, and back, of this book cover. In her love of nature, (S.S. Originals), Theresa, has painted all types of natural wonders, including, wildlife in our oceans, and in forests, or on the African plains, thus, focusing our attention, on many endangered species. We are reminded, once more, of man's activities, on planet earth.

I am also grateful, for many presentations, debates, and articles, by various experts, lecturers, and journalists; and for comments by average citizens, who provided relevant, and sometimes, controversial, topics, for discussion, throughout these pages.

CONTENTS

The following is a presentation, and a discussion, of political, and social, issues, in different parts of our world. As the United States has been the principal protagonist on the Iraq war, updated reports on the perceived, chaos, persisting in that country, will be outlined. That topic has been discussed, over, and over, by many thinkers. Opinions from all over the world, but also, from the majority of Iraqis, indeed, suggest that, since the US occupation, chaos everywhere, has ruled, in Iraq. Because of recent events, at home, and overseas, America's policies will feature prominently, so that people in all walks of life may analyze, and debate.

However, as suggested in "Mirror Reflections = =Mirages", our society desperately, needs, many leaders who are honest, and who are willing to invest time, and resources, *in dialogue, and in finding common ground, and much less time in confrontation, and in useless, tragic, or immoral, wars.* Thus, according to commentators, there are ongoing, behind the scenes, discussions, between US officials, and insurgents, in Iraq. This is, as it should be, and, it is commendable. But, for political gain and, for public consumption, authorities, in the US, UK, and other countries, *have often stated that, they 'do not have dialogue with terrorists, or insurgents'!* Such double talk, and disparity, between words and actions, and manipulation of people, or facts, in that manner, serves no purpose, and should be universally condemned. In recent years, we had heard similar comments from officials in several countries, but especially America, and Israel, that they would never hold discussions with certain groups, for example, in the Middle East. *That is often a demonstration of poor leadership qualities.*

In that previous book we also referred to the stigma of persisting racism, and discrimination, in parts of the world; but then, in 2005, came hurricane, Katrina, that struck a vicious blow at parts of the southern coast of the US. That word 'racism', but also 'discrimination', surfaced immediately, as critics, and most people, *accused the Bush administration of failure to lead, failure to act properly, in a real (not imaginary) emergency!* We also commented, in that book, on a special commission that, was supposed to investigate the events that led to the Iraq war. Apparently the results of these investigations were *ordered withheld until after the 2004 presidential elections, in the US (was that to shield a president?).* Critics accused that it was purely for political traction, so that the incumbent republicans would not risk embarrassing discoveries.

In a similar fashion, in the US, the Bush administration had been facing many other investigations. These included, the 'White house leak' affair, under investigation by special prosecutor Fitzgerald. It has been in the news for well over a year. Once again, it was alleged that, the trials on Libby (the right hand man of Cheney), in connection with that leak, had been postponed to a date, much later than the 2006 elections! Critics again, made sarcastic remarks that, 'people in high places', in this American 'oligarchy', tried to make certain that republicans, facing re-election in 2006, had all the advantages, no matter how many rules needed bending! Then, in February 2006, there were reports that, the Libby defense team, had allegedly testified *that he had been told to divulge secret data by his boss! Are these revelations astounding, or what?*

Many have also debated, or written, on, the scandalous influence of money in American politics; how *Mammon* is ruling, supreme, over the American political scene, much more than in any other country; just as dictators *rule, supreme, over dictator states.* Except, this time, it is money, and the lobbying scandals that accompany the hundreds of millions, of dollars, that pour into US politics. There is yet, another, investigation, into lobbying activities in this country. Critics have already accused that these scandals penetrate into the halls of congress, but also deeply, in the Bush administration, itself. *Can anyone, in America, expect justice, on these scandals? Where, is, the arm, and the oversight, of congress? Are all the above examples, a clear demonstration, of a democracy on the brink?*

As reported by many, this US administration had orchestrated this Iraq quagmire, single handedly. But there have been other collaborators, such as, UK, Israel, former Iraqi expatriates, and other, lesser, players. *What did Americans, and what did most people know, about Iraq, in our march to war?* That was a form of introduction to the program, 'Now', on PBS, with David Broncaccio, and his guests. They presented recorded parts of Powell's speech, for the Bush administration, before the United Nations. That speech has since been ridiculed by many, both at home, and abroad; but Powell might have sensed pressure, 'from high up, the government ladder', to give such a speech. The more one reads, and hears, about the machinations in this Bush administration, the more sinister is the appearance, of some of their policies. Mr. Wilkerson was a guest on this program, and *he was a former Bush administration official. He surprised most of his audience by an amazing admission that (on Iraq), he had participated in a hoax, on the American people, on the United Nations, and on the international community! He felt terrible about that, he said!*

Experts have alleged that the Bush entourage had fabricated information to achieve their goals, to help them declare war! Mr. Kay, an American investigator on weapons, in Iraq, in the early days of the occupation, reportedly stated that, *he was embarrassed when he realized what 'fabricated minutiae', US officials had used, to accuse Iraq of possessing weapons of mass destruction, and to invade that country!* During this program guests also said that, US officials probably knew that much of the propaganda material they were pushing on the American people, **was false!** Americans, everywhere, must remember that, these are statements coming from former officials in this government!

They also suggested that, Bush officials, reportedly, relied on information supplied by a captured, Al Qaeda, operative, who had spilled such details, perhaps, under torture, in Egypt? The ugliness of these perceived plots, becomes more sinister, when we hear that as investigations into these government scandals become more intense, officials keep on leaking certain, bits of information, to the public, to distract the attention of Americans, even though such information, supposedly, had previously been 'top secret'. Thus, as the investigation into the 'White house leak', got closer to Cheney, and to the White house itself, lo, and behold, *we suddenly heard of spying activities on American citizens, by this government! Was it by accident that such information was not given out, before?*

Many have since announced that the manner in which such spying was carried out was illegal; and reportedly, early in 2006, the American Bar Association, also stated that Bush had probably acted outside the law. How did Bush officials react? Why, naturally, to try to justify their spying, they allegedly, announced, how they had foiled a terrorist plot, *in 2002, mind you,* to attack the tallest building in Los Angeles, trying to inflict casualties. That certainly might be true, but *for many cynics it might be just another game, of tricks. If it happened in 2002, why would Bush officials agree to its release now, in 2006, just when the administration, was being criticized from all sides, for activities that may have been outside legal boundaries?*

Several, obvious, questions come to mind, of interest to both the American people, and to the world community:

1.Will American officials, now, justify, attacking, and invading, another country, causing destruction, and thousands of deaths, of the innocent, on the basis of fabrications; or on questionable information, given by a prisoner, who might have been subjected to abuse, or torture? *And, are these officials preaching to the American people, **about values?***

2. Are the congress, and the justice system, in the US, so paralyzed that nobody seems capable, of uncovering the truth, in all the scandals we read about, and present it to the world?

Hans Blix of the UN had informed the Bush administration that, his investigators had checked out areas in Iraq, identified by US officials, as concealing prohibited weapons, *and they found absolutely nothing there, that was threatening to the US, or that Iraq was connected to Al Qaeda!* Reports on US preconceived plans to invade Iraq, now include the famous memo from government offices in London- - -!

3. In America, are people, of power, often, above the law, so that nobody can conduct an impartial, thorough, investigation, into these matters?

4. And, in America, if there are officials who had participated in a hoax, or in deceit, resulting in illegal activities, or in an unjust war, or whatever, are they often rewarded with medals, with promotions, or with teaching positions in universities? Is that going on, here, in "our democracy"? Is it going on in all countries, developed, or, underdeveloped?

In 2006, CBS news also featured more disturbing reports, on corruption activities, in the US handling of the Iraq messy, situation. They alleged that billions (with a 'B') of dollars that, were given to contractors, for projects in Iraq, *were unaccounted for!* This money, did not belong to the government, to be squandered, it was tax money that belonged to the American people. They stated that 'people simply carried away loads of dollars in wheelbarrows, or in sacks'; and, under present US government policies, some contractors landed 100 million dollar contracts, even though they were thoroughly incompetent, and deceitful. Guess what? They still continued to work for this US administration, these reports alleged. A few individuals had been accused of bribery and corruption; but the amount of contract, money that was, unaccounted for, had already, reached, about 8 billion dollars. To most people with common sense, these revelations, coming one, after another, must raise many, serious questions, about this form of US government.

In early 2006 we witnessed Palestinian elections, intensely touted by this US administration. *They were, closely, monitored, by the international community, and the Hamas, group, won an overwhelming victory.* Some critics claimed that it was a type of 'slap in your face', response, to the US, and Israel, because of the longstanding fighting, and instability, in the region, and the suffering of the Palestinian people. In February 2006, news agencies reported that, the US, and Israeli, governments, would not accept Hamas, as the truly elected government, of the Palestinians. It was true that, those officials had stated that, Hamas, must first renounce violence, and must accept the state of Israel, to live in peace, side by side, with an independent Palestinian state. However, the US, Israel, and Palestinian representatives, had never been able to reach an accord on very important issues, such as, *those numerous Jewish settlements on Palestinian land, the specific boundaries for a Palestinian state, and on the status of Jerusalem.*

We could pose a relevant question for sensible people, in America, and the rest of the world, to ponder. What definition of 'democracy', do the Bush administration, and Israeli, government officials, choose to follow, with regard to the Palestinian impasse? Or are they simply opportunists, and change their own definition of democracy, from week, to week from month, to month? Under American domination, and continued pressure from 'Washington', Iraq has had multiple elections within a short period; the governing body there, has almost become a farce, as they have not been free to make their own decisions. There is little doubt that, the ideal of 'democracy', for Iraq, is laudable, but according to many experts the future for Iraq looks bleak, indeed, because of the imprint of a United States boot.

Let us reflect on that word, 'democracy'. An example of domestic 'democracy' was thrust upon us in February 2006, when vice president Cheney, of the US, accidentally shot his friend during a hunting trip, hitting him in the face and chest. However, what is relevant, here, is that, news reports alleged that, law enforcement officials did not react the way they would have reacted, if it had been another American citizen, in that predicament. The Bush administration was accused of continuing on its path of intense secrecy, as it had been doing all along, and no reports were given to the press initially, and the story was muddied a great deal. It was pointed out that in such accidents, other US citizens, and all witnesses, would have been interviewed, and investigated, promptly, and the scene of the incident would have been scrutinized as well (not many hours later, when people had plenty of time to compare stories, they said). But, reportedly, law officials had acted quite differently, for a vice president, why? Is such behavior consistent with a 'democracy', or an autocracy?

And, on a different story, a United Nations report, in February, called for the closure of the US prison at Guantanamo (Cuba), as it was essentially a 'torture facility'. Such, allegations, on the torture of prisoners, had also been made by many, human rights, groups, in the past. US officials denied those accusations; and here, again, as a reflection of our bizarre 'democracy', those reports were rejected by the Bush administration. That is fine, except that US officials *should no longer claim to be able to show other countries, the way to true democracy.* As we continue to hear of scandals in government, it becomes obvious that both in America, and in other countries, the meaning, and value, of democracy, had been forgotten.

United States senator, R. Byrd, spoke before the senate on the spying scandals in the US, pointing out how this republican administration had traumatized the people of this country, and many in congress (can we add, and the rest of the world?); and how some members of congress had implied that, if this president had acted outside the law, 'then, perhaps, we should change those laws'. *That is amazing!* Is that the caliber of politician we need in our world, today? You do not change the law in such situations, but you demand immediate, impartial, complete, investigation, and an attempt to achieve some form of balanced (not corrupt), justice.

On the PBS program, 'Now', with Broncaccio, they discussed how Bush talked about reforming 'pork' projects in the US congress, but his inaction was louder than his words. For example they showed that republican president Reagan, had vetoed bills with gross 'pork' projects in them, whereas, president Bush had vetoed none! Other shady tactics were presented, such as, a senator who had stopped a bill in the defense budget, to shield pharmaceutical companies from lawsuits; but that, the senator had also received many thousands of dollars, in campaign donations, from that same industry. You might ask, what has the pharmaceutical industry to do, with a defense budget bill? Ah, those must be the quirks of political machinations, going on in most countries, apparently? In America, there have been some members of congress, who have genuinely tried to reform the corrupt system, the influence of money, but they have usually been voted down!

On the above TV program, they continued to discuss how thousands of these 'pork' projects were regularly slipped into important bills, in congress, often in the middle of the night, sometimes before a period of recess, so that no member of congress had time to review that legislation, before it was passed! Under this republican administration, reportedly, these pork allocations had mushroomed to over 27 billion dollars (that is with a 'B', of taxpayers', hard earned, money). *A few examples mentioned were, money for a dog kennel, for a teapot museum, for an indoor rainforest, for a bridge to nowhere, and on, and on, and on.*

With all this, the US government could not find sufficient funds, to prevent a disaster like "Katrina", or to provide prompt assistance, and relief, to thousands of unfortunate victims of that destructive hurricane. On news, and talk, shows, everybody seems to talk about the corruption of money in the halls of congress, of the United States. Thus, many have called the Abramoff scandals the 'tip of the iceberg'; and most educated people know only too well, *what lies beneath the surface of an iceberg- - -!*

With all these revelations, and allegations of corruption, in the system of government, in America, do we need to consume ourselves with possible corruption in the UN, or in the governments of China, the former Soviet Union, N. Korea, Syria, Egypt, African nations, the Palestinian authority, and more. Yes, they have plenty of corruption in these countries, but firstly, should we not study our own reflection, in the mirror?

As regards the Palestinian elections, reports from the United Nations, and from the Carter center, were unanimous that, those elections were fair, free, and democratic. What did people in the Bush administration want, perhaps, not a true democracy? Would they rather produce another form of dictatorship? It was alleged that they were conniving another election in the Palestinian regions; and if they did not result in candidates, approved by the US, then another, and another! Many have claimed, that, is a recipe, for disaster. Is it that Washington officials, can only accept an election result, if the elected members are prepared to bow down before America's demands, to be in total agreement with the United States government? *Most sensible people know what that is, it certainly is not democracy- - -! It is akin to imperialism, all over again!* Did we witness another debacle in elections in 2006? Yes, in elections in the troubled country of Haiti, again, the winning faction, there, was not what the US had hoped for. Will pundits in Washington attempt to topple them, as well?

In February, Iraq's prime minister, after a meeting with Britain's foreign secretary, strongly suggested that, the US, and Britain, ***should stop interfering in Iraq's politics, in the formation of its government!*** Most people around the world had sensed for some time, that, this US government had been domineering, controlling, and interfering, in the affairs of Iraq, in spite of the propaganda of "free elections". Also, reports continued to reaffirm that the Bush administration has been negotiating with Iraqi insurgents, because they knew perfectly well that, without the cooperation of factions of insurgents, *there would be no peace and democracy, in Iraq!* And many critics have stated that failure in Iraq, would amount to a form of defiant response, to the policies of the Bush government. According to most world experts, *the United States was losing the fight to try to win the* hearts and minds, of the Iraqi people. In a poll on the Internet, a full 70% answered that the US should leave the Iraqi people alone, to form their own government! *Is that not what democracy is all about?* Did the Bush administration tell the Iraqi people that, they invaded their country, and removed S. Hussein, to bring them democracy? Or was it, once more, to seize Iraq's oil, as many thinkers around the world, had believed?

In 2006 we also had the publication of cartoons satirizing the prophet, Muhammad, and millions of Muslims saw that, as an insult, and a provocation. It resulted in rioting, and much violence, in many countries. A Vatican cardinal criticized the publication of those cartoons, and the growing trend to make fun of religious symbols, in general. Destruction of life, and property, cannot be justified, but religious provocation should not be condoned, either.

It is true that we must value, and protect, freedom of speech, and freedom of expression. However, with that freedom must also, come, a deep sense of responsibility. Insulting the religious sentiments of a segment of our society, shows disregard of such sentiments, and should not be acceptable. We do not need censorship; what we need is, to exercise a high degree of self discipline in the day, to day, practice of our freedoms. In the following chapters, we have also touched upon, religious intolerance. In a recent 'America' magazine, writers referred to a priest murdered in Turkey; a Hindu mob attacking a bishop in India; we have witnessed religious disputes in Iraq, in Iran, in Lebanon, and in Saudi Arabia; and Christian patriarchs had informed the new Palestinian leaders that they would extend their cooperation, but they wanted full religious freedom; and we had vandalism of churches, mosques, and synagogues. *Yes, even today, religious intolerance, and discrimination, persists worldwide. That is regrettable, and we need to remind ourselves that, if we truly believe in freedom, and democracy, then, people should be free to nurture their beliefs, and practice their faith.* We are not talking about cults that can be anti-social in character, and harmful to society.

Leaders of nations, and government officials, in general, in any country, cannot possibly, *talk of values, of morality, of human rights, of freedom and democracy, and be believable, and trustworthy,* if, at the same time, they embark on preemptive wars; on kidnappings of innocent people, or 'suspects', for rough interrogation, through 'rendition'; on the abuse and torture of prisoners; on spying on citizens, at home, or abroad, without due cause, or due process of law; on the practice of nepotism, bribery, and corruption, and the excessive influence of money on the running of government institutions, or on the electoral process.

On the question of social justice, many writers have highlighted the widening gap, and inequality, between the 'haves', and the 'have not'. That topic is also discussed in these pages, not only as it refers to nations of the 'west', or as a contrast, between the richer, developed, countries, and the poorer, third world, countries. No, it refers also, to the 'haves', and the 'have not', in India, Pakistan, China, former Soviet Union countries, in Latin America, and the Middle East. And, yes, it refers also, to Africa; most African countries are extremely poor, but there, too, we find much social disparity between those 'who have', the ruling class, and those who 'do not have', the masses, who are ruled, and sometimes, are also oppressed, as happens in many dictator states.

A comment by Fr. John Burger, in Columban Mission, magazine, was noteworthy. He was discussing the passion of the Church, for justice. He said that, "Injustice, and poverty, rarely come about only by misfortune, or by accident. *They are precipitated by structural problems such as, corruption in society, or the gross misuse of political, and economic, power". That statement applies so well, to what is presented in this book!* In the February 2006 disaster, in the Philippines, where mudslides entombed a village, with hundreds of people trapped underneath, we witnessed, once again, an outpouring of humanitarian assistance. The United States government promptly dispatched military personnel, and equipment, to assist, to search for victims, and try to save lives. Many have recommended that those who are well, off, show greater acts, of charity, love, kindness, and altruism, towards those who are in need, and suffer. If politicians, everywhere, continue to focus on such humanitarian assistance, to countries in need, we would not have to be concerned with terrorist attacks, against the 'west', or elsewhere.

No sooner had the section on inter-religious intolerance, and strife, on the previous page, been completed, when, on February 22, 2006, news reports overflowed with comments, about the bombing of a Holy shrine in Iraq, and the subsequent bombing of several other mosques, in retaliation. This was another sad, tragic, day, for Iraq, and for the US. Once again, these events focused our attention on the concerns of Pope John Paul II, *when he told the Bush administration that, if they stayed on course, and attacked Iraq, it could result in terrible consequences!* Some experts had suggested that this increased sectarian violence had brought that country to the brink of civil war! And many, had viewed this, as a direct consequence of US government bungling, and obsession with, S. Hussein; when any disagreements, and false assumptions, by the Bush administration, could have easily, been handled, by the UN, without an invasion, and occupation, of Iraq.

For several thousand years, people worldwide, were accustomed to being under the boot of their rulers, be they monarchs, emperors, sheikhs, autocrats, plutocrats, dictators, or the barbaric tyrants of old. Then came the birth of America, when a group of people rebelled against the unjust dictates of the English king. They believed in a better life for the people in these States, in the New World. They believed that, "all men are created equal, and that they are endowed by their Creator with certain unalienable Rights; that among these are Life, Liberty, and the Pursuit of Happiness" - - -the Declaration of Independence. *"That whenever any form of government becomes destructive of these ends, it is the right of the people to alter, and abolish it".* These sentiments in the Declaration were not unique, as the English had used similar thoughts for their revolution against a 'tyrant'; and before the revolution, in France, thinkers had concluded that, *a ruler should be permitted to rule only through an agreement with the people!* We have strayed far from those concepts, and, surely, we must get back, on the right track.

February also brought us the winter Olympic games from 'Torino', Italy. It reminded us how in past years, men, and women, from many countries, competed in various sports events, setting differences, culture, and politics, aside. Yes, rivalry existed in the past, it still does. But some of the participants developed camaraderie, beautiful, lasting, friendships, and even closer relationships. In recent years sports assemblies had been marred by the intrusion of politics, in the games themselves; by the influence of money; in the judging of contests; and by individual national groups wanting to win more medals than any other group, perhaps, no matter what; and then, there was the use of performance enhancing drugs, by the athletes. In spite of all that, the venues of sports have always been a welcome respite from the struggles of humanity. At such gatherings, groups of athletes, and their families, from many parts of the world, were able to overcome untold hardships, just 'to get there, and be able to take part'! They bridged over many misunderstandings, and sometimes, opposing ideologies. *Do we not need politicians, all over the world, to be more like them?*

In the following pages, let us, together, embark on a journey, an arduous one, to identify, some of the problems, and *search for answers to many difficulties, facing all humanity, on planet earth.*

I

INTRODUCTION

It was French Philosopher Diderot who observed that we cannot look on the sheer beauty of a butterfly, a butterfly's wing, and not acknowledge the existence of God. Over the years scientists had written about the beauty and complexity of Mother Nature, and the wonders and vastness of the Universe, through the naked eye, or binoculars, or telescopes, and more recently the amazing Space photography from the Hubble telescope. We could glance at a myriad twinkling stars, planets, galaxies, comets, nebulae and much more. Others have commented on the complexities of cells under the microscope, plants, the beauty of pristine forests, coral reefs in the oceans, and so much more. All of it awe inspiring, and they often described how all these things induced one to conclude that there must be a Supreme Being holding all together. Others hold to the theory that it is all part of the process of evolution, over millennia of selection and adaptation.

We will now fast forward to the 21st century, and we have a commentary by Brian Fanelli "US Politics in a Galaxy far, far away". This analyzes the latest Lucas movie, how it was awash in political meaning, much of it applicable to what is going on today, with one party controlling the administration and congress in America (republicans); and, the same could apply to any other country. And one gathers from all this that what is happening is not good for our people, for the country, or for our world.

There was another movie with a powerful message "The Day the Earth Stood Still". The gist of that story follows: A spaceship lands in the US, and an alien appears at the door of the craft, as a humanoid in a space suit. Instead of a peaceful welcome, he is faced with an army of soldiers, machine guns, tanks and all types of weaponry. They were ready for a confrontation, or so they thought. The alien looks on at that scene, and walks towards the crowd, soon there was shooting and he is wounded, is taken to hospital but manages to escape. After this act of aggression, a giant robot appears at the spacecraft entrance, he surveyed the scene, as his laser beams focused on that military might. When he let go, guns, rifles, soldiers, even tanks, vanished into thin air. Military personnel could do nothing but gawk in awe, a military armada faced down by a single robot.

We assume that those leaders thought they would be attacked, that they would seize that superb technology that the world did not possess, and they would prevail. The alien survived through the intervention of the robot, then he lectured the earthlings thus: Where he came from, they too had seen violence and many wars; but in their wisdom leaders of other worlds decided to create an army of sophisticated robots such as the one accompanying him. These were programmed to destroy anyone and any planet planning on any form of aggression or war. They had enjoyed peace and harmony ever since because nobody was capable of altering the programming of those robots, once installed. He warned earth leaders that they had a choice, to cease their warmongering and adopt peace, or the interstellar army of robots would annihilate them as they had become a threat to the goal of peace in the universe. This is paraphrased somewhat but it relates to events in our world, with constant friction and wars between nations over many years.

Another old movie dealt with confrontation between the US and a North African nation. One scene showed a former US president telling another official "their fate rests in my hands, and I will decide by tomorrow". He was referring to actions the US would take against that nation. Such statements and descriptions as in these movies, do seem to portray what often goes on in the international arena, belligerence and arrogance that never seem to end, *and we wonder why our planet has been beset by so many tragic events throughout its history.*

The US and a few other countries have the capacity to help solve difficulties faced by so many around the world. America is a vast, multi-ethnic nation, with a people endowed with energy, with a wealth of resources, advanced in technology, and riches beyond comparison. True, that wealth has often been misapplied, and much of it is simply squandered. But we could become a beacon not only to show the way to proper democracy, and freer societies, but also a way to overcome hardships, for those who are burdened to come for help. Such an attitude by some nations could change our world beyond comprehension.

Although this book describes much ugliness in our world, most often the result of man's misguided actions, we need to keep focused on that ugliness simply because if we refuse to do so, humans are apt to repeat mistakes over, and over. In spite of all that there is much beauty and serenity in nature, all around us, if we cared to look and nurture it. The jungles and forests with their varied echo-systems are still teaching us to this day; and the amazing number and variety of plant and animal life is cause for reflection. If we look at the insect world, all types of animals, at the oceans, flowers and the trees, at the birds in the sky, we cannot but wonder at this awesome nature that surrounds us. Did all of this happen by accident? Hardly. Those who have studied and worked closely with, gorillas, chimpanzees, birds, porpoises, whales, household pets, and more, can tell you how much these creatures can associate and understand. Others will state that there is no intelligence there, yet others, will dispute that. Take the example of a simple budgie in the home. If you spend enough time with them they get to understand your requests very well, they give love, they practically talk to you, but not in so many words. And what about man's best friend? Not enough can be said about these, there are not enough words to describe the wonderful relationship of dogs to humans. There have been many stories, books, and movies, about these beloved pets.

Previously we had reported on the aggressive stance of some officials, and the continuing efforts of the US to militarize the Cosmos, besides the accumulation of more, and more weaponry, yes, weapons of mass destruction. Now, Russian officials have announced that because of the US administration's star wars program, they would not discuss tactical nuclear weapons control with any nation that deployed such weapons in outer space. That was obviously aimed at the US. That is how serious US officials, and the weapons industry, have been, in their discussions on the worldwide control or eradication of weapons of mass destruction. What they wanted was to control them for other countries but never for themselves. If that is how we want to achieve world peace we still have to learn to do much better. We have a long road ahead of us.

Now, consider some of the recent worrisome headlines, as most of these refer to America, but they could equally apply to other developed or underdeveloped, countries.
'The greatest Democracy that money can buy'
'The buying of the president-2004'
'Outsourcing the Pentagon'-the military
'Prescription for Power'—an army of lobbyists for drug makers ensures their legislative dominance.
'A Nation of Pharisees-A Nation of Hypocrites'-referring to the US
'A Cry for Freedom in the US Senate'—In this speech US senator Robert Byrd reminded us that many had written of what could happen if men without the courage of their convictions, simply sat back and let themselves be swept away by a powerful majority. And then he quoted Orwell, on Liberty: "If it means anything at all, it means the right to tell people what they do not want to hear".

About mid-April 2005, Marla Rutzicka, an American activist, was killed in a roadside bomb explosion in Iraq, a tragedy. She had fought for help for innocent people in Iraq and in Afghanistan, injured or killed, by US or coalition forces, or who were caught in the crossfire between insurgents and our forces. A CNN commentator said that *she had done more good for the people of Iraq, on behalf of 'we the American people'*, than all the politicians, diplomats, generals, soldiers, and other emissaries, put together. All these others had been filling our screens with propaganda and rumors, about the good the US government had done in these countries! She had done much more. When members of the US media, had the guts, to talk to the average citizens in those countries, they heard completely different stories, more like those recorded by foreign news media.

In this connection there was a piece on the Internet, that "Politics is supposed to be the second oldest profession, I have come to believe it bears a very close resemblance to the first-----". In 2005 there were disturbing revelations about activities by US authorities that many called illegal. As if we needed to hear more bad news, after what has gone on in the past few years, the economy, record deficits, the falling dollar, health care, and the chaos of Iraq. These scandals too have an impact on our global family.
One dealt with the US government *keeping a secret fleet of aircraft, without markings that could easily identify them*. Allegedly, these were used by US secret service agents, to seize so called 'suspects' in other countries, and transport them to secret prisons in third world countries, for interrogation (for most, that meant torture). They would be kept out of the jurisdiction of US courts. Countries receiving such prisoners were listed as Egypt, Morocco, Pakistan, Turkey, Uzbekistan, even Syria, and where else? Yet, another dark side of the US political system, this so called 'democracy'. In June 2005 Italy ordered the arrest of 13 alleged agents of the CIA, a US secret agency; they were suspected of helping in the seizure of an Egyptian imam, in the streets of Milan, in 2003. Prosecutors

believed it was the CIA plan, to be able to take such suspects without court orders or due process. Italian authorities accused that this was against international laws, but we have been told before that the US recognizes no international laws.

Another report dealt with the 'Economist Terrorists', as some had labeled them, special agents of the US government, who would visit leaders in underdeveloped countries, and tempt them with offers of financial aid, to build their infrastructure projects such as dams, power plants, roads and so on. Most of the projects, were completed by personnel provided by US corporations, and these countries were then heavily indebted to America. After a period these 'hit men' US agents, would again visit the leaders in those countries to discuss repayment of that debt. It was alleged that they informed those leaders that they could ease the debt burden *by voting with the US on such and such a motion before the UN; and with their granting territory in their country for US military bases to be located there!* Are such reports true? Is this what the stature of the US has fallen to? If true, is it any wonder that we are so resented and held in disdain, by people everywhere. It would be another example of glaring imperialism, of bribery, blackmail, and rampant corruption. It is also an example of America practicing another form of slavery, is it not? Such activities are not for 'national security', they are considered illegal and immoral by most nationalities. In recent months we have been assailed by speeches from some officials, on values, justice, and on freedoms. Surely, it is this, and not what some pundits have called, envy of lifestyle, which has caused so much hatred, and so much upheaval, in different parts of our world. Americans have suffered the consequences of a system run amok! Readers may think these are just idle rumors, but in August 2005 the president of Paraguay issued a statement denying that he was planning on having an American military base in his country. Why would he need to issue such a denial according to news reports? Is this more of our imperialism at work?

There were more disturbing headlines such as, 'Islam under Siege', 'Bush and Iraq: mass media, mass ignorance', 'The environment is in trouble, and the religious right does not care', the latter from Bill Moyers, renowned journalist, who received the Harvard medical school annual Global Environment Citizen Award. And from British papers came these: 'Fiddling while Baghdad burns', 'How to stop civil war'. 'Sunnis in crisis over Iraq constitution', 'Millions embezzled at Iraq ministry' (under US control and occupation), 'The lie behind the lie', referring to the start of the Iraq war. Then we had senator Robert Byrd's 'A Troubling Speech', referring to president Bush landing on that aircraft carrier, "war is not theatre, and victory is not a campaign slogan" Byrd said, and he continued, "Today I weep for my country"! Are Americans listening to these urgent messages being proclaimed in our country, and from around the world? Senator Byrd added, "Stopping a strike at the heart of the senate", "Reckless administration may reap disastrous consequences". He said that he could not help, but compare the description of the dignity of president Abraham Lincoln at Gettysburg, with the flamboyant showmanship of president Bush on that carrier, "The USS Abraham Lincoln". Those were powerful words by this great senator!

The cause for freedom championed by senator Byrd also brings to mind another old movie "Mr. Smith Goes to Washington", that is familiar especially to most older people. It was about a fictional young senator who fought against the forces of corruption in, or outside the government. This could have applied to any other country. He used the art of filibuster to deliver his message and achieve his goals in the senate. Byrd emphasized that democracy can flourish together with filibuster, how traditionally, the senate had always rejected limits placed on debates. That the senate was the watchdog, because majorities can be wrong, and filibuster can highlight injustices. He compared what the republicans were trying to do in this country, to dictator states, and there have been many others who have made similar comparisons, he is certainly not the first.

John Paul II, in his book 'The Pope Answers' quoted Gandhi, when he said, "Christ does not belong to Christianity alone, He belongs to all of us". Right! By perseverance and peaceful means Gandhi had advocated, he had helped topple the oppressive yolk of the British Empire. It was not considered oppressive by the British, but the Indian people argued that it was, as did most citizens under any form of imperial control—in Africa, Latin America, Middle East, Asia, etc. Present day humanity would be wise to consider history, because some fundamentalist Christians have been criticized as being extreme in their thinking. Many statements by the late Pope are so valuable in this day and age. Certain Christian leaders had been quoted as saying that Evangelical Christians have ready access to heaven, whereas many of the other faiths do not, unless they learn to accept Jesus. But in answer to questions, they were then forced to admit that nobody knows for certain God's mysterious ways. And, according to scripture, did not Jesus speak repeatedly against the teachings of some of the 'high priests', in those ancient times? Yes, that quotation from Gandhi could be directed at some of our preachers today.

Every so often, we have had great men and women appear on the world scene. Another quote from the Pope Answers, is from Albert Schweitzer, "I don't know what your destiny will be, but one thing I know: the only ones among you who will be really happy, are those who *have sought and found how to serve*". Then, we are also reminded of Martin Luther King in America's history, he courageously continued to push in the struggle of the black population against segregation, subjugation, and discrimination, that perfidious cancer in society. Some of it, not as glaringly obvious, or in the news, persists to this day. That famous song from the civil rights movement, 'We shall overcome, we shall overcome, some day', then resounded from the rooftops. M.L.King paid with his life, when he was murdered, as have been many other great leaders.

US representative Cynthia Mckinney from Georgia, spoke in congress lambasting the horrors of war, and the fact that businesses are permitted to profit from wars. Many around our world, expressed similar views, in disgust. She said when workers and CEOs, when generals and members of congress, earn only the same wages, as the soldiers in the trenches, then perhaps there will be no more war. Right! She presented large photographs that had been splashed worldwide on news media, of the gross abuse of prisoners at the hands of US armed forces personnel (and others reported by the British).

She stated that she had been strongly advised by leaders in congress, to maintain decorum in the chambers. Well, she asked, looking at these pictures "what are we doing, what are our leaders doing, and when are we going to stop it- - -"? This was a powerful presentation by this lady. How can these leaders in government talk of decorum, looking at photographs of what the US had done to Iraq, and what was done at Guantanamo, in the face of so many accusations leveled at this nation's leadership. Using decent sounding words like 'detainees', 'enemy combatant', 'rendition', and other forms of trash, will never camouflage or erase the evil perpetrated in certain quarters.

Another congressman Charles Rangel, reminded us that the Iraq war was the greatest fraud perpetrated on the American people. He compared it to the evil that had led to the killing of so many Jews in world war two. But then, we have heard many others in the past few years, both here and abroad, compare the US to the regimes of Stalin and Hitler, why? What a stigma indeed! Are we doing anything, to try remove even the slightest possibility that they may be right---?

With a view to the numerous revelations, vìs a vìs the status of our world today, and that of the US, presented in this book, and in a previous one, "Mirror Reflection= =Mirages", it is important to include another quote from 'The Pope Answers' by John Paul Two. It is by Rev. Fr. Pedro Arroyo, "Do not the thousands who are dying of hunger in India, Africa, Bangladesh, or Latin America, have more urgent need of bread, than we have of luxuries"? What a statement for wealthier, developed nations, for the world bank, and for the group of eight, to take to heart and do something, for once----! Not simply talk, and do nothing; or if they do something at least see to it, that the really needy people get it, not the elite in those regions, or our own corporations (Disaster Capitalism)!

Professor M. Mamdani discussed his book 'Good Muslim, Bad Muslim' on a C-Span TV program. He made several interesting points. He said that some thinkers in Muslim countries, and others, concluded that to move forward a State must resort to political violence, not unlike that adopted under former regimes in China, and the Soviet Union, and also in the previous Western countries, under colonialism. Quite a statement! Then, they began to identify 'good violence', and 'bad violence', our violence, their violence. How correct that was, as we tend to do the same today, good wars, bad wars, good dictators, bad dictators. Thus he said, most officials in America use 'good Muslim, bad Muslim', but they do not refer to their religion, Islam. Rather, they use good *to mean pro-American Muslim, and bad to mean anti-American Muslim, because in their view it is all centered about America!*

Can governments, can politicians, avoid confrontation, avoid threatening, belligerent speeches, so often used in recent years, by officials in the US, and North Korea, and others; that were much more common in the past with the former Soviet Union and China, when we in the West harshly condemned them for it. Can they do these things, work closely together, to achieve peace, justice, and harmony? Yes, they can. We have seen evidence that when disasters (the Tsunami, Katrina), an epidemic, earthquakes etc.

strike, people in many parts of the world try to help each other, across national boundaries. There is the international Space station where scientists from many nations have cooperated extensively, and a remarkable feat, the station, is now in orbit, miles above the earth. Astronauts from several countries have traveled to it, spending a few months at a time. When the US shuttle was grounded after a tragic accident, the Russian space agency pitched in, and was able to keep that station supplied, until the US could mount another shuttle mission.

Then in August 2005 came a report by Barry Massey, in the Florida Times Union paper, marking the anniversary of the US atomic bomb attacks on Hiroshima and Nagasaki, in Japan. It behooves our youth everywhere, for the future of this planet, to keep these memories alive, as has been done for the holocaust victims of Nazi Germany. Because humanity has since committed more atrocities on a massive scale, in Rwanda, Sudan, all over Africa, in Latin America, and other countries. . If for no other reason than to prevent repetition of these dastardly acts, to eliminate weapons of destruction, once and for all, and to vilify such acts of violence as the evil they represent! Protest marches to commemorate this anniversary were held in the US and overseas, but especially in Japan. A survivor, Koji Ueda was quoted " No more Hiroshima, no more Nagasaki"! He said the atomic bomb survivors were determined to keep their stories alive. We can only hope they will receive many blessings, and many more years in which to perpetuate their efforts, and that many others, younger, will join them in their cause for peace and justice.

Activists gathered near Las Vegas, Nevada (US), near the atomic bomb tests sight, and Oak Ridge, Tennessee, near a heavily guarded weapons industry. As usual, government officials and military personnel arrested some of the participants, they did not want the world to see that some Americans care enough for this fragile world of ours, certainly much more than government officials. Those protesters were only pointing out inhumane activities by the State, whether that takes place in the US or in any other country. That report also quoted Masado Hashida who was a teenage girl not too far from the bomb that was dropped on Nagasaki. She had been knocked unconscious and when she came to, her surroundings were no longer recognizable, and she saw a person trying to stand "barely human-like, burns and swelling making it impossible to tell if that was a woman, or a man- - -"! There have been many similar descriptions, of such scenes of devastation and suffering over the years, in articles, in "Hiroshima" and in many other books. The evils of war at the hands of any power, we must never forget. The US was the only nation to attack with nuclear weapons. In those days we were not told much of the many casualties among the innocent. As has been stated often by many, it is never in the interest of the victor to give accurate figures of innocent civilians killed in wars. It has no propaganda value! How many times do we need to hear that? Amazingly, reporters who recently flew over the target area of hurricane Katrina, in the US, also compared what they saw there to pictures they had seen of Hiroshima after the bomb.

Protesters in America also gathered at the Los Alamos nuclear research facility. To their credit demonstrators acknowledged in placards "We are sorry for Hiroshima and

Nagasaki", something no US administration has had the moral courage to state publicly, and formally acknowledge that we were wrong-----'No More'! Pope John Paul Two, in his greatness and humility asked for pardon for past misdeeds by the Catholic Church, but we in America, are not repentant enough, or humble enough, to do the same. Finally, that article also showed a group of US veterans with messages in favor of what the US had done, dropping atomic bombs. Simply, that demonstrates that Satan is still busy working amongst us, here on this earth; that some people do not accept the moral concept that you cannot use evil means to achieve a good end.

The whole question of Iraq will be dealt with more extensively in the book, but an Iraqi delegate had accused the Americans of hijacking their constitution process because of all the pressure and meddling by US officials. There had already been two delays in the artificial dates forced upon them by the US. The Bush administration denied that, as one would expect, but most people with intelligence have been saying all along that they will continue to call all the shots, and pull strings, in Iraq. No, this is not the face of freedom and democracy for Iraq, anything but.

Then there was the episode where an American evangelist with a large following in this country committed a serious breach of ethics to say the least. News reports alleged that he had called for the assassination of the president of Venezuela by the US; may the good Lord help us all! Not so long ago this man had campaigned for the presidency of the US but some of his critics had considered him poorly qualified; and others stated that such people would claim that they had received a message from God himself, to do this. It created dismay even within the republican administration, and so the evangelist soon issued an apology. After this, the disaster from hurricane Katrina over New Orleans and elsewhere was well publicized, and Chavez of Venezuela announced plans to help as best they could. That must certainly have exposed that preacher's lack of charity or true Christian principles. What makes people behave in this manner? Do they read from the Bible and Jesus' teachings; and do they preach about them? Another well known, and more level headed, preacher, Rev. Jesse Jackson, visited the Venezuelan leader and stated that what the other man had done was immoral and illegal.

Many are quite familiar with a prayer of St. Francis, for those, who are not, they will find his words enlightening, as will all politicians everywhere:

>Make me a channel of your Peace
>Instead of darkness, Light
>Instead of despair, Hope
>Do not let me seek to be consoled, as to console.

Other teachings in Christian and other faiths, tell us that 'Love sees no evil, that Love is fulfillment'. And a strong belief of Blessed Mother Theresa of Calcutta was that the way to Christ is through love for our fellow human beings.

Such thoughts and words could inspire all on this fragile planet, to set differences aside, to come together to try resolve our problems, with humility, with justice, and in peace.

IX

From a chronicle of events discussed in this book, and a previous one, one could conclude that human beings are destined to keep on blundering, the blind leading the blind, as the saying goes. Yet, when you consider the mismanagement, falsifications, and corruption in governments, across the world, from their top leaders, all the way down; the extreme dishonesty and corruption in business corporations, as profits always take precedence over ethics; when you watch the continued degradation of the environment; when you realize that millions of our fellow human beings have been left by the wayside as there are few, really good, Samaritans for the task; when you read about the many confrontations, uprisings, and actual wars, since world war two- - when you consider all that, and more, you begin to understand, that our planet is beset by enormous problems that must be addressed. Scientists, theologians, experts and thinkers from different walks of life, have been telling us for some time, that society had been stampeding in the wrong direction. Most had indeed sounded the alarm, a long time ago, that human beings needed to change course, and soon.

SOCIAL JUSTICE

Critics have often pointed out that leaders in The United States of America, and in Europe, have sometimes exhibited double standards, in deciding when to intervene in crises situations in Africa, or in other regions. When, and where, should they intervene? Professor K.R. Himes, of the Boston College Theology department, discussed parts of the compendium on social teaching, of the Church, in 'America' magazine. His comment that "Human beings should be considered in their fullness, not simply in their political or economic dimensions", should be directed at politicians around the world, in developed and underdeveloped countries, alike. Because, if most of these were to get it right, our world, through a most effective United Nations, would be in a much better position to deal with dictatorship States, with poverty, starvation, and disease; and with such tragedies as genocide or ethnic cleansing (whichever term politicians prefer to use), in their earliest stage, before tens of thousands of people have been murdered, or injured, and hundreds of thousands forced to flee as refugees.

And in the same journal Fr. Thomas Massaro discussed those teachings in the context of 'Work and Markets', as they emphasized that if the economic policies of developed countries were genuinely concerned with the protection of workers as recommended, then those workers would find a greatly improved environment in the workplace. That is true, and actually, quite contrary to what goes on in the US and other wealthier nations. There, executives and other top echelon personnel, receive most of the rewards. He mentioned how Pope Paul VI in the "Populorum Progressio" encyclical, *had severely criticized the capitalistic system;* and Pope Pius XI in "Quadragesimo Anno", *advocated changes in the ruthlessness of competition, for the good of humanity as a whole.* The writer concluded by pointing out that the challenge was "to tame the forces of globalization for the benefit of all". As many experts have stated, this *is not* what has been going on in our world, and it is obvious that many of our Popes have been referring to it, in their writings, trying to guide humanity towards better days ahead. However, large sections of our society all over the world, had failed to heed such advice, and we have paid a price for that.

Another editorial also in 'America', commented on the delicate balance of the US Supreme Court, trying to maintain government neutrality in religious affairs, as it should be; but also recognizing the role that religion had always played in American life. Other developed countries face similar balances in the freedom to practice a religion of choice. In America, we have had debates on the Ten Commandments, and Christmas scenes, being displayed in public areas; prayers in school or other public places. Many favored such practices, others objected to government intrusion in religion. At the other extreme, in some countries, as Saudi Arabia and Pakistan, and others, the freedom to practice a religion of choice barely exists; and reports from India suggest there is significant discrimination. The history of man teems with stories from periods when, Christians and non-Christians, alike, were put to death because they would not agree to change their faith, they could not forsake allegiance to their God. These were some of the darkest pages in our history.

Leading up to the hoopla surrounding the G-8 summit, in Scotland, the Sunday Times of Malta in an article, reminded us that it had been decades since the magnanimous 'west' had started organizing such meetings, and movements, to change the face of poverty in Africa, to make it a thing of the past! Truly, some of the poverty in that country, and the suffering, was caused by corrupt politicians in various countries. But this article pointed to some $150 billion, in subsidies, *to farmers in Europe and the US, and other rich countries, at the same time, those same countries created barriers against food exports from the poorer countries!* Where have Mr. Blair and Mr. Bush, and other politicians been, all these years? Blair was now cheering for Africa, and also Mr. Chirac of France, and other present and past leaders. Why then, had they done so little that was visible, that had been constructive? We need to remember that many of these countries in Africa, were once under the boot of European colonial powers, hence European nations may bear more responsibility than America. Mr. Blair, who helped Mr. Bush launch the Iraq war, is now talking about 'moral imperatives'---is that another example of hypocrisy? Reports in the "Independent" showed that Norway was, proportionately, providing most overseas aid, at .87% of gross domestic product; UK came in at .36%; and unbelievably, the US came in at .16% of GDP! Yes, politicians have got it all wrong. Many expressed surprise to hear Britain's Gordon Brown announce that they were leading the charge! What charge? Then US officials said that they were giving the most in total amount; what paltry excuses! These reports were not discussing amounts but rather, they were focused on percentage of GDP. It was back in 1992 that at an Earth summit they had set a target of .7% of GDP, for overseas aid, and 15 years later it was only Norway that had met, and exceeded, that goal. But both Blair and Bush had found plenty of cash, to be able to attack another sovereign nation, and create chaos! Is that decent governing, or is it scandal and lack of caring? Let the reader be the judge.

In 'Mirror Reflections' we pointed at incompetence and hypocrisy among many governments including those in the west, but the above article specifically highlighted corruption in much of Africa itself, and thus it re-emphasized that there was plenty of blame to spread around, to explain the crisis on that continent. They referred to governments in Zanzibar, Malawi, Swaziland, Kenya, Zimbabwe, and many others. They were noting the use of Mercedes cars for the leaders, their wives, and concubines. There were awfully huge residences, excessive luxuries, and a penchant for high immorality and lust! One could be tempted to conclude that, people in the 'west' need not bother with countries harboring such terrible leaders. When we hear that, it is not difficult to understand why Africa is beset by crises, why their people are so poor, and why they are forgotten. But that writer also added 'that there was plenty of immorality abroad', because poor countries should not be allowed to wallow in debt. Neither should they be burdened with the luxury of being ruled, in many cases, by leaders whose first, second, and last name, is 'Jack' (as in the Ripper).

There are many reasons why protesters at that G-8 summit felt that their freedoms had been infringed upon by British authorities; they were only making their voices heard on behalf of Africa, but they were being muzzled. How did British authorities react? They said they needed to control a group of anarchists; at least they did not call them 'terrorists', as they might have been called in the US! As the Malta Times emphasized there was plenty of blame for everybody, in the rich countries, and the corrupt leaders in those poor countries as well. Most of us, in the developed nations, cannot use that as an excuse, that their leaders were stealing most of the donations, in any case; and therefore we should not keep sending aid. As has been pointed out previously, we have landed humans on the moon, we sent robots to mars, there is a remarkable Space station in orbit; the US has numerous spy satellites in Space (and presumably other countries too), we have sent probes into Space, and on July 4, an American probe ventured inside a comet, for scientific studies. And China is also beginning to explore outer space. If we have performed such magnificent feats (western nations, Russia, and now China), should we not be able to get a consensus of people, politicians, financial experts, charitable groups, church leaders, and together, plan how to get aid to the desperately needy in those countries; at the same time thwarting any evil intent by the corrupt leaders, in those same countries. Or indeed, if we have to, we can arrange their overthrow, as we have sometimes done, even without ample justification.

In the correspondence section in Time magazine, a reader said that progressive leaders had now understood that the problem with development in Africa, was not only corruption and poor governance, and with steady commitment Africa could gradually stand on its own feet. Another reader, shrewdly reminded leaders in developed countries that Africa's *resources had contributed significantly to western wealth, as the continent had been exploited, sometimes brutally- - -!* A speaker on a C-Span TV program sensed that Africa would not change until the public became better informed, and to do so, they needed independent media, an independent electoral process all over the continent, and an independent judiciary. These would expose corruption, and offenders would then be duly punished.

Besides other issues, the G-8 summit was purportedly organized to deal with Africa, but at the end of the session little had changed. There was the usual, pompous talk about increasing aid, but activists quickly showed that much of it was not real money, *as it was aid that had already been promised in the past, but the time frame had been too long.* The leader of South Africa proved to be more sympathetic to the G-8 group, and he was then accused that he was playing politics with those influential world leaders, to the detriment of his African brethren. In particular critics accused, that the help offered for Aids, was again, too little, too late. Guests on a CNN program said that Bush had only contributed $4 billion, out of the $25 billion in aid alluded to; and they added, that $4 billion was simply a repackaging of past committed money! On such a background we must always remind readers that America has been spending well over $450 billion per year on the military, on weapons of war; and then we offer a paltry, repackaged, $4 billion in aid for the poor! *America, where are we heading, or are we already there, in the abyss- - -?*

On global climate change scientists again criticized the group of eight, for doing nothing, and for refusing to recognize the urgency. A spokesman, for BBC, stated that Bush had changed his attitude the absolute minimum he had to, on that topic! They agreed to dialogue with India and China, but there was no force put on the US to reduce its emissions, or for G-8 to provide more money for such projects. Who was talking about corruption, on which continent- - -? On the question of heavy subsidies by rich nations, that had victimized poor workers around the world---*on that, they did absolutely nothing!* To say the least Blair, who had hosted the group, had expected a much better response, and was greatly disappointed.

In July 2005 the much-publicized live-8 concerts were held throughout the world, mainly to try pressure those group leaders to do something about the tens of millions of our poor. They predicted that about 1 million people would attend, and 200,000 were reported in London's Hyde Park concert alone. As is usual, in our present culture, they announced that it would mainly consist of rock and swing music. What has happened to lovely and decent melodies from the past, did they not have a place in such a large concert for a noble cause? Would they perhaps, not act as an additional drawing card for attendees? The organizers let it be known *that they were not seeking charity, but they were asking for justice!* There is such a free, and democratic society, in the 'west', that now wherever our leaders gather, they must have a police crackdown, they need thousands of police and soldiers on guard or on patrol; and they keep protesters miles away from the venue. Why is that, if our society is supposed to be open and free? And, when G-8 leaders meet in excessively luxurious surroundings, to be pampered ad lib, to discuss the desperately hungry and poor of the world, *does that not portray an ugly contrast, a paradox?* Are these not symptoms of what is wrong with our society? And should we not rush to make it right?

When we discuss social justice we obviously need to concentrate on lesser-developed countries; but also on the developed nations of the west, because of the wealth and lifestyles therein. Amongst them the US features prominently, as it is the largest and the richest. We look at actions by those rich countries to help alleviate so much misery and injustice on our planet. But there have been glaring problems within individual countries themselves. On a C-Span TV program on Afro-American influence in politics, speakers pointed out that presently, in Washington DC, USA, all the power was in the hands of right wing republicans, and Afro-American elected officials had little influence. They emphasized that for those powers to work well in parliament, or any other political center, some of that power should flow to the streets, to ordinary people. There was a new twist to justice, in America, that focused on crimes committed during the civil rights movement of the black population, their struggle for justice. Much attention was given in the media, to the 2005 arrests and trials of suspects, in crimes of murder committed many years ago, that had remained unsolved until now. Crimes perpetuated during many years of oppression by white folk on the Afro-American people. Most of those crimes had been committed by young, white people, and had gone unpunished. Some of the perpetrators had since died, and those now being prosecuted for those crimes were aging. Juries faced hard decisions trying to render a just verdict, after so many years of neglect, and when so many witnesses, and much evidence, had been lost. It was amazing, that although in many of those crimes, the KKK (Ku Klux Klan) had featured prominently, now people tried to testify that as an organization, the KKK had done a lot of good for the community. That may be so, but you cannot tell that to the black population in those days, as KKK had been guilty of committing many capital crimes. In June 2005 a Mississippi grand jury convicted a ringleader in the orchestrated murder of 3 civil rights activists, some 41 years earlier! The latter, had been, ambushed, by, the KKK, they were beaten, and shot. The stories of "Mississippi Burning", were revived as that state had been a hotbed of violence, and oppression against the black community. But even now, some critics stated that the jury only convicted of the crime of manslaughter, and refused to convict of first-degree murder. Others said, it showed there was still a lot of work to be done, in Mississippi, even though much progress had been achieved in 40 years!

On the topic of civil rights, former president Lyndon Johnson, had spoken before the US congress in 1965, urging them to quickly pass his civil rights bill, then before them. Many in congress were conspicuous by refusing to applaud Johnson's speech, and one could assume that most of them were republicans. He emphasized that history would surely judge the nation by action taken by congress. And he reiterated that the passage of such a bill was long overdue, it had taken over 100 years! He said our true enemies are, poverty, disease and ignorance, not our fellow man; and several times during his speech, he intoned the famous words 'we shall overcome', restating that 'ours was one nation'.

One would think that such barbaric acts depicted above had long been relegated to the distant past, not so. In Maryknoll magazine, David Strong described the murder of Notre Dame de Namour missioner, Dorothy, from Ohio (US), in the rainforest of Brazil; and this was fairly recent. She had gone to the Amazon region to help peasant farmer families, who had moved there in a government sponsored settlement plan. But big landowners, the land barons, were angered because they wanted, that, same land, for, logging operations, and cattle grazing. As she was helping these poor families, she was also urging the government to protect them, and therefore she was at odds with these 'land barons'. Middlemen hired 'pistoleros' to kill her, according to these reports. The peasant families called her 'their protector, and she was no more'! This is also a country where, in the past, one heard of orphaned, disenfranchised, youth, street people, who were summarily murdered by 'groups unknown', under a previous government.

A different, tragic, commentary in the European press dealt with the practice of sexual mutilation of women in some underdeveloped countries. Critics lamented the fact that the UN, the west, and society in general, had failed to stop these practices, once and for all. On the contrary, they claim, some of these people had migrated to western countries and continued this illicit practice from their cultures, and governments had been slow to deal with culprits, and to stamp out this brutality, perpetuated out of ignorance. It is against their religious teachings we are told, and therefore a process of reeducation would be essential. Again this comes in the realm of cultures and values. We cannot, and should not force western values on other societies. But for many of these people, after years of colonial rule, by the west, has so little been achieved by example, by education and exchange of ideals? In showing them perhaps, that there are better ways in life. In some countries women are still abused, and treated as inferiors, in some instances no better than a piece of furniture. Even in the era of Aids, we have not yet taught them that safe sexual practices or abstention, can prevent serious disease, many years of misery, and even death, resulting in thousands of orphans around the world. It becomes a vicious cycle from which there is no escape. In 'Mirror Reflections' we made a strong plea for the countries in the west, to help the poor in our world; a plea, for the larger countries to divert a substantial portion of their military budgets, for humanitarian causes, instead.

We did not intend for such aid to be in the form of cash donations alone, because that could further enrich corrupt leaders and corporations. Cash is certainly important, as is debt forgiveness so often advocated by the late Pope John Paul two, a saintly person. But, such help should come in forms often adopted by president Carter, and his Carter center, and by missionary groups, in their global efforts. Improve education, develop decent health care and access; teach works in infrastructure; improve agriculture in such a way, that would generate greater, and better products; improve water supplies with access to clean, safe water; better housing; a better business climate with less corporate abuse and greed (the US could learn from that as well). Simply put, opportunity for more people to get out of conditions of squalor, and perhaps one day to venture into a small enterprise of their own. And last, but not least, the teaching of, and having access to, aspects of Faith, **but** only if, and when, the people express a hunger for such information. We cannot ram our values down their throat under threats, as was done in the early years of imperialism.

That is how we help millions of people in our world, who are dying because of inadequate help from countries that could afford to do much more, for our brethren. In the US we just saw the tragedy of hurricane Katrina where many died because the federal government was badly unprepared and not caring enough, even for its own citizens, according to many critics. Recently Africa was in the news a lot, perhaps another opportunity for sound bites by the group of eight. But, there are others besides Africa, and we have failed them all. Africa is the most glaring! The recent Asian Tsunami was another good example, where countries talked big, like the US, UK, the EU, etc. (mainly sound bites, photo opportunity, for the politicians). They talked about all the millions in cash, and donated goods, that were being given. But according to critics, although those countries had promised hundreds of millions soon after the disaster struck, as of this writing, little had reached the people themselves, those who had suffered and who needed it most! That is what experts talk about when they criticize the west. Why do we continue to perpetuate such inhumane policies? Talk is cheap we all know that. Action requires courage, determination, it takes guts, it calls for honesty and decency, and love for our fellow brethren.

The Sunday Times (UK) carried an article by Salman Rushdie, when he too, discussed the rape and abuse of women, in Pakistan, at times group rapes, that often go unpunished, and reports suggest it occurs in India as well. Those rapists often talk of male honor! The article also points out how president Musharraf of Pakistan pretends to be fighting terror, and visits president Bush in Washington, but at the same time he permits terror on women in his own country. Surely our Washington officials knew about that, or is it one of the many instances when we gladly close our eyes? Thus we have leaders of western countries who would like to reshape the Middle East, whilst they are on good terms with the dictator of Pakistan. How many times has that region of the world been reshaped? Both the US and UK maintain close ties to both India and Pakistan, there is trade, there are arms sales, yes, and a plethora of out-sourced jobs from the US and other countries. It does not bother them that human rights organizations have found human rights abuses of their people in those countries; and particularly against women.

On the home front, a CNN program featured 'Judging Justice', when guests discussed the shaky justice system in the US, which had received much criticism, both here and abroad. They stated that, 'we cannot be pleased', when justice takes a kick-in-the-teeth, and they were referring to the M. Jackson trials. For weeks we had been bombarded with news clips on this high profile trial for alleged pedophilia. Previously we had numerous reports in our media, on priests being charged with pedophilia. There were comments by prosecutors, and the defense team was emphasizing, that, the jury must be able to believe such and such, 'beyond a reasonable doubt'. That, to many, raised memories of another high profile trial a few years ago, where an ill-fitting glove was splashed on TV screens all over the world, by a defense team. There have been many high profile trials on prominent families, politicians, film stars, and so on. To critics this suggests one type of justice for one segment of society, and another type for the rest of the people, two justice systems in America. Similar uneven handed practices come to mind from the Israeli-Palestinian conflict; from the old South Africa with its Apartheid system; other middle-eastern countries; and from the caste systems in Asia, and other disparities in many parts of the world. In short, the constant use of double standards, one for the haves, and the other for the have-nots!

Professor M. Mamdani discussed his book 'Good Muslim, Bad Muslim', and the shift in the cold war of the 1970's; the Portuguese colonial power collapsed, and those African colonies gained their independence; but US foreign policies that had given rise to terrorism groups, had started even before that. American policy makers had determined that they should no longer become involved overseas, but they could persuade others (mercenaries), to do it for them. He said that Reagan's philosophy became such, that right wing dictatorships could be embraced, whereas those of the left wing should be overturned. He added, the Reagan doctrine wanted the destruction of evil by all means, there was no middle ground. That was how Apartheid South Africa gained strength and gave rise to a violent terrorist movement. Then there was Nicaragua, and others were to follow, overthrow regimes! It was from all these events that nationalistic groups learned terror methods; but in so doing, he said, some of them degenerated and lost track.

He suggested that after the US defeat in Vietnam, officials decided to contract violence outside (the proxy wars), either supporting them, or actually they ended up creating them. He gave as example the heavy involvement of America's CIA in the Afghanistan resistance movement against the Soviets. We live in a world where there is a single hegemonic power (US), and any major power must be held accountable, otherwise it can destroy at will. He also pointed to the irony in the present Bush administration justifying violence overseas, with the excuse of bringing human rights to others; whereas it violates human rights in the US itself. Others had made the same accusation about Bush, that he has been doing these things, by using another excuse, 'National Security'! From the above argument we assume that after the cold war, the US military budget should have plummeted, but instead, the billions of dollars continued to climb, because the military industrial State, the national security State, wanted to maintain the status quo, to find other adversaries. This had driven US politics for many years as thinkers around the world had long maintained!

Other problems for America were investigations into the last presidential elections, of 2004. According to 25% of those polled, there was evidence of irregularity in the state of Ohio, not a small number! As many as 52% of voters reported having trouble voting, in other words, there was attempted voter suppression, and it was often directed at minorities. What type of freedom and democracy are US officials promoting in other countries, if we have trouble finding them, in our own backyard? Are such reports, the examples we have given them? Why were those Ohio elections certified as fair, and above board, if they were not? Were the powers that be, the elite, so desperate that another republican administration should be elected in America, that they would resort to anything? Is there anyone who believes such behavior is true democracy?

The League of Women voters featured a program on the Carter-Baker commission on election reform in the US; we want to tell others how to run their governments and their elections, when we have not taken care of our own glaring irregularities! Not yet! They stated that *the country needs massive reform of the electoral system, because it was in very poor health.* There was lack of proper funding and equipment, lack of fairness across the US, lack of encouragement for increased voting among the public (one of the lowest voting rates in the world), there was an improper registration system, long lines at voting stations, and much, much more. They said, if many corporations ran their business the way US elections were run, those organizations would go bankrupt in no time at all. A California professor added that the above was an embarrassment to the nation. With all this, once again, why was the election of a president certified in 2004? We need answers from the 'independent media'! 40% of eligible voters do not bother to vote in presidential elections because they feel they cannot make a difference, that the outcome was already decided, and that money in the US was the single most important factor! This was a league of women discussing the commission reports on our elections. Yes, we need much house cleaning ourselves, before we climb on a pedestal, to pontificate to Russia, China, Venezuela, Iraq, Iran, Syria, Lebanon, Palestine- -before we attempt to show them how to run theirs! What utter hypocrisy, is our foreign policy? They have been clamoring for reforms in UK as well; so apparently we, in the west, need to solve our problems first, to be more effective in convincing others.

We also had another incident reflecting on justice, when in 2005 congress moved to make it a crime for someone to burn a US flag in protest. Critics immediately claimed it was another assault on freedom of speech and freedom of expression. We have known that freedom of speech was strictly controlled under tyrannies and various dictatorships. We are now trying to adopt some of their tactics in the US. This is a question wherein in the past, the US supreme court had ruled that it was legal, it was a form of freedom of speech, to burn a US flag, if this was the form of expression someone selected. It seemed that those on the right fringes would stop at nothing to advance their sinister agenda. True, we should not encourage anyone to burn a national flag, but neither should we trash people's basic civil rights and freedoms, by such legislation! Various forms of protest are important, and should be protected, if carried out in a responsible manner.

Yet another blow to civil rights and personal freedoms in America, came when the supreme court ruled that local governments had the legal right to seize private property, homes, etc. and give them to others for development, *if it was for the common good!* There is the catch. The laws of Eminent Domain used to imply that governments could seize private property at a fair price, to build public facilities for the common good, such as hospitals, schools, railroads, and so on. But now, that had been reinterpreted to mean they can give it to private developers to build shopping malls, and condominiums, which enriched the developers, and on which the government could collect increased taxes. The latter, was now called 'common good'! It depended on whom you asked. Justice O'Connor gave her withering dissent on those opinions, because with this ruling the government was free to take from those who had little, and give it to those who had a lot, the haves, and the have-nots! Whatever happened to the American dream? Under Eminent Domain the law usually applied to blighted areas, that were becoming an eyesore, and these could be developed and improved for the common good. But now, attractive, decent looking areas, could be seized in this manner because some business tycoons carried weight with politicians.

On the PBS program, 'NOW', with David Broncaccio, the emphasis was on the owners of such 'condemned' homes who would not receive what their property was worth, because under the law the government declared them blighted. At the same time wealthy developers favored by crooked politicians could rake in millions of dollars in profit. Who is conning the public? In this program they showed senior citizens in tears, they had lived in their homes 30 or 40 years, there was nobody else they could turn to, for justice and protection, from Big Brother! That court decision had been a major blow; one couple so involved, were determined to fight on in the courts, to fight Big Brother, even if it cost them a fortune to do so. Most Americans may not be fully aware of what has been going on--are these not symptoms of dictator states?

Another bizarre report came from the British newspaper 'Independent', where they alleged that Dick Cheney of the US, some years ago, had voiced disapproval of the release from prison of a prominent personality, Nelson Mandela, of S. Africa. Is that not amazing? Here is a man (Mandela), who had fought hard against oppression, and was a voice for justice, freedom, and democracy for his people. He paid for that by being imprisoned for many years under the Apartheid system, that was then, S. Africa; and Cheney, a prominent US politician, was opposed to this man being set free, according to the reports. If true, many were bound to ask, how could anyone compare Cheney, to Nelson Mandela? Are these not more symptoms, why we have such a troubled world? Because of the type of people who assume leadership roles, when they are not properly qualified? We need to understand that when there is rampant dishonesty, political chicanery, and the ugly influence of money, in America, or anywhere else in the so-called 'advanced west', can one imagine what could be uncovered in third world countries, that never gets to independent media.

At least in the west, sooner or later, usually much later, some of those scandals, and corrupt practices, do get into our news reports. Do Americans remember the fanfare of the Bush administration, the photo propaganda, as they rammed through congress a senior citizens prescription drug bill, supposedly at a cost of some $350 billion? This charade of a bill was said to help our suffering seniors. Well, according to guest speakers on 'Now', on PBS, that figure quoted by officials, as of 2005 alone, had reached at least $700 billion! Amazing! Someone was allegedly playing dirty games with the American people, to force republicans to pass that bill, simply for political gain, as usual. Most of the seniors had never understood what the bill was about, and reports suggested that the only winners were the pharmaceutical industry, the republican dominated government, and their lobbyists! Certainly not the people!

An editorial in 'America' magazine also dealt with many social issues in our world, as their writers often do so well. They pointed to reports from the US and other wealthy countries, of individuals making huge expenditures on trivia. An example quoted was the purchase of Mother-Baby bracelets for $12,000 each—they urged all of us, to consider that, in the context of thousands of babies and children around the world, dying of Aids, other diseases, and starvation. Then there were college students in the US, who needed residences for 2, 3, or 4 years; and for refurbishing such temporary residences, families hired decorators to spruce up students' rooms, with furniture, large TV sets, etc. at a cost of many thousands of dollars, the haves and the have-nots. When we hear such revelations we also wonder about Christians who raise tens of millions of dollars for their churches for 'evangelization'. Does not evangelization also mean we should care for our brothers and sisters wherever they are; to always show mercy and compassion? Was it not Jesus who told people that He did not ask for their sacrifice, but He asked them to show mercy!

Social injustices have been rampant everywhere; in the west, we often hear criticism of conditions under military dictators, in Asia, in Africa, in Latin America, the Middle East, etc. But our better-developed, more 'civilized', western nations, have glaring social problems of their own. Injustices in most societies, are as old as history itself. In 'Night

Comes to the Cumberlands', Harry M. Caudill paints a picture of poverty and neglect, amongst the mountain settlers of Appalachia (US), in the early nineteen hundreds. It describes how when the vast wealth of mineral deposits in the region (mainly coal), were discovered, capitalists from the northeast traveled to the area, they appeared polite, with a quiet demeanor, trying to be helpful. But they quickly persuaded the landowners to sell them all the mineral rights beneath their lands. The author pointed out that these shrewd industrialists knew that with increasing transactions, the value of land would go up, and so would property taxes for the local government. But they would owe no taxes, as they bought only the rights to the minerals beneath the surface! The mountaineer landowners would be stuck with owing the increased taxes, and they would see little or none of the riches that would accrue from the mining of those vast mineral deposits. Thus the plight of these folk was to remain as if they had come from ages past. Rarely did they believe that their children needed advanced education, if they remained in that region, and decent facilities were not available anyway. School buildings were badly outdated, but even in those days, they said, when bond money was available, a substantial portion went to athletic programs, as children seemed to find those, more attractive than academics. Thus, in school systems in the old days, as it still is today, athletics seemed to receive too much emphasis, sometimes to the detriment of more essential academic studies. Again, though some of these reports pertain to the US, they are encountered in many other countries as well.

Social injustices have come in different guises, including elements of religious intolerance, persisting to this day. Columban missionaries have felt the need to constantly work with Pakistan society, to increase understanding and acceptance of each other's faith. That, perhaps, could provide the foundation for a better society overall. In a communication, president Carter referred to their work on human rights injustices, and again this was about Pakistan. A United Nations representative tried to help a woman get a divorce, after many years of abuse (and torture was described). They agreed to meet with the woman's mother, who arrived with an uncle and another driver, who promptly shot and killed, the woman seeking the divorce (these countries continue to use the honor ideology preferentially, to abuse women). Carter gave another example of a sociology professor in Egypt, who was trying to register people to vote. He had been imprisoned in the past for 'activism'. He was arrested again (Egypt, too, has been a dictatorship), but through involvement of the Carter center, and others, he was acquitted. Yes, tyrannical, dictator states, are dotted all over the globe, call them terrorist states, if you will; but US officials have cordial relations with many of them—surprise! That is why so many thinkers, and other experts, have long maintained that US foreign policy had actually given rise to terrorism, just as the Israeli-Palestinian conflict had, and the years of colonial rule, of ages past.

Another article in Columban magazine dealt with society's attitudes towards the older segment of our population. It mentioned how, in Japan, many years ago, old people were put out of the home, sometimes abandoned in the mountains. Things have improved considerably since then, but there have been periodic reports of acts of discrimination against the elderly in both developed and underdeveloped countries. Fr. Paul McCartin stated that "devaluing elderly people in our economy-based society, dehumanizes us all". The article goes on to say that we cannot be fully human unless all people are respected. There have been many reports about senior citizens barely able, to make ends meet.

After the catastrophe caused by hurricane Katrina on the US Gulf Coast region, an entire city, New Orleans, was about 70 to 80% under water, by most estimates. Criticisms of the Bush administration and all levels of government were harsh, as they should have been. About the 8th day, federal officials kept on repeating how much they were now doing, sending millions of this, millions of that. Much too late! Most of the American people and many others, from around the world, had condemned the poor response, the incompetence, of some, in the Bush administration. Responding massively on day 7 or 8, was too little, too late. That would be considered very poor for underdeveloped countries, imagine for the US! It will not bring to life hundreds who may have perished because of drowning, dehydration or from lack of medical help! There were many who had accused Bush of lack of leadership in a crisis, similar, they said, to the first several hours after 9/11, inaction. Others came out saying that it was not the time to place blame, the elite, protecting the elite; and the US keeps heading down a slippery slope. Yes, of course, you have to assess blame, because the buck stops with the men at the top, the leaders of nations. You do not postpone such actions in the hope that most people would soon forget what you did not do.

As many officials and politicians do in democracies, and dictator states, alike, even though they may have failed in their leadership roles, they are always quick to make certain the media can portray them touring devastated areas, comforting the afflicted. This is the type of corruption or ineptness, in any government, experts are always writing about. In the US, both republicans and democrats, called for an immediate investigation, with public hearings. But as the US no longer had a democracy, in the real sense, the Bush administration announced committee hearings, *and behind closed doors, if you please!* They did not want the public to hear about the failures of the government on Katrina. The right republican wing wanted to make it right with the American people because the polls were showing them in a very bad light; but sending in the cavalry on the 7th or 8th day can never make it right, when they should have been there as soon as the storm had passed! Allegedly, according to reports, Bush administration officials told their people that, although they were late in responding, they must get out there now, and show government agencies in a positive light! Another example of lack of caring.

During the first week or so, after this hurricane catastrophe, we heard experts from various professions talk about *how Katrina had bared for all Americans to see clearly, the racial and class divide, that was alive and well, in the United States of America.* It had been there all along, but some citizens and many in government, simply closed their eyes, and pretended it did not exist. Most of those devastated were poor, black, and also the elderly! Many were poor before, and after the storm they were left with nothing. What was the common thread through hundreds of comments? That nobody from the federal government had come to help, not a single agency representative. This time, all these scenes from New Orleans were amply splashed on news reports for the whole world to see! Then, the government agency FEMA announced it would distribute debit cards for $2000 to victims of the disaster, they caused such utter confusion that within 48 hours they had already cancelled the program! Some other approach would be adopted, this, when people needed help, and fast. Some headlines in news reports, were these, 'Seventh day of Hell', 'Catastrophe', 'How Bush Blew it'! Then there was 'The Duct tape man', referring to the person Bush had just appointed to the federal emergency agency. Apparently the man had advised Americans to stock up, on duct tape, in case of terror attacks with chemical or biological weapons! He was soundly ridiculed for that piece of advice.

On September 9th, after both president Bush and vice president Cheney had visited the devastated area, they were praising agency directors for their hard work; but the voices of critics continued louder, so one of the directors responsible, was removed and transferred to Washington, 'to plan for future disasters'---! Readers would think that such a person would be fired, not so, many governments do not function like that. Actually even in western countries, officials who may have run into difficulties, are often moved around, or promoted, in all branches of government. The director, who was dismissed over Katrina, has since spoken out, that he had been made the scapegoat; that he had warned his superiors, and the Bush White house, about the seriousness of the hurricane, long before it made landfall, and they had not listened to him.

In 'Mirror Reflections' this writer discussed problems with health care for the elderly, and this can be encountered in many countries, large or small, rich or poor; more so in poor countries. But regrettably, it occurs also in the US, the richest. Thus, past stories from Japan about the plight of the older generation, may still ring true, for present day society, because 'we often measure the significance of people by how much they can produce and consume', **consumerism!** The elderly would not fit in well. But as we have learned in recent times, if we start discriminating, or if we start a preference or selection trend, young over old, blonde over brunette, tall over short, light skinned over dark, if we do that, then society would surely rush headlong over the precipice! If we cannot be properly responsible for the poor, the hungry, the disadvantaged, of our society, what type of a future could we expect?

In an essay on the Lehrer news hour, on PBS station, R. Rosenblatt referred to the attacks on London, that were followed by officials warning people to be on the look out, to be on the alert for anything- - -suspicious behavior, language, abandoned packages, and so on. He emphasized that those events were serious, but so were the attacks on our liberties, such as the US patriot act, with its attacks on out freedoms, snooping on our activities in public libraries. He concluded that *we have to be alert there too, we must protect ourselves from such extreme acts by governments- - -!*

OUR TROUBLED WORLD

In this uncertain, troubled world of ours, various crises, or disagreements, can become aggravated, because of erratic foreign policies adopted by government officials of nations. As an example, the US had often praised Uzbekistan, and maintained friendly relations with their government, in spite of gross human rights abuses in that country, and tyrannical behavior by some of their leaders. It seems that we have heard often enough, that if we need those countries for military bases, or whatever, we can readily close our eyes to many abuses, and to oppression of their people. However, in the United Nations calls were increasing for investigations of Uzbekistan, but their president had rejected the idea, as one would expect. In May 2005 there were violent protests in the former Soviet states of Uzbekistan and Kyrgystan, the usual scapegoats were 'Islamic extremists' and 'Terrorists'. Many civilians were killed, by heavy machine guns used, by the authorities, in Uzbekistan; and streets were littered with bullet casings according to European news media. But there was no immediate comment, or condemnation, from the US administration, on those reports 'mum' was the word.

Fresh reports, had emerged, of US soldiers abusing Afghan prisoners near Kabul, and it had angered president Karzai; and in recent months resistance to US occupation forces had increased as well, with many anti-American protests in Muslim nations, including Pakistan, a close US ally. In 2005 it was announced that first lady Mrs. Bush, would travel to parts of the Middle East, and reports claimed she would try repair some of the damage the US had suffered through all this, perhaps she could do a lot more good, than US policies had done.

European papers had reported that witnesses saw Uzbek soldiers fire indiscriminately into crowds, killing hundreds of men, women, and children; that blood, and body parts were scattered everywhere. The leader of Uzbekistan issued a statement that he had not ordered them to fire. Did the US believe him? In the past, that leader, and others like him, had been described as virtual tyrants, but we, in the US, 'did business' with such as these! Did Mr. Bush, or Mr. Blair, feel that the above actions were as bad as Saddam Hussein's? Why did they, and most at the UN, not call for the immediate overthrow of that tyrant, and bring him to justice? Was it because he 'was a close ally of the US', and we must never forget those military bases----? Those double standards again! This Uzbek leader took a cue from US government officials, and from Israelis, when he said that, 'they only fired on terrorists'. Another tragic chapter in the troubled history of the US!
In that part of the world, there was another report, about the president of Turkmenistan, who had bought for himself a Boeing jet airliner, worth $150 million (*note, from an American company*). It was custom built for him. In our previous book we had described the plight of the poor people of Turkmenistan, and their 'democracy', or lack thereof. And we referred to US, and other leaders, playing 'friends and allies', with such dictators, wherever it suits them.
Also, in 2005, president Putin of Russia, organized several meetings with leaders of western nations, for celebrations commemorating the world war two victory over Nazi

Germany. He was reported to have lambasted the Baltic States for their political demagoguery, thus souring the atmosphere of those meetings.

This same year there was also the death of the elderly, ailing, king of Saudi Arabia, and the portrayal of his burial ceremony in a plain grave, according to their culture, contrasted sharply with ceremonials in the west. The chain of command and succession, were already in place, and experts suggested the transition would not likely usher in policy changes in that kingdom, with respect to relationships with the west, with America, and with neighboring Middle Eastern nations. British correspondents expressed concern about the oil industry, because of some instability inside that kingdom. There was a large population of young people, and those with rigid Islamic leanings, had long resented the royal family, because they allowed American forces on their land.
In August, we also heard of the helicopter crash, and the death of the vice president of the Sudan, and some of his associates. He had been instrumental in drafting a peace accord between the north and south, Muslims and Christians. Soon after this, violence erupted, but violence was never far away in the Sudan. Reporters said it threatened the fragile peace, although critics had repeated that there was no real peace, because killings in the Darfur region, had continued all along. The ethnic cleansing, where witnesses claimed, that the rebels, were assisted by the Sudan government, in their barbaric acts. Women were raped and taunted, that they would give birth to a lighter skinned child. This violence in the Sudan, had killed about two million people, over a period of a few years, and created millions of refugees. Faced with such reports, one has to ask why Bush, and Blair, decided to go after Iraq? True, there had been several thousand killed there, as well. But, what about the systematic ethnic cleansing in the Sudan, was that not a greater humanitarian crisis, than Iraq? Was it because of unpleasant memories, on Sudan, from the days of the British Empire? Or, was it the oil riches of Iraq, for America's tycoons, as so many critics had accused all along?

Next, according to European news reports, Britain and the US, were warning Iran 'that it must abide by its international obligations----or else'! It is noble to require nations to abide by international agreements; *but how is it that US, Britain, and Israel, and others, are not also required to abide by **all** international obligations?* We can pick and choose where to enforce international laws! Ah, there is that problem again---a continuous use of double standards! One form applies to the rich and powerful, and one for all the rest. In the world of dirty politics, what is good for the goose, is not always good for the gander!

Author Rev. Fr. R. J. Neuhaus, with several books to his name, appeared on a C-Span TV program, to discuss one of his works, and answer questions. His statement that Europe was dying likely surprised many; that Christian moral attitudes, were quite low; that birth rates had plunged immensely, so that in some countries, the percentage of those over 60 or 65 had rapidly escalated. He referred to Germany, France, Scandinavian countries, and also Italy. On the other hand, and many would disagree with him, he pointed to America as a predominantly religious society, adding, *but confusedly so.* Many around the world, are bound to agree that America is perhaps confused; that there is too much going on, that does not fit in well, with sincere feelings towards religion. He emphasized that for its vitality the church must remain independent from the state. That, in countries where there was close interdependence between church and state, it did not always work out well. He pointed out that the Catholic, Christian church, takes nothing for granted; it takes nothing away from humanism, but rather, enhances it. In answer to a question on Iraq, if that war was just, he would only comment that perhaps, *on the basis of what information we thought we had in 2002, perhaps it could be called 'just'*. Many would argue with him that such wishy-washy opinions by the church on war, had led to more uncertainty and violence, because some are always ready to find excuses, and point to church attitudes on violence and wars. But, he failed to elaborate on the fact, that, high officials in our own government, put out lies and fabrications, lots of them, to try to justify the war on Iraq. Where was he when Powell made his ridiculous presentation to the United Nations for the US? Surely, he had read about those infamous London memos? On the other hand, Pope John Paul Two, was against this war to the end, because for him, there were always peaceful means, first, to help resolve international problems, to avoid inflicting so much suffering on humanity!

Reporters also discussed an interview with the secretary of the People's Committee for Security in Libya---he had stated that the bad, negative image, on Libya, in the western press, was false propaganda. We had often heard that, in the past. He denied reports of political imprisonment in his country; they had invited many press personnel from many countries, and they were allowed to investigate freely, and found none of those allegations. He told reporters, that unlike in many countries, his government was really representative of the people, because 'our people made most of the decisions concerning their country's policies , and so on. They were free to speak out, and express their views, in the various congresses across the nation'. Now, we can criticize such talk coming from Libyan representatives; on the other hand, in the US, we claim a government 'by the people, of the people, for the people', *but in real life, it is none of that, as experts have pointed out that money, and special interests, control our government. A government by the few----!* This Libyan Secretary claimed that there was no other country where the people had such authority to make decisions (and if true, he may well be right, but only, if true). About this time, the son of Col. Gaddafi, of Libya, was on a trip to the Middle East, and he announced that he was not likely to succeed his father. That was an interesting statement, considering the history of friction between the 'West', and Libya. From the above, we realize that we have markedly differing assessments of global political situations, one from certain pundits, in the 'west', and one from Libya itself, very different interpretations, indeed.

From a small country, we found this report in the Times of Malta, by K. Zammit Tabona: "When you live in a country where nepotism is rife, contractors hold governments to ransom, and the population is largely dissatisfied with the way its taxes are spent"---. We presume he was talking about Malta, and we mention the Islands of Malta, because this country will feature prominently in later sections of this book. However, the above quotation could be applied to most countries, could it not? Whether large, or small, from north to south, or east to west, most have politicians that are shadows of the same, as far as behavior patterns are concerned. Thus, in this book, we feature Malta as one of the smallest, the US as one of the largest, and countries in between, some are considered rich, others, quite poor.

The struggles between Israel and the Palestinians remained in the news arena, as they resumed negotiations towards a peace of sorts. US authorities were still having disagreements with Syria, with the EU, with Iran, with N. Korea, and many other nations, that was nothing new. A blip on an Islamic website hinted that the Al Qaeda leader, Zarqawi, may have suffered injuries during an attack by US forces. This may be true, but if western officials believe all they hear, they would be called a bunch of puppets, to say the least. Time will tell, where lies the truth, because the attacks on US, and Iraqi forces, had increased considerably by the spring of 2005. We have heard many times that the factions opposing the US, and their supporters, and battling for their freedoms, are many and varied, and they are said to have differing ideological backgrounds. They all claim they wanted to rid themselves, of an occupation of their country, by the Americans. But in doing so they should not use illegitimate means, on innocent people. In conflicts, as in wars, all sides put out misinformation, lies, and propaganda.

We heard more sound bites on efforts in the Middle East. The usual, photo opportunity, was provided by media, when Bush met with Palestinian leader Abbas, something he had refused to do in the past, and he announced that the US would give the Palestinian authority $50 million in direct aid. But critics reminded the public that such a sum compared with a few billion Israel received each year from the US! More of those double standards are seen here, in US policies. Still on the Middle East, May of 2005 produced more reports on Iraq. Now, most in the world, and increasing numbers in the US, called it chaos, and a quagmire, whilst the Bush administration kept sidestepping this issue, and preferred to embellish it with 'we are making steady progress'. But nobody else seemed to see that! *That was a complete disconnection, between US politicians and their people, and the rest of the world.* By now, over 1700 US service personnel had been killed in Iraq, and in one month alone, over 600 Iraqis, most innocent victims. That is anything, but progress, the president and our generals, surely understand that! In June an attack was reported to have killed the most American women in a single blow, since the war started. Many are now calling for an end to this unjust war, to start bringing troops home, to set a timetable for withdrawal. It is regrettable for America that a strong opposition in congress, did not muster a powerful grass roots movement, from the very beginning, to prevent this war. *Those 1700 (and climbing) young men and women would not have lost their lives for weapons of mass destruction that were not in Iraq, and for a threat that never even existed---!* Because of mounting pressure from the media and his own party, in August of 2005 Bush decided to speak out more, on Iraq. His ratings at the polls were the lowest ever. Thus, for the first time since the Iraq tragedy, he was actually heard mumbling the numbers of US forces that had been killed- - *and the world could easily see that he was most uncomfortable doing it!*

There were elections in Iran, labeled 'Axis of evil' quite often by the Bush administration, and there too, an odd turn of events came about. Some in the west, particularly in the US, had predicted that a more moderate leader would emerge from the Iranian elections. But to the surprise of US pundits, it led to a run-off between the more moderate candidate favored by the west, and a more conservative, religious candidate, who had obtained about 6 million votes in the very first election. It was also reported that the more moderate candidate was very wealthy, and had spent large amounts of money on his campaign (how like some political campaigns in western nations); whereas the people claimed that the more fundamentalist candidate was of poor background, he lived in the same modest house for many years, and they called him 'one of us, the struggling workers'. Forecasters were predicting that this guy may well win, not exactly what US officials had been hoping for. And he did win with some 60% of the popular vote, a much greater mandate, than the Bush administration claimed for themselves in the last elections in US, with barely 51% of the vote.

The British Sunday Times discussed persisting and increased corruption all over Africa, including South Africa, previously pointed out in election campaigns in the west, as an example of major efforts at a democracy of sorts. We have to admit that under Mandela, South Africa had made great strides, but since then it had taken some backward steps. As in the US, when international groups give S. Africa poor ratings, officials there quickly object. Many of their ministers had been accused of scams involving many fraudulent travel expenses. Again, this is also similar to abuses reported on officials in western nations. By 2005 these reports claimed that 76% of S. Africans believed that corruption had actually increased under the ANC. There was criticism because the government had clamped down on the media, in an effort to sweep problems under the rug. Is that any different from most western countries?

We also had accusations of oppression under Mugabe of Zimbabwe. In the most recent travesty, he had ordered the bulldozing of hundreds of homes, mostly of people who supported his opponents. There, he seemed to have taken a cue from the Israeli government that, for years, had the policy of bulldozing dozens of homes of Palestinians opposing the Israeli occupation of their lands; and who had been struggling for their freedom from subjugation for decades. And many critics had accused that the US and other western nations, had turned a blind eye to their plight. It was alleged that Mugabe had ordered the arrest of thousands among those who were protesting; he claimed he was cleaning up the cities; whereas human rights groups had labeled him a tyrant. Some in the west have given terrible examples to third world countries, by their behavior.

Elizabeth Davies wrote in the 'Independent' on the curse of gold, whose quest had fueled rape and slaughter in the Congo. Regional warlords, *and international companies*, were among those benefiting from access to the gold rich areas of that country. On the other hand, the local people had suffered ethnic slaughter, and torture. In 'Mirror Reflections' much was discussed on the troubled areas of our world, aggravated by flawed, selective, often capricious, foreign policies of wealthier nations, in the west. Also, how corrupt corporations, doing business in such underdeveloped countries, take advantage of the people and close their eyes to all types of human rights tragedies.

Another disturbing piece of news dealt with 5 children, in Britain, who allegedly had attempted to kill a five year old, boy. Such revelations from Britain were most unusual at one time. Previously we had referred to high rates of violent crime in the US; but now, media in Europe are reporting significant crime waves there as well, why? Could some of these trends be exported from the US to Europe, or vice versa? In tiny, Malta as well, once a bulwark of Catholicism, there has been visible shifting in the opposite direction. Past solid Christian values are being relaxed by many, and in some cases seemingly abandoned. Crime has increased, capital crime, once almost unheard of there, is no longer uncommon. True, there has been an increase in illegal immigration, a serious problem for a small country like that; and sociologists had long maintained that an increase in crime often accompanies such upheavals. It is said that drugs are now easy to come by, and a report claimed that 'guest houses' for prostitution, were now readily available, and the authorities could not do much to curb this scourge, or to control the use of drugs. Another report alleged the presence of white slavery in Malta, involving young girls usually coming from Eastern Europe. What a tragedy for this island, so markedly different from stories of the old days! Thus, by trying to emulate practices in wealthier countries, do we call that progress?

The newspaper 'Independent' also carried stories from the Hague trials on the Balkan wars. At the trial of Slobodan Milosevic, a video was shown of the outright murder of Muslims. This video, taken *by one of those committing these atrocities, also showed an orthodox priest blessing these murderers, the notorious paramilitary 'scorpions', as they were leaving, (what a perversion of religion)!* Then, short clips showed this Srebrenica massacre, where several young Muslim males were gunned down, and those criminals even had the gall to record it! However, *two alleged leaders from these war crimes, Mladic and Karadzic, were reported still at large.* Whilst the US and UK, and others, did little all these years, to insist on their apprehension, and to bring them to justice. Bush and Blair were desperate to remove Saddam Hussein of Iraq, for his crimes; and they are so quick to demand expatriation of other suspects, whereas these other Serbian criminals were allowed to go free all these years! Besides, we remained on friendly terms with the leaders in those countries, who likely knew something about the whereabouts of those criminals. Is it any wonder that the US is accused of double standards much of the time. How can anyone see justice in such a bizarre foreign policy by many governments of the west?

On the Lebanese scene, for many weeks, politicians in the US and UK, had pressured Syria to leave Lebanon (never mind the numerous countries that American imperialism had expanded into, with military bases). After the Syrians had exited Lebanon, a prominent journalist there had been assassinated, and there was more upheaval. This raised the question, if Syria was now gone, who was behind the continued instability? By September 2005, there were more reports of bombings, and casualties. Was it not Pope

John Paul Two who had warned president Bush of the risk of destabilizing the Middle East? It has not been going well.

Time magazine carried an article by Saar who had served with the armed forces for several months, at the Guantanamo prisons in Cuba. What was striking in these reports was the first hand knowledge of what was going on, as the whole world had been accusing the US of illegalities and abuse of prisoners, against all human rights, and international laws. Apparently, one such prisoner had cut his own wrists, and in his own blood, left a message to be translated for the Americans, *"I committed suicide because of the brutality of my oppressors"*. Now, most sensible people would conclude that this was strong enough evidence of what actually had been going on, in these US prisons. Is that not the reason why the international Red Cross had broken its silence, and also accused the US government of mistreatment of prisoners, and of trashing the principles of the Geneva Convention. But human rights groups have been even harsher, in their criticism. There was evidence of large numbers of attempted suicides. These inmates would not do this, in large numbers, without good reason, would they? These reports cited at least 350 suicide attempts in 2003 alone at Guantanamo. Does the US government keep our citizens well informed on all such developments? The Red Cross should investigate all other facilities under western control, and all other nations as well, to expose and publicize all wrongdoing. And at the United Nations, officials should keep bringing these matters up, for action, and resolution.

That report emphasized how the US constantly under-reported such suicide attempts at its facilities- - -*corrupt government or military officials, or what have you, disguised the actual numbers by calling suicides "manipulative self-harm"!* It is likely that only American officials would believe that such pitiful gaming could deceive the citizens of our world! And to use taxpayers' money for such deceit and deliberate misinformation, only confirms the degree of corruption, and lack of ethics. Most honorable and decent people, would conclude that here was a man who obviously thought he was going to die, and decided to leave a message in his own blood, on his cell wall, plainly for someone to see, translate, and transmit, far and wide. Many of these inmates had complained of being beaten without cause, according to these reports. Because of all this, surely most would be inclined to believe this man's story, that he was telling the truth! Most importantly, here, he was **not** referring to brutality by Russians or Chinese, or by Libya, or Turkey, or North Korea; not even by Saudi Arabia, or Cuba! *No, none of these, he was writing about the brutality by officials of the United States!* How will we face up to that, before the courts of the world, and above all, before God Almighty?

Coincidentally, in June US officials announced that a group of congressmen and journalists, would visit the prison at Guantanamo, to see for themselves, and they would eat the food served to the inmates, and listen in to an interrogation process. No doubt, this was because many reporters around the world, kept hammering on this topic, and it had been embarrassing for the Bush clique. But, honestly, government officials must think that citizens of the world, including the US, are morons. That is the problem with many in our government, they feel they have a monopoly on good ideas, on intelligence. We ask the readers, how many would believe US officials, after all that has happened? Such a visit as the above, to that prison, would be well controlled, by US authorities (the same, as in dictator States); the date is set, and they are expecting these visitors, well in advance! The food served would obviously be decent. *And do officials in the US really believe that anyone expects them to carry out an interrogation, with abuse and brutality, in front of an audience, of congressmen and journalists? Come now, America, you know much better than that- - -!*

An Israeli personality had long been critical of Israel's occupation of Palestinian territories, and the mistreatment of Palestinians. It is a troubled world indeed when we keep hearing of the mistreatment of people everywhere, even by so-called civilized societies. What have we come to- - -? This personality had continued to accumulate stories for news reports, or for books, or even to document some of them in movie strips. In late June 2005, he was continuing his work when Jewish extremist groups were causing mayhem, as Israeli soldiers were trying to keep them out of their settlements in Gaza, as these were scheduled for total evacuation by Israel's occupation forces. This gentleman reaffirmed that many Israeli soldiers had indeed complained of the treatment meted out to the Palestinian people, so much so, that some had continued to disobey their orders. And, he said, 'there is no such thing as a benign occupation'. Right! And we can say the same of the US occupation of Iraq, after the so-called preemptive war!

How did man's aggression and belligerence develop, and does it usher in the decline of humanity? Man's inhumanity to man, goes back to ancient times through archeological discoveries; to the days when Homo Sapiens, (dare we still use Homo Sapiens?), learned to assume the erect posture. They soon learned to use crude stones, or crudely fashioned clubs, as weapons. Down through the ages, through biblical descriptions, to the present, our barbaric acts have persisted. We only progressed from those rocks and clubs, to more brutal means. In those historic days, most fighting, or battles, had been fought 'mano a mano', hand to hand. Now, we hurl death causing bombs, or missiles, from miles away at sea, or on land, or in the sky. We have heard officials stating 'how well' our forces were performing in war. That is how far our values and morals had declined. Before we continue to talk of morals and values, we need to remove all skeletons and cobwebs, from our own closets first!

History records ruthlessness in the various empires, the dynasties of the Pharaohs, in Rome, Genghis Khan, by the Chinese, and Japanese, under the feudal periods in Europe, the Ottoman Empire, and on, and on. In more recent history, we had the French, Spanish, and British empires; and some experts now claim, we have an ongoing American empire. There were the horrors of world war one, and world war two; of the Korean and Vietnam wars; the war of the Balkans; and now, Afghanistan, and Iraq. We have people on all sides, particularly in the US, all the way up the chain of command, who have stated that they *must not have legal restrictions on how to interrogate detainees!* But these same people add, 'they will be treated humanely'. Are we talking here, of officials in civilized societies, you ask? Yes, but these are also the same people who clamor about values and morals. Therefore, we need to ask the following- - -Is it humane to keep prisoners naked, ridicule them, and their religion; set dogs on them, so that some had been bitten (evidence given at trials); place them on a stool, with hoods on their heads, and a noose around their neck (and electric cords attached?); keep them in very hot, or very cold environments; keep them in chains, in cages, worse than animals; deprive them of food and water, deprive them of sleep; use lights and noise to drive them crazy, so that some of them commit suicide; and do all this, through long hours of interrogation and terror. Do citizens of the world realize that officials in Nazi Germany were put on trial for similar acts as these, some much harsher, some less so? What about the above acts, in the present? Or are imperial powers always beyond the reach of decent laws, and with them, anything goes?

Consider this - - - which is more humane and charitable, to summarily execute your captives; or to keep them alive, abuse and torture them, so that some become insane or die, as a result, and do that, day after day, week after week, month after month? All these, mind you, without due process, without charges or trials, without access to families or lawyers. Let, readers, judge, which is more humane? *Did we mention civilized societies-?* None of these actions is humane, and they should all be, equally, condemned.

Andy Rooney of '60 Minutes', a CBS program, discussed the obscene budgets of the US military, and we cannot repeat this often enough, simply, because of the enormous good that could be achieved with that money, in our country, and parts of our troubled world. He showed aircraft, ships, submarines, at a cost of a billion dollars each! Then we saw graveyards of hundreds of planes, ships, and other military hardware, all going to waste, as obsolete! And our military and defense industry, constantly want more and more expensive weapons of war. Many critics here and abroad, had often stated, that as long as our politicians are beholden to corporations because of the corrupting influence of money, these evils in our society are perpetuated everywhere, not only in third world countries, or dictator states. A United World body with integrity (a rare commodity) needs to come together, and put a stop to this madness!

What is it that has caused humanity to stray so badly off course; to lose the sense of distinction between right, and wrong, between good and evil? Why has there been, and still is, so much violence in the journey of man on earth? This brutal history goes back to ancient times, to the sacrifices of humans or animals, 'to appease the gods'. There were men battling each other to the finish, till one or both were dead. Then came the horrors of spectator sports, perhaps the most famous being the Colosseum of ancient Rome, with gladiators going at each other, in pairs or in groups; and wild animals set loose on Christians in the arena, their prey. And the degenerate audience was using these spectacles as entertainment! Many stories and movies have been produced on this topic, such as Gladiator, Spartacus, Ben Hur, and more. Animal activists point to remnants of savagery in our world, to this day. There have been cock fighting, or dog fights, with an audience, for monetary gain; then there is fox hunting, deer, and bird hunting, as a 'sport' when for sport, they could easily use artificial targets. True, in some instances numbers of certain species must be kept under control, only because man has usurped so much of their natural habitat. There is the ongoing 'entertainment', with an audience, of bull fighting, that so many have condemned and tried to get banned. Others claim that boxing, and other forms of fighting, with potential for injury or death, are perhaps also remnants of what went on in man's past. A well-known US personality, with brain injury from such sport, was Muhammad Ali. There have been movies depicting fighters in third world countries, performing for a gambling audience, even till one of them was injured or killed; how much was true history, it is hard to tell. Then in other areas we had the practice of voodoo, whereby there was the belief that spells or curses could be cast on someone causing discontent, or harm. With such bizarre activities, and reports from many parts of our troubled world, is it any wonder that we are still hearing of mistreatment, abuse, and torture? And one has to assume that many such behavior patterns, are completely hidden from the public domain! Many groups around the world had called for a total ban on such performances, making them illegal, and subject to prosecution; but they have had limited success, as such activities persist to this day.

In some cultures, in Africa and elsewhere, they had the ritual whereby a young man could only establish his manhood, by stalking a wild animal in 'a hunt', killing it, and bringing it back to the camp or village. Then, came the 'famed white hunter' of the imperial days of Africa, India, and elsewhere. These 'brave' souls, sometimes with a supporting group, would stalk and corner a wild animal, a Lion, or a Tiger, for the kill. With high-powered rifles, often from a safe distance, they were considered brave, and fearless, according to romantic tales of the past. And why was all this killing, going on? Often, to have homes 'decorated' with trophies of mounted animals, or heads, or with skins of various species of animals! The new European invaders to the discovered land of America brought these same traits with them, and they hunted animals not simply for food, but for monetary gain from pelts, and at times 'just for sport', as already alluded to. They slaughtered so many of the free roaming Buffalo, that the animal came close to extinction. Many of the wild animals on this planet had neared the same fate, before we learned the blunders and errors of our ways. However, many animal and plant species had already disappeared from our environment, according to scientists, millions of them!

In old times, indigenous people only took from nature, what they needed for the survival of their families, or what was needed for the village. Any animal that was killed provided sustenance, and they made use of most parts of the animal, little was wasted. An old TV commercial, on behalf of the environment, remains vivid in our mind. It depicted a venerable, old, native-American Indian, the lines of years of experience, well etched on his aged face. He was walking by a pristine stream, only to find, as he rounded a bend, here or there, discarded items of trash (man's intrusion on nature). But he then climbed a hill and looked down at the valley below. *The camera then focuses on his majestic face showing copious tears flowing freely down his cheeks; the valley below was littered with numerous carcasses of slaughtered Buffalo, they had been skinned, and left there to rot.* A powerful scene that spoke volumes, no words were needed for that moment - - -!

What is it, that has caused it all? Is it a genetic marker of savagery? Or, is it a degenerate tendency of humanity, where we have misused our God given talents, and free will, and took the wrong path a long time ago, 'the fall of man'? The path, that has led us away from God and His basic teachings - - - goodness, love, mercy, and peace. As Mahatma Gandhi had stated so well, "Did Jesus not come for all mankind"?

There were even more thought provoking news bites and headlines, from the British newspaper Independent, and the reader must bear in mind, that these are only from a handful of issues: 'Bush under pressure to increase debt relief for third world'; 'Gordon Brown (UK) stepped up the pressure on Bush, to agree to a huge increase in debt relief'; and here are some that should stimulate debate among politicians in the US, UK, and the rest of the world: 'T-shirts available in UK, made from American cotton, and produced in Chinese sweat shops'; 'How the multi-billion dollar farm subsidy is destroying Africa's cotton farmers'; 'The WTO last year ruled that America's cotton subsidy was illegal'! If so, why did the WTO not take immediate action against any country breaking international laws? There is more: 'How the US is stitching up Africa', and British consumers reap the benefits as well! My, my!

Then we were shown satellite photographs taken 30 years apart, over parts of Brazil, China, and Spain. These pointed glaringly to the devastating deterioration in the landscape, vegetation, forests, etc., thought to be the direct result of greenhouse gases emissions, and global warming. And we have all seen pictures in the past of the melting of polar ice caps. Do Bush and Blair, and the group of eight, and the international monetary fund, and the world-bank people, *do they ever listen to experts? And above all, do they care?* And, finally, here are some more headlines, as regrettably this could go on indefinitely: 'Africans not included'- -this could have referred to the decision process by the group of eight, over the past several years. 'Three facing prison for the torture of a girl for being a witch'- - -my, what is our world coming to? 'The disappearing Tiger'; 'We need a new generation of leaders in Europe'- - -this perhaps, to change the course of our world for the better, particularly if the US keeps on the wrong track. This last, referred to the 'NO' vote in France and Holland, on the EU constitution. They feared that a snowball effect could follow. France's Chirac, and Germany's Schroeder, were to meet (without Blair of course) to try sort out some of these difficulties, for Europe as a whole. But, at last count, there were now, 25 members in the EU, not just 8 or 10. Gentle leaders, is it not time to put differences aside, to agree on plans to mould a better Europe, stronger, more prosperous for all, and united?

And also in the news from the US, were even more disturbing reports on the republican administration attacking the Public Broadcasting System, for being 'too liberal'! That; they were biased against conservative issues, and the Bush administration. What utter nonsense! We must presume that another news station, Fox News, would be perfectly acceptable to this US government, only because this one, had been called by many, 'a perfect mouthpiece for Bush'! This is yet another sign that people around Bush, want to silence any, and all, balance and freedom of speech in America; and that is why the republican controlled congress wanted to cut funding for public broadcasting. Republicans had been attacking the program 'Now', with Bill Moyers (now retired), who is one of the most respected journalists in the country. Public survey polls revealed that 75% of those polled felt there was no bias in public broadcasting, that it was balanced reporting, and rendered a valuable service to our citizens. In these programs one seldom sees any trashy or violent stories depicted, as are so often seen on other television channels. This was going on in the US, but it is the same administration that tried to silence Al Jazeera, in Iraq; that was the democracy, Washington pundits claimed they had brought to the Iraqi people, through attacks, and an invasion of their country. If these patterns are found in the US, and in third world countries, are they then found in the rest of the world? Does it also portend more trouble for our disturbed world?

There are not many who doubt that our planet is in trouble, most of it engineered by human beings. We have also experienced shake-ups in the sphere of religion. The Catholic Church, especially in America, was rocked by many scandals relating to pedophilia, by some of its priests, and for the longest period all major media would not let up on these stories, as if they had planned to gang up, on Catholics. We witnessed the capitalistic marketing of religion on television, and other media outlets, again mostly in the US. Evangelical preachers had raised millions of dollars in this manner. But this was followed by disturbing revelations that, some 'preachers' had associated with prostitutes; some had their own church jet aircraft; others lived in luxury, with very expensive suits, in mansions, some of which had bathroom gold fixtures, for extra ornaments! Was that the modern way, to try to bring the faithful around, to show them the right path? With such thoughts, a blip arrived on the Internet that seemed quite appropriate, author unknown. It went like this: 'if you attend a church meeting without fear of harassment, arrest, torture, or death, you are more blessed than almost three billion people in the world'! Another went like this: 'if you have food in your refrigerator, clothes on your back, a roof over your head and a place to sleep, you are richer than 75% of this world'! Are these not amazing? Do we note troubles around us that must be addressed, soon?

Many people, including those in government, often hold to their 'beliefs', as being the only right ones; and thus, they want to force those values on the other side, because ' they are superior'. They are wrong! If the other side claims that their 'beliefs' are the only right ones, and try to force them on the 'west', they are also wrong! Somewhere there is a middle road, that of dialogue, education, that of exchange of ideas in a peaceful manner. We can always learn from each other surely! Differences are never solved by wars, by assassinations, targeted or otherwise; by kidnappings or murder; by rendition as invented by the US government; or by terrorism. *Historically, these have aggravated problems, never solved them.* A recent example is the Iraq war. Experts here, and in most countries, believe it did not help terrorism, as Bush officials claim, that it had made it much worse, and had created more violence, not only for Iraq, but also for other countries.

Yes, indeed, from the preceding paragraphs, one can conclude that many changes have taken place in the world, all around us; and regrettably, these changes, are often in the wrong direction; whether they occur in large, or small countries, in developed or under-developed areas; in so-called democratic, or dictatorship states, or in monarchies. Whether they come from the left, or the right, they are, yet, moving in the wrong direction. Society must come together, under a strong, united, international body, a revitalized United Nations, *fully supported by all,* to get ourselves back, on the right track! Our troubled world needs all of us, to work together, for the good of mankind as a whole.

LOOKING AT POLICIES OF THE UNITED STATES

A former president of the United States, James Madison, is quoted thus: "We have staked the whole of our political institutions, on the capacity of mankind for self government, upon the capacity of each and all of us, to govern ourselves, to sustain ourselves according to the Ten Commandments of God".

Another historically famous president, Thomas Jefferson, worried that the courts would overstep their authority, and instead of interpreting the law, would begin making law, in other words, an oligarchy? In that context, should we not consider what the Supreme Court did in the 2000 presidential elections? Did they indeed, overstep their authority, when they unduly intervened, in the recounting of the popular vote in Florida? Many would agree that they did. And recently president Bush referred to his selection of a judicial candidate, and said he hoped the senate nomination process would be *dignified.* Many must have wondered how *dignified,* were some of the decisions his administration had made in the past few years. A guest on 'Now', a PBS program with David Broncaccio, also referred to an address given by George Washington. He had emphasized some of the danger signals for his country- - - national debt, party factions, and a divided country! It is astounding, today, that what such a great, historic figure, as Washington, had feared so much, many years ago, has descended upon America, at the present time!

And participants on another 'Now' program, discussed actions by politicians that can undermine freedom. They viewed an exhibit, and also mentioned a book on the same topic, "The Design of Dissent". They affirmed that *dissent means democracy, and suppressing dissent is tyranny.* The exhibit contained a picture of Bush with his mouth covered in a thick coat of black oil. That cartoon had significant implications re the Middle East. They talked about how the media in the US had been extremely passive, in always bowing down to the federal government, in the past several years.; and how, when there was fear, power (the government) can do anything it chooses, it can repress, it can intimidate, and thus can instill even more fear!

In July 2005, White House press conferences were finally dominated, at least for a short time, by the press corps trying to pin down a spokesman for Bush, to get him to give one definitive answer, on the White House leak, about an undercover CIA operative. Rove, the right hand man of Bush, had apparently been named in criminal investigations; as well as a senior person working for Cheney. The pathetic answer by that spokesman was zero, he kept stating 'that he had nothing to announce', *as it was an ongoing investigation.* But he was quite willing to talk ad nauseam, about meaningless white House propaganda issues, as soon as he could get reporters off that subject. One wonders if reporters could walk off, together, from such a conference, and thus deliver a strong protest; and repeat that gesture, until they sense some fairness, in the government's dealings with the press. Officials were obviously anxious to deflect public attention from this scandal. Thus, how do so-called civilized nations portray themselves? There is a lot of information within these pages, but there is much more. There were weeks of controversial reports on the above scandal of the White House leak, and the choice of a possible judicial nominee by president Bush. Some officials may have had wakeful nights dreaming up plans on how to get rid of this mess. By July 19, we had reports on how our magnanimous politicians work, both here and in other countries. To get the media and the public off guard, and off the scandals, it was reported that Bush would announce the name of the justice nominee, and it would be at least one week ahead of schedule. Is that serious government business, playing politics with such important issues? Critics promptly announced, that it was all a ploy to distract the nation. Sure enough, within twenty-four hours, of the naming of the potential justice, all major US networks had discussions on the name of the judge, on all their programs; *not a word on the White House scandals, and on that right hand man of Bush, who had been all over the news lately!* There, is a great example of how corruption in media ownership works, in association with political chicanery. It is a disservice to our people, it is also the absence of true democracy.

In victory during conflicts, even if one wins, there is always a profound loss; there is death and mutilation; there is destruction, and so much suffering. One poster in the above mentioned exhibit, linked consumerism to aggression. In "Mirror Reflections= Mirages", this writer discussed the abomination of an ethic that accepts, that business climates and corporate profits, would improve significantly, from wars and their miseries. This is a sad fact of life. Then they also emphasized how repetition, such as 'the president wants to save social security'- - -if you repeat that often enough, many gullible Americans get to believe it. Whereas many critics, and analysts, had concluded that the Bush programs would actually destroy social security, not save it! In the past it was always desirable to question authority, but now it seems to have become archaic. They wondered what had happened to famous ideals, that an end, does not always justify the means. Commercial advertising in America, gives the false impression that acquisition of wealth means happiness. Because our people have become so sensitized (brainwashed?) to advertising spins or bites; *they have likewise, become sensitized and accustomed to political misrepresentations.*

For example, reports on the Internet showed that president Bush and other officials, had claimed success with the patriot act, with anti-terrorism laws, resulting in some 200 convictions, related to terrorism, since 2001. However these reports claimed, that on closer analysis, there were only 39 convictions connected to terrorism or national security; most others only dealt with minor infractions. Talk about spins, and misinformation!

August 2005 ushered in the passage of a transportation improvement bill in the US congress. Reporters claimed that it was particularly remarkable, that both democrats, and republicans, had introduced many more billions in that bill, than Bush had asked for, all of it going to pet 'pork' projects in their districts. One comment revealed that although the two major political parties disagreed on most issues; but on the question of 'pork' they were in full agreement, they all got something. A few brave souls had voted against such a padded bill; others who had voted against some of the president's agenda, had pork money taken away from their districts, and it was given to somebody else, 'more cooperative', those who had become, yes-men. When readers encounter such revelations, they are bound to ask why US officials still deny that there is corruption, bribery, and blackmail in US politics, as is found everywhere else, unfortunately. Who is right?

An amazing news release from Europe, in May 2005, alleged that American CIA officials in 2001, had instructed their members to deliver Bin Laden's head in a box of ice, let alone that he was still at large, and we had changed our tunes about him, several times, already. If this is true, it reflects once again, on our questionable conduct in the international arena, on the depths to which 'civilized' countries had deteriorated. Then again, it also reminds us that barbarians of old, used to adopt such measures, not heads on ice of course, but in a sack! It does not portray America in a good light, does it? But, neither do other revelations in this book.

There has been much rancor between the Bush administration and rogue nations, as they like to call them- -North Korea, Iran, Syria, at one time there was Libya; and at times, they turned on Russia or China, typical US foreign policy. As regards N. Korea, for world consumption, our government officials had often stated that they refused to participate in one-on-one talks, with the N. Koreans, on dismantling their nuclear program, but only in six party talks! Some of this was apparently simple pompous behavior, because since then, reporters have shown that there were six party talks indeed, but within those, the US had one-on-one talks with the N. Koreans, contrary to its publicized policies. That 'humble pie' may yet cause administration officials a powerful indigestion. Thus, we had foot dragging for months, or years, and in the end, the Koreans got what they wanted, anyway. We could have started talking to them years ago, as many experts had suggested. The Chinese and South Koreans wanted the Bush clique to adopt a different policy towards N. Korea, but the Americans were not interested, they said.

It had become a foreign policy maze. An article by R. E. Powalski, in America magazine, points out that the US strategy in the last few years had not worked at all. Clinton had tried to get Bush officials to expand on agreements that had already been reached with the Koreans, but the Bush administration showed no interest. The author stated that the perpetuation, and worsening, of that crisis, was caused by this administration alone. On the other hand, the N. Koreans had been angered, by Bush calling them, 'Axis of evil'; and by the suggestion that the US could preemptively attack, even with nuclear weapons (everything was on the table), any country they considered a threat! Quite naturally, the N. Koreans took that as a direct threat against them, and instead of calming the situation, Bush officials had escalated the dangers immensely, by their bravado speeches, the so-called 'Bush doctrine'. By the third week in September 2005, the Koreans signaled that they might consider putting their nuclear program on hold, pending further negotiations. Thus, finally, talking, instead of a posture of demands and belligerence, was perhaps beginning to bear fruit. Time will tell.

On the PBS program 'Now', with David Broncaccio, participants re-visited the issue of prisoner abuse, because it was not only taking place at the US Guantanamo prisons in Cuba, and in Iraq or Afghanistan; but, they said, we have mistreatment of prisoners in our own country as well. They referred to conditions in many prisons as unconstitutional, cruel, and inhumane; and that, could change a prisoner with only minor offenses against him, into a hardened criminal. Experts had called our prison system, punitive, rather than a rehabilitation program. And, once again, they quoted previous reports of prisoners being abused or tortured by military personnel, and some of them dying in US custody. If such reports were about a third world country, our magnanimous leaders would clamor for the UN, the whole world, to investigate, to prosecute, and punish responsible parties, all the way to the top, and for sanctions against those countries. Well, how about the fabrications by the US and UK, regarding Iraq, and Saddam Hussein's intent? Critics have been asking for some time, what about the gross misdeeds by some of our own officials? Why are the 'free' news media not running wild, with such worldwide interest, news coverage?

Another tragedy in June of 2005, was in our reports, once in a while we do get more open coverage, after all. These reports alleged that US doctors at that, now infamous, Guantanamo prison, assisted interrogators by providing guidelines on ways to increase stress levels, and suffering, of those inmates (let us remember that many, here and overseas, called it torture, by the US), some of whom were totally innocent to begin with. They tried to force them to 'cooperate'. What a ghastly black eye for America, if this is real, for the government and the military, to use the noble profession of Medicine, for their dastardly intentions! Therefore, we ask, once again, *do readers see the shadows of what doctors reportedly had done to prisoners, under the old Soviet and Nazi regimes?* A psychiatric association official said that such behavior by physicians, would be unethical, and illegal, by medical professional standards; *and it had been so, since the days of Hippocrates!* Our fellow Americans, if you cannot wake up to comprehend, and try to stop, these dangerous trends, surely you will be dragged down to the depths of despair.

President Clinton had stated that globalization needed to work for all people, something the late Pope John Paul, had emphasized many times. And on Iraq, Clinton recently said that what we did in the beginning might have been wrong (might - -?), but now our people need to move forward; to stop criticizing the Iraq war, and work for peace in the region. Are these more examples of the elite, covering for the elite? This writer has agreed with Clinton on many matters, but we cannot, we should not, stop criticizing what the US did to Iraq, and by now we all know those solid reasons! It was immoral, against all international laws, and we killed tens of thousands of innocent people! *Can we tell them, that it is time to move on-?* As yet, we have not heard from the US, and the new Iraqi governing body, how many innocent people had been killed, precisely how many? Surely we must have accountability for our willful, misguided actions. To stop all criticism, would be a mistake, it would be like acquiescing, and encouraging more, similar, tragic, mistakes.

However, we agree with president Clinton that we must work hard, for peace and justice, in that region finally solving the Israeli-Palestinian nightmare. But we can do that, and still criticize the misdeeds of any government, large or small, whether here at home, or abroad. We must remember that *dissent implies a healthy democracy, always.* For example, recently media and also, some of our officials, have been critical about authorities in Aruba, being so secretive about the possible murder of an American woman. True, that case was still under investigation. But why are the media not awash with details of so much secrecy in our own government? We often hear nothing but, 'no comment', 'it is still under investigation', or 'it is for national security', and on, and on!

Senator Robert Byrd, a well-known United States orator, gave a thought provoking speech, 'A Cry for Freedom in the US Senate'. This referred to the present republican majority in the US congress, trying to eliminate the practice of filibuster for certain issues before the senate. This is the art of limitless debate to try to defeat any legislation, with which the minority opposition disagreed, when this was the only tool left it, against a solid majority. Otherwise, it would become a dictatorship, right? The trend of his talk was, that we risked becoming an imperial power, and a tyranny; because the party with the majority would try to ram through any legislation, on the American people. Those concerns about such risks, had been expressed by many other writers, as well.

Byrd also quoted Ronald Reagan, a former president, where he said, "Freedom is a fragile thing, and never more than a generation away from extinction". And Byrd said, he was not discussing the grandiose freedom talk, with far-flung foreign policy goals, referring to the US administration; but the freedoms here at home. He pointed out that it was the persecuted, the disadvantaged, those who are poor, and downtrodden- -they were the citizens who needed the strong protection of an unbiased legal system. He emphasized how members in government would be derelict in their duty, if they did not dissent, because the country was now so polarized and politicized, that *dissent was being discarded as obstructionist.*

Another US senator, Tom Daschle, had lost his seat in the 2004 elections. Money was flooded into his district by republicans, it was alleged, to ensure his defeat. Money talks! He spoke before a large university student body, and he reiterated that something was terribly wrong with a health care system, that leaves 45 million people uninsured, when most of them depended on the emergency rooms, for their health care needs, a very expensive form of care. The US could do much better, and he pointed to the obvious advantage of a universal healthy care system, as is found in most industrialized nations, for all their people. He also mentioned that many Americans had the misconception that all was well with the US electoral process. Students then commented how things were terribly wrong with a system where Gore had received the majority of the people vote, but Bush got to occupy the White House. Daschle affirmed that we needed to do a better job at educating people on the existing problems, with the electoral process, and perhaps, he was suggesting, with our democracy? All this, was met with loud applause from the vast audience in those halls. Another author, Rev. Fr. J. Dear, during a lecture at a different university, expressed how all religions are rooted in non-violence; and he raised the question whether we can call ourselves Christian, if at the same time, we support war and nuclear weapons, or corporate greed, or systematic injustice and executions. He said if we did that, we would have joined the ranks of the blasphemous hypocrites.

In the United States increasing numbers of our citizens are at odds with their government on the Iraq war, and on flawed foreign policies by their officials. Perhaps as a result, the military had a serious problem in recruiting candidates for their 'voluntary armed forces'. Most of the youth, did not wish to join, and risk being sent to Iraq; apparently, that was becoming the glaring truth. Their number of recruits had fallen short in 2004-2005, even as television reports showed that some of the techniques used by the recruiting officials were highly questionable, to say the least. *They alleged, that sometimes recruits were rushed to sign papers that they did not fully understand.* With the numbers of US forces scattered around the world, they created the back door draft, as it was labeled. US officials had announced that they did not want to re-institute the draft, in the country. But, through this other 'draft method', the military could refuse to discharge soldiers who had completed their tour of duty. Others had past discharge papers, thinking they had finished with the army, only to be sent re-enlistment orders. Others, who had long 'retired', were also brought back, some in the 50's, and some others with disabilities, it was stated. These orders included women with babies a few months old! As expected, these matters received a great deal of media exposure, so that potential recruits were forced to use much needed finances, to hire lawyers *to fight big brother in the courts.* What type of democracy and freedom are we talking about? Ask these young men and women.

Another embarrassment for America, occurred in May 2005, when anti-US protests erupted all over the Muslim world, as European papers reported that US soldiers had desecrated their Holy Book, the Koran, at the Guantanamo prison. One paper quote read: "the Koran defiled by the dirtiest of hands". Such comments hurt America's image, once again. These incidents, like the prisoner abuse, will continue to have a snowball effect. Anti-US protests had increased in Afghanistan as well, when we had been told that things were much better over there; and when the 'poppy' had remained the only source of income for thousands, and when the poppy business was the strongest ever. Most people in that country, had remained extremely poor, jobs were scarce, reconstruction efforts had been trivial, all under a US occupation going on 3 years.

These reports on the Koran were so serious, that US officials tried to downplay the news release, that it was not true, and a magazine that had broken the story, tried to retract the comments 'because there was no absolute proof' (did that sound like government coercion)? Would such assertions by the US government be believed, after much of the world had been accusing some of our officials, with fabrications? Besides, there were so many photographs on the US military abuse of prisoners, shown around the world. Allegedly, even Pakistan officials had not believed the retractions by an American news periodical, and demanded further investigations. Because world opinion against the US was mounting fast, in June both Bush and Rumsfeld gingerly announced that, in any case, they did not want to keep those detainees, but what would they do with them? And they alleged that those that had been released, had gone back to fight Americans. One cannot but wonder how they received such information. Most psychologists had long maintained that when you mistreat those in detention, you end up forcing them into behaviors, more serious than they originally were. Some officials suggested that perhaps America could send them to other countries. Why, so they could be abused or tortured even more? There were other headlines in the British press that the pentagon had admitted the abuse of the Koran by a prison guard; but they had initially issued a denial. But as this insult had caused such an uproar in the Muslim world, US officials announced, that after 'an investigation', they concluded it was simply an accident. This commentary in the papers, with tongue in cheek, described the following.

A soldier had been urinating near an air vent behind a wall, adjoining a holding cell of some of the prisoners, when, accidentally, the army alleged, air currents forced the urine through an air vent, into the cell, and it splashed the detainee and his book! Some of the news reports had previously mentioned that the book had been flushed down the toilet. We cannot tell if this was true reporting, or just a bizarre jibe at the US government, but it is doubtful that anyone will believe it. They will likely be laughing their heads off, at such preposterous stories put out by the US government. According to the Sunday Times, Amnesty International's annual reports had recently branded the United States prison at Guantanamo, "the Gulag of our times", and millions in our world had already agreed with that description. C. Rice, for the Bush administration, was forced to admit that the persisting bad news had become a serious problem for our government.

A Chris Matthews program, Hardball, on MSNBC television station, featured noted journalist Bill Moyers, and the discussion started with the US government slashing funds for Public Broadcasting, because 'they were too liberal'. Many asked, what do the Bush people want? What is wrong with that? They do not welcome criticism of the State, either from within, or without. Is it not freedom and democracy, that you show all sides of the story? Then they pointed to a Time magazine article on how America presently had a government by the few. They lamented that so many democrats had voted for the Iraq war, giving the Bush administration carte blanche. And they reiterated how, these days, it is difficult to get into politics unless you had millions of dollars, to begin with. They showed that many in our country cannot make it economically, but the elite in Washington, and corporate CEO's, do not like to hear that, because they want Americans to believe that everyone is doing well in the US, even if it is not true! Do our people really swallow such misrepresentation? It is called brainwashing! And then Katrina came, and the events in New Orleans, and it really exposed the dark side of this great country.

Neither did the elite wish to publicize the fact that some 80 million Americans had a difficult time paying their bills, that is more than a fourth of the entire population! Republicans conservatives, the extremes, had tried their best to undo 'the new social deal'. In "Mirror Reflection", this writer discussed such issues at length, how some of the elite, everywhere, can lie, fabricate, misrepresent, so that people are manipulated, and are fed a steady diet of propaganda. Therefore, things are made to appear better than they actually are, whether it is the economy, or education, or health care, or the war, and on, and on. Such discussions, as the above, seem to corroborate what many have been stating for several years. Does society ever try to change course, and improve? Bill Maher, on that Chris Matthews program, commented how most wars *are entered into, following a series of lies;* and that in the Iraq case, those who wanted that war so badly, should probably have been the ones to go to war! Then Maher stated that we could witness a senate shut down, because 'it could not get any worse than it already is, in Washington'. These comments are worth noting, especially as they are so disturbing; those on the right will call them controversial and leftist, (whatever that is supposed to mean). But many others will realize, that such reports reflect much of the truth, of what is happening in Washington, today. What has gone wrong with that welcoming symbol, the statue of liberty that beckoned, to all who sought out these shores? Where is the 'free press'?

On another PBS news hour, with J. Lehrer, guest speakers accused Bush and Blair of rendering a disservice to the community, when they continue to say that terrorists attack us because 'they hate us', when it is the policies of the US government, in particular, they are fighting against. Other critics have also accused the US, of behaving like the new Empire of the United States. Today, our world still festers with the cancerous effects, on millions of people, of the boot of empires past. American officials vehemently deny such talk, but critics point to the presence of American interests, and military bases, in dozens of countries, not unlike the days of 'glory' of the British Empire; except, for some of those citizens in those countries, it was not considered glory. Neither is it 'glory' for the people now inundated with this US presence, as we have learned in recent years. In 2005 US officials were debating military base closings, and it came out, loud and clear, that in Germany, many in that country, had resented all the years with American presence on their soil. But others had welcomed it indeed, as an economic and cultural arrangement, yet others, did not welcome any of it.

The behavior of some in our government had hurt our relationships with much of the world. There are those, who only pretend to be our friends, because of what they could get from us; others, pretend to be friends mainly, because they fear us. But many have grown to distrust, and dislike, the United States, according to reports from around the world, they consider it a pariah. They always emphasize, they do not have issues with the ordinary folk, but the governments ruling and dictating, over America. It was certainly not like that, in the past, was it? Then, the vast majority looked up to the US, and as noted, millions had sought out these shores. How else would we have become a melting pot, of many races and ethnic communities? We do need trustworthy leaders, leaders with genuine solid values, not just those that are imaginary or capricious, for political gain, and for the votes of a particular moment. Such leaders are there, and they must come out in large numbers, to show that **Mammon** will not continue to dictate politics in America. They should take the reigns of this country, whether they are from the right, the left, or the center, and regain us the respect and admiration of the world, as it was once. This, truly, could help maintain peace and stability, and justice, not the accumulation of weapons of destruction, by any country, or countries; because working closely with all nations (then truly becoming our friends), *we could eliminate most of the root causes and discontent, in our world today!*

There were also reports in 2005, on more investigations into the armed forces of the US, this time, dealing with the air force academy, because of alleged religious intolerance. Previously, this academy, the navy, and other military groups, under the Pentagon, had come under fire repeatedly, for sexual harassment and abuse, and sometimes for racial intolerance as well. There were many news reports on the sexual abuse of female recruits, and apparently, those at the top, seldom did much about the problem. It was always announced that 'the matter was under investigation'. These, and many other incidents, raised the question, again, of what had happened to the stature, and stability, of America? What was going so terribly wrong, with some of our government agencies?

And, on the steamroller tactics adopted by the Bush administration, the program Hardball, on MSNBC, with Chris Matthews, had senator Robert Byrd outline, how the majority republicans hoped to appoint certain judges to the bench, with extreme ideologies on the right, and how some judges could be forced into the supreme court of the land, (by eliminating filibuster)? This attempt at eliminating filibuster, had been labeled 'the nuclear option', and the destruction of free speech in America. Once more, are these not shadows of Stalin, and Hitler, as had been suggested by so many? Byrd continued, that the republican so-called constitutional *option, was in reality, an unconstitutional option.* He complemented 14 senators, 7 from each major party, for forging an agreement to stop the destruction of the senate, and freedoms in America. He said that they were in those chambers, elected by their constituents, and the constitution had always granted them the power to speak, for as long as they had strength and voice to do so, on behalf of a cause they fervently believed in, and "for the people"! *Whereas, they continued, the Bush administration was trying to stifle voices.* Then, they said, today it may be restriction of speech, and the election of judges, tomorrow it will be social security, education, health care, etc. Another senator, Carl Levin, pointed out how both sides should recognize the value of bipartisanship, but he said, it could not be a one way street, that is not being bipartisan.

Senator Dick Durbin discussed how some religious zealots were trying to force 'their moral values', on the population of America, by selecting judges who are likely to lean to the extreme right, and by restricting debate. He pointed to certain areas that had given rise to bitter debates in this country, both in congress, and within the judicial system, such as, women's reproductive health issues, as contraception, and family planning, abortion questions, stem cell research, the use of Medical Marihuana, and many others- -all these provoked intense disagreement. Obviously, most of us have differing opinions on these issues, but on many others perhaps a consensus can be reached, if it benefits mankind, and does not contravene moral beliefs. All in all, such debates, even if prolonged, should never be labeled 'justice denied', as some republicans have been accused of doing.

Governor Howard Dean, leader of the Democratic Party, has been outspoken, on political issues, on the Iraq war, and had caused consternation in some circles. However, he had voiced problems that people everywhere, wanted to hear, and the youth responded favorably, in large numbers. If more politicians had emulated Dean, critics maintained that the last election would have had a different outcome. Senator Biden had also been harshly critical, as had many other congress representatives, of the mistreatment of prisoners in US custody; and he, and many others, had already called for the closure of the infamous Guantanamo. Meanwhile, American officials had continued to protest the comparison of actions in the US, to the Stalin or Hitler regimes. Some have pointed out, that if we object to those comparisons, coming at us from all over the world, the answer is, we should stop behaving like those evil regimes! As long as we behave like them, those comparisons will only become louder, and more persistent. As July 2005 was upon us, we could add that as we celebrate 'Independence', once again, we show the flag, we sing patriotic songs, we see numerous fireworks displays, and many other external manifestations, *but at the same time, we keep on doing some terrible things; things, that are not good for our citizens, or for our world!*

Scandals for the present administration, in Washington, were never far behind. In 2005, we also had the tobacco industry being hit with heavy punitive damages (some 100 billion dollars), by the courts, for concealing details that for 50 years, they had allegedly conspired to get smokers addicted to their product, tobacco. All this was debated on one of our television programs, and readers might conclude that is as it should be, right? Suddenly, critics alleged, the US justice department announced, that those damages awards, would be greatly reduced, to 10 billion dollars! They said, this smacked of the heavy hand of the Bush administration, interfering even in the American judicial process. If this is true, is it what we call *freedom and democracy?* This, it was alleged, because republicans had always been considered pro-corporation, and not pro the citizen at large. Thus, they would still be pro-corporation, no matter how dishonest they might have been? A witness on that program, in this tobacco litigation, said, *they had felt the heavy handed pressure of those in high places, to change, and substantially soften, their testimony, against the tobacco industry! Is this what we call justice, these days, in America?* Other witnesses also commented on the continuing wrong doing by some of the tobacco companies, in spite of previous court orders issued against them. For example reporters claimed, funds charged tobacco companies for smoking cessation programs, and children smoke-free societies, had never been paid.

Rev. Fr. J. Dear had written extensively on the ethics and the morality of war. He had been active in a movement to try force the US government to shut down Los Alamos, that infamous establishment for the proliferation of nuclear weapons, instruments of mass destruction and death. He also questioned the morality of clergymen as they bless soldiers, going into action, killing and maiming the guilty, but also the innocent. There are many who are bound to be in agreement with his positions, in this area of ethics.

In 'America' magazine, Fr. J. R. Conroy, A Jesuit priest, wrote 'A Veteran Remembers' and made some very enlightening comments. Before joining the priesthood, he was in the armed forces as a young man, and served in Vietnam, thus seeing first hand, the experience of combat. He pointed to the "violent rupture of relationships by death"; and the difficulty in understanding the long-term consequences of being involved in war. He added how he became 'one of his generation's skeptics *about American foreign policy and decision making*'. He emphasized how MacNamara, the secretary of defense at that time, was concerned about doubts and mistakes made in the Vietnam war; but he had lacked the transparency to come forth with those misgivings at that time. Rather interesting comment, that! Likewise, Conroy felt that the Iraq war veterans will have the same skepticism about their government, and it had already begun, much earlier this time, than during the war in Vietnam.

Renowned journalist Bill Moyers, gave a keynote address to the national conference on media, when he said "Because what we are talking about, is nothing less than rescuing our democracy, that is so politicized, and it is in danger of being paralyzed and pulverized. I was naive I guess, I simply never imagined that any Public Broadcasting chairman, democrat or republican, would cross the line, *from resisting White House pressure, to actually carrying out their policy*". The chairman of Public Broadcasting was charged with being too pro republican administration, and therefore was not allowing balanced reporting on issues. In a democracy, should an individual in such an important position, not be asked to resign, or be fired immediately? It so happens that before the end of 2005, that individual had indeed resigned, but news reports also showed that a majority of the top positions at Public Broadcasting had been stacked with conservative candidates. About this same time, a caller to a news program commented that he had never seen so much cronyism, as in this Bush administration. Many critics of recent events in the US had pretty much agreed with those comments. Most media owners obviously leaned towards whichever direction they liked, and they did. But, historically, Public Broadcasting had always been presumed to remain totally independent, to provide fairness and balance. It is, in most countries, except in dictator, totalitarian States!

Another revelation in the realm of US politics was the purported identity of the former 'Deep Throat' personality from the president Nixon era, and why he had kept his secret for so long. This was to do with the person who had leaked information on illegalities being perpetrated under the Nixon administration. Many continued to praise 'Deep Throat', others, criticized his actions. Some on the right, government officials, and former Nixon aides, continued to label him a traitor! Why a traitor? Others claimed that most Americans considered this guy, a hero! His critics said that he was bound 'by professional ethics'. Ah! Had these ignoramuses considered that ethics should not comprise concealment of serious criminal activities, at the highest levels of our government, or any other government? As we have often reiterated, *we are not holier than any other society, far from it!* Ben Bradlee of the Washington Post said "for people to talk of immorality regarding Deep Throat, for doing what he did, makes me laugh". An editorial said that had the individual remained silent, Nixon might have succeeded in one of the most serious abuses of power, by an American president. Were the London memos on the quagmire of Iraq, another form of Deep Throat, for our US government, yet again? Not really, because the revelations of those memos were like an open book, as to what went on with the Iraq machinations! When we the people need them, *where are the great independent media- - -?* Why are they not beating drums for a worldwide, transparent, investigation, with the immediate release (not years later!) of **all their findings.** No classification for 'national security' garbage should be permitted. That is genuine freedom and democracy in action, and what it stands for. And whilst we are on this subject, why is it that the United Nations, and the World Court, has been so mute on all that went on in Iraq?

Newsweek magazine had an article on the need of the military to always tell the truth about the facts on the ground in Iraq, and we presume, on any other military action. What about the need for politicians to always tell the truth, as well? It showed the cover of a book on Vietnam, aptly entitled 'Dereliction of Duty'. Then the question came, "Do they tell the truth"? Another statement in that article was striking: "How then to explain the different versions of reality in Iraq that came out of the mouths of Bush administration officials, and of senior generals on the ground, in Iraq"? Others had pointed out this glaring disparity, especially from overseas. All this came on the background of that comment by vice president Cheney, *that the Iraq insurgency was in its last throes, this was also echoed, by Rumsfeld, using different wording perhaps.* These statements came, as more, and more Americans, and Iraqis, were dying. They were criticized both at home and abroad, for such comments. Newsweek also had a disturbing photo gallery heading that should induce debate worldwide: "The devastating aftermath of 6 Iraqi children whose parents were shot before their eyes, by US forces". The heading read thus: *"Instantly orphaned"!* Is this what the administration in Washington, our politicians, and our military, have been calling 'collateral damage'; and we want this hidden from people everywhere? Where, on this earth, is the American conscience, and the conscience of the whole world- - - -?

Certain mediocre television commentators have occasionally stated that those who cannot say nice things about the US, and the US military, should just keep their mouths shut. That is the lopsided mentality of US reporters, and the arrogance, that had led them to such poor coverage in balanced news, in the early days of the Iraq war. They were highly criticized for blindly following the dictates of Washington. Likewise, even with mounting criticism on the prisoner abuse, in June, President Bush still claimed that the detainees were 'justly imprisoned', and that they were treated humanely! What about the true meaning of the word, just? All this seems to be out of touch with the rest of humanity. Is it any wonder that America is now looked upon with disdain, suspicion and with fear. These are not exactly the qualities we would like other nations to hold dear, regarding America.

In the face of increasing attacks against US and Iraqi forces, in June, the administration kept on reiterating how well we were doing in Iraq. It appeared like 'the lone ranger' of

America, as hardly anybody believed such propaganda anymore. On a news report we saw a US general, chest covered in medals, so that you could barely discern his coat, stating that the American people needed to support the troops, because they were making good progress! Again, did this man think he was talking to a bunch of citizens who cannot see the truth, who cannot use their intelligence? Former soldiers who had served in Iraq then commented on how the US had done so little for the infrastructure of the country (most of it destroyed by US attacks over many years), and how poorly off were the vast majority of Iraqis. They stated that American forces had occupied the best areas of their cities for themselves, palaces, etc. They showed videos of US personnel fooling around in S. Hussein's palace and pools. Is all that, not truly reminiscent of what former imperial, colonial, powers had done? Do we want to try to convince the world that we had no imperial motives? Some of these servicemen said, look, we have been in Germany and other places (Japan?) some 50 years, since world war two, so, why not Iraq? *Ah, there is some truth ----!*

There is a colossal canyon gap between Bush administration policies, and opinions from the rest of the world; there is also a major disconnect, between the US government and the American people, as evidenced by the following. A guest on MSNBC news said Bush needed to take off his rose colored glasses, and he needed to take a dose of reality, of what is going on in Iraq, and around him. A constitution in Iraq, going nowhere, US coerced and instigated. The major factions in Iraq were splitting farther apart; and our soldiers, and Iraqis, continued to die each day. There was no real progress and Americans were waking up to the truth! This writer has written against the Iraq war since before it was even launched, as had many others. Here are some comments from a single issue of National Geographic, in its correspondence section. 'Since when does America hold prisoners without trial'? Could we add, since the invention of the patriot act? And 'they are flown thousands of miles to a hell hole'! Now, contrast that statement, with vice president Cheney calling it 'like prisoners living in the tropics'! Another said that the US government invited reporters to Guantanamo, *but allowed them to see only what was designated!* We knew that all along! The world knew it was a trick that only the dumbest of the dumb would believe, just like those used by N. Korea, Iran, S. Hussein when he was in power, and many others, no better, no worse. They are all the same when it comes to political chicanery and publicity. Another said 'thank you for drawing attention to the huge waste of money at Guantanamo bay', that we should quickly give it back to Cuba! And an important one, 'How can we be a beacon of democracy'? Ah! Similar thoughts were previously expressed by many Americans, and by thousands of writers overseas.

June 2005 brought another disgraceful reminder of US politics, as with any rich country, when guests on a news program discussed the revolving door phenomenon. How, top US government officials, in large numbers, after retirement, *seem to accidentally find well paying, senior positions, with large US corporations, that do enormous business with the US government.* And the millions of shareholders in those companies had put up with these shenanigans for years. That is another good reason for increased voter protests against these corporations, who pay millions to their officials, and millions in political campaign, and other, various contributions.

There are certain corrupt politicians everywhere, but they expect people to believe that there *never is a relationship between those jobs offered retiring government officials, and any favors such corporations might have received, from those same officials, when they were wielding their powers!* Come now, not many of us are endowed with total stupidity, are we? Another sad commentary this year, and attacks on democracy, has been, the Bush administration trying to force congress, because they had voting majority, not only to renew the controversial patriot act, *in its full capacity, but actually to also add more teeth to it, so to speak!* Critics and citizen's rights groups had continued to mount a barrage of attacks on the abuses in that same patriot act. Members of congress need to get off their behinds, and walk out of the chambers in protest without voting, if that is the only way they can have a voice in the present congress as it exists today. *Many have stated that it had grown closer to a totalitarian regime day by day.* A caller to a news program stated that cronyism in this administration was unbelievable, and he seemed right on target. It was an astounding news report, that, soon after a top head of an emergency agency had resigned, because of criticism of his performance, over the Katrina disaster, it was announced that the Bush administration had rehired this guy, as a consultant for emergency planning evaluation. Amazing? Cronyism, indeed, if it is true!

At a Press Club forum, on C- Span, with noted journalist Dan Rather, a question focused on the fear of competition in major news rooms, and one amazing statement stood out. There was a fear in US news rooms, that if they opened a newscast with international news, instead of American news first, their ratings could plunge; or that was one possible explanation for the plunge. That would be in line with comments from Europe, that in America, people were not receiving proper coverage of international events, compared to the rest of the world. Is that not another sad reflection of journalism in America today? A highly placed personality in US politics had stated in the past, "Those people who were willing to trade freedom for temporary security, deserve neither". That is quite relevant to the US patriot act debates, and it strikes at the heart of the many problems of modern day America.

Critics also pointed to the energy industry that spends six dollars in lobbying, for every dollar in campaign contributions. Why do you think that is? The influence of Mammon, all the time! Influence in legislation that might prove beneficial to corporate America, we must never forget that; and eventually, through that mighty revolving door, beneficial to the legislators themselves, perhaps, do you think? There was a disclosure about some members of congress, who are in committees responsible for energy legislation, but they also own, directly, or indirectly, substantial personal investments, in those same energy sectors! And critics pointed out such policies, yet, in another direction; there is no end to the corruption of money. This one revealed, that presently, some 250 former members of congress, *held high paying lobbying positions with major US corporations; thus, they can lobby congress, their former alma mater, on behalf of those same corporations, now their bosses.* When we hear all these revelations about our own government, do we honestly need to look at the behavior of governments in other countries? Have we not just been shocked into realizing, that we have colossal problems of our own? *Is that not like seeing the speck in our brother's eye, but you fail to see, or refuse to see, the beam in your own?*

US officials also continued to criticize the lack of security in international borders, such as Syria, with its neighbors, and the Afghanistan-Pakistan borders, and so on. But the US itself had spent billions of dollars, which other countries do not have, on homeland security, so-called, and there are persisting reports of porous borders in the US to this day. Even with such reports, we hear government officials blowing their horns, telling the American people, how much they had done to protect the country, how well they had spent our billions in tax dollars. Give us a break! Politicians tend not to give Americans sufficient credit for their intelligence, why is that? Many experts, as well as, ordinary folk, had called for a change of tone in Washington, a change of direction; it is needed urgently as one can gather from the following comments.

Yes, we have experienced many difficulties through the years, all one has to do, is to look, to search, and to read. 'Night comes to the Cumberlands' by Harry Caudill, has been mentioned in these chapters because, in a way, it is quite relevant to some of these discussions, man's behavior, politics, assaults on nature, corruption, and more. He referred to the 1940's and 1950's important coal industry, destroying the natural scenic beauty of the land (he was describing parts of Appallachia, but undoubtedly there were many others as well), and destroying the environment. Then, strip-mining had added further insult, to injury, all over the countryside, and some of the author's statements were most striking. 'It is scarcely conceivable, that such vile and crumbling structures (as existed in parts of the US), could be found in use, in any of the new nations of Africa, not even in the chaotic republic of the Congo'! Amazing, here is a writer in 1962 making comparisons of the US to Africa; and these days, we have heard many comparisons made, to Stalin's Russia, to Hitler's Germany, to the Sudan, to dictator states, and more. Have we changed so little, in 40 to 50 years? He described how from the air, and high mountain peaks, the terrain was nothing but a land covered in ugly scars, left behind by the coal industry's mining efforts. He mentioned the serious injuries or death, among the miners, and how "these broken men were part of the price America paid for her industrial preeminence, although Madison Avenue firms never mentioned them, in their expensive advertisements"!

Here were more symbols of corporate greed and corruption, even back then! Other comments were, how tourists would not want to drive on roads, with heaps of trash littering the sides of the roads. Refuse was dumped by the public, but also by hauling companies, either on the creek beds, or down into the ravines! Streams had changed to yellowish, trickling muck; and there was not a single tract of decent forest left, in that area, he said. In that environment, people suffered much, 'but the local city councils appeared oblivious to the blight cast upon their region'! Local efforts in the realm of education had fallen by the wayside. For example, the author pointed out how politicians were struggling to find funding for classrooms and school programs, such as teachers' salaries; but, even then, they managed to vote $257,000 in bonds, for a gymnasium. As is often the case, priorities were all wrong. Thus, most of their people became candidates for different welfare programs. Caudill said, of the local political environment, "It tells a story of the breakdown of democracy, and of the growing dependence, and futility, of the population". That was some 50 years ago, are we doing more of the same, today? Have we changed so little, and have we learned any lessons?

Throughout much of 2005, and before, crises continued to emerge, in the sphere of politics, and policies, of the United States, *both within the country itself, and in the international arena.* In September, reporters announced that a leading republican, congressman, had been indicted by a grand jury, in his home state, alleging illegal activities on his part. Now, politicians always preach to the public, that our judicial system, with grand jury participation, represents the ultimate in justice. That is, until that system happens to point at them, or indict them, then, they are quick to turn against it. Thus, another, right-leaning politician, hastily appeared on a news channel, to announce that it was all political gaming. *It was, and by a grand jury?* He said, that particular republican, was a good Christian. Right! *Had this character ever heard, that Christians too, have been known to go astray, to sin? Had he ever been told of the lives of some of the saints? Had he heard of the words of Jesus, when, during His days on this planet, He called 'hypocrites', some of those who 'thought' they were being holy, and religious?*

We were also told of another republican, in the senate, who had become the target of investigations, for possible illegal activities; and we previously had the right hand man of Bush, at the White House, being investigated for leaking secret information. We understand that these activities go on, in all political parties. But, here was, not one, not two, but three, top republican politicians, facing alleged unethical, illegal, behavior charges. They all claim they are completely innocent, and one has to wonder! It seems, that when it comes to the movement on the extreme right, they are all walking on holy ground! Here is one statement heard recently on a news report, by a retired security official, "Politics, is dirty, dirty". That says a mouthful, right there. It is not this writer, making these comments; this is not coming from Russia, or China, or Europe; this was from an American security official., and there have been numerous others, as well.

If we needed further proof, about some of the reports in this chapter, Mother Nature provided it all, when hurricanes Katrina, and Rita, struck. The cheap talk about homeland security, about how well our government was performing, how well they were spending our funds; about how great our justice, and lack of discrimination, had become - - - it was all laid out, bare, by those massive storms, for the whole world to see, and just marvel.

UNITED KINGDOM

This section on the United Kingdom will deal primarily with the period around the Iraq war; the decision making, before, and what has followed since, in the context of British politics, and Blair as the current prime minister. But one would have to touch upon, ever so slightly, the glories of the old British Empire as well, because in this text, we refer to the plight of many third world countries under European colonial rule. Authors have written much, on the glory and might, of the British Empire, when British influence extended to all corners of the globe; when a world map could be seen literally dotted all over, with areas under Britain's rule. It covered many parts of Africa, Asia, the Middle East, to islands scattered in the Mediterranean, the Caribbean, and in the Atlantic and Pacific oceans, and more. Larger areas comprised the Indian sub-continent, Australia, New Zealand, and Canada. Farther south there were the Falkland Islands, in the proximity of Argentina; these a few years ago, were the source of another conflict, when Argentina sent an invading force to claim these tiny islands, as their own territory.

As far-flung as Britain's sphere of influence once was, that episode brought home present day realities, as Britain's widespread tentacles, had shrunk considerably; and its military forces were concentrated mainly around the mother country. The 'Falklands' felt they had been invaded and occupied, and the consensus of the population announced its allegiance to, and preference for, affiliation with the mother country; and thus, they requested help from England. Even at those enormous distances, Britain still dispatched a force of ships, and military personnel, and those islands were soon retaken, but not without losses. But it also reemphasized the fact that the old days of glory of the British Empire were gone forever. Many prominent people had decried the loss of the empire, among them Winston Churchill. America now, finds itself with armed forces and ships scattered all over the world, and it too, started experiencing difficulties of its own. It has been labeled an imperial power, even though it has exerted such influence, for a relatively short period of time.

Many children, and even adults, who in the past, delved into the educational hobby of stamp collection, used to treasure stamps of the British Empire. Some even limited their collections to those specific countries. They were amazed at the beauty and variety of those stamps; the color, the scenery, the exotic flora and fauna, the names, and the image of monarchs, ruling over England and its empire. Times have changed, as have the names of many of those countries, once they regained their independence. Some even went to the extreme semblance of nationalism, by wanting to change also the names of streets, towns, buildings, and so on. Yes, humans can go to extremes, and they often do. Most countries, even though under a colonial power, had a remarkably good relationship with England, and the British expatriates on their soil. Some, including the Indian sub-continent, parts of Africa, the Middle East, experienced a growing nationalistic trend, and could not wait to loosen their bonds with England, and become fully independent. Many, maintained very close ties, even after becoming independent, and the British Commonwealth of countries emerged. Some small countries had very close ties to

England, that spanned many years, in the case of Malta, it covered the historic periods of world war one, and world war two.

During world war two the British people were fighting for their very existence, and for Europe. England alone, with assistance from countries within the empire, (Australia, the Indian sub-continent, New Zealand, S. Africa, Canada, and many others) came forward to face the onslaught of Hitler on Europe, as European nations became involved early on. England and France declared war soon after Hitler's forces attacked, and other nations in Europe, and all British Empire nations, joined in. Large numbers of forces from all over the empire, and supplies, were sent to the European continent to stem the German advance; but after the collapse of France, England and its allies, were facing the enemy, more or less, on their own. America had not entered the war but was providing assistance with war materiel. Many from Britain, and commonwealth countries, have precious memories, of the Battle of Britain, when heroic pilots turned the tide on superior German forces, and the much feared, German invasion across the Dover channel never materialized. That battle was won, but the war was to go on, in other fronts. There were names, like Dunkirk, where large numbers of allied forces were facing the advancing Germans, with their backs to the sea. Heroic efforts by an assorted armada of ships, boats, anything that could float, crossed over the channel from England, and rescued the vast majority of those forces, and they could remain in the war efforts.

There were other names like El Alamein, Tobruk, and more, as the allies tried to stop the continued spread of Hitler's forces, as they had conquered most of Europe, and were also in North Africa. Then, Hitler decided to turn his attention on Russia, 'The Eastern Front', and he made the serious mistakes of a previous emperor, Napoleon, he was spread out too much, facing too many fronts. After the Japanese attacks on Pearl Harbor, in 1941, America declared war and fully mobilized to face the Japanese forces, and sent forces to join in the European war theatre. Later, as the tides of battle began to change, British soldiers referred to the desert battles in North Africa, as 'clean wars', as there were no civilians involved, simply the armies battling it out in the desert. Each side respected the other, and they reported how in that sphere of war, prisoners from either side, were treated well, and with the respect they deserved. It is refreshing to hear such comments coming from soldiers, considering what was to come later, with news of the holocaust, the intensive bombing over Germany and Tokyo, and the atomic bombs dropped by the US, in all these, civilians indeed, became targets. And today, we witness the cold, push-button wars, where leaders are detached and not fully engaged. Now, too, we still bomb civilian areas, hospitals, churches, shelters, anything that we suspect, might hide an enemy! This was perpetrated in Korea, in Vietnam, in Afghanistan, in Iraq, and for the longest time, in the Israeli-Palestinian conflict, not to forget the many tragedies in Africa, and in the Far East, as well.

There was also Malta, in the center of the Mediterranean, surrounded by German forces in Europe and N. Africa. There too, was the Battle of Malta, where British and Maltese forces, with a smattering of commonwealth personnel, were desperately trying to hang on. Besides Maltese servicemen, British armed forces personnel lost their lives, protecting the island, as did many civilians; and many more, were wounded. Heroism was not in short supply, under such adverse circumstances. The enemy was determined, through constant attacks, and a blockade, to starve and exhaust the entire population, that they would be forced to surrender. Those Hurricane and Spitfire pilots seemed, at times, to achieve the impossible. Then, there was also the heroism of people in the British navy, and the merchant ships, as they tried to bring desperately needed supplies to Malta; they knew they would make a most dangerous crossing, under heavy attacks from the sky and the sea. Many perished, but those supplies did come in, over a period of many difficult months, facing such overwhelming odds. Malta, with the support of Britain, never capitulated. Many of the stories of some on those ships, may never have been told! Survivors and their families had many tragic memories, to live with all these years, but family members passed on their story, no doubt.

On such a brief background look at the British Empire, and later the Commonwealth, we then fast forward to the spring of 2005, when the British were on political campaign trails, several months after those in the US. By comparison, election campaigns in Britain last for much shorter periods; and although the influence of money is still there, *Mammon* does not appear to rule supreme, as it does in the US! News reports claimed that Blair was distancing himself from Bush, as much as possible, and there was little mention of Iraq, and less crisscrossing of the Atlantic. Supposedly the economy had improved under Labor, but there existed problems with education, with a decline in health care, with hospitals, and the cost of living remained very high. The British were now also considered to have one of the worst personal savings rates, competing even with the US. The misadventure of Blair in Iraq, remained most unpopular in UK, and they faced such headlines as, "service sector slowdown adds to economic gloom".

Blair still managed to squeak in a win, but that was no great surprise, really. Many voters were not sure what they could switch to, in the Conservative party. Sure enough, after his reelection, early in June, Blair was across the Atlantic visiting Bush. Reporters asked him if it was pay back time, if he wanted Bush to pay him back for his support on Iraq. It was said that Blair wanted Bush to support his efforts on Africa, and on the environment. However, critics said that Blair was not likely to get much from Bush. Also, because public opinion in Britain had already tainted Blair as a lame duck prime minister, and his party was hurt badly at the polls. He might have to consider resigning before too long, for the sake of the party. Blair, though reelected, was very unpopular with his people. Likewise in the US, June polls showed that 52% of Americans thought Bush (though reelected) was doing a bad job as president; *and importantly, most Americans now believed it was not worth going into Iraq!* What a shame, that all these people did not join the rest of us who protested against the start of the war. Losses have been too high, and the problems for that country had increased, not lessened. Hundreds of Iraqis were not dying each week, or each month before we attacked them, and occupied their country. They are now, because America had become a magnet for a strong anti-occupation resistance movement. Some, might be terrorist inclined, others, have been labeled religious, and others, nationalistic.

The late Pope John Paul two, in his holiness and wisdom, had repeatedly advised the Bush administration not to start this war, but the Washington elite thought they knew better *and look at where the US and UK find themselves, now.* Although Bush kept talking of a 'coalition', everybody knew, including the Vatican, that America was making all decisions.

Although European news media carried headlines with 'Blair wins another term', he ended up with a greatly reduced majority from before, and it was said, he had been punished, by his people, for Iraq. His popularity remained very low; forecasters predicted he would not last out his full term in office, as he was crippled and would have to step down (*that is something rarely done in the US*). A spokesman for another party in UK stated, that Blair had been punished "for lies, lies, and for all the people you had killed in Iraq". Those were harsh words indeed, from another politician, leveled at Blair; and we presume he meant soldiers killed in Iraq, as well as, the thousands of innocent civilians. Similar comments were also heard from families of British soldiers who had been killed.

In a previous book "Mirror Reflection= = Mirages", we had predicted, indeed hoped, that the Brits would deal with Blair, for his actions, better than the Americans had done with Bush; and for his becoming a stooge, more or less, for Bush, a sad day for Britain. It seemed that those predictions written in 2003, had come to pass in some respects. On the other hand, Bush was returned to power with a bigger majority, that republicans, including Bush, called a mandate. In reality, it was anything but a mandate, when barely 51% voted for the president, and 50% of the voting public, had not bothered to exercise their right to vote!

The world may never understand those actions by Americans. But, once again, it was alleged that the last elections might have been tainted. Whilst the first election, (2000), was fingered, by critics, as a stolen election. Most people know, only too well, that the corrupting influence of large cash donations, and other favors, had always been a problem, in US elections. And now, it seemed, that might also be true, for Britain, and, no doubt, for most other countries, as well. We have often been told that 'people get the government they deserved'. How true! About the time of the UK elections, home made bombs exploded outside the British consulate in New York, and there was speculation as to its significance; but it momentarily disturbed the British financial markets.

It did not take long for members from Blair's own party to suggest that perhaps he should step down; and news media continued to point to the weakened state of the Blair regime. Of the two protagonists of that war, Bush and Blair, Bush remained very unpopular in many parts of the world; and large protests were organized against him, in most places he visited. He traveled to Europe to participate in the large commemorative celebrations of victory, in world war two, particularly in Russia. It was hinted that Bush was trying to mend fences, as best he could. Critics claimed he had to do this, as Iraq was going so badly for him (up to 60 insurgent attacks per day); and many countries continued to condemn America. However, when Bush visited former Soviet Union States, he was well received, and some reporters wondered if that was, because of what assistance those governments had hoped to obtain from the US.

According to Time magazine reports by McAllister, people's gripes against Blair, were because of his arrogance, contempt for any constitutional process, and a willingness to bend the truth to get his way! *My, my, and many concluded, that description could well apply to Bush, and to other leaders in this world of ours!* The writer added that most Brits felt nothing but disdain for their man, *and his legacy was permanently damaged.* Charles Kennedy, a liberal democrat, said that the effects of Iraq were very corrosive on the government, and for Blair. An advisor said, we were punished for Iraq, and there is nothing Tony can do about it! Opponents regretted, that in spite of all this, labor still managed to squeeze in. Some had also predicted (as in the US), that millions of voters in UK would not bother to vote. As we recall, when the US tried to force democracy on others, they had commented that their citizens wanted democracy, but not one patterned after the US (and now, would they include, UK)? How about that, just when those countries, tried to remain, shining beacons of 'democracy', for the rest of the world.

The famous memos leaked from ten Downing street, in London, had caused large numbers of Americans, and many in congress, to question even more, the methods used by the Bush administration, 'to take us to war'. Critics alleged that the memos suggest, that, before any UN debate had taken place, *before the president had spoken to the American people, before his talks with Blair, Bush, according to British officials, had already decided to take military action against Iraq, to remove Saddam Hussein!* As one would expect, both Bush and Blair, denied those accusations implied by those memos. But at this point, not many people, around the world, believed either of them, because of what the US had done to Iraq; because of allegations of fabrication of intelligence, to justify the war; and above all, there were no weapons of mass destruction, as Bush and Blair, had pontificated! Incidentally, does not the information in those memos, confirm, that Blair had become a stooge for the US?

By June 2005, the number of Americans who believed it was worth invading Iraq had dropped to 42%. The protests against the war in Britain were large, compared to America, that was a chasm between the two nations; but they were increasing in America as well; and worldwide, people still remained opposed. That reminds readers of comments from overseas, reported in the previous book, that, when it comes to self-discipline, by the US government, 'what is good for the goose, is not always good for the gander'! In other words, any party in power can seek disciplinary actions against their opponents, or at times, choose to close their eyes to gross misconduct by their own members, depending on which direction the winds are blowing! Thus, protesters here, and abroad, reacted to those memos by again raising the specter of impeachment. One UK headline read 'When will Americans get off their ass, and start to impeach'? And many had called for some type of action, by the US congress.

An article in Newsweek by John Barry and Mark Hosenball referred to behind the scenes disagreements between Bush and Blair, on Iraq. The London memos obtained by British journalist Michael Smith, showed that Blair aides thought the Bush plans for the Iraq war were "hastily conceived, too optimistic, and legally shaky"! Worldwide, many had long questioned the morality and legality of that war. The amazing, unbelievable, question remained, why had the US media not been filling our news with those revelations, week after week, and keep on the pressure, until something is done by congress. That should convince our people that media are indeed biased, and have been for some time; they are no longer independent, and it is not a free press. In public, Bush and Blair seemed to agree, but in private there was much they did not concur on. Much more than Bush, the British were indeed worried about the aftermath of war. How right they were, and how terribly wrong were those in the Bush administration who insisted on going ahead! Leaked comments, as: 'the intelligence, and facts, were being fixed around the policy of invading, to remove S. Hussein', says it all- - -! Where were the US media? Are not many left, who want to desperately protect the freedom of the press? Will Americans finally be convinced of the warped policies going on in their government, just as in other nations?

Here is another example of the 'values, morals, and integrity', of some politicians in the so-called developed, civilized, countries. According to London Sunday Times reports, (Michael Smith), on the Internet, *ministers in UK were warned in July 2002, that Blair had already agreed to back military action, at a summit with Bush,* at his Texas ranch, at least 3 months earlier. The briefing for those attending a meeting of Blair's inner circle, in July 2002, emphasized, *that since regime change was illegal, it was necessary to create the coalition, which would make it legal.* Oh, Mr. Blair, how many more devious twists, in your policies, might be uncovered? It behooves all of us, in 2005, to realize that these plots were not the works of leaders in Russia, China, Libya, N. Korea, Iran, or Syria, not by Arafat or Chavez, most of whom had been called a few uncomplimentary names, by officials from the 'west'. No, this unheard of degree of connivance, and fabrication, had been coming from officials, particularly in US, but also from some in UK. They likely had spent nights, trying to come up with ideas on how to thwart international laws, and human rights laws, and how to proceed against the decisions reached at the UN.

A comment by a reporter in 2005, on an international news station was striking, that officials in US (and UK?), were working hard to uncover blunders, that led to the argument, to wage war against Iraq. Now, they are calling them blunders-- -! Those arguments by Bush and Blair, were all wrong, correct? A country has been ravaged and raped, close to 1900 of our young men and women had been killed, others from Britain, and other countries, and thousands of innocent Iraqis! What now, Mr. Blair? And that hour-long speech by Colin Powell for the US, now repeated on our TV screens, will go down in history, as one of the most blatant, false assumptions, and many had already called them, outright lies! This, by an official of a once great nation- - but, is it, now?

In "Mirror Reflections" we wrote about the corruption of money in US politics, how it had always played a major role, in election campaigns. It gave the impression, that, the role of money was more important, than the competence of the various candidates. There were always large corporate donations in US campaigns, and reports that those companies, usually received their pay-back, one way or another (legislative favors?). Now, in that same Sunday Times paper, we also got a glimpse into corruption in UK elections as well! We had always understood the corruption in underdeveloped countries, but here, we are talking about two supposedly, civilized, and prominent, nations. Throughout history, we have learned that corruption existed in all civilizations. In the US and UK it was usually well finessed and hidden from public scrutiny. It has been disclosed, how for years, in UK, those who contributed 50,000 pounds, or more, most of them, ended up receiving titles, or honors, and so on. A committee that investigated such abuses, had been disbanded by Blair, of all people! These abuses happened under all parties in power, as is often the case. Thus, we cannot state that, 'those other third world', countries, were the only ones, with corruption in their governments. That is certainly not correct! But, some in the west, such as the US, picked those they preferred to shake up, such as Iraq.

Why did Blair go along with those plans? He continued to claim it was worth it! Critics maintain that such forms of corruption have always been around, both in the US, and UK, and elsewhere. Historical data suggest that scandals have existed, involving leaders and politicians, at all levels of power, Caesars, presidents, prime ministers, monarchs, sheikhs, dictators, even some highly placed church officials, professionals, and corporate executives, as we have recently learned. It is not found only in backward, poor countries, it is everywhere. In the west, we had learned how to manipulate it, or that is what some politicians believe. That is the only difference, between 'us', and 'them'. Such information is often 'classified' by governments, the excuse being 'for national security'. Thus, scandals can be perpetuated forever, and people are kept in the dark. Or they decide to get on with their lives, and leave politicians to their own games, as often happens.

In June 2005 there were more reports of UK memos, and these again suggested that Bush and Blair, had been less than candid with their people, surprise! They also confirmed, as most world experts had accused all along, that it *was Bush who wanted to start the war, and the British knew there were no plans for post war Iraq.* There must be some truth in such memos, in spite of denials by certain personalities, because of the suffering the people over there had endured for more than two years. What was Blair thinking, many have asked, that he would go along with such a scheme? A man, who initially seemed to be so amicable, clever, the right man to lead the country. And now, some 90% of Britons say they cannot believe a word he says! The obvious question becomes, why is he still prime minister?

Many of these revelations had come on another facet of British life, in 2004, and culminating in 2005, that of prince Charles announcing plans to marry Camilla. That too, unleashed all type of speculation as to their having a civil wedding, perhaps. Could it take place in the church, or would it be both? Would the Queen attend both, or one, or perhaps none, of those ceremonies? Would the stature of the monarchy survive, after this? Considering, that in recent years, young members of the royal family had been the cause of much adverse publicity that, perhaps, shook the foundation of royalty. Many in America, of all places, began to comment that the monarchy had become obsolete. Is that because there are those, in America, and elsewhere, who never miss a chance to meddle in the affairs of other countries? Butting in, where they do not necessarily belong!

True, questions were raised around the world, including UK, whether prince Charles should remain the heir apparent to the British throne. But all this gossip was obviously not addressed by Charles himself, or by the royal family. The Queen, herself, must have had periods of sobering reflections, over a number of years, about some of the revelations on members of her greater family. We recall, that before the divorce of Diana, from Charles, gossipmongers had a field day, about the continued relationship of Charles with Camilla; and many of the tabloids had raised questions, if it had ever stopped. Others suggested that Charles had caused Diana heartache over a number of years, that her fairy-land wedding, had not been that, at all. In recent years, after Diana's tragic death, some were changing their view, in the sense that, Charles deserved some happiness, and he had been very active in programs on behalf of charities, and the environment.

As in the case of president Kennedy in the US, many rumors had persisted on the events surrounding Diana's death, and conspiracy theories. It was announced that lady Diana had written letters, that she feared she might be killed, and that it would be from a car accident of some type. And reports also suggested that British secret service agents, were stalking her in France, and that the driver of the fatal car crash was, perhaps, on the pay of the British secret service. Books on this topic have been written as well. After a thorough investigation, French authorities had concluded, there was no conspiracy, and that it was an accident, caused by speeding, the driver being under the influence of alcohol. Other news reports had accused the French of handling the tragic incident poorly, and of giving the victims inadequate emergency care, something they denied. They showed that the injuries sustained were so severe, that survival would have been unlikely.

The father of the man, who was killed with Diana, continued to insist that there was a conspiracy, and that they had been murdered, according to media publications. Here again, we are dealing with rumors, gossip, and innuendo; but as mentioned by many over the years, we are also dealing with the elite and powerful. Wherever the country, such people, have the wherewithal to conceal, and to move mountains. Thus, as in the case of Kennedy, so with lady Diana, it is most unlikely that there will be answers to satisfy everyone. Some will keep on asking questions, others will keep on writing, and criticizing. By spring of 2005 there were more revelations that in Britain, full, and impartial investigations, would take place, into all these alleged activities. They were requesting all evidence from France, including the car wreckage, and any available data on the use of alcohol, drugs, or other medications. The conspiracy theorists had let it be known, that it was all planned in advance, because of the relationships of Diana, and the remote risk of there being, eventually, a 'royal' baby, with a Muslim background. On the one hand we assume that some of these speculations are preposterous, but, on the other hand, these theorists, will continue to doubt that the investigations by British authorities, were really 'open and impartial'. But then, do we recall, all the stories surrounding 'Deep Throat', in the US, and the enormous scandals those events had dealt with? With all the news surrounding the royal family, some extremists continued to call for the dissolution of the monarchy, but in the United Kingdom, they were definitely in the minority.

Then, came Thursday, July 7th, 2005, a sad day for the British people. One day after London had been chosen to host the next international Olympic games, European, and US news media, and the Internet, were full of reports on a succession of explosions in London's underground train system, and a double-decker bus. Early releases suggested that 50 had been killed, and as many as 700 injured. Shock and confusion were prevalent around the groups of people involved, and the areas hit. British authorities blamed terrorism, and said they had received no warning; that it appeared coordinated, and was meant to disrupt the G-8 summit in Scotland. That was pure speculation, however. Blair was quick to call these acts *barbaric* - - -that, they are, Mr. Blair, and it is a tremendous loss, as in the case of NY City, Madrid, Bali, a loss, for all the families who had suffered from these tragedies. The average citizens always pay the price for wrongdoings by politicians, as critics would state. Mr. Blair, surely must realize, that his actions, and those by Mr. Bush, who launched a preemptive, immoral and inhumane, war on Iraq, killing or maiming, tens of thousands of innocent people, *must have seemed equally barbaric to majority world opinion, and certainly to the world's Muslims.* Or is it, that what 'we' do, is, always right, and what 'they' do, is always wrong? **No, these actions are always wrong, whoever carries them out!**

Intelligence reports had suggested that London might become a prime target, for attacks, as terrorists were experiencing difficulties entering the US. In past years, Britain had numerous bombing attacks by the Irish Republican Army, and innocent victims were then, also, often involved in death or injury. Mercifully, that conflict had declined, since the two sides began to talk to each other, and trying to resolve their differences. As in many worldwide struggles, Irish nationalist groups had long fought for a united Ireland, without controls from England. Repression and subjugation, real or perceived, are often the causes of resistance movements, and of uprisings.

On a BBC program via C-Span television station, a commentator said that when president Bush announced, "if you are not with us, you are with the terrorists", he did Bin Laden's work for him, *that, and the Iraq war, had attracted numerous recruits to their cause according to world experts.* A British member of parliament, Galloway, reaffirmed that when Bush and Blair, spoke after the London attacks, they were still trying to justify their own actions in Iraq, even during such a tragedy in London. As many others had done, Galloway, again emphasized that we need to remove root causes of terrorism, and he accused BBC spokespersons of being in a bubble, as many politicians do, and that the vast majority of his constituents had agreed with him. The BBC spokesman promptly cut off Galloway in mid sentence; there is a good example, as in the US, of freedom and democracy, in 2005! Galloway, with many others, had long believed that what the US did in Iraq, with Blair's help, likely, caused more violence, not less, around the world, more terrorism.

That BBC announcer seemed to be taking Galloway to task, because he dared to suggest that perhaps Blair's support for Bush, on Iraq, was connected to the London attacks. Have Britain, and the US, now come to a such state, that, if their leaders are responsible for serious mistakes, that lead to illegitimate wars, let nobody dare to criticize, or even question? Come now, the leaders at BBC ought to know much better than that; or, are the 'free' media empires, in both the US and UK, being muzzled?

Within 48 hours of the London tragedy, it was obvious from British news, that recovery from such disasters is a slow process. As with New York, we saw videos of people on the streets, holding photos of loved ones, asking if anyone had seen them. It appeared that initially, the deepest subway, at King's Cross, was presenting problems, because it was deep underground, there was intense darkness, communication difficulties, smoke, lack of fresh air, wreckage, and vermin everywhere! They feared that many bodies could still be in the wreckage. This demonstrates that when disasters strike, help and recovery, can be very slow, and this is seen to a greater degree in poorer countries, such as the recent Asian Tsunami. But, we are now witnessing that in rich countries, often with sophisticated equipment and technologies, there too, some disasters can present enormous hardships, for the people. Many in London, had already criticized their government for being too slow, for lack of proper organization, and for lack of information being given to those affected. This is very much like reactions from people in America, when disasters strike. It is well recognized that in the poorer countries, people suffer more intensely, for much greater periods of time; but they all suffer. In poorer countries they often depend on some degree of assistance from western countries. Within several days of the attacks, British authorities had information on the suspects, that some of them were British born Muslims, and they were all suicide bombers. It was revealed that some had attended schools in Pakistan.

Commentator Mark Scheuer, on the same BBC program, also stated that we should not have gone to Iraq, to start with. And he reasserted, as others had done, that they do not attack us because of the way we live (as the Bush people tried to claim), *but rather, because of our behaviors, they hate our foreign policy- - -! Right on target!*

According to the 'Independent', in the beginning, members of parliament issued no criticisms, but later, those at odds with Blair's policies, came out swinging. One headline read, 'Iraq factor returns to haunt Blair'. A former member of parliament, also stated that we talk as if the bombings are evil, but everything we have done was just fine, it was good! Not so, the statement continued, especially when the UK had been an accomplice in the slaughter of large numbers of civilians in Iraq! Other critics were clamoring, "Please do not tell us, that the bombings in London, had nothing to do with Iraq"! This article also referred to a briefing paper, by a think-thank, due to be published soon, warning that Britain had laid itself open to attacks, by acting as a 'pillion passenger' to US foreign policy. *There is that criticism again, about US foreign policies!* It was true that some radical Muslim groups were in UK, but the majority of traditional Muslims had disavowed any connections with their ideologies, and remained law-abiding citizens. Minority groups in UK complained that after the bombings, hate crimes against them had increased. Blair and Bush, as well as, Howard, of Australia, continued to deny that these attacks were connected to Iraq! *What else, can they say, they had to protect themselves.* Other sensible leaders around the world had always blamed such actions on America's decisions to start that war. As Blair issued stricter measures and tough policies (as had been done in the US), critics said that in Britain 'we have freedoms and liberties, we have presumption of innocence, till proven guilty'! Many thought such comments were a jab at what had been foisted on the American people, by their government, the patriot act!

A 'Daily telegraph' report by Philip Sherwell, reads, 'Britain and America clash over tactics', and it referred to terror suspect, Aswat. American authorities, as usual, wanted him sent to a third world country, but the British refused to allow that, on someone with UK papers (they know, as everyone does, that the purpose, is usually, for torture techniques, right?). American officials, hide behind, innocent sounding words, like, *rendition, detainee, enemy combatant, and other trivia, but is there also an absence of conscience and morals?* Most are aware that the secret seizure of people (considered highly illegal by many), and flying them to other countries, is for the sole purpose of harsh interrogations, and possibly, torture. British officials had sharp differences with their American counterparts, because they *would not participate in such controversial schemes!* Controversial? That is too kind a word! *Thinkers, and other conscientious persons, would call those American tactics, criminal and barbaric.* Americans continued to state that Aswat was a suspect, in the bombing, in London, but the British again denied it, saying, "it was rubbish to suggest that Aswat had anything to do with the bombing". There is that divide again, as US officials push ahead with their seriously flawed, foreign policy, which had been the source of much trouble, in our world today.

As happened after New York, following the terrorist attacks in London, there were several false alarms, resulting in the evacuation of people. They were also issuing warnings that the group or groups responsible, could strike again, that everyone should be vigilant. London authorities also announced that it would be weeks or months before all the victims could be identified. Blair said that in past attacks mistakes in identification had been made, and they would follow the coroner's advice and do the right thing, this time. In London's streets one continued to see a fairly large number of pictures of those still missing, people were distressed, and complaining about the terribly slow pace! But, British authorities were indeed fortunate, when, two weeks after the first attacks, there was another attempt, but this time the bombs did not go off. Police were able to collect . lots of evidence, and after several days, a number of Muslim males were in custody. Reporters claimed, that, some, in the Muslim community, provided useful information.

British reports also suggested that instead of terrorist sleeper cells, around the world, as assumed by the US and UK, now, some believed that Al Qaeda may be recruiting Muslims born in specific countries, such as UK, they may be reasonably educated, and may have felt marginalized, for a variety of reasons. They would recruit such youths, and indoctrinate them, how to carry out these attacks, which would include suicide bombing. Experts believed that this would make anti-terrorism efforts much more difficult, as these individuals would have no significant markers, they would not be known to authorities, except for their ethnic background, the fact that they were Muslims. But then, there are millions of Muslims, scattered in cities, all over the world.

Blair and his clique, wanted to follow in Bush's footsteps, and after the London attacks, issued tough, shoot to kill, orders, for terrorist suspects. Undoubtedly many Britons agreed with him (as they had, in America, with Bush), because they had just been attacked, and there was also that second botched attempt. But, most in Britain, had much more common sense, they valued justice and human rights, and they would not agree with such broad, drastic measures. Mr. Blair had been blinded in following Bush, on Iraq, and he was about to make more mistakes.

Sure enough, on July 22nd, a British correspondent reported that plainclothes security officers had spotted a man coming out of a house under surveillance. They decided he was a wanted suspect, and followed him into the underground; they said he was wearing a thick padded coat, running and acting suspicious, vaulted over a gate, and ran into the train. Witnesses stated that the security people, then rushed him, *held him, and immediately shot him 7 or 8 times, obviously killing him!* Initially officials denied he was connected to the attempted bombing the day before. But, by July 23rd, the British announced *regrets, and that it had all been a terrible mistake, the man they had killed was not a suspect at all.* Until now, to their credit, British authorities were quite prompt, once they had realized their error, but there was more to come! Other governments such as the US, under similar circumstances, usually only admit that it is a security matter, and 'it is under investigation'. It would take some time! Thus, such officials would hope that the public, and the media, would soon forget such incidents. However Mr. Blair and Mr. Bush, surely must realize that when such blunders are committed, and innocent people are killed 'by the State', we simply cannot tell their families 'we are sorry', and get away with it. Is that supposed to solve everything? The offer of money, to maintain their silence, would be an added insult to grievous harm done.

British police are known worldwide because, by and large, they perform their duties without carrying or brandishing guns. Unlike the US, and others, where such forces are seen carrying guns wherever they go. And the latter, often fall into the trap of shooting first, and asking questions later, much too late! A small group of British undercover officers are armed, and they were the ones involved in this killing. All over Britain, people realized what happened, and they were dismayed, that this should happen in their country. There was a dead man, and accusations of racial profiling, looks, and so on, especially from Muslims; and the fear that such incidents would likely increase. Although the British said they were sorry for what had transpired, the man was identified as a Brazilian youth, totally innocent; he was not a suspect at all, and his family was devastated. As expected, Brazilian authorities demanded answers. Unfortunately, the bullies in the 'west' seem to get away with anything, don't they? Within a couple of weeks or so, there were more disturbing revelations from Britain, with allegations that the chief of security over there, had been dragging his feet, and concealing important information concerning this case.

It appeared that the hastily put out initial reports by the authorities, were not factual, and gave misrepresentations. Witnesses said *the man was not wearing a thick, padded coat that could have hidden bombs. They showed pictures of his body in the train.* He was not acting suspiciously, *he was not running, as the police claimed! He walked slowly, even stopped to pick up a paper.* He had no idea that he was being followed by security, why should he, he was totally innocent! After all, this was England, right? Again, he had not vaulted over the gate as was stated, he may have rushed to catch the train on the platform, as most people do in London, every day! Witnesses continued that as he entered the train, security followed, they manhandled him, and they said, *"they simply shot him"!* No warning was given, no trying to detain the man, *instant murder! You can hardly call it, not deliberate!* It was not with 1 or 2 shots according to those witnesses, but 7 or 8, all at close range. There was no consideration for high morals, here! Has Britain, like the US and Israel, also degraded to the point, where they will shoot first, and not bother with the truth, with trying to establish, guilt or innocence.

These events had continued to generate news for a while. There was mounting pressure in the UK about this murder of an innocent Brazilian man, and the alleged lies given out at first, by British authorities. To compound the ugliness of that behavior by officials in Britain, the man who leaked the truth to "Independent" news, about these events, was promptly dismissed! Mr. Blair, will heads roll, at the highest levels of your 'police State', just as quickly? Does it appear that both the US and UK (note events on Iraq, and now this, and the White House leak, and there is more), now must live a life of lies, to protect their own government officials? Mr. Blair, are UK policies such, that hundreds may be mistakenly killed, as they rush into the underground, to catch a train? Thousands do that, every day, will they be considered 'acting suspiciously'? If not, then, those officials were acting upon profiling data, a dangerous thing to do. Blair had announced tough measures against extremists, including immediate deportation; but critics complained that such powers would be abused, and civil liberties would be trashed in the UK. Now, consider what has already been perpetrated; and news on this tragedy had suddenly disappeared from our media; and in the US we heard nothing of the final outcome, why? They say, birds of a feather, always flock together- - - -!

On both sides of the Atlantic, government officials, and some others, are increasingly seen with flags in their lapel, intoning patriotic sounding words, and perhaps using the sorrows of those who had suffered death and injury, and other losses. They use all these, allegedly, to try scare the opposition, and to drown out critics. They do not want to hear persistent criticisms of their blunders, and they do not relish being shown the error of their ways. They do not want critics to trumpet the chaos that politicians had been responsible for, and for which normally, there would be some accounting. Where are the media, why are they not following these events intently, and uncovering answers, for the public, such media, as- - - BBC, CNN, Independent, PBS, C-Span, and others?

THE EUROPEAN UNION

Several years ago, some countries in Europe had forged a type of Union, The European Union, EU, the original six members being, Germany, France, Italy, Holland, Belgium, and Luxembourg. This was, to improve their economy, their culture, across border trading, and tourism. There were many discussions about a single monetary system, changes in certain laws, easier access across borders, and more. Things progressed quite well, and in recent years the Union had been expanded, and more recently, the number of countries, was increased to twenty-five. Those, included, some countries formerly under the Soviet Union, and some small countries such as the Islands of Malta. Then, there was also much talk of preparations, for another large country, such as Turkey, a predominantly Muslim nation, to join the EU, so that the East would really meet the West, so to speak; and thus, see the merger of remarkably different cultures, in agreeing to such a bond, which would be a first.

In the spring of 2005, the EU experienced a double set back, in the failure of motions for the formation of a constitution, and drawing up a budget. According to the French paper, Le Figaro, this 'revealed a deep sickness in the old continent, that the European leaders still refused to talk about'. Many in the old countries were shocked, that the French had voted 'no', on the constitution; and soon after, the Dutch referendum delivered a similar verdict. Other countries had been in favor of the constitution, and the drawn plans for a budget. In Britain, word soon spread, that this was not the time for, their own referendum, as it would likely fail, as well. Much more discussion was needed, it appeared.

These were tumultuous times for Europe, because they had tried hard for some years, to develop a powerhouse, perhaps to act as a buffer to the US, or any other major entity to emerge on the world. Some experts had felt, that it would be a rough road ahead, in sorting out their many difficulties. Others, had known for some years, that European nationalities had certain individual characteristics, such as, culture, language, pride, and so on, that could present major obstacles, to the formation of such a strong union. But most of the citizens had faith that the stumbling blocks would be overcome, in time. Many believed, that a united, strong, Europe, was of paramount importance, for progress on the world's economic front, for the United Nations, and for preservation of world peace.

However, skeptics, and critics, said that the expansion of, the EU, was not without other elements of corruption. Leaders of this union appeared to strike deals with various nations vying for membership, squeezing some here, others there; making strong demands on some, whilst closing their eyes to abuses, and undesirable traits, in others. There were many factors for the prospective candidates to consider, their economies, the gross domestic product, infrastructure, rate of employment, pollution, justice systems, human rights, and more! In other words, we see that corruption is encountered, in large or small countries alike; wherever one looks in politics, corruption seems to thrive. We heard reports on most of the newer candidates for membership, to the EU. From Turkey, there were objections to their harsh suppression of opposition groups, and of human rights abuses. Some had accused Turkish authorities of using torture, to this day. But, Turkey had expressed a willingness, to discuss, and work with, all the problems that had been raised, and also announced that it was already making good progress in some of those areas.

Also in the spring of 2005, were some disturbing reports on Malta, a fledgling EU member. This small nation has many significant problems as well, many of which one would have expected to be well on the way to resolution, before accession to the EU. Apparently, exceptions and deferments, had been made here as well, as with many other countries. So, where are the unified standards people are to go by? Is that why, citizens in some of the older member countries, had raised many objections? One glaring objection, for Malta, was that people there, have persisted in the savage practice of shooting birds, any kind of birds, even Sparrows, mind you, that had the misfortune to venture on their island. These darling creatures, in their migratory patterns of travel, across oceans, see a haven where they feel they can rest and feed, before continuing on their journey. What a mistake! Along much of the Maltese coastline, one can see numerous bird entrapment sectors, and hunter concealment structures, everywhere. It is a disgrace! *As these creatures fly in, exhausted from their journey, shots ring out, and the birds are no more!* Reports suggest there are some 37,000 registered hunters in this small island nation. No political party has had the fortitude to tame their misguided habits, in this author's lifetime, or that of many others; and one would have thought that such abuses had to go, before access to the EU.

Visitors to the island had condemned this practice for a long time, and their comments had regularly appeared in the local papers over a period of 40 years, but to no avail. Many pictures of slaughtered birds were often featured in the local press, but critics said that government officials had done little to curb the abuse. During a recent visit we saw many reports of such shootings, the birds being left on the ground, where they fall, a Seagull, a Lark, a Blue Heron, anything! *Should the EU not demand much higher standards from its members, if it is to have any future?* Otherwise, it would soon deteriorate, into a third rate organization.

Stories from Europe suggest that when voters were asked to express opinions on the EU itself, many of them did not hold the EU in high regard. Why? That is disturbing as many of these States had tried so hard to form this partnership, where they were hoping to include not, only the economy, but also, defense, as well as free borders. Many had assumed, that it would have provided a counterbalance to the might of the US. Some of the new entrants to the EU, had a fragile economy, others, had emerged from years under the control of communism. Some had remained relatively underdeveloped; whereas, others had experienced over-development, with haphazard building programs; no proper planning in place, and a taxation system in disarray. Besides, most of them tended to be fired up, with that entity of pride, in their independence and their individualism.

For example, one can see that in some countries, building permits are granted, with no regard to uniformity, and are likely subject to corruption. They may be granted for say, 5 stories in height, but instead, the builder erects 7 or 8 stories, and no action may be taken by authorities, often, because of the influence of money, power, and politics. They always go, hand in hand. Another example is, when a ground level area, in a building, may have a permit for a restaurant, but before long, the owner also starts a disco entertainment (without permit), with the resulting crowds, music sounds, and rowdiness, to the distress of anyone living in that building, above. Again, the police, and responsible agencies, either do nothing, or are too slow in acting. One can also see buildings with a historical heritage that are taken over, and soon converted into 'modern' steel-concrete-glass structures, that can be an eyesore. All this can result in a façade, with buildings from 2 to several stories high, side by side, the new, with the very old. That can present quite a sight.

What else may be seen in some of these countries? Garbage dumps that can become miniature hills, with significant pollution; roads in disrepair; water and electricity, and telephone services, that could be modernized. Water and electricity may be turned off, several times each week. There is poverty, and homelessness, in some of these countries, as is found elsewhere, in the west as well. Did such countries hope to alleviate some of their own problems, by joining the EU? That may be the case. In some instances, job opportunities are scarce, hence the fear in parts of Europe, that people would move across borders in search of work, and become a cheap source of labor. There are many in these European nations, who believe, that they should firstly resolve their own problems, because they created them, to start with; and other countries should not be saddled with the added expense of providing solutions. Many of these citizens felt that their own people, must achieve better education levels, and reach certain standards of civilized behavior. Perhaps the more progressive members in the EU, saw this coming, with some of the newer members joining their partnership, hence the negative voting on the constitution; and other difficulties being encountered, at this time.

And what about the practice of using bottled water, wherever you go in Europe? Is that for the health safety of people? There is ample technology, to produce safe, pleasant tasting, water, as in the US, Canada, and elsewhere. Why does everyone offer bottled water in Europe? For third world countries, the assumption is, that you need bottled water, for your own safety, because of serious, water borne, diseases. Is that now applied to Europe as well? *Or are these, corrupt practices, to support industries, dealing in such products?* Is that, how Europe will nurture, and protect the environment, in future? Tens of millions of bottles, mostly plastic, are consumed every day- - *even, if some of them are recycled, these products have been shown to be serious sources of pollution, resulting in the degradation of our environment.* That is not the way to protect the environment, in the west! Many parts of Europe should have good, natural sources of water, with appropriate treatment facilities, as needed. In the past, most of the citizens did not feel the need for bottled water, what went wrong?

Spring of 2005 brought troubles to the political fortunes of Italy's Berlusconi, and that country's economy had faltered significantly. Berlusconi, and his team, had been dealt a blow in recent elections, the economy could not be revived with a 'quick fix'; and he had allied himself with America's Bush, on Iraq, a move that was most unpopular, with the majority of Italians. Many in that country, could now say that he deserved more, than just a set back, at the polls; perhaps, he too, should be accused, of leading the country down the wrong path; and assisting in a war, on another sovereign country, without good reasons, and on a basis of an alleged conspiracy of lies. As if the Italians needed more proof, in July insurgents warned Italy, once again, to leave Iraq, and Berlusconi announced, that Italian forces would start leaving the country in September.

In the British paper, The Sunday Times, some headlines read as follows: 'Blair will kill off EU', that is, after the rejection of the constitution, by voters, in France and Holland. 'While Blair plots'; 'Thinking the unthinkable as Euro trembles'; 'Let the Turks in to finish off the Euro Super-state'; 'New dawn fades for latest Euro members'; 'Old Europe dithers'! In one single day, such headlines reflected the sentiments floating around, after the negative results of the first two referendums. According to newspaper articles, after those voting results, Blair would also try to kill the EU constitution. Even efforts by chancellor Schroeder of Germany, to save the day, would not likely succeed. Reports continued to refer to the EU needing to appear more open and transparent, allowing television cameras, as they had met behind closed doors, up to now. Hardly anybody could object to such demands, in these days of much talk on democracy, and open societies, the need for transparency should be obvious. Britain was the second largest contributor to the EU, and therefore Blair would continue to exert his influence in the decision process. Polling in Britain, had also demonstrated, that a referendum at that time, would almost certainly be defeated, there as well.

We cannot but wonder why critics do not wish to see the EU, become a super-state. Why not? How else could they provide some balance to the super-power of the US; if they set their minds to it, and ironed out their differences, they could become the super-power of the New World. France and Italy and Germany, were the original founders of the EU; and according to these reports, Germany had some doubts about being closely associated with a weak economy, such as Italy, and that perhaps it would abandon the EU, if things went wrong. Many felt there was a bit of tug-o-war going on, with France and Germany on one side, and Britain, on the other. Thus, there was a sense, that, with UK assuming the EU presidency soon, matters could lean towards the British position. These reports, further alleged, that, the British, had long been reviled, by France and Germany, 'as bad Europeans'. Many of their members perceived, the entry of poorer and cheaper countries, as a threat to their stature, and their standard of living. We have often heard these arguments in the context of globalization, and free trade agreements in the Americas.

There are so many aspects that could cast shadows on an entity, as the EU. Leading up to the G-8 summit, the Sunday Times reports reemphasized, why we should all worry, when police stop, potential protesters miles away from where they want to go, using legitimate fears of terrorism, for illegitimate ends. We have heard that often enough. For instance, in the US, there has been much criticism that when the government is experiencing problems, or their ratings are falling, in the public's view, they raise terrorism alerts, or *announce that they had 'credible evidence', of a threat against a certain facility.* Therefore, in the US as well, protesters are often kept miles away from important venues, from gatherings around the president, and people are always pre-selected! There is no such thing as a really open forum for the president, in America; it is all smoke and mirrors, the speeches, the so-called town hall meetings, etc. Has it reached the same low levels in Europe? In the same paper, another report reflected on the UK, where a Muslim officer had joined the police force, and had filed reports that he had been victimized, and had received racial insults. The authorities denied this. This man had graduated with a law degree in UK, and was amongst the highest A-level students for that year. The reports continued, "His allegations are a potential embarrassment to the authorities". The EU had prided itself in promoting justice, fairness, and the uplifting of human rights. Once more, it was alleged how such incidents were not always fully investigated; and we recall, similar charges had been made against the US. It seems that governments tend to make it a habit, to sweep under the rug, anything that may shake up their egos!

Another disturbing news release on the EU, on the Internet, was the possibility that Washington might have been interfering in the internal affairs of the EU; *it is not unusual, for America, to interfere! They make a habit of it.* They referred to a London-Ankara-Washington axis. EU leaders should ask London to tell Washington to get off the bandwagon of meddling in the political affairs of Europe. Many European leaders have rightly been disgusted with Washington trying to push its own demands. Thinkers have felt that America desperately wanted to control the world! For example, in October reports suggested that Turkey was still receiving warnings, on its human rights records. There were other discussions going on in Europe, on 'open skies' agreements, on tendencies towards protectionism. There were also allegations that some of the European states had attempted to disguise the size of their budget deficits.

Blair of UK had his hands full, as he was preparing for his day in the limelight as president of the EU. Some, perhaps, looked to him to guide the Europeans in the right direction; and also hoped to see a renewed leadership role, for the original founders of the EU. Another Internet report dealt with a briefing in Brussels, by Dominique Moisi, adviser to the French Institute on International Relations. Present pressing problems were identified as the constitution, a budget, and other disagreements between some of the countries. Certain comparisons were made, with the old, powerful, republic of Venice, when they stated, 'Europe must not go the way of decadent Venice'! They talked about the possible decay of an entire continent; how its political system, and constitution were anachronistic (similarities to the US?), ' that there was a vain frivolity of living, a carnival of both pleasure and frustration'. The main theme of the report was the inequality between the haves, and the have-nots, and again, that was amazingly similar to present day America, and other nations. They decried the pessimism that often turned to protectionism. They commented how the beginning of decadence appears charming at times, for civilizations, but then they cannot keep decay from taking control. They may become concerned that petty nationalism would expose weaknesses in the European projects, and that perhaps, there was not a strong enough sense of 'European patriotism'. That is surprising, because so many in Europe, and elsewhere, had hoped that Europe would get its act together. If they are talking of decay in Europe, and many believe there has already been much decay in the US as well, one wonders who will assume a leadership role next, China? Ah, that is not so far fetched, as some thinkers had already reached such conclusions.

In 'Mirror Reflections- -Mirages' we had pointed to America's increasing problems with scams of all types, identity thefts, many directed at the elderly and most vulnerable; and a terrible decline in the quality of service. From UK and other parts of Europe, we now learn, that they too, have seen their quality of service become a shambles, and they have experienced a major increase in scams and identity thefts, there as well. Their economy had strengthened, whereas in the US it had been struggling for a few years. But prices of goods in UK were very high; and Germany and Italy had their own difficulties also. Their higher rates of unemployment were disturbing, indicating that these were uncertain times, for good, 'old Europe'.

One could get a glimpse of what was going on in Europe (nationalism, indifference, and so on), from something as simple as a musical contest. In May 2005 we heard much, in Europe, about 'Eurovision', the song festival from many European countries. It was fascinating to watch, but such a production had its own problems as well. Greece finished in first place, and tiny Malta came in second, and Romania was third. But, what we heard from many countries, were good imitations of hip-hop, swing type, pop music, Anglo-Americanized, if you will. Most of these presentations sounded much like a shadow of the other, a terrible taste in music, and perhaps, it did not even deserve the title 'song festival'. Although it was a competition for the best song, and singer, most of the acts had lavish supporting casts, background singers or a band, and extensive stage effects. There were also some performers in sexy outfits, with sexy gyrations. Chiara, from Malta, with her presentation, "Angel", was one of a handful of solitary singers, with no supporting cast, or lavish stage sets. Such secondary stage effects should not have influenced the placement of singers, but they might have attracted some votes as well.

What was also troubling, in the voting procedures, was the appearance of corrupt tendencies, that left little to the imagination. Countries were not allowed to vote for their own candidate, but only for candidates from other countries. However, citizens in individual countries, *had a tendency to vote heavily for their neighbors, or for those with strong political affiliations with them.* It was so flagrantly obvious, as we watched the program, that, commentators predicted which country was going to vote for which singer, to give the largest block of votes to their neighbors. It was a poor showing for the EU, even in such activities, as an art venue, which should have been honest, and impartial, and enjoyed by all. It demonstrated, once again, that countries with smaller populations (Europe), can be just as corrupt as larger ones (US, and other countries).

According to some commentators on this European festival, little Malta deserved to win that contest; but surrounded by water, as it was, it had no close neighbors, so to speak, to vote for its candidate, as neighbors were seen to vote for each other. Is that not amazing? If dishonesty exists, even in a song festival, in entertainment, is it any wonder, then, that there is such overwhelming corruption, and dishonesty, in politics, in business, and in so many other activities, such as, sports. In the past, we had also heard reports of cheating in television parlor games, where awards were given.

And on the Internet, other reports suggested that Blair would be performing a juggling act, to try to obtain some type of a consensus, from the 25 EU members; because there were several pieces of legislation that needed attention, and Blair would have the presidency for the next 6 months. One contentious topic was that, Britain had the highest, per capita income, in the EU, but had one of the lowest financial contributions to that organization. How like the US, with its contributions to the UN, another major world organization! And Britain had been receiving rebates of a few billion Euros each year; and now, Germany, and France, had insisted that those, needed to be significantly reduced, but Blair and his group continued to raise objections.

That briefing by D. Moisi, in Brussels, besides comparing the EU, to a possible decaying Venice, made another comparison of the EU to Switzerland; and this too, was presented in an unfavorable light. One could not agree with the latter conclusions, by Moisi, because the reasons given, were that Switzerland, had remained neutral, had stayed out of many major disputes or wars, for the past 60 years. *What, on earth, is wrong with that philosophy?* The speaker suggested that Switzerland was only able to maintain its status, because during all those years, it had agreeable neighbors who had decided to respect the Swiss neutrality. However, other experts had previously pointed out, that, Switzerland had followed the right course all along; it had maintained peace within its borders, its citizens enjoyed a very high standard of living; it managed to preserve a healthy economy; and it most likely enjoyed a genuine, democratic government, with greater partnership with the people, and the most stable in our world, today. *Perhaps, more countries, including the US, and Europe, could learn a valuable lesson from Switzerland, right?*

In the individual members of the EU there are always political considerations as well, that is, the changing of the baton, at election time. Germany's Schroeder had a close one recently, and critics were still debating the winner or winners, of that one. German representatives were discussing the crisis within the EU, and emphasized that the union could not continue to donate money to member states, when they gave nothing in return; it could not be a one-way street, and gestures had to move in both directions. They pointed out that corporate tax could not remain at 19%, that they needed an equitable tax system, so that everyone paid a fair share (have we heard that before, in reference to the US as well)? That would apply to small, and medium enterprises, large corporations, and to individuals. They reiterated that each EU, member-State, should be in a position to send something to their headquarters; and they mentioned that the value-added tax, present in much of Europe, might need some reshuffling. As they had been running a deficit, they felt that the EU must push for a balanced budget, and the sooner that was achieved the better it would be, for all member States.

In the National Catholic Reporter, Sister Joan Chittister, OSB, put it this way, "It is good news that Europe is past its age old rivalries between the Hapsburgs, and the Bourbons; and they are deep in the process of trying to form a European Union, rather than a series of competing dynasties". Good news indeed, for Europe, and there are many who wish them, full speed ahead! Hopefully, they will soon be able to overcome their nationalistic distractions, and their differences. Let us remember that major nations have come into being from a veritable melting pot of ethnic groups---America, Australia, Canada. So, why not, a European Union, that would encompass the richness of many cultures?

THE MALTESE ISLANDS (MALTA)

Why include Malta, in a discussion, such as this?

It is included, because we have written about larger countries, such as the US, Russia, China, and India; also about continents, such as Africa; those that are rich, and those that are poor. And as a nation, Malta is one of the smallest, and its economy, and standard of living, would place it about the center. It had faced constant struggles for freedom, and its history is one of the richest anywhere.

The Maltese Archipelago is situated between southern Italy and North Africa, in the center of the Mediterranean, a region full of history. The land area is a little over 300 square miles, and a population estimated at around 400,000. To those with a background in history, it brings memories of bravery during world war two, when it was plunged into a major international conflagration, as Britain declared war on the German-Italian axis, after Hitler's armies invaded non-threatening, neighboring countries. To others, it evokes gallantry, and memories of the Knights of St. John-Knights of Malta, fighting for Christianity against the Ottoman Empire. And especially to Europeans in modern times, it has become the holiday island, for vacation and relaxation, and beneficial sunny weather. This writer hails from the island of Malta, and the memories of those wartime years remain vivid to this day. We were then part of the British Empire of nations, and many countries were still under colonial rulers, at the start of world war two. Since then, however, there have been many national movements, everywhere, that ended up freeing many from the yolk of colonialism, from whichever source.

The Megalithic temples of Malta remain unique; and archeological excavations at numerous temple sites date some of them to about 4000 to 4500 BC. These temples indicate that the people of ancient times were peaceful, well organized, and self sufficient, even so far back in history. How is it that we have deteriorated so much- - -? It is presumed that Neolithic farmers, from the region of what is now Syracuse, in southern Italy, had reached the islands about 5000 BC. Pottery discovered at Ghar Dalam, in Malta, was quite similar to that found in those regions of Sicily. The 'Temple Culture Period' commenced about that time, and these temples continued to attract worldwide attention. One of them, The Hypogeum, of Hal Saflieni, is a one of a kind gem, an archeological treasure. It is considered so unique, that, thanks to assistance from world heritage groups, strict conservation efforts are now in place for this Hypogeum, with climate controls, restricted lighting, and controlled numbers of visitors. Something Malta had not done in the past. These Megalithic temples, and the legacy of the Knights of the Order of St. John, have endowed Malta with a rich heritage, in both art, and architecture. Later on, in the Bronze period, people from Italy and Greece had migrated to inhabit these islands. There are also numerous cart ruts, coursing deep, in solid rock, all over the island. These, too, have been the source of much archeological debate, and are considered the work of Neolithic man. Some of these ruts go into the sea, others go right off rock cliffs, so that it was theorized, that traffic existed between continents, at one time. Others had concluded that geological upheavals explained the sudden termination of those cart ruts. Then, it was also taught, that these ruts had been painstakingly started by hand chiseling of some type, and then, carts or sleds drawn by man, rendered them a permanent impression on the terrain.

At a later period the Phoenicians traveled extensively throughout the Mediterranean, and settled in Malta about 800 years BC; and after them, the islands had come under the influence of the Carthaginians. The might, and power, of Rome was growing rapidly, and its domain extended all over southern Italy and Sicily. They defeated the Carthaginians, and Malta passed into the sphere of the Roman Empire. It thus, became a province of Sicily around 216BC. There are, preserved Roman villas, showing the elegant standard of living, of the Romans, during that era. But Malta was not treated as a conquered people by Rome. It was during this Roman period, as recorded in the Acts of the Apostles, that St. Paul was shipwrecked on the Island of Malta in 60AD, as the Romans were taking him to Rome to stand trial. It is written that the passengers and crew, of that boat, had all survived, and were treated well by the local people. And it was during this stay, that St. Paul converted the Islands to Christianity.

In 395AD Malta came under Byzantine rule. And then the Arabs conquered these islands about 870AD, and remained in control, until the Norman, Roger, Count of Sicily, defeated them, in 1127, and ruled over Malta, as part of the kingdom of Sicily. The Arabs were finally expelled. But under them, the standard of living for the people had remained high. After the Norman Conquest, Christianity flourished, and became the main force on the islands. Later on, as Malta was passed to several feudal overlords from Europe, the local population was sometimes treated poorly, and conditions deteriorated. The Maltese language, which had a Semitic foundation, now became influenced by all these other entities, from Europe, to make it, the unique language it is today.

The Order of the Knights of St. John lost Rhodes to the Turkish armada during the continued expansion of the Ottoman Empire; they had been driven out of the Holy Land, went to Cyprus, and to Rhodes. They requested a new seat, to call home, from Emperor Charles V of Spain; but at first had not considered Malta, an ideal location, for their purposes. They had been without a permanent home for a few years, until they took possession of Malta, about 1530AD. The Turkish forces continued to carry out attacks against them, so gradually they began to improve the island's fortifications, as they were quite inadequate. In 1557 Jean de la Vallette, became Grand Master of the Order in Malta. The Turks increased their attacks, trying to eliminate the Order for good; and thus, they launched the Great Siege of 1565 against Malta. They had sent a huge armada of ships, differing numbers had been quoted, but all agreed, that to the local population, it must have been an awesome sight, hundreds of ships against a tiny island. The Turkish force was estimated at 40,000, and it was reported that they had brought with them some 100,000 cannon balls, of all sizes. The defenders of the Maltese Islands numbered about 9000. Documents state that, the Knights by themselves, could not have held out very long, without the help, and courage, of the local population, including those already in active service, and women and children. The elite had already left the islands, proceeding to Sicily, to await the outcome of this major confrontation.

One of the important forts (fort St. Elmo) fell to the Turks, after a prolonged battle; there was heavy loss of life on both sides. When the Turks turned their attention to another fort (fort St. Michael), at the end of June, reinforcements, small groups of Knights, and Spanish troops, reached Malta, to assist the defenders. The battles continued between the Turkish armada, and its forces, on the one hand, and the Knights, and other defenders, behind the fortifications. Then on a fateful day, *the 8th of September*, more reinforcements from neighboring Sicily, managed to break through, and land on the island. Although the Turkish forces were still far superior, they were demoralized; they might have misinterpreted the significance of the relief forces that had arrived. The islands and the defenders, had not been defeated quickly, and forced to surrender, as they had anticipated would happen; and they had lost large numbers of their Turkish comrades. Thus, it is recorded, that on the *8th of September 1565, they boarded their ships, and left the Maltese Islands!* The Knights of the Order of St. John had won a most important victory for Europe. The Knights and the local citizens had also suffered heavy losses, in manpower, and the devastation of the island's fortifications, and other structures. Some historians have since theorized that, besides the determination and bravery of the island's defenders, perhaps another factor might have forced that hasty retreat by the Turkish forces. That is, the possibility of impending severe storms, that might have severely impacted such a large armada far from home. As is customary in historic events, debates, and conjectures go back, and forth, and they are certain to continue.

In such violent wars between the Knights, and the forces of the Ottoman Empire, brutality, sometimes from both camps, was not unheard of. According to history recordings, the invaders had sustained substantial losses. To strike fear in the defenders across the harbor, behind massive bastion walls, they killed prisoner knights, beheaded them, and attached their bodies to wood planks, which they floated across the water towards the defenders. They assumed that when those defenders saw this, they would panic into surrender. However, it had the opposite effect, as the knights and other defenders, became even more determined to fight to the end. And they too, responded, with similar acts of barbarism, to strike fear in the Turks. It was said, that at one point, they killed some of their Turkish prisoners, beheaded them, placed those heads inside their cannon, and fired them at the enemy camps. Such was the viciousness of the battles of old times. We have not been doing much better today; our actions are different, but the rampant killing of the innocent, with the guilty, and the destruction inflicted by all sides, are still barbaric; as is the demolition of people's homes, without just cause.

Following this great siege, and remarkable victory, of 1565, the Knights of St. John drew up plans, to strengthen the fortification even more. And they also laid the foundation for a major city, that of Valletta, the capital of Malta, so named, after Grand Master La Vallette. When he died, he was buried in the crypts of the cathedral of St. John, within the city walls, as that was considered the Conventual Church of the Order. Disraeli had been quoted as saying, of Valletta, "A city built by gentlemen, for gentlemen". Some years after these historic events, the stature, and the importance of the Knights, as a fighting force, declined significantly. Thus, they were eventually, overrun by the French forces, commanded by Napoleon, in 1798. He also spent several days in Malta. For the Maltese, the struggles continued, the invader was different, that was all. Local insurgents, and British troops, aided by British and Portuguese naval forces, blockaded the main harbor, and forced the French to surrender. Thus it was, that by 1814, Malta had come under British rule, but it was emphasized then, "that it was, by the will of the people".

The Maltese islands were involved in world war one, when many of the war wounded were sent there, besides there being a large garrison, in Malta, as well. Different factions within the population, soon began to emerge; those who favored closer ties to Italy, those who wanted even closer ties to England; and a substantial, nationalistic faction, that began to spread the fervor for nationalism, towards achieving an independent nation.

And we mentioned elsewhere, then came world war two. In those early days of the war, Malta was ill prepared to fend off a mighty adversary, such as Germany. The British air force, in Malta, had 3 'Gladiator' fighter aircraft, aptly christened Faith, Hope, and Charity. They were no serious challenge for the renowned Luftwaffe, back then. Faith, because the people were very religious, and placed themselves in God's merciful hands; the defenders, were fighting a power, that had launched a war without cause, and they were defending their own land. Hope, because, in spite of great odds, there was hope that they would come through the ordeal, that England would continue to provide assistance. Charity, because there was a strong sense of camaraderie, that the allies would be there, for each other, no matter the hardships. There were a number of guns aimed at protecting our skies, and perhaps our seas, if called upon. And, once again, in those fateful days, our citizenry was ill equipped, with an assortment of hunting rifles, pitchforks, and other odd armaments, as an imminent sea invasion had been predicted. That is how weak, and vulnerable were these islands at the start of world war two. But the invasion never materialized. Later in the war, a few Italian E-Boats attempted a speedy assault on ships in the Grand harbor, but they were spotted by the gun defenders, and were soon blown out of the water,

Because of Malta's weak defenses, it had also been assumed that the Germans would launch a parachute assault as well; but as these islands are so small, it was postulated that such an attack was unlikely, because many of the parachutists would end up in the sea quite likely, and many others would encounter heavy small arms fire streaking up towards the sky. Such attacks, or invasions, were therefore not attempted, once our defenses had been strengthened. The air force received its Hurricanes. Spitfire Squadrons arrived later, and these became more of a match for the Luftwaffe. Military personnel, from other countries in the British Empire, arrived to assist in the defense of Malta. But the advances of the German army, in Europe and North Africa continued, and the plight of the island became more precarious. The incessant attacks took their toll on buildings, and people alike, and many aircraft were lost on both sides.

The German Stuka bomber pilots, demonstrated their bravado, by diving down to their targets, often with deadly accuracy. Other German, and Italian aircraft, unloaded their bomb loads from considerable altitude, resulting in random destruction. Although, an actual invasion never materialized, a very determined enemy enforced a virtual blockade. Food became scarce resulting in austere rations. The population suffered much; and malnutrition, and certain diseases, increased., as so often happens, in prolonged wars. Parents scrounged to provide some degree of nourishment for their families. 'Victory' kitchens, organized by government agencies, sprung up everywhere; and these provided meager sustenance. A 'black' market soon thrived for certain commodities, although these practices had been declared illegal. Ammunition for the defending guns, on the islands, was also rationed. That was the plight of Malts in the early stages of world war two!

The German forces were stationed in Sicily, within an easy hop of Malta; and the boot of the Nazi regime was being felt over most of Europe, and parts of North Africa. With certain countries, Germany had engaged in various non-aggression pacts, so to speak. As their forces were amassed across the Dover channel, in France, Great Britain was gearing itself up, as best it could, for a final assault, and the invasion, that many felt, was coming. Since the war, historians have argued the reasons, why German leaders had hesitated, and never crossed over to England. One explanation was that, perhaps the lack of initiative to go after England came from Hitler's pondering, on what the United States would eventually decide to do. That country had not yet entered the conflict in those early stages of the war. Then, there was also Russia. Perhaps for similar complex reasons, they likewise, never invaded Malta. Instead, they marked the island for havoc and destruction, and for starvation, hoping to force them into surrender. Malta was indeed, a thorn in their side. With Axis forces all around the Mediterranean region, this British/Maltese fortress, continued to launch forays against the enemy, by air, or by sea.

Readers may ask, how could a small island as Malta, survive, when surrounded by what appeared to be invincible forces. It was because of the bravery of the citizenry, the British, Maltese, and a smattering of other defending forces, that such a feat was accomplished. Convoys of Merchant ships tried often, to run the gauntlet, from Britain to Malta, only to be mercilessly attacked by German U-boats, or the Luftwaffe, with the heavy loss of life, and shipping. But they absolutely had to try replenish, the island's depleted supplies of food, and ammunition, or else surrender. Whenever possible, small amounts were transported by plane, or by submarine, but obviously these were insufficient, by themselves.

When the locals heard, often by word of mouth, that another attempt would be made to bring relief to the beleaguered nation, people would congregate in churches all over, for private prayers, or special services, to ask for Divine assistance, for those trying to make the run, to cross over those perilous seas; and perilous, they were! People would also stand on vantage points, trying to spot early on, any surviving ships approaching closer. Occasionally, a crippled ship, aided by Destroyers or Cruisers, would be spotted, not far from the entrance to the Grand harbor, trying to make the final passage, for some protection. Cries of joy, and encouragement would go up; and scores of volunteers would rush to the wharfs. As soon as the ship was safely secured to the moorings, they would hurriedly assist in the unloading, before more attacks would come from the enemy, to finish the job! Some of this was not unlike scenes we have all seen on our TV screens, of people trying to escape from East to West Germany, across their no-man's land, and the dividing wall. Many did manage to escape over the years, until that wall came down; but many other East Germans, were spotted by their guards, and would be shot. Thus, it was, that even then, people on the west side, shouted encouragement, for the escapees to reach safety. This was after world war two, but the struggles between East, and West, were to continue.

In the early phase of the battle for Malta, the arrival of one Merchant ship, even though crippled, provided immediate respite of sorts, but more food supplies, and ammunition, would be needed, if the island were to survive. Yes, all that, and a steady supply of fighter aircraft, and the courageous airmen to fly them! One desperately needed convoy was called 'Ta' Santa Marija', the convoy of St. Mary, as the faith of the Maltese came to play, when they beseeched the Lord for help, and for mercy, in those dark days. They prayed to the Blessed Virgin Mary, and their various patron Saints, for intercession on their behalf. Whenever possible, as ships entered the harbor, the whole area was enveloped in a smoke screen, to make the ships less vulnerable from the air, at least for a period.

One episode involved the British aircraft carrier "HMS Illustrious", that had been hit by a German air attack. With an escort, it managed to limp into the Grand harbor, to its moorings, close to the magnificent ancient bastions (heritage of the Knights), that grace the harbor on most sides, to give it some protection. However, the enemy knew that it had reached safety, and were determined to finish her off. More attacks were launched from Italy, and the ship was hit again, with loss of life; but following repairs, it survived to fight another day. The old three cities of Malta, and the capital of Valletta, were repeatedly hit during these attacks, as they were so close to the harbor. The toll was heavy. A grand structure, the beautiful Opera House of Valletta, was destroyed, and regrettably, to this day, it had not been restored. Numerous homes, churches, schools, hospitals, shelters, anything, were hit during constant attacks on Malta. The unique Dome of Mosta church, one of the largest in the world, sustained a direct hit. Several people were in the church praying, at the time. A large bomb penetrated the domed ceiling, leaving a large hole, but the dome did not collapse; the bomb crashed to the tiled floor below, creating a huge crater. There were no serious injuries, as it did not explode, and it was declared a miracle.

In those early months of the war, many citizens, young or old, volunteered for service, and if not accepted, performed other types of volunteer work, to help in the war effort. There were air and sea spotters, air raid wardens, black out inspectors, to make certain all lights were put out; there were shelter supervisors in some places, and more. Younger individuals who had been turned down, sometimes performed tasks as look out, for air attacks by planes that might have sneaked in, to enable people to evacuate buildings, and move into shelters, particularly in schools, and other public buildings. Those were very uncertain times at the beginning of that war. Many European countries had been over-run, by German forces; the famous French Maginot Line, had a reputation of being the ultimate in defense lines, and presumed to be impenetrable. With such a build up, it was both a disaster, and a disappointment, when the wily Germans managed to locate weak areas to penetrate, and attacked the French from the rear as well. With the collapse of the Maginot defenses, France soon surrendered. On such a backdrop, it was assumed that the clock, of capitulation, was also ticking for Malta. This was not to happen, we were ravaged, but survived. As mentioned in the previous book, "Mirror Reflections= = = Mirages", because of staunch resistance, and nationwide acts of heroism, sacrifice, and much suffering, the island was awarded the prestigious George Cross by King George VI, of England, to the nation, considered a rare award, for an entire population. And president Roosevelt, of the United States, also awarded a special citation, for what was achieved, on this Mediterranean island.

In May 2005, James Holland had a commemorative report, in the Times of Malta, on the air battles over Malta. It began, "By the end of May 1942, after one of the most concentrated and protracted aerial blitzes, of the war, to date, Malta was on her knees". And it appeared that fears of an invasion kept recurring. Some British pilots heading for Malta were not sure what to expect. One comment by such, a pilot, newly arrived in Malta, rang loud and true. "The tempo of life here is indescribable- - -living conditions, such as food, sleep, and all ordinary standards of living, have gone by the board. It makes the Battle of Britain- - -and fighter sweeps, seem like child's play, by comparison". That said it all, about Malta. Some incidents were not uncommon, such as a woman, soon expecting to deliver her baby at home; but as a bomb hits close by, she must seek out a better shelter, for that purpose. Another woman was also expecting to deliver, but because of numerous air raids, she gave advance warning to her midwife, and they went to a safe cave where the delivery was successful. Such was life, with constant air raid sirens blaring, as many as 30 attacks per day! In due course, the allies were victorious, and world war two ended. Some years later, Malta gained its independence, and tourism was to become a major industry.

According to reports of meetings, held in 2005, between the president of Italy, and the prime minister of Malta, the two countries had been cooperating on many projects. Historically, Italy always had close ties to Malta, temporarily blemished, by Mussolini's alliance with Hitler, during world war two. These leaders discussed improved relations between the two countries, and the programs that Italy was assisting with; some 200 companies were operating on the island. Work was already in progress, on modernization of the infrastructure, food safety, maritime controls, environmental protection, tourism, restoration of artistic heritage, and so on. The Italian president pointed out, that there could be other projects, such as, Telecommunications, Pharmaceuticals, Elections, and environment friendly technology. How wonderful!

Many of the European Union countries have much house cleaning to do, including Malta. There, the economy has been on a bumpy road, there is a significant budget deficit, and the cost of living is very high. Noise pollution is a problem, and the people do not seem to care; neither do the police, and other government agencies, to some extent. Cars, buses, motorbikes, trucks, at times zoom, screech, and blast their horns, with abandon, some with radios blaring. There is often a haze over the island, which is likely a result of major pollution; it is not uncommon to see the ocean and beaches, with lots of trash, which could easily be avoided. The numbers of cars, for the size of Malta, is hard to believe, as well. Thus, wherever one goes, cars are parked everywhere in the streets, because with many of the structures being quite old, garages were not built, with them, in years past. Therefore, they now park cars on one side, or both sides of the street, sometimes double park; and also park, where no parking is permitted! Trying to navigate some of these roads can be a challenge! Laws are, seemingly, often ignored; and any punitive actions taken, are not strong enough, to act as deterrent. Sometimes people do whatever pleases them. Only recently, measures have been taken, to try to eliminate smoking from public buildings. Many roads are poorly paved, and in many countries these would pass off, for country lanes. Traffic signals are few, as are pedestrian crossings; and the latter, have been the scene of locals, or often tourists, being injured or killed, because drivers are cavalier, they speed, and can be undisciplined.

Dogs often litter in many areas, on the pavements, as in tiny Malta, large tracts of grass cover are unknown; there may be pooper-scooper laws, but nobody seems to know about them. For years, walking along some of the promenades was called, 'strolling through the tulips'! It used to be, that potholes, and the uneven surface of roads, was an invitation, to disaster. Many buildings are in a sorry state of disrepair, paint peeling, cracks in masonry, rust, collapsing balconies, and more. Other so-called, high-rise buildings, are an eyesore, and seem out of place. A huge Hilton hotel complex has also been erected, complete with a multi-story tower. For this project, they destroyed a lovely coastal area with wild flowers, and a rocky shore to the sea; this was public land. The hotel group took it over in spite of protests by environmental groups, because government agencies gave permits to the builders. The wilderness areas on the rocky shore, were blasted open, to form a channel, to allow sea water to go inland, to form a yacht marina, as part of the hotel complex. Allegedly, the ploy was, that these wilderness areas would be restored later on, for the public. You guessed right, it never happened! It was never restored to its former wilderness attraction. That coastal area, the marina, and the entire complex, were enclosed within a boundary, with walls, and gates, as private property!

It has been said often enough, that if you have wealth and power, and you know the right people, everything is possible, and there are no restrictions. This applies to most countries, large or small, democratic, or otherwise. For example, there was a piece in the local paper, about a visitor to Malta who was waiting for permits to build an addition, on his second home. One of the locals told him, that he did not have to wait, to just go ahead and do it. When you hear these things, what can you expect? Most will tell you that driving on Malta's roads is like navigating through a maze. Because of this, and the large number of automobiles, accidents have increased dramatically, and it is a miracle that they are not even higher. Traffic in illicit drugs has become a business, and with that, crimes of all types have soared, as well. With all this, will the brotherhood of the European Union, help improve some of these statistics? Time, and history, may tell the rest of that story.

This is an island, that for its size, is likely, the best endowed, nation on earth, with an artistic heritage, that is unequalled; steeped in a rich history; and there are numerous archeological, and other treasures, as described above! And yet, for many years there was utter neglect of these heritage sites that, in most countries, would have been protected with great pride. This could become a steady source of income for any government, with an eye towards improving the standards of the entire country. For example in the US, in St. Augustine, Florida, there is a single fort (San Marco), similar to the magnificent bastions on Malta, built by the Spanish colonialists, in a later period. The monument is impeccably preserved, and is a famous tourist attraction, with visitors coming from all over the country. When we referred above, to that huge hotel complex, how could any government issue such permits, for structures that are so esthetically out of place? Was it, because the government was at the mercy of contractors and builders, as happens in so many countries? Was it the usual corrupt influence of power, and money? Many of the older homes, have been demolished, only, to be replaced by taller, more modern, structures, such as, apartment buildings. Why would any responsible agency act so irresponsibly? One argument given is, that the communities need space to expand, as the area is so small, and they can only expand upwards.

Letters, to the editor, are seen regularly in local papers, usually from visitors- - these, deal with noise, and other forms of pollution, dust and trash at many sites, dirty beaches, and the regular killing (or trapping), of all types of birds, more or less, year round! If they complain to the police department, quite often, no action is taken. On one such occasion, a policeman said that, the loud music was not a nuisance to them (even though it is against the law), and therefore the complainant should be the one, to take the offenders to court! Nonsense, why have laws to protect the public, if that was the case.

When you visit Malta, there is indeed, dust and litter at too many places, but there is always a great deal of construction going on, in many of the towns. In other countries as well, where there is construction under way, there often is dust and dirt around, as we have seen in parts of Europe, and the US. But in many countries, society is better organized, and they are also, better equipped to handle such expansion. They have much more space, in which to expand. Malta's streets are rather narrow, built in periods when the automobile did not exist, and they were meant for horses and carriages, as in many parts of old Europe. In such narrow streets, with numerous parked cars, when two cars approach each other, one is compelled to go in reverse for some distance. On one occasion, neither of the drivers would give in. One got out, and said that it was not a problem; with that, he pushed the side mirrors of both cars, inwards, saying: "now we have more room to pass"! Such is life, in an overcrowded, overbuilt, lesser developed, nation. One hears much talk by local citizens, and writings appear regularly in the press, on problems with the environment, pollution, and, of course, politics play a major role as well; and these are a part of any topic that one might consider opening up, for discussion. Then, what about water, decent, potable water? Without desalination plants, for reverse osmosis of ocean water, the island could no longer sustain the population it presently has. Rainfall amounts are inadequate, there are hardly any reservoirs, no springs, no rivers or lakes; snowy mountains do not exist, and neither large tracts, of forest covered, land. Small groves of trees are few and far between, and that makes the appearance of Malta from the air, especially, quite barren. It had been reported that when the government tried to plant a number of shrubs and trees, many of these, would quickly disappear. However, over a period of many years, some progress has been achieved, with a few park areas being created, and long stretches of, well planned, promenades, along the ocean.

Some would argue that the education, and culture, of many, among the local population, needed restructuring; as is needed, in many, underdeveloped, European countries. With tongue in cheek, a writer had apiece in the Malta Times, about building a villa cheaply! The land area he desired to have, was simply there, so he helped himself, and marked the boundaries for a plot, to build upon. He 'managed' to get hold of blocks of stone and cement, here; and paint, somewhere else. What did he do about tiles? Why, he helped himself to some of the tiles lining the walls of tunnels! It was inconvenient to have to collect them at 3am, but he managed quite well. He then helped himself, to bathroom, and other fixtures, from buildings, and hotels, that were under construction, and so on! Before long, this man's villa was a show place! Undoubtedly, this was a parody, of sorts; but it reflects, how in many countries, large segments of the population still require much education, and a change of bad habits. How often have we noticed, that, in developed or undeveloped countries, rich, or poor, items in restrooms, and other public areas (such as trash bins, and toilet accessories), keep on disappearing. *That is the culture of the 'me' society, and nobody matters. It is prevalent amongst many, including in the United States of America, in large or small countries, alike.*

Because of the frequent reports on the shooting of birds, many visitors have written that they would never return to Malta, and they would try to discourage others, from visiting there, as well. That is a sad commentary on the island! Others wrote, that they would publicize this inhumane activity on Malta, and thus turn people against wanting to plan vacations, there. If thousands of tourists, were to adopt such a stand, surely then, the government would be forced to act, without always considering the votes of these hunters, to the detriment of everything else. Yet, others, wrote, to urge the protection of the rights of these hunters, to practice their sport, and hobby! *How dare they, such backward looking people, call that ruthless killing of birds, a sport, and a hobby- - -!* That reveals only too well, the lack of proper standards, and lack of values, that seem to prevail. Many of these hunters seem to follow no season, no laws on limits in numbers, or of types of species, as far as they are concerned, anything goes! Some critics had called them, barbarians, and savages, and that, may not be far off the mark! It is also true, that some of the hunters have acted responsibly; but as all these letters of complaints, continue to appear, year, after year, it can only mean that no laws are being followed. Government officials could have stopped this practice a long time ago, with the services of police, soldiers, and undercover agents, in different parts of the island, on patrol. When such criminals are caught, then, the penalties should be severe enough, to teach others a lesson, they cannot easily forget. This is done in other civilized countries. Because of the lack of such discipline, some third world countries have had serious problems with poaching, and killing, of majestic wild animals; some of them are now on the brink of extinction. For example, in Malta, a fine of a few thousand pounds could be imposed; and the seizure, by government, of all weapons, cars, boats, and other equipment, with, or without jail time. Periodically, these items could be, auctioned off, by the government, with the funds applied towards the protection of birds, and the environment.

In most countries, this would act as a great deterrent, and citizens would not break the laws so readily, for fear of being caught, and because of the consequences. On America's highways, and other roads, it is not unusual to see notices forbidding littering; and the penalty could be a fine of $300 to 1000, just for littering, mind you! Often, that stops people from throwing trash, out of passing cars. Yes, people still break the law, but it cuts down on the problem; and when they are caught, they pay a hefty price. The warnings against hunting, or fishing, in forbidden areas, are well publicized; as are such activities, when carried out, out of season; or the possession of a certain number, or, a type of species, that, are, not permitted, to be taken. Yes, indeed, people can enjoy the richness of nature, but regulations must exist, and they must be obeyed, for the benefit of all.

Like other, much larger, countries, tiny Malta has also experienced, illegal migration of people from North Africa. They either land along different parts of the coast, or they are spotted in territorial waters, on the high seas, often, in unsafe boats, and are brought in, to safety. These boat people have been arriving for a number of years, and lately, the numbers have increased considerably. Malta is a very small country, and cannot possibly provide jobs for many illegal immigrants. Ostensibly, many of them report, that they were trying to reach Italy, or other parts of Southern Europe, to seek asylum; but many end up in Malta, the first tract of land they spot. It has obviously created a strain on the local economy; and local papers are pointing out, that the Maltese people are now, also experiencing the specter of racism, and intolerance, not encountered before. These are dangerous signals, in difficult times.

Some of the topics discussed in the preceding pages, are boldly emphasized in some of the following headlines, in the papers, during a recent visit to the island. 'The Rape of our villages'; 'A Sad Day'-this referred to the cutting down of 400 year old Carob trees, and other types, for so-called, development; and as far as one could judge, there was no government action to stop this, and severely punish the offenders. 'Dirty Beaches'. 'Employment, a fundamental right'. 'Arrests, in Drug raids'. Farmers, Landowners, in fierce battle over land'. 'Vandals remove country road signs'. 'Least Educated work force', this was drawing comparisons with the EU. 'Farmers in free fall'. 'Inexcusable service'. 'Loud Music'. 'The Hague program-Ten ways of improving our lives'. 'Kalkara valley, a monument of shame'. 'Leaders of the Commonwealth Nations, to meet in Malta'. 'The Asphalt Jungle', this of course could be applied to many other countries as well. 'Ask not, what the country can do for you', a Kennedy quote, used, because of the utter selfishness, of some of the people. 'Another call to ban spring hunting', and this, headline, accompanied more pictures of dead birds, that had been killed. Regrettably, actions taken, by various governments, on this hunting debacle, have been negligible. All these headlines are from the month of May 2005, and they are pretty much in line, with many sections covered in this book.

"Home Truths From Abroad" appeared in the Sunday Times of Malta, and was written by Howard Hodgson, an Englishman, living in Malta, and UK. He described remarkably well, what Maltese, and visitors alike, have been describing, about the direction that, Malta had followed. He writes "Imagine their shock (visitors), when they find areas of Valletta empty, and decaying"; "when they drive past half built, concrete shells"; "when their impression is completely marred, by rusty cars, fridges, freezers, and even oil drums, dumped indiscriminately, to ruin the beautiful landscape". Then, they view some of our wonderful artifacts, or monuments, and see them neglected, or vandalized. You can now also see, where some developers, have been permitted to use adjoining walls of ancient forts, or bastions, to build private projects, such as apartment buildings. In most developed countries, this would be unheard of! Is this, what passes, for progress, in Malta? *Is that how to protect, and preserve, ancient, heritage, sites?*

This article, by an outsider, who had a second home in Malta, bares only too well, some of the deplorable goings on, in the island of Malta. Besides trying to secure help, from European nations, it behooves the Maltese, to learn an important lesson; that they must all pull together. That they must all pay, their fair share of taxes; and that all those who break the law, would be equally punished, no special treatment, for the elite, as happens too often, in many countries. All citizens, and visitors, need to take great pride, in the island, and maintain clean streets, and beaches, and stop all acts of vandalism. Such acts of neglect, and ignorance, do not hurt outsiders, but they hurt the local people, above all! Then, perhaps, many aspects described in the above article, and others, referred to, in this book, *would no longer be an eyesore, before those who are trying to enjoy, their visit to this Mediterranean jewel, of an island!* The islanders could then be justly proud of their membership in the EU, and sense that, they too, had something worthwhile, to contribute, to that expanding Union of Nations!

CONSEQUENCES OF PREEMPTION: IRAQ

In May 2005, a British member of parliament (Galloway) was summoned before the US senate, on accusations stemming from scandals, to do with the UN oil-for-food program. American officials had alleged that he might be guilty of participating in those activities. European news media featured extensive interviews, with Galloway asserting his innocence, in all that. He was looking forward to going, to Washington, *to blast them for their lies, and setting up a smokescreen, simply to divert public attention, from what the US had done in Iraq!* He told senators, in no uncertain terms, that what the US had done over there, was all, wrong; and what he, and many of his colleagues had been stating, about Iraq, all along, had been proved right! It was quite an exchange between Galloway, and those senators. Do members in our government have any shame?

Much of the press in Europe favored Galloway, that, he had won handily, over a bunch of senators. Many critics had maintained that the American fixation on the oil-for-food program was, indeed, to distract the UN, and most world governments, from the chaos the US had caused in Iraq; and the tens of thousands of innocent people killed, the suffering, and the utter destruction. There is no way, US officials could hide complaints by Iraqis, that, they had no clean water, no electricity, no health care, no decent infra-structure, all because, of American attacks; and that their streets were no longer safe! Iraq was not a terrorist haven, before, but, since the US occupation, it had become a major one. Galloway had called the accusations against him, by this administration's committee, 'utterly preposterous'. He asked those senators, why they had not consulted him, before making such allegations. He said "now I know that the standards had slipped in Washington, over the last few years". How right he was, too! The whole world has been aware of that, but unfortunately most Americans did not seem to care.

A CBS commentator stated that most of the recruits for terrorism had come from Sunni regions of Iraq, where the US had a strong presence. And a guest on PBS news hour, with Jim Lehrer, said that for some Americans, war had become a distant memory, as they had become concerned with other matters. But there was *the silence of war; the names put out on that same program, night, after night, of the very young, men and women, in their prime, who had lost their lives; in that sense, war was not a distant memory, for many American families!* Yes, for them, that war was still going on! A US general also appeared on that same program, and listening to this character, made it appear that Iraq was a huge success story. That the Iraqi government was working, that Sunnis were changing their views, that, their economy was picking up steam. But, most people, here, and abroad, would disagree, with what that general had to say! All he could do, was, to keep repeating, over, and over "we did a good job"! He said that they had captured important insurgent leaders, and that, is often repeated, by US officials, even, as attacks keep on increasing; and the number of deaths on both sides, keeps climbing. Listening to this fellow, made one feel that the US government, and military leaders, had no idea of the realities on the ground, in Iraq, and of opinions from around the world. At the same time, an official on the ground, in Iraq, stated that they might kill one insurgent, but then three others, take their place. That was much closer, to realities on the ground, in the Iraq quagmire, not the platitudes of that general.

Author, and lecturer, sister Joan Chittister, referred to good news from Kuwait, where some political reforms were taking place, with an increase in registered voters; and a woman had been appointed to a cabinet position. And, she added, they had done it themselves, *'we did not have to bomb them, to make it happen'*. She said, 'but the country, we did bomb, to spread democracy, *does not have it, not really, not independently (of the US), not without violence'*. On imposing democracy from the outside, Chittister called that, **the most Schizophrenic of concepts!** There is little doubt that, millions here, and overseas, agreed with her presentations. It has already begun, in American policy fashion, the US controlled Iraqi governing body, announced, in September 2005, that Saddam Hussein had already "confessed" (members of the Iraqi governing body, was that obtained through torture?), to ordering the execution of Iraqis. Within a day or so, the chief lawyer for Hussein, denied that their client had made such confessions. People everywhere need to remember, that the US administration had kept Hussein imprisoned for many months, without proper contact with lawyers. This is not that Hussein might not be guilty of many crimes against humanity, but to point out the type of democracy, and justice, we had been demonstrating, to the people we came to liberate from oppression. Towards the middle of October, there was much talk of the new elections taking place in Iraq, to be followed, finally, with the start of the trials for Saddam Hussein. This resulted in many opposing comments, all around.

Much of what had been going on in Washington since the debacle, in Iraq, had turned out to be mostly bad policies, and bad politics. With regard to the possible UN oil scandals, nobody would object to impartial investigations, if criminal activities were suspected. Unfortunately, some things that go on, in Washington, can be just as bad, or worse, than the scandals themselves, at the UN; at least those are the opinions of many thinkers around the world. No country would consider such investigations, carried out by the US government, as 'impartial investigations', certainly not in the climate of suspicion of the US, that, had prevailed for the past few years! Such investigations should always be carried out by, a well recognized, world body. As we have heard from many reports, both, in the US, and abroad, corruption thrives in many countries, but also in the US itself.

Around 2004, there was an interesting period, when US officials started accusing a well, known, Iraqi expatriate (previously very friendly with Bush administration officials), of corruption and criminal behavior. He was before the news media extensively. It was alleged that he had deliberately given false information to the US government, to force the war against Iraq, and Saddam Hussein. Such manipulations have certainly taken place throughout history. Except, that this war had drawn criticism, and condemnation of America, from all over the world. Although the US government had threatened this man with arrest and prosecution, it was alleged that they were not able to touch him, because of his power, and popularity, in Iraq! *On the contrary, he remained a figurehead, over there, he was very active in local politics, and attained positions on the Iraqi governing body.* These are more examples, of machinations, and corruption, in politics everywhere, even in countries, in the process of undergoing major changes. Thus, the saga of Iraq continued to unfold, as US foreign policies remained even more suspect.

Iraqi security, and US forces, continued their daily attacks against insurgents; or by the latter, against the occupation forces, and on Iraqi civilians, in suicide attacks. Iraqi police, or anyone cooperating with the US, became ready targets. European press reports showed, that in one May attack alone, by US forces, about 9 US soldiers had been killed, and some 100 insurgents, this in a single day. Had US officials truly, announced, that we had brought Iraq, peace, and democracy, and justice, in the past two years? US-Iraqi initiated information continued to issue steady propaganda, about progress in Iraq, how they were disrupting the capacity for the enemy to attack; but other sources kept repeating that daily attacks were on the increase; and deaths and injuries had increased on all sides, especially Iraqis. And more, and more, Iraqis, were being arrested as 'suspects'. Was that, a US demonstration of democracy, arresting, and detaining, hundreds of people? Would the US, and the Iraqi government, eventually arrest most of the Sunni population? *Would that, bring peace, and democracy, to Iraq? Some Muslims have gone as far as accusing the US government, of trying to stir up war, so that Iraqis would end up fighting each other, instead of fighting Americans.* Where lies the truth, in such chaotic environments?

Millions of people around had expressed amazement at the reelection of Bush in the US; but, in short order, polls in the US, had turned unfavorable for Bush, with 45% saying he was not honest, or straightforward. Now, 40% considered Iraq the most important problem facing America; and a majority of citizens felt that Bush was not doing a good job. Since these figures were announced, there was more bad news from Iraq, and on the home front, and criticisms of Bush's performance had increased dramatically. Mind you, all this, *was even before the Katrina disaster at home!* The 'Observer', had a commentary on a book, "Secrets and Lies", by Dilo Hiro. He analyzed political lies, distortions, and confusing reports that allowed the United States and Britain to launch an illegal war on Iraq. Hilo gave convincing evidence *that Bush had been determined to invade Iraq, on almost any excuse, soon after his first election.* Similar accusations had been made by, others, as well.

Articles in the Sunday Times suggested that increasing violence was pushing Iraq to the brink of civil war, and suicide bombers kept on coming. This, instead of the peace and goodwill, Bush and Blair, claimed they had brought the Iraqi people. Bush administration, and military, officials, and the Blair clique, should read such reports more often; and here are more- - -'corpses are found by the dozen, as police join death spree', by James Hider, from Baghdad. Apparently, Sunni corpses, including that of a cleric, had been found; they had been handcuffed, tortured, and shot in the head. Our 'free' media could ask, if this was the way US officials had taught Iraqi police, and soldiers. Other Iraqi men were left in a van, without ventilation, in temperatures of over 100 degrees, and they suffocated to death. The Iraqi ministry had admitted to this. Bodies are often discovered, seemingly of innocent people, Sunni, or Shiite, they are murdered and dumped on the streets. These articles alleged that senior Iraqi officials had admitted that, frustrated security forces, mainly Shiite and Kurds, sometimes tortured, and executed, 'suspects'; **sometimes- - -?** Mr. Bush, Mr. Blair, did such atrocities occur on a daily basis, under Saddam Hussein; was that one, of many, reasons you gave, for attacking the country, and putting Hussein on trial? Well, what about those, committing such atrocities, now? Will they also be put on trial?

Powerful voices of Shiite clerics were coming out, condemning all that violence. Ayatollah Sistani had 'blinked', it was said, at the present Iraqi government, and that was the only reason, it was still standing. But another cleric, Al-Sadr, stated that 'the occupation was a problem, that Iraq was not independent--- that the American presence was causing most of the trouble'. And many experts had also expressed similar views. As late as August 2005, the US was still claiming to have bombed houses, with insurgents in them, and had killed many of them. But, this time, Baghdad security officials contradicted such reports put out by US officials, and said that many civilians had been killed. The usual, gross disparity that exists, between what US officials state, and what others claim, had actually happened. It had reached a point, that hardly any foreign government officials would believe anything reported by the American government. Just like so many in UK, had stated that they would never believe anything Blair said.

According to Associated Press reports, on the Internet, the Iraqi ambassador to the UN accused US marines of murdering one of his relatives, and demanded an investigation, and justice. He said that the young man was, escorting marines, to a room, in the house they were searching, to show them a rifle without any ammunition. The ambassador claimed, that when the marines had left, the young man was found dead, with a bullet wound in his neck. It is difficult to get at the truth, whenever there is a repressive government, or occupation; examples of this have been, Iraq, Israel with the Palestinians, Egypt, Jordan, Sudan, Saudi Arabia, and many more. In underdeveloped, poorly governed, countries, it is not uncommon for people to disappear; but this has happened in developed countries as well, as has been reported all over Latin America. A fair question would be, how many such stories are out there, whenever there is a military occupation, and news media, and the public, might never hear about them! *That is the true calamity!*

Around October 2005, we witnessed the type of democracy, as forced on the Iraqis, by the Americans. Shiite factions, within the Iraqi government, were accused of "fixing" the referendum for the coming October vote, in such a way, that it would be impossible to vote against it, and defeat it. In other words, *it was a fixed election, even before voting had started.* Sunni factions immediately objected to such fixes, and threatened to boycott the elections altogether. Announcements by members at the UN were also critical of the changes made by the Shiites. Kurds were reported at odds, with some of the Shiites. What type of democracy had we brought to Iraq? However, to their credit, reports suggested that US officials possibly applied pressure, to the Iraqi governing body, to remove the changes, that they had 'fixed', in the constitution. This, could have been done, because most of the Sunni population, had boycotted previous referendum elections. If such a boycott were repeated, the US administration would look pathetic, before the whole world! Well, the Iraqi, constitution, elections, in mid October, were without much violence; but with a very heavy US, and Iraqi, military presence, and enormous restrictions, placed on the country. This should not be called, freedom, and democracy, *it came out looking much more like a dictatorship! And sure enough, as most of us expected, as votes were being counted, there were serious accusations of election fraud.* Most in the world, expect US, and Iraqi, officials, to deny that, but they are not likely to be believed.

Other news reports showed the American vice-president Cheney, stating that he could not understand why people were criticizing the US, for the Guantanamo (Cuba), prisoner abuse scandals; and, Mr. Cheney, the gross prisoner abuse, in Iraq? He said that the prisoners in Cuba had a new facility, there, and they had spent a lot of money on them (that word, money, again!); and that those detainees were comfortable, and were treated very well! *It was as if they were in the tropics, they could eat all the food they wanted! Would readers guess, if anyone believed him - - -?* Now, here is the vice-president of the US, at great odds, with all experts from around the world, and with many in congress, including his own party! **His assertions were at odds with the UN, the EU, the international Red Cross, with all Human Rights groups, with Amnesty International, and more!** Therefore, would people believe such political rhetoric? There were also reports, of Iraqi security forces, torturing their own Iraqi prisoners, in Iraq, to force confessions out of them. Is it any wonder, that the Iraqis would now do such things as well, after all the reports before the world, on the US abuse of prisoners in Iraq, in Afghanistan, at Guantanamo in Cuba; with reports of several deaths, and numerous suicide attempts, among those detainees, in their prisons. *America, America, what has become of your morality, of truth, of the recognition of good, and evil, of your conscience?*

By early 2005, more than 1700 US soldiers had been killed in Iraq, and those numbers were to increase even more; and that was more than double, the deaths listed as our other book "Mirror reflections = = Mirages", went to press. Several hundred Iraqi civilians had been killed by insurgent attacks, in a single week; and civilians are reportedly also killed on a regular basis, by US forces, and by Iraqi security forces. They rarely release those numbers to world media. Although a semblance of an election had been forced on Iraq, by the US, this was under a foreign military occupation; and there were accusations that, they were the usual corrupt elections, under a domineering foreign power. Many considered the resulting officials thus elected, puppets of the US government, and rancor among the different factions had persisted.

There were many past reports of 'torture' techniques, used in the former Soviet Union, in China, N. Korea, Morocco, Saudi Arabia, Turkey, Egypt, Israel, Pakistan, Libya, and many more- *are we saying that such evil activities are still going on, even in the US?*

According to Human Rights groups, any investigations carried out, on these abuses, can be highly controversial, as high-level personnel are seldom implicated; and low-level staff members, are usually made the scapegoats! This is injustice, this often happens in corrupt societies! We are expected to believe that those low level staffers made those decisions, all, on their own. If all this is true, according to world reports, are we not also portraying, images of tremendous injustice, and corruption, in the 'west'?

Senator Ted Kennedy, on Iraq, had emphasized how US defense secretary Rumsfeld had committed one blunder, after another, and suggested that it was time for the secretary to resign. Writer Paul Craig Roberts, stated that after the invasion, "the arrogant Rumsfeld found out, that the generals were right", there were not enough regular troops for the job, and therefore the National Guard had to be called up for Iraq. Vice president Cheney had also announced that the insurgents were on their last throes, but nobody else seemed to know that! A US general who was actually in action, in Iraq, disagreed with Cheney, saying, that the insurgents were still strong, and not on their last legs, by any means; and that could be judged, by the number of the attacks, and their coordination. Such statements were also at odds with some of Rumsfeld's comments. At this congressional committee hearing, Kennedy referred to the secretary's many errors in judgment, and he asserted how in baseball, three strikes, and you are out of the game! And, once again, they pointed out, how public support for the war, in the US, was rapidly heading south. The month of May had seen the most car bombs in Iraq, in a single month, with 77 attacks. After all the lies and misinformation, we had been hearing from various sources, it was reported that, Rumsfeld had stated that, we must always give the truth. All these months, we had many top United States officials, and others, telling Americans, and the whole world, about weapons of mass destruction in Iraq, about biological laboratories, about Iraq obtaining nuclear material from Africa, about Iraq being an imminent threat; *and now, we are asked to give the truth? Do they understand what the truth is?* Will our media ever fight for the American people? They had received much criticism for being partial to this US administration, and for improper news reporting.

There was yet, another blow to US prestige, when the World Tribunal on Iraq (WTI), according to European reports, continued to meet in many different countries, with the culminating session planned for Istanbul, Turkey. They planned to call president Bush, and Prime Minister Blair, to account, in a global awareness campaign. In Brussels, they displayed a large banner saying, "President Bush, the World holds you Accountable". My, what an unfortunate legacy, for our country, that was. WTI officials wanted as many countries as possible, to climb on board; and they accused that some of them, including tiny Malta, were burying their heads in the sand, for fear of the US! These officials informed the public that they were soliciting testimony worldwide, to use as evidence at this tribunal.

Whatever name, people have applied to Iraq, chaos, extreme violence, quagmire, nightmare, anarchy, they are not laudable names. It certainly does not reflect the birth of democracy, at the point of a gun; and many experts have asserted this. Critics have said often, through this process of elections, that, America could not bring democracy to Iraq, by forcing artificial datelines , on the Iraqis, purely to satisfy the political whims of a republican administration in Washington. The Bush people had cajoled them into meeting one deadline, after another; into forming a temporary governing council, then setting dates for certain other 'elections'; *then they forced them to meet another dateline for the famous constitution, which was a failure.* Any reader, with any intelligence, can judge that all this, was a prescription for disaster; we shall see. They are constantly trying to rush, and compromise, because of American pressure. Blair too, in the UK, had been taking more heat, because of his support for Bush, on Iraq. But what did he do after the London attacks? He was being magnanimous, when he went about pontificating, "that we had the UN mandate, to do, such and such". Now, he finds it convenient to hide behind the UN! That was a poor performance on his part. When the Iraq war plans, were being fabricated, it would have been honorable, if most of Blair's party associates, had resigned, as British foreign secretary Robin Cook had done. He showed, he was a man of courage, and principles. If most of them, in UK, had done that, then, Bush and Blair, would not have been so cavalier, to push another war, on this planet!

An Iraqi council member stated, 'they were learning about democracy, it takes time; they did not need artificial dates'. He said, "yes, Mr. Bush, you won; now, leave us alone, to do our work, right"! *This Iraqi, council member, hit the nail on the head, with a simple statement! Washington pundits could learn valuable lessons from him!* That was amazing reporting. And in another report, a member of the Kirkuk development group, in Iraq, claimed that the present elections over there, were not likely to be democratic, *because the existing governing body (forced by the US), did not fully represent the people!* This contrasts sharply with Americans, including the military, who might have been brainwashed into believing that everything was progressing very well. Average citizens never learn of elements of corruption, and shady dealing, by officials in government, whether they are in developed, or under-developed countries. On the PBS television program, 'Now', with David Broncaccio, a guest discussed how he had spent 20 years in the army, and had served in Iraq. He emphasized *that citizens could certainly be vocal against the Iraq war, and still, fully, support our troops, (contrary to US official propaganda).* He said that most Americans, including soldiers, did not know what we were doing, in Iraq; that our forces did not have the resources they needed; and that there was no clear strategy. And they again pointed out, that the original reasons given by Bush to go to war, were simply not true. Instead, they were now telling the American people that we are fighting terrorism. How was the US government defining success in Iraq, and what were the final goals? These questions, as critics have asserted, had never been answered by this administration; but there was considerable flip-flop, over a period of many months.

On a CNN program, a team described their visit to Iraq, to meet with people over there; to get their views (possibly uncensored by the US). But a reporter said, that of all the Iraqis he interviewed, not a single one had told him, that they were better off, under the occupation; or that things were progressing nicely. A prominent Iraqi said, that the problem with the Americans, was, that , when you asked how many soldiers they needed, for the task, *they did not know;* if you asked when they would bring real peace to Iraq, *they did not know.* And if you asked them when they would leave the country, *they did not know! This Iraqi concluded that the Americans did not seem to know anything they were doing!* Coming from a prominent citizen of Iraq, that, certainly, was not complimentary. Another man stated that they had a strong sense of nationalism; but now they realize, that, although this was their country, they were under an occupation. All this, and more, was obtained from Iraqis themselves, in all walks of life, *and not from the elite in Washington!* At the other extreme, we have American government officials, members of the military, and politicians, constantly touting the progress made, and how the Iraqis were better off! *But, nobody believes that, the Iraqis do not believe it, why?* Most Iraqis, on all sides, seemed to agree, that the idea of giving democracy to Iraq, under US influence, and pressure, was ridiculous.

About this period, there was an amazing letter to Time magazine, commenting on rumors about a peace prize for president Bush. The writer said, "that it would be laughable, if it were not so sad. Bush used lies, and distortions, to make a case for the invasion of Iraq".

As noted elsewhere, in the UK elections, Blair had tried to concentrate on domestic, and other foreign policy issues; and to distance himself, from what he had done in Iraq, by allying himself with Bush. Thus, Time magazine had several comments on Blair: a British woman from Lancaster, said, "I think Blair is a lying bastard. But I do not see the point of voting any other way". What a shameful legacy, that is, for Blair, as well as, for Bush. Such comments echoed majority opinion, that in spite of Blair's many faults, at this time, conservatives were not in a position to do much better, for the UK economy. The conservative's Michael Howard said, "on the one thing on which he, Blair, had taken a stand, which was taking us to war, he did not even tell the truth, on that"! Another caption on Blair read, "If he is prepared to lie, to take us to war, he is prepared to lie, to win an election". Right! There were other headlines in British papers, such as, 'Blair lied, and lied again'; 'Blair's dark days, as Iraq war erupts'; 'Final proof that Blair deceived the nation, on Iraq'! With such sentiments expressed by his own people, and by others, would he have the courage to resign? Time will tell.

With such public reaction, it is still hard to understand how this man was returned to power, though humbled at the polls, as was Bush in the US, with his many faults, and misrepresentations. We repeat, as it is so important, that many have maintained, that, 'the people will get the government, they deserve'. Why is it, that, leaders of nations are seldom held accountable, except by the so-called "victorious", as happened after world war two, at the tribunals; and we are about to witness, a spectacle of a trial, for Hussein, in Iraq, which, according to some world opinions, will be anything, but, a fair trial, in a true democracy.

The much, touted, (by American officials), quick, three week, war, that culminated, with the collapse of Baghdad, had turned out to be no significant victory, but a nightmare. Let us remember critics stating, that, a country with over $450 billion, in its military budget (US), was going against a country (Iraq), with a $4 billion, military budget! Yes, many had now called Iraq, a quagmire, as it entered into the third year of conflict, chaos indeed, ruled, and people continued to die, after three years! Many had blamed the Bush administration for single handedly creating a hotbed of terrorism, as well as, resistance fighters, fighting a common enemy, an occupation force. These increased numbers had come from the Iraqis themselves, and others entered from neighboring countries, to join in the jihad. They had heard US government officials, and at least one general, possibly, others, call this Iraq war venture, *another crusade.* This only angered Muslims, even more, worldwide, because of past tragic connotations with the brutality of the crusade wars, in years gone by, all in the name of religion. Again, this time, both sides have brought religion into the equation! That is a sad commentary, for our society, that we are still using wars and killing, and attempt to bring religion into such evil acts. And this is being perpetrated, in the twenty first century! Throughout all this, Britain's Blair continued to support Bush, on Iraq, undoubtedly, he felt they were together, in the swamp, and it was too late, to withdraw.

The compendium of the Doctrine of the church, referred to elsewhere, emphasized the duties that leaders had, to promote peace, *and to find alternatives to war.* A news item in America magazine, outlined a conference between Muslims, and Christians, and they had concluded that the *sanctity of human life was the only responsible position for people of faith.* Surely, the republican right wing, can understand that they were not only talking of abortion, but also of the killings in wars, and other forms of killing. Therefore, they called on the US, and other countries, to eliminate all nuclear weapons, with appropriate plans for verification. On the contrary, the US government had continued to develop new forms of nuclear weaponry. Those on the extreme religious right are often absent at such debates. Professor Dianne Bergant, also in 'America', wrote on "What a wonderful World", and she pointed out how, more, and more, of our intelligentsia, are questioning whether the masses, once they get rid of their illusions, would continue to volunteer, to die for their empire! *Because in the end, she said, we are likely to be destroyed, or disintegrate from within!*

Did we mention lies, half-truths, and misinformation? There was that incident, where, an Italian journalist was freed, unharmed, by her Iraqi captors, through the intervention of an Italian, secret service agent. They were driving towards Baghdad airport, to be flown to Italy. They were repeatedly shot at by US troops, at a check, point, she was wounded, but her rescuer was killed. Italians everywhere were angered, and wanted their government to immediately pull out Italian forces, from Iraq. The journalist gave interviews to international reporters, and claimed that the US government was lying; that they had not been speeding; and they were given no warning; and, she said, the Americans knew we were coming, and they kept on shooting at us! Other critics said, that, her captors had warned her to be on the look out for Americans, because of what they might do! Others, said, that the Americans would not want the world to hear, *what this journalist had to report, on American activities, in Iraq!* Italy's Berlusconi was embarrassed, and felt insulted by the US action. But, Berlusconi had behaved like a pawn, in the hands of Washington, and he portrayed himself as a poor leader. Readers might wonder, and rightly so, why journalists everywhere do not keep pounding, on such a topic, as this, of that Italian journalist, on the injustice, and the corruption. *Do we have a free press, or is it all smoke, and mirrors?*

A CNN program focused, on some US newspaper reports that had to be retracted, in recent months, because 'they had not got it right'. But, interestingly, the guests on that program, agreed, *that most US news media had been lax in their job, before the Iraq war, and also in the early days of the war.* They were not questioning enough, of their government; and they were not constructively critical, of the reasons, and techniques, used by this White House, to attack Iraq! They had done much better in the United Kingdom, because there, *some of their media channels remained truly independent.*

Overseas reports suggested that some 100,000 Iraqi civilians had been killed, and US troop fatalities were steadily increasing. British, and other fatalities, were fewer, but there were losses, nonetheless, in this US initiated war. That same CNN program, also told the story of an Iraqi male civilian, and his wife, when, his family group had been shot at, by, American soldiers, *and all their children had been killed, and the man lost a leg!* The man, and his wife were, both in tears, as they described how some American corporations arranged to bring them to the US, for treatment. They said that many Americans had helped them, in their tragedy, and they were so grateful to them. Then, he added, *that the American military will not admit that they did something terribly wrong, and immoral, firing on their family group, and killing the children!* Are we seeing more examples, whereby, governments compound the damage, and the problems, and civilians step in, to try to bail out, our own governments? We know, only too well, that the military has always tried to justify their actions, the reasons for their behavior, no matter how ghastly it might be! Likewise, they claimed 'good reasons' for shooting at that Italian journalist, and killing another innocent man, her rescuer. There have been numerous reports in the international press, on errors committed by US armed forces personnel. British reporters had commented on the rough tactics by US soldiers, that they had easy 'trigger fingers', shooting first, before asking questions.

US and Iraqi forces, continued to announce, this, or that, offensive, against insurgents. By now, people knew, quite well, that many were actually freedom fighters, not necessarily insurgents. They were battling the US invader, in their mind, similar to, freedom fighters in Palestinian territories, freedom fighters in Afghanistan, formerly against the Soviet invaders, and now, against the American invaders. There have been many freedom fighters in past struggles, including many in world war two, all over Europe. Surely, they were not terrorists? The Iraqi forces, taking a cue from the US, began assigning ridiculous names to their offensive actions, as if that would make them cleaner, and less violent; as if the innocent victims, injured, or killed, would feel less violated!

All the optimistic releases on Iraq, by the Bush administration, and by republicans, and by Blair, in UK, had **not** come to pass, and the war was not going well, in 2005. And, on the other front, in Afghanistan, the situation had deteriorated there, as well. In June of 2005, a US helicopter was shot down, in the mountain region, and some 16 US servicemen, had been killed. A group of special, forces, personnel, they were trying to help, were reported missing.

The Internet also had some remarkable headlines, on Iraq: "Iraqi death squads sweep the country"; "Ongoing slaughter in Iraq"; "Arsenal of Hypocrisy". Hypocrisy is everywhere, in politics, but this one referred to, US recruited Nazi intelligence, to help with the Space program, *to fight future wars!* As was stated before, some will sleep with Satan, if it helped them reach their goals.

In the spring, of 2005, British papers leaked a memo that, *alleged, that the Blair government knew that Bush had decided to remove Saddam Hussein, of Iraq, a full 8 months before the war!* He was ready for war, even before he told the American people, before he had approached the United Nations! Many had already stated that those actions by Bush, were nothing, but a sham. People, do understand that, simple talk, of 'values', is real cheap! This recently leaked memo was causing serious consternation, on both sides of the Atlantic! They had made a mockery of the Bush administration, agreeing to meet, with the emissary from Pope John Paul two, who had tried his utmost, to preserve peace. Bush met with that emissary, only days before the launch of this war! Now, we hear of the 8 months, referred to, above! In "The Shield of Achilles", in America magazine, Drew Christiansen, wrote, how the late Pope never tired of repeating, *that war destroyed lives of innocent people, and left behind, hatred, and resentment.* The author added, how, "The architects of war received presidential medals, and were rewarded with high-level positions"! Such reports, lend credence, to dozens of statements, over the last year or two, from all over the world, that, the Bush administration had, long ago, decided, to go after Iraq, whether Hussein was still in power, or not. That is why, many in Europe, and elsewhere, believed that it was all, for Iraq's oil, and for the benefit of US corporations! After what has transpired, surely, readers will now be able to judge, for themselves.

On a CNN program, guests again discussed news coverage, in the US, why, the above, juicy information, on the leaked, UK memos, had not been seized upon, by all media outlets. One respondent said, being quiet, for now, might mean that they are collecting all they can, on that particular topic, before exploding. We certainly hope so, for the survival of any semblance of independence, in our American media. We have not witnessed any 'explosions', in the US media, since the Iraq war started! They have been playing, dead! They are bought, and paid for, as critics have alleged. Iraq, had certainly uncovered the cancer, of heavy handed, media control, in these United States, just as we find in totalitarian regime states. A few journalists had issued warnings to our people, but regrettably, these, had gone unheeded!

AS POLITICAL WINDS BLOW

In "Mirror Reflections = Mirages", we had discussed how the wealthiest countries, and also others, could channel significant portions of their military budgets, to assist in disaster areas; and give aid to millions of the needy, the poorest, of the poor, and the hungry of the world. We could do that, and provide personnel, equipment, planes, ships, trucks, and other means of transportation, needed. This, instead of launching, wars, resulting in destruction, and loss of life. Recently, Naomi Klein, wrote a disturbing piece about *'The rise of disaster capitalism'!* Why, most of us, had, probably, never considered such an entity. She stated, "But, colonialism is dead, or so, we are told"; "There is, however, plenty of destruction- - -countries smashed to rubble, whether by so-called acts of God, or, by acts of Bush, on orders from God". Thus, now, instead of the help, and acts of good will, proposed in that previous book, we read about further plans, for the rich, and powerful, countries, to abuse the poor, and disadvantaged. And recently, as part of the US, had been reduced to rubble, by Katrina, and Rita, we heard from countries all over the world, even the extremely poor, offering to help, the victims, in America, in any way they could. What a lesson in Charity, that was, for our leaders, in the 'west', to ponder!

Klein quoted Herman Kumara, from Sri Lanka, who said that 'the funds received for the benefit of the Tsunami victims, *were directed for the benefit of the privileged few, not the real victims'!* And he also warned that Sri Lanka was now facing a 'second Tsunami of corporate globalization, and militarization'. The United Nations needs to forcefully, condemn such practices, if it hopes to project any semblance, of a world body. On Indonesia, and East Timor, Klein wrote, how such countries were considered unstable, and, therefore, humanitarian aid funds, targeted at, those areas, were handled by the World Bank. The excuse, they said, was, to disburse those funds responsibly; *and that usually meant, by slashing public sector jobs, and lavishing money on foreign consultants, that, the Bank insisted, must be hired, by those governments.* That is how intensely corrupt, society has become, according to a standard of western philosophy. The system of, I will scratch your back, if you scratch mine. Seldom is there any true altruism!

Klein continued, how in Afghanistan, the World Bank refused to release money to the government because of corruption, *but it preferred to give it, to equally corrupt, government organizations, usually foreign based!* President Karzai had blasted, wasteful, and, unaccountable, foreign contractors, for squandering precious aid, meant for Afghanistan, and its people.

Similarly, according to Klein, Honduras, Guatemala, Haiti, Nicaragua, and others, have all been under the thumb, of so-called, global relief, financial institutions. Following disasters, the poor, those without a voice, ordinary citizens, are often displaced; whilst the rich, the powerful, and the elite, move in, and take over. Klein wrote how Condoleeza Rice, for the US, had sparked much controversy, when *she referred to the Tsunami disaster, as a 'wonderful opportunity that had paid great dividends for us'!* Needless to say, many were horrified at the idea of a highly placed, US official, treating mass human tragedy, death, and suffering, as an opportunity to reap profits. This is another disgraceful example of capitalistic behavior, in such societies. But then reporters had shown how the Bush clique had often opened their mouths, and put their foot, right in. This is not uncommon, as had been quoted from many writings. Comments made by US officials, the merciless bombing of Iraq, and Afghanistan, even in civilian areas, it was called 'shock and awe'; on the horrific destruction, the killing, and the so-called progress, in the war, it was, 'we performed magnificently'. On the abuse, and torture, of prisoners, by the US, and British, we heard 'we are investigating'. Whatever happened to great leaders, who were ready to announce that they bear full responsibility (even to the point of resigning?), for the actions of all those under them? The buck stops here. Have we heard any 'Mea Culpa', from London, or from Washington, lately? Certainly not, not from present day politicians!

Naomi Klein, further commented on how, the rise of a predatory form of disaster capitalism, "used the fear, and the despair, created by a catastrophe, to engage in radical social, and economic, engineering". Such, mischievous planning, by any country, or countries, should not be tolerated, by a unified, well-founded, and successful, world body. Perhaps, for many countries, some social, and, economic, change is, indeed, desirable; but under what conditions do capitalistic societies embark on such a program? How many strings are attached to various ventures imposed, and what may be the adverse consequences on the local people? Klein added, that, in many of these disaster areas, it is the World Bank, already devoted to poverty alleviation, *through, profit, making, that leads, the charge.* Have we not heard numerous reports on the corrupt US contracts, given to Halliburton companies, for Iraq, and the many criticisms leveled at that company, and at the Bush administration? Did the US government ever adequately investigate those allegations? Or, was it all swept under the rug, as usual? Why do such companies continue to receive lucrative contracts from our magnanimous governments? Should our 'free' media not pursue investigations of such matters, till a decent answer is obtained?

In those countries struck by tragic disasters, have critics investigated, why, privatization, 'that disaster capitalism', enriched a handful of fat cats, but always left the masses behind, in poverty, and misery? Is it, an accident, that, these disaster, capitalists, are usually foreign based, from the 'west', and often in collusion with their friendly politicians, in power, at that time?

Author Prestowitz, in "Three billion new capitalists", wrote about the US being an economy, perhaps, on the brink, on life support; and how, when it collapsed, it could also lead to a global economic collapse. Why is it, that so many, had graded the US economy, with an, 'F'; was that, because it was true? He commented on how US influence around the world was on the decline. On a CNN interview, he said, *that in 2005, US officials were criticizing China, on its military build up (US, criticizing China?), but, at the same time, America was borrowing 2 billion dollars a day, from China, to keep us going!* (Did he say, 2 billion)? It so happens, that many other experts worldwide, have written on the erratic patterns, of US policy shapers; and that, this, probably meant the gradual fall, of America, as the only major global player. *And, that, may well be, for the good of our planet!* Others, have previously mentioned, what an article, in America magazine, recently summarized, on the book, "Collapse", by Jared Diamond; how, in the present trend of US policies, one could read parallels between ancient Rome, and America, 'The Decline and Fall of the Roman Empire'. Because, many, in America, especially, those in high, positions, failed to see, the writing on the wall. The signs are all around us. Katrina, Tornadoes, Floods, Wild Fires, Drought, Earthquakes, our Poor, and all those lacking decent health care, and an education, are only small reminders! Not to, also, point fingers at, the utter corruption, at all levels of government!

Commentator Jim Sinclair, wrote about UN reports, on certain blueprints, that might end up, being traded on the black market. Readers could ask, what is the big deal? Simply this, that, those blueprints dealt with specific steps on how to build, a regular (or a dirty) nuclear device! He was critical of Big Brother becoming involved in a secretive filing system that, 'was accumulating extensive personal information, on all of us, those who breathe, and on some, who do not'! He told us that the FBI listened in, to all types of conversation, on our citizens, supposedly investigating terrorism; and sometimes they tapped phone lines of the wrong persons! He also pointed at the US government, drastically reducing, punitive damages awarded against the tobacco industry, calling that, 'more evidence of *authoritarian free enterprise'!* With regard to our economy, Sinclair had predicted, that before the end of 2006, we might all be adversely affected, by a falling US dollar, and rising interest rates. That the Australian reserve Bank, had warned that, the current calm in financial markets, could signal the coming storm, for the world economy. Thus, it was bizarre that US officials, in some of their comments, would insult China, a country holding large amounts of America's debt!

Even since the war on Iraq, we have witnessed many tragic events beset our planet- -there have been many natural disasters, of all types, in all corners of the globe; repeated terrorist attacks had been carried out not only in Iraq, or Afghanistan, but in many other areas of the world, by some, who had felt, that certain leaders, in the west, had victimized, the brotherhood of Muslims. There have been economic upheavals, and the US financial markets, had tumbled severely, since Bush first came to power; a partial recovery had occurred, but the US economy had continued to struggled, under a heavy deficit burden, the largest in history. But, at center stage, remained the cycle of violence, and uprisings, and the ever present, Israeli-Palestinian crisis, that, the US administration had, initially, been accused, of ignoring. A Time correspondent emphasized that the commission investigating the faulty US intelligence, on Iraq, came nowhere near assigning blame; no names of senior personnel were reported, who might have seriously erred, or deliberately lied; and importantly, no heads had rolled, according to those reports. That always suggests to people around the world, that those in high places, with power, can get away with anything, whether it is in the US, or UK, or elsewhere.

We also heard reports on Haiti, in 2005, that US supported death squads were in action, over there. True, we have terrorism in our world; but, are certain actions by some, in the west, part of the cause, and have become, part of the problem? In the past, many had written about governments in the US, UK, and others, supporting dictators and tyrants, when it suited their policies. Are authorities in the US, still at it? Here are a few, recent, disturbing headlines from the Internet: 'Supreme court in Haiti (right wing) overturns dozens of convictions of Haitian military mass murderers'; is this now taking place under the umbrella of US, and UN protection? Was it not the United States that orchestrated the removal of that country's elected leader, president Aristide? *Is this what we have given the Haitian people, instead, death squads, and, a tainted court?*

Other headlines read like this: 'Earth Matters takes on Bush administration lies, and deception, regarding global warming'; 'An eleven year old boy shot in the back, by US armed, death squad Haitian police, as he attempted to go to school'; 'He is one of the world's leading dissident voices, in opposition to the wealthy, influential, repressive regime, in Saudi Arabia'- - -this referred to an ex-Saudi citizen, now in UK. The latter, was from Ian Masters', commentary, in 2004, on Saudi Arabia, whose autocratic leaders have been chummy with the US, dining, and holding hands, with our president, it was all over the news! Noting all the above news items, did US officials state, that they absolutely had to attack Iraq, to remove Hussein, the leader, there?

Many officials in the US, and others, have been quick to agree with Amnesty International, when their reports critically targeted other countries, such as, Russia, China, North Korea, etc. But, when that same organization, criticized the behavior of the American government, in the treatment of prisoners, or for other US activities, that were questionable, our officials were always ready to call those allegations, reprehensible. That eternal attitude by American officials, that we are better, we are cleaner, we can do no wrong. Some have called those double standards, bizarre, going all over the political map. The elite, in powerful, nations, can think that way, because they often defy international laws, as well.

It seems that materialistic, capitalistic, societies, had predetermined, how certain governments should act, how to adapt laws to suit themselves, the elite. Thus, those who are wealthy, politically powerful, and well-connected, can usually travel, freely, and spend lavishly, wherever they go. Others are going to be closely scrutinized, perhaps restricted by countries still enforcing visiting visas, and some will undoubtedly, be discriminated, against. Some have already accused the US of ethnic discrimination, particularly since the US, had been attacked, by Muslim oriented groups. Similar accusations have now been directed at UK, Italy, Germany, and others. France had received much criticism regarding its past activities in Algeria. Large ethnic populations have now entered, or have tried to enter, all these countries, since world war two.

Is any of this, giving Americans, a sense of safety, and security? Not likely because, in spite of the chaos, difficulties, and much hassle, at US airports, many have reported numerous loopholes in security. We had previously discussed inefficient security at some locations; and, we emphasized that it is very important, to stamp out terrorism, and other acts of violence, not only in the US, but also, worldwide. However, it can never be achieved, by committing acts, of even greater violence, against those we condemn. Following the attacks in London, we heard that the authorities there, would be studying tapes from thousands of cameras all over London, to try to obtain some leads. There it was again, Big Brother, in action, in the US, UK, and other places, thousands of cameras surveying the public. We did not like it, when it was going on, in Stalin's Russia, or Hitler's Germany; but we are seeing the noose tightening, more, and more, in western society. Critics have accused that the United States had many satellites spying on cities, and their citizens, scattered all over the world. For them, such acts were called tyranny, for us, it is the right thing to do! *What type of Schizophrenic, behavior, is that?*

Many have debated, how greater efforts, should be expanded, by the UN, group of eight, the World Bank, to eliminate the roots that breed despair, and terrorism, that is, poverty, hunger and starvation, inhumane treatment, millions of refugees, and a sensation of alienation, and discrimination. Proposals on how to tackle these, 'epidemics', had been made; and it was concluded, that when these tragedies were well under control, then, most of the causes of terrorism, would have been removed. There are few experts who believe that terrorism is adopted as a 'calling, as a quasi profession. Others had claimed that some terrorists are drugged, and indoctrinated in the belief, that if they sacrifice themselves for the cause, and die, they go straight to heaven to meet their virgins. Was that another fabrication by some of our western elite?

In some countries the question of airport security had grown, like paranoia, and where does, that, lead? Do we become, more, and more, like a police State, when we hear of thousands of cameras surveying the public at large? We have numerous reports of the US government, and many companies, collecting all types of personal data, on all our citizens. A news release by the Center for Public Integrity, showed how foreign companies, now, paid, to influence US policies! Thus, it is not only US corporations who employ infamous lobbyists, to do their bidding in Washington; now, they can come from other countries, as well, with, their, millions, of dollars! They mentioned how the 'privatization of Romania's oil industry had enriched the well-connected, and the corrupt'. Is that anything new? We have all heard that the powerful, and corrupt, can often get their fingers into most ventures, they set their eyes on. It has always been that way, and it goes on, to this day; you ask, in Iraq, as well? Why, we had that example of an Iraqi personality, who had been chummy with the US government, and is now steadily climbing the ladder of the Iraqi political machine!

The clashes between East, and West, go down through history, the most tragic, in recent memory, had followed the establishment of Israel, with the displacement of over a million Palestinians from their land. National boundaries have moved, back, and forth, over centuries, and this often occurred following wars. This one, too, in the Middle East, was followed by wars between Israel, and its neighbors. It has been stated, that all along,

Israel had the heavy, handed, support, of, the US and UK governments. And what was common knowledge was, that, Israel received massive assistance with weapons of war, mostly from the US, but at the same time, their Arab neighbors were ignored, to a significant degree. The latter, then turned to the Soviet Union, China, and other nations, not sympathetic to the US. In the meantime the Palestinian refugees had continued to struggle with the humiliation of, refugee, camp life. Clashes between the Jewish and Palestinian people, in that region, had persisted for over half a century; and all these events gave rise to various resistance groups, some of whom, resorted to the extreme tactics, of suicide attacks. Regrettably, the targets of such attacks, often, had no consideration for innocent civilians.

Many thinkers believe, that, the Israeli-Palestinian impasse, and the Iraq misadventure, forced many Muslims around the world, to direct their vehemence particularly at the US,, and also those supporting America's policies abroad. There are many politicians in America, who have long believed that our policies needed changing, badly! Although some governments in Muslim countries had tried to maintain cordial relations, with Israel, and with the west, millions of their citizens, had continued to foment, and such intense resentment, had festered for years. On a television program, speakers suggested that in the past, Israel had been accused of using torture, in as many, as 90% of Arab prisoners arrested as 'suspects'. Writer, Harbury, commented that, in the history of torture, since Korea, and Vietnam, it had become obvious that torture did not work. There was an apparent reference to torture techniques, used by the US, in Iraq, Afghanistan, and Guantanamo, in Cuba. Such reports could not have calmed the anger felt, by those Muslim insurgents. This chasm, between the governments in those 'friendly' Muslim countries, and their citizens, was cause for concern. Efforts by Israel, and the US, to revive dialogue in that region, after Arafat's death, have had limited success; but the political situation remained unstable.

European reporters discussed the move by Palestinian leader Abbas, to invite militant factions into the Palestinian government, to help fashion solidarity, and peace; thus removing the excuse for Israel, to refuse to withdraw completely from Palestinian territories. However, government officials in Israel, and the US, condemned such inclusion, of those groups, in the government Abbas was trying to organize. Israel, and the US, always insisted, that, any planning for the Middle East must be on their terms. Thus, in October 2005, on world news, Abbas warned Israel not to interfere, in Palestinian elections, and the formation of a Palestinian government; that it was none of their business. Others, did not tell Israel, how to organize a government!

As an added historical note, one cannot but wonder why news media have not commented, recently, on any final reports on Chairman Arafat, as he was a figure in that part of the world, for so many years. People remember well, how officials in the US and UK, had demanded investigation, and publication of medical reports, on one of the candidates in recent elections, in the Ukraine. Government agents thought these would foster public unrest, which they did, and perhaps sway the voting public. Some in the west, wanted to make certain that news releases on 'poisoning', and 'attempted assassination', were kept before the public; and allegedly, they tried to implicate Russia, and perhaps, embarrass president Putin. This led to massive street protests during the last Ukraine elections, with complaints of fraud taking place, there. Have we not heard of fraud allegations, in the US, and UK, elections, as well, and in many other countries? Those double standards by some, in the west, never cease! Past reports, that Arafat may also have been poisoned, and those surrounding the mystery of his illness, and death, were, seemingly, quickly suppressed. Why did the same people, who instigated news headlines on the 'poisoning' of Ukraine's Yuschenko, why did they not do the same, for Arafat? That, would simply be called, fairness, and justice, if they still exist, anywhere. Otherwise, we are demonstrating the wrong attitudes towards justice, and charity, to the people, we claim we are trying to help. Or is it that accusing finger, again, of one set of standards for the US, and Europe, and a different standard for the rest of the world? Unfortunately, that is precisely, what over a billion Muslims, around the world, have always asked, are we listening?

Although the Middle East had been most unstable, at least the Israeli and Palestinian leaders were still talking, and the violence had decreased noticeably. Israel's Sharon, had formulated his plans for Jewish soldiers, and settlers, to leave Gaza, and those settlements would be dismantled, or destroyed. That is yet another bizarre enigma, why destroy settlements they had used for years, why not simply hand them over, as a gesture of, goodwill, and charity? Sharon was immediately accused of wanting to dismantle the smaller settlements in Gaza, leaving, much larger ones, in the west bank, with the support of the US administration. Critics reiterated that Sharon would not get away with that, without the full support of the US. But, even this first gesture, in years, by an Israeli leader, was met with protests from the Jewish settlers, themselves, with resulting violence. These rumors, and accusations, never, cease, in that part of the world. Some of his own people went as far as calling Sharon, a traitor; but he managed to gather enough support, from members of his government, to go ahead with his plans.

When Israel's Gaza pull-out commenced, in the third week of August, as expected, Jewish settlers protested, and resisted, because 'this was always their land'; and many Israelis from other parts of the country, descended on the area of Gaza. They struggled with soldiers, chained themselves, pushed, and shoved. Some threw liquids, allegedly including acid, at soldiers, and police. Here, again, was noted, the, disparity and tremendous disconnect, in comments by US officials, and US media. These Jewish settlers and other intruders, causing mayhem, were simply called ultra-nationalist, Israelis, they were not criminals, certainly not terrorists. They were defending their settlements (which were Palestinian territory). Whereas the ultra-nationalists in Afghanistan, in Iraq, or Iran, those are usually referred to as terrorists, by US and Israeli officials, and most US media. They were called that, even if they were protesting against US attacks, or a US occupation of their land, or fighting an invader; *they were quickly lumped into one group, terrorists! They were not simply called, ultra-nationalist*! In the above Gaza upheaval, a Jewish settler, took a gun away from an Israeli security officer, and promptly fired, killing Palestinians. Now, consider this, how many US officials, or how many in the US media, had immediately called that, a terrorist act, by those Jewish extremists? *The answer is none, at least not that we could hear them, loud, and clear.* Do people understand the constant uneven handedness, in foreign policy by the US, and UK, for that matter. Perhaps it is not as blatant, in the UK, but surely, they seem to follow in copycat fashion. It is the above picture that many, in our world, see, or hear about, month, after month, year, after year, never ending!

Through so much verbal exchange, on Iraq, on the Israeli-Palestinian negotiations, on Syria, on Iran, and Pakistan, and more, an imam was featured in a European paper, and he had this to say, regarding war and peace, according to Islamic teaching, from the Qu'ran. 'That fighting is legalized, to eliminate injustices, and to secure the sanctity of places of worship, for all faiths. It is also allowed, to secure justice, and to save helpless, and oppressed people. During war, it is forbidden to kill anybody who is not engaged in fighting'. He also added, that, "we condemn all kinds of terrorism, whether by individuals, by groups, or by states". Then he added that, occupation, barrier walls, social, and political, injustices, violation of human rights, disdain of Muslim dignity, provocation of Islamic religious sentiments, and discrimination against Muslims, all these, *will not eliminate terrorism, but rather, will escalate it.* Once more, most people of conscience, with an open mind, will find such comments, enlightening; sentiments that have been echoed by many others, in our advocating for more dialogue, and less confrontation. There are those, in the west, who quote similar values as these, but it is obvious that not all sides, to these conflicts, have followed *the rule of right, or wrong.* We have glibly stepped over the line, and allowed matters to escalate, on the pretense of fighting terrorism, on the excuse of national security, and defense. Have we reached a point of 'no holds barred', the point of no return?

Then there was the famous G-8 summit in Scotland. Before that meeting had even started, leaked memos implied, that Bush administration officials, had forced the G-8 group, to water down, statements, on Global warming. They insisted on removing words like, *threat to humanity, that global warming had already started, and that man was responsible.* Thus, although there is plenty of scientific evidence, that global warming *had indeed started,* and that it had become a very serious threat, what did US officials do? *Mr. Bush, announced, that America, was already taking action, the nation was spending more on research into climate change!* US governments do not like to restrict big corporations, the usual large campaign contributors to politicians. Bush had refused to sign the Kyoto accord, and in some countries, news clips had labeled him, the Toxic Texan; and he had been referred to, as, the *most anti-environment leader the world had ever seen!* What a sad legacy, that is! He was seen in action again, after hurricane Katrina, when numerous Americans accused him of inaction, but after the storm had passed, reporters stated, that he was quick to relax environmental regulations on gasoline blends, allegedly, to help the battered oil industry.

The question that comes to mind, is, why did the G-8 leaders bow down to the requests by president Bush, and soften the wording, of their summit reports? Was it 'business as usual'? Mr. Blair, you were hosting that meeting, could you have taken a stand, perhaps, on something you believed in? Can the European Union take a strong stand against anything, for the sake of the rest of the world? There is much more to our world, than just the US, and Europe, is there not? They all know that the US, is, by far, the largest polluter, and also the richest country; therefore, it can afford to curb pollution, and punish all polluters, to the extent of the law. But, the heavy influence, of money, campaign donations, corruption, and close 'nepotism', type of association, between government, and big business, *makes these efforts at pollution elimination, a 'pie in the sky', dream.*

Although there have been regular, and massive, protests, at these meetings of the richest nations, those leaders met, year, after year, talked of solving poverty, and hunger, but seldom did anything, really constructive, to solve those problems. Security forces often, used extraordinary violence, against those protesting, at such venues. And young people traveled to them, from all over the world, to express their views. Governments tend to crush freedom and democracy, at these meetings, and keep protesters away. But, such behavior by those, in the west, is not unlike, what was seen previously, in China, or the Soviet Union, or even North Korea. That is not freedom and democracy; neither is it the open society, so glibly, voiced, by the US and UK. Is it the protesters who always provoke the security forces, or is it the other way around? It depends on who is giving the reports. For example, at the Scotland summit, security forces were shown clashing, with those gathered to protest, even before the meeting had started! And those in charge of the G-8 summits, in the various countries, have always referred to protesters, as anarchists, trouble, makers, or leftist, why is that? Surely, those going to so much trouble to be at these sites, had good reason to try to express their views, before these leaders?

Consider for a moment, that in the past, there were many protests in former Soviet Union countries, in China, in Africa, in other parts of Asia, or Latin America. The authorities in those countries attempted to crush the protests, fighting ensued, and some were injured, or killed. Leaders over there, as in the case, of, the US, and UK, called those, protesters, anarchists, and criminals. But, how did western officials react to those events, especially with regard to China, Russia, and a few others? *Why, they called those governments repressive, and tyrannical! Who is right? Is it the pot, calling the kettle, black, all over again?* If those other countries suppress protesters, it is oppression, and tyranny (which it well, may be); but, *when we, in the west (US and UK), suppress similar protesters,* **why, we are only enforcing the law, and removing, or arresting, anarchists, we are not tyrants!** When we do it, it is never oppression! Does anyone notice the constant spin, and propaganda, in all this- - -?

For our own sanity, and for us to be credible, we need to acknowledge our unbelievable, and sometimes bizarre, policies, around the world. The American government, and the British, often, take the lead, in criticizing, governments in other countries; and, to be sure, some of the criticism is well founded. We had mentioned Russia, China, North Korea,

Syria, Libya, Cuba, and others; seldom, Israel, Saudi Arabia, or many rogue nations, with whom these 'powers', had maintained good relations, either because they needed their oil, or they have military bases on their land, or they have substantial business deals, with them. In the cold war era they used some of these countries, to help oppose communism. Now, we are using them for what other sinister purposes?

In these pages, we have referred to many reports, in the past year, or two, on prisoner abuse by US, or British, forces, and these involved some deaths, as well. Allegedly, 'impartial', investigations, were, carried out, on both sides of the Atlantic. The most serious reports were about prisons in Iraq, and Cuba, under American forces control. These reports were recently reviewed, on 'Now', Public Broadcasting Program, with David Broncaccio, with new revelations. Guest speakers mentioned that America's, FBI, had been investigating, allegations, about the abuse at Guantanamo, Cuba. They reported that prisoners had been chained, hands and feet, to the ground, in a fetal position; other, chained prisoners, were left there, for 24 hours, who had defecated on themselves; yet, others, who were also chained, with the air conditioning being turned off, so that the temperature reached 100 degrees, or higher, and they were almost unconscious! *If this was truly, an FBI report, as outlined in this program, is this, what, US officials, at the highest levels of the Bush administration, have told the world, 'was humane treatment of prisoners', by US forces- - -? Have we degenerated to such extreme, base, levels? These questions need debate, and answers.*

Civil Liberty groups have also asked important questions. If we are going to be fighting terrorism, indefinitely, will we imprison these people, we have detained, forever, without charge, without trial, and without regular access to families, or lawyers? Does anyone call that, freedom, and a democratic society? Do we think, we can keep on, deceiving, those, in the rest of the world?

AS OTHERS SEE US

Are most views of the 'west', and, particularly of the United States, from around the world, negative? No, certainly not, but a good percentage, are, indeed, negative. Foreign policies that are bizarre, flawed, and uneven handed, admittedly, had an adverse effect, on opinions of the US, coming from overseas. Worldwide, they became overwhelmingly negative, *after what was called, 'the Bush war on Iraq'; and, 'what he had done to our world'.* It should be the other way around; views from the outside, on the west, and on the US, should be overwhelmingly positive. Those reports, and photographs, of prisoner abuse, by US, and British, armed forces personnel, had also, severely blemished, our image; more so, than, government officials are willing to admit. Many reports had claimed that terrorism had increased as a result, and recruiting for insurgent groups had also increased. In fact, some claim, that there are now so many suicide, bombing, attacks, that these groups never seem to run out of volunteers, who are willing to sacrifice themselves, for the cause.

Following the recent London bombing attacks, authorities there, tried to piece together, the reasons why, locally born citizens, would give rise to, 'home grown terror groups', so to speak. They emphasized that, even if some of those young men had attended college, in UK, Muslims there, were three times more likely to be unemployed, than other Britons. Some had also attended radical schools in Pakistan., and then they decided to participate, in a jihad, in the UK. From their investigations, officials confirmed that recruits, had also increased all over the world, and they were now, more readily available, to join these conflicts. It had been shown, that, in most countries, such young, Muslim, males, were furious at what America, and Britain, had done to Iraq, a predominantly Muslim nation; that millions of their brethren had suffered so much aggression. It was concluded, that was how they came to join the insurgent groups; they had seen the old struggles of the Palestinian people, and now, they had Iraq. They felt they had their reasons.

On a PBS news program, guests commented that, if Abbas, of the Palestinian Authority, failed, because of the impasse, with the Israelis, it would, indeed, be a failure of the Palestinians, but also, of the Israeli, and US governments. And a speaker on a CNN program, responded to questions on why insurgents had continued to fight in Iraq, and in Afghanistan, bringing chaos to those regions. He implied, that there was now, so much instability, that these situations could still be confronting the next, several, United States presidents! And therefore, the US needed to address the reasons, why these people fight; not to simply go after them, because they are fighting! That was an ominous forecast, but it is precisely what experts, here, and abroad, had been stating, all along.

As one would expect, Bush, and Blair, *had rejected any connection between, their actions in Iraq, and the increase, in terrorism.* There was nothing else they could say, when you look at the facts on the ground, in Iraq, in Afghanistan, and elsewhere. According to a London Sunday Times report, Chatham House, a research organization, had concluded, that Britain's involvement in Iraq, and Afghanistan, had enhanced propaganda value, recruitment, and funding, for Al Qaeda; and also, made Britain, a likely target. They added, that Britain's *efforts to combat terror had been hampered, by its closeness to America's policies!* How many opinions do people need to hear, they have been coming at us, from all over the world, and from various experts, and other personalities. As if to lend credence to such reports, Bush's own performance approval ratings, in July 2005, had dropped to 44%, the lowest ever; and they would go even lower. Reporters from UK also wrote, that, during a visit by president Jimmy Carter, he had admitted to them, that the prisoners who were detained at the US facility, at Guantanamo, Cuba, was a disgraceful situation; and that the Iraq war, was unnecessary, and unjust. Following on all the above, new polls were released in the US, in October 2005, when people were asked if new elections were held now, how they would vote; *only 39% said that, they would still vote for Bush; is that, not amazing?*

There were other, recent, reports, on officials from North Korea, and the United States, calling each other, names, that were not considered, too complimentary, as mentioned elsewhere. But, at least, the so-called six party talks had resumed, even with the usual political chicanery. In the National Catholic periodical, author Sister Joan Chittister, highlighted the good news, that the South and North Koreans were talking to each other, rather than maintaining old, cold war, hatreds, that were long gone; *and they were often, fabricated, to begin with.* When we hear such reports we must again wonder, if these are more examples of our disastrous foreign policy, as it has a long history of missteps, has it not? Those talks are aimed at getting North Korea to dismantle its nuclear program; and it was reported that the North Koreans demanded that the US remove its own nuclear weapons from South Korea- - -!

In a previous book, "Mirror Reflections=Mirages", we had outlined the extent of corporate corruption, in western countries, especially in the US, as many scandals had become exposed, in our media, in the last few years. Most had believed that those at the top are seldom held accountable. However, since then, to the credit of the justice department, there have been successful prosecutions, of senior corporate officials, with some sentences being handed down. Yes, it had taken several years of foot dragging, but perhaps, certain corrective actions have been taken, finally; we shall see. Some of these American corporations had global reach; and others were, more, or less, international in scope. For a while, there was an outcry, that, those officials should be held accountable, for the huge losses of their employees, their clients, and investors. For our own people, and for those in the rest of the world, it is important to see that justice is served, in the corporate world, as well.

An Internet report focused on US officials criticizing Public broadcasting system programs. Writer D. Ulmann stated, "these folks do not realize how limited our access to news is, in the mainstream media, in the US today. Even CNN, has different coverage in Europe, *there, they include world news*". Similar thoughts had come from others, overseas. She quoted from a speech by Bill Moyers, "- - -even covering stories, that made princes, and priests, uncomfortable". That was referring to genuine freedom of the press, in a healthy democracy. She congratulated David Broncaccio for filling in, so well, those giant shoes of Bill Moyers, on the television program 'Now'. This is one of those programs that republican circles had objected to, because they dared to criticize administration elite, in Washington. Many writers had concluded that news, in America, over the past few years, could no longer be called, news; it had embraced a significant touch of republican, party, propaganda; and many blamed that, on some of the journalists themselves, but also, on the media owners, as they did most of the dictating! There were a handful of exceptions, perhaps, where big brother, did not control all of it! When you travel to other countries, it is striking, to see, totally different, news, reporting from Europe, from Canada, even from lesser, developed countries. There, apparently, they have more, truly, open forums, than we see over here, where they are organized, and controlled. In this regard, a note arrived from a friend in Europe, thus, "how does it feel to live in a police State"? It was directed at those living in America, and although it was meant to have a touch of humor in it, it had a shock effect. We could not be comfortable, because this was the image our government officials had projected, of the United States, and it has become a serious problem, for us, and for the whole world.

A report of June 2005, also reviewed how 'detainees' were handled in the US. It could be done with the secret agency, FBI, and then by armed forces personnel; or, as has been reported, in a completely different manner, by sending them to facilities in other countries, usually, third world countries. As mentioned previously, reporters have shown that all types of 'interrogation' techniques had been used, on these persons, until they were forced to break down, one way, or another. Although some of these 'detainees' may have been well trained, after considerable pressure by US forces, or by others, they eventually break down. Therefore it came as no surprise that most human rights groups, had continued to call, all of this, inhumane, and illegal, and some called it 'torture' of prisoners, at the hands of US officials. The United Nations had joined in, and asked that the American Guantanamo prisons in Cuba, be opened, for free, and impartial inspections, by UN, and other international representatives. The UN, itself, had also received reports of systematic, inhumane treatment, and even torture in those prisons. This was yet another reflection by the international community, on US policies, and behavior patterns.

A statement, on CBS, television program, '60Minutes', stood out. That the United States had become a chain store for guns, for the whole world. That was not a complimentary picture at all, because our officials talk, or pretend to talk, about controlling weapons; but it has been alleged that we give, or sell, weapons, to many countries, above, or under, the table! If the government does it, one would then assume, that many, in the weapons industry, did it as well. Scandals in Washington, dealing with military and defense spending, were recently written about. Critics pointed out, how there were always, many pork barrel, spending projects, buried inside such defense bills; for example, to eliminate a type of snake in Hawaii (in a defense bill?); to renovate a special center, at a military base, that had been shut down many years ago; and many more, unbelievable, gimmicks.

Question: in whose pockets does all that money go? Reporters stated, that once such a bill had been approved by congress (*with all the pork, and fat, in it*), those, other items, that had been added, as extras, to the bills, cannot, be removed. And such bills are often voted on, without members of congress having the time to study them adequately! Thus, officials responsible for military budgets, compensate for such 'pork' allotments, by cutting back similar amounts of money, from other important items for the military. Is that how our system of 'democracy' should work? Others, looking in, from the outside, must wonder why 'we the people', do not have more power in governing, for example, as we had read, about Switzerland. Should the media not try to uncover who benefits from such pork item dollars, especially as this had been going on for decades? Why has it been allowed to continue, without the laws being changed a long time ago? Is it because the almighty, power, and money, dictate everything that goes on, in Washington? As both major parties participate in such mismanagement, has it always been a question of the haves, and the have not?

The voices of critics of Bush administration, policies, had grown louder, both in the US, and overseas. Bush had nominated Bolton to be US ambassador to the United Nations. Readers must recall how nepotism works in the US (as in many countries), at all levels of government; if you scratch my back, I will scratch yours. No, these shady affairs are not seen only in third world countries! This was another rocky road for this administration. Republicans, in parrot like fashion, wanted him approved quickly in the senate; democrats objected, and stalled, as it was alleged that there were skeletons in that man's closet. He had made disturbing statements in the past, and his attitude towards subordinates left a lot to be desired. It was then claimed that Bush would try ramrod, his nominee, in, by executive powers, during senate recess! That is how the people's business is served in Washington; and that was precisely what president Bush did. Critics said that Bush was sending an ambassador to the international body, *who had not received senate approval, and he was supposed to represent the interests of all Americans.* And they added that Bolton was going there, as 'damaged goods'. Many also criticized that Bush, and republicans, had never held the UN in high regard, in any case. What image does all the above portray, for all those looking at America, from overseas?

Jason R. Rowe wrote in 'America' magazine on, "Some forgotten lessons", where he zeroed in, on similarities in US actions in Iraq, and El Salvador. In El Salvador, Archbishop Oscar Romero had been murdered. And a UN sponsored commission concluded that, it had been, orchestrated by officers within El Salvador's, US funded, military government. The Archbishop had defended the rights of the poor, and he ran afoul of the regime, there, by publicly denouncing its perpetuation of injustices, and repression of human rights. Before his death, the Archbishop had written to then president Carter, asking him to cut off military aid to the El Salvador government, because it was being used to repress the people. But, the author went on, that aid had continued at a rate of one million dollars a day. Romero was described as perhaps, the most prominent of the Catholic martyrs who had arisen in Latin America, in the 1980's.

As did many other commentators, in "Mirror Reflections=Mirages", we deplored the policies of American governments whereby, when aid was given to Latin American countries, *it often went to, very oppressive, tyrannical, officials; seldom, did any of it reach down, to the poor.* Thus, no matter who was in charge, in Washington, these policies were continued for many years, supporting evil, with the false presumption that, some good would come out of it. Well, we know exactly what happened, from history; and now, we are repeating our blunders in Iraq, and elsewhere. The above article also specified, that those martyrs in Latin America, had exposed *"the dark side of these US policies"*; as the US government gave its support to the oppressors of the poor, backing dirty wars, coups, and human rights abuses, *by some of the world's most repressive regimes.* Is it not astounding, to hear such reports, and to witness, those half-truths, or worse, that were given by members in the Bush administration, as their pathetic reasons, to attack Iraq? All these events ran against the myth of the 'US and the cold war', the writer continued. Perhaps Americans can learn that, although, Saddam Hussein had been used as a convenient excuse, for an early 21st century debacle, with daily massacres, 'by them', and 'by us', *history suggests that, US behavior patterns have been, quite similar, with our neighbors to the south; our policies towards 'good dictators', when contrasted with those policies towards 'bad dictators'.*

Surely, people remember many reports on El Salvador, Nicaragua, Chile, Guatemala, Peru, Colombia, Panama, Grenada, Haiti, and how many others? The infamous School of the Americas had generated controversy, as it was allegedly used to train military, and security personnel, from Latin America. Our politicians, and the military, had contrived a name change, to hide behind, for that facility. It had been uncovered, that, some of those trained recruits, had returned to their countries, 'to practice' their newly gained techniques, and engaged in the oppression, and killing, of thousands, of the poor, in those countries, most often, native peasants. Even if they had been warned, perhaps repeatedly, by Americans, against such tactics, according to many human rights reports, that is exactly what they had done. Many of our own citizens have written about that particular school, and what it stood for; many others had protested, some had been roughed up, by US security, and some had also been arrested, and imprisoned.

Archbishop Romero was, by no means, an exception, but he was perhaps, the, best, known, high, profile figure. There have been numerous other reports, of nuns, priests, indigenous people, and ordinary citizens, who had been murdered. Many others disappeared, and their families never learned anything about their fate. For people looking in, from the outside, such a history would look dark indeed. Ours, is truly, a dangerous world, a disturbed world, and any super power can be dangerous, ineffective, and counter productive, if it has not mastered the art of governing, of getting along, of proper diplomacy; the art, of preserving peace, with justice, for all.

Another program on CBS '60 Minutes two', dealt with US secret service activities, and techniques, under the provisions of the so-called, Bush-Ashcroft, patriot act. This time, it involved a Canadian (is there no end to our problems?), who was picked up by US secret service agents in New York city, and detained. As these characters usually do, they never informed his wife, or allowed him due process. He was "accused" by American officials, of having Al Qaeda connections, and of visiting one of their camps; but he denied all their allegations. Here, our citizens need to remember, that under the US justice system some prisoners had spent several years, on death row, sentenced by the courts, and were later executed by authorities; but on further investigations, those prisoners had been found innocent of the crimes they had been charged with, *after they had already been killed by the State!* This Canadian man's wife contacted her Canadian embassy, and they were able to track him down; and they assured her that they planned to get the Americans to release him to Canadian authorities.

However, tyrannical methods used by secret agencies, are not found only in police states, because, even in some western countries, certain corrupt techniques are beyond anyone's imagination. But that is not expected in western society. This man had been taken at night, and flown to Syria, as 'a suspected terrorist'! The Canadian man, told the Americans, that he would be tortured, according to reports; but that, too, fell on deaf ears. US officials may conveniently announce, that they warned Syrians not to employ any torture techniques, but to intelligent people, that would be seen as nothing but, political garbage. It would also uncover US authorities, that, they were well aware, that, torture was being used, in certain countries. Presumably, that is why they send detainees to these places, many would ask? The man was interviewed on the '60 Minutes' program, and he told them *that he was indeed tortured in Syria.* When the Syrian ambassador was confronted with this information, he naturally denied that this man had been tortured. *What else would this politician say, before world cameras!* The commentator asked the ambassador if that was not the only reason US officials had sent him to Syria, instead of returning him to his country, Canada! The ambassador was trying to be evasive, but replied that they had investigated fully, and informed the Americans, that they found the man to be innocent; that he had no connection to Al Qaeda, or to terrorism.

For our readers, this would be another example, a sad one, of how others see us! Some US officials often lambaste the machinations of 'the Axis of Evil', when they refer to Syria, Iran, and others, in those epithets. *But when they need those countries for their sinister purposes (Iran contra affairs?), according to critics, US officials knew very well, how to do business, even with Satan, himself!* Meanwhile months had passed, and fortunately for this poor man, people in Canada began to protest, and it reached the chambers of Parliament over there. The Canadians demanded an explanation from the Bush government, for behaving in this manner, instead of returning the man to Canada as had been requested, originally. He was a Canadian citizen! Readers might recall that this US administration had been accused, in many parts of the world, of unusual arrogance, of going it alone; hence the trouble it had generated everywhere.

All this finally received the attention of US officials, and this man, Arar, was just as suddenly released, and returned to Canada. It is another example, of many, of a superpower with little knowledge of what proper behavior really is like, on the world stage; and has been accused of being a bully, of the frequent use of threatening language against other governments. Syrian authorities had obviously tried to curry favor with the Bush administration, and they would bend over, backwards, to do what was asked of them. They could have refused, and told the Americans to return the man to his country, Canada. This is the corruption whereby superpowers, out of control, keep other countries, under their boots, to do their bidding. One would, also, not be surprised, if Syria took advantage of 'torture' techniques, whether that topic was brought up, or not; they wanted to 'cooperate' with the Americans! The entire disgusting affair can only be laid right at the doorstep of the US administration, nothing more! By the time this so called 'prisoner' returned to Canada, it was said that, he had lost over a year, of his life; and he continued to insist that he was tortured, and suffered physically, and psychologically, because of those despicable acts, by US officials.

In this book we have referred to reports on, *unmarked, fleets, of US, secret service, aircraft, that were used to surreptitiously, fly such 'suspects', to third world countries; and critics have maintained that the sole purpose for that, was, the rough methods of interrogation used, which could include torture!* And such reports, had alleged that, US government officials had done this, to hundreds of 'suspects, but there is no way, one can confirm the exact figures, because of intense secrecy within the US government itself. Readers might ask, why does congress, and, the courts, not, put a stop to it, and force the administration to release all documents, so that real justice could be served? One major reason is, that, in America, there is no longer a truly free press, or decent journalism; and US officials are allowed to hide behind the words, 'classified', and 'national security'; and they do that, at every opportunity they get! Those were precisely, the deceptions that had been used in the case of Arar; officials would not release full details, because the case was, 'classified'! American officials often accuse our perceived 'enemies', of using human shields, to hide behind, when we are doing the same, or much worse; we hide our many grievous sins, behind fanciful facades, yes, human shields, as well!

To the credit of this Canadian, and the citizens who supported him, news reports suggested that he had found credible, and well placed, attorneys, who recognized gross injustice, and abuse of power. They were suing American officials, including Ashcroft! There were many, who had hoped, that, justice would be served in such situations; and in the long run, such justice, might help the health of this nation, and unite our fractured society. As in the case of the prisoner abuse scandals, the world has witnessed once more, how low level personnel are often made scapegoats, whilst top officials are seldom tainted. In corrupt societies, such officials are often moved around, and promoted! Our 'military-industrial' complex had, unfortunately, been accused of many such incidents, of promotions.

When such, scandals, are uncovered, by media, even in the US, officials usually respond that 'they were unaware', that torture was used in such, and such, a country; but most critics would not likely believe them. Many had also criticized US authorities for going to such extremes, when they should have interrogated such 'suspects', in the American justice system. It might be flawed, but it is still a much better system, than that, in most third world countries. In some 'dictator' states, there is nothing, in place, that could be called a justice system. Readers can readily judge how murky these political manoeuvres had become, with lies, and deceits, at all levels of government everywhere. Therefore, we should not be surprised that our own justice system had uncovered all sorts of corruption, in corporate America, as well. Corruption and dishonesty, seem to be pervasive; *as one justice official had put it, 'it is not a single rotten apple, it appears that the whole crate is rotten'!* Right!

And then, as if the many missteps of mankind were not bad enough, Mother Nature, also came, to reveal its wrath! During the final days of August 2005, hurricane Katrina struck with might and fury, as it crossed over the southern portion of Florida in the US, inflicting significant damage there. On their journey from the African coastal areas, these hurricanes hit various islands in the Caribbean, and sometimes other parts of the Americas. Florida was a state that in 2004 was pummeled by 5 major hurricanes, resulting in severe destruction in much of the state; hundreds of people had not yet recovered from that. But Katrina was not done, this time either; as it entered the Gulf of Mexico, gathered strength, and pursued a north, westerly, course. After a couple of days over warmer waters, it reached a category 5 hurricane, one of the strongest on record. And as a category 5, and soon after it reached land, a category 4, it struck a devastating blow at the states of Louisiana, Alabama, and Mississippi, in the United States. The old city of New Orleans was hit hard, and the levees protecting that city were breached. Water poured out, adding to the huge storm surge that hit those areas; so that most of the city was inundated with 8 to 20 feet of water, destroying buildings and other structures, cars, utilities, anything in its path. Air photography revealed city streets with water up to the rooftops of buildings, cars overturned or completely submerged.

Adding to the disaster was an announcement that the water was very dangerous, a sludge mixture of water, with oil, chemicals, and sewage, pouring in from damaged structures. It was anticipated that for many of the local people, especially in the poorer neighborhoods, it would be a total loss of their homes, and all their possessions; but the disaster struck wealthier neighborhoods as well. There were also gas leaks with sporadic fires, here and there, making aerial videos most eerie looking- - -vast stretches as far as the eye could see, were under water, with scattered plumes of smoke from those fires. Reporters said that as much as 80% of the city of New Orleans was under water! As often happens in disasters, including the US, the ugly side of man surfaced, and there was much looting, and other criminal activities, to further hamper rescue operations. But there were also many people who helped others in distress, with volunteers coming from all over. Then there were disturbing reports, that in such catastrophes, individuals and their families, are initially completely on their own, and could not expect much help from their government. This was another clear demonstration of the haves, and the have not; many who were well off, had left to stay with family, or friends, or in hotels. *Those without means watched the devastation, and as the water level rose, they ended up in their attics, or on rooftops hoping to be rescued in time!* Some of the media kept on reporting on the destruction of Casinos; but those represented luxury, it was not what the suffering masses needed to hear. They also showed some people in front of the cameras, sobbing for long periods, as they described their losses, and their plight. That is not right, such reporting should be kept very brief, the main purpose being, to solicit others, to offer help. The rest of the story could be told with the people off camera.

Beyond any doubt this was a colossal disaster, much like the Asian Tsunami, not that long ago. Damage had been extensive in at least three states where the hurricane had made landfall; but as the storm advanced northeast, it spawned tornadoes, causing additional destruction in other states further north. If any country could cope with disasters, the United States should be able to do so; but it had already been predicted that this would be a major challenge even for this country, for the affected areas- - -no electricity, no drinking water, gas leaks, rising water everywhere, damaged sanitation facilities, garbage and debris making roads impassable, some roads were heavily damaged, and tens of thousands of people were left homeless, and without jobs to go to. The American government can muster technology, equipment, and manpower, and it has the financial resources (although it is burdened by massive debts at this time). But in spite of all this, large numbers of ordinary folk suffer the most, as they do not always get the desperate help they need. When disasters strike, leaders promptly announce that government assistance is on the way! In the US they talk a great deal (all political talk) about the Federal Emergency Management Administration (FEMA), and the National Guard (Armed forces units). But in such disasters words are easy to come by; complete help, and relief, that, is a different story. Several days after the catastrophe had struck, in New Orleans, reporters said that they talked with many people on highways, or other areas, *and those people complained that they had not seen anyone from a government agency; nobody had come to tell them where to go, or how they could get help, they had no home! Nobody had given them water or food!*

During the 2004 hurricanes, there were the same announcements about the help that was being provided by the government. They do provide some help, but many people today, one year after those tragedies, in 2004, still complain that they have no home to go to, and they continue to struggle to put their life back together again. That is not good enough. It is not a good reflection on our government, surely. *Will it be the same for the victims of Katrina, and soon after, came Rita?* A commentator stated that this disaster was so overwhelming, that no amount of planning could have prepared government agencies for what had happened. Thus, politicians may be quick to appear before cameras, as they should; but then people are left to suffer for months, or, perhaps, years. Some never recover! Here are more reasons why, when the public is asked to rate the various professions, for competence, integrity, and so on; year, after year, politicians are invariably, at the bottom of the barrel.

As conditions continued to deteriorate around New Orleans, there were reports of anarchy setting in; it was called a total breakdown of systems, after the second or third day of the disaster. There were many reports that authorities were unable to cope, that people were trapped in buildings by the thousands, surrounded by rising waters, many of them elderly. Through so much suffering, there were the customary political spins, with politicians before cameras, and announcements that president Bush would terminate 'his vacation', two days ahead of schedule! Imagine, through such a massive disaster, the president was still on vacation. His advisors had goofed off, rather badly, on that one! Arrangements were being made for him to tour the area by helicopter. In most instances all this does nothing, to alleviate any of the misery, of thousands of people, to provide much needed relief. Instead, politicians need to stay out of the way, but make certain that there is plenty of help, in the form of cash, and materiel; personnel, armed forces staff, all the necessities and equipment that would be needed; *and this should be made available immediately, not 2, 3, or 4, days later!* That is how politicians can be most helpful in such situations, and, above all, *make certain that the people they have in charge, and advising them, are well qualified, not just, political cronies!* We, all, see, too much of that.

What is even more sobering is this: if countries like the US, and other rich, western, countries, also, face great difficulties, and suffering, when disasters strike, can anyone imagine what goes on in third world countries, and dictator states, under similar circumstances? There, hundreds of thousands, perhaps millions, are usually devastated, and thousands lose their lives, as in the case of that Tsunami. There is a president in America, and other politicians, most often republican, who, together with some business leaders, and other leaders in third world countries, have totally ignored the repeated warnings by scientists, and other experts, on the destruction of the environment. These had demonstrated, that there have been major climate changes on our planet, and we must rein in polluters everywhere. To all this, it had been alleged, that, president Bush stated that, we needed more studies on climate change, to determine the causes; and thus, all those leaders continued to downplay those warnings. Since Katrina, there have been other disasters with loss of life. There were serious floods and mud slides in Guatemala, with villages being buried, and total destruction, in those areas. Then came the October earthquakes in the Pakistan-Kashmir regions, with awesome devastation, where estimates were, that, over 50,000 had lost their lives, and millions were left homeless, in the mountains, facing harsh weather conditions.

As the world outside, looked in, at America's response, to natural disasters, news reports showed the reactions of the people affected, to the actions, or lack thereof, by their government. And through all this, there was another mess, building up, on the domestic, front, *the White House leak investigations!* They had dragged on for some two years, and were placed before a grand jury, where two reporters were ordered to divulge the name, or names, of persons, from the Bush administration, who had exposed the name of Valerie Plame (Mrs. Wilson), as an undercover agent. On the basis of promised confidentiality to their sources, the two reporters initially refused to give out those names. That was quite honorable, some thought, in the face of a judge's threat of a jail sentence; and when they were surrounded by so much corruption in Washington, anyway. Perhaps, more politicians should follow, by example, to protect the truth. Indeed, in July 2005, a female reporter was sent to jail, because she claimed to want to protect her right to privacy, and a promise to her clients. The other reporter, a man, was freed by his source, from the promise of confidentiality, and was thus able to testify before the grand jury. What could happen, next? It was alleged that a suspect of leaking information, was Rove, the right hand man of Bush, at the White House; but another top administration official mentioned, in this scandal, was Libby, the right hand man of Cheney. *There, it was, two top politicians attached to the president, and vice president, of the United States, suspected of possibly leaking information illegally! And possibly there were others?* The next pathetic, legal, mumbo jumbo, was quickly put in place, by the republican side, it never fails. This included the fact that the agent might not have been mentioned by name, specifically, *but only as Wilson's wife, and that the high official at the White house, did not know for certain, that she was a secret agent!* Come, now, give us a break! Do we have to keep reminding our officials, that Americans are much smarter than they think?

Readers know by now that the whole murky affair started when ambassador Wilson was reporting, *that, some of the reasons being presented, by the Bush administration, for the attacks against Iraq, were simply not correct!* That is, the reference to weapons of mass destruction, and that Hussein was trying to obtain nuclear material from Niger, in Africa! In his official capacity, Wilson had investigated this, and found it to be untrue; and he gave the true facts, as he found them! Reporters had suggested that people in the Bush circle did not like that report, because, as we know from the London leaked memos, *Bush had apparently already decided to go to war, long before! The pieces of the puzzle appeared to be fitting together!* That is how the smear campaign against Wilson had started according to critics, and that led to leaks on his wife. And now, we know, that all these fabrications, and lies, had also led to the imprisonment of a reporter, for what? Was she truly doing her job? Two years had been expended, using large amounts of tax dollars, in an alleged, sophisticated cover up, within the US government! Have the American people lost confidence in Washington, as we are reminded so often? It would not be at all surprising, because of the perceived dishonesty, as seen in these stories, and rumors, over the past several years. Have they lost faith, that, things will ever change for the better?

Reports on MSNBC television station suggested that since the name of Rove came out, there would be many calls for his resignation, or he should be dismissed. That, even, if he was absolved, of committing a serious crime, he did not deserve to have security clearance. Americans recall the Bush administration announcing that there would *be full and prompt cooperation with the investigation.* And many critics said that as Bush's right hand man was implicated, and Cheney's right hand man, then White house staff would continue to try to deflect any serious consequences, away from the president. As usual, Bush's press spokesman started refusing to answer direct questions, as did the president, because 'there was an ongoing investigation', and we must not pre-judge! Before that, they had let it be known, that the culprits would be dismissed. The swamp in this republican administration, had become much more ominous! Does all this, reflect on justice, American style? And are the US, and UK, now, teaching justice to developing nations of our planet? What, on earth are we doing? Do we know? These reports also alleged that the republican national committee had been trying to discredit Wilson himself! Those are more examples of dirty politics, at their worst. *If most of this turns out to be true, one can assume that Washington pundits no longer want to hear the truth, to hear honest answers, is that it?*

In October 2005, another amazing revelation, dealt with Judith Miller, the N.Y. Times correspondent, who had been jailed, for a few months, for refusing to name the sources of her information. But, lo, and behold, after serving time, to protect the confidentiality of her sources, reporters alleged, she informed the independent investigator, and the grand jury, that she had been given permission, by her sources, to answer questions. *It was also alleged that she stated, she could not remember who had given her the name of the US undercover agent! Is that amazing, or what?* Many journalists were quick to question the credibility of Miller, at this juncture, and the airwaves were full of comments, thus: had she been too cozy with Bush administration officials; had she been too eager to tout their line, on Iraq, all along, and on weapons of mass destruction?

This, again, focused on the ugliness of US politics, and some of our politicians, before the whole world. In another section of this book we commented on lifestyles, and extreme corruption, amongst the elite in third world countries, notably, in parts of Africa, and other regions. But, are we really, much better in our behavior? Citizens everywhere know only too well, that many leaders waste enormous resources, of the people's treasury, with their plotting, and alleged illegal activities. A news 'blip', in the Guardian paper, on the Internet, by Mark Tran, referred to Bush's right hand man, Rove, that the noose was tightening around him, in that investigation. He was said to have cancelled an appearance, in support of a gubernatorial; candidate, 'because of a scheduling conflict'! It was then alleged that it looked quite bad, for the Bush administration.

On October 28, the independent prosecutor, Fitzgerald, gave his findings after 2 years. He announced that the grand jury had handed down five indictments on Libby (Cheney's right hand man), *which included charges of perjury, and obstruction of justice.* That same evening, most guest speakers on Larry King Live, on CNN, except for a republican congressman, agreed, that it was most serious for the Bush administration. Libby announced his resignation, which was accepted by the president! The independent prosecutor indicated that the investigations had not been concluded, *and should proceed, because the charges were extremely serious!* The questions that critics kept asking, centered on whether there was any proof, that the leaking of the name, was an act of deliberate malice. And the fact, that, it could have a bearing on the false statements made, to take the country to war! Most speakers indicated that Rove, the right hand man of Bush, although not charged, remained under a cloud of an ongoing investigation.

Many writers have long pointed out that the goings on, in this Bush administration, were much more serious, and grave, than what president Clinton had been accused of. Americans need to consider what the republicans in congress, attempted to do, to the

Clinton family. They connived news leaks, prolonged investigations, pushed for impeachment proceedings, and kept digging up personal data, that had absolutely nothing to do, with managing the affairs of the people, responsibly. Now, compare all that, with the republican travesty, of trying to sweep under the rug, the numerous, alleged, scandals, in the news, on the present republican administration, in Washington. *Ask yourselves, is there justice today, in America?*

Most speakers on that Larry King program agreed, that Bush was now, significantly weakened, as a president; and he needed to show all Americans whether he was going to change, and how! Then, an important question was posed; does this president Bush have the personality, the capacity, to make the right changes for the people, and for the country? On the CBS '60 Minutes', television program, guests *with personal experience as undercover agents*, were all highly critical of this White house, for the serious damage they had inflicted, by leaking Mrs. Wilson's name. Mr. Wilson, on that same program, added, that he believed the White house had decided to go after him, by targeting his wife. She had protected her cover well, for 18 years, and was 'shocked when she first saw the newspaper article by columnist Novak'. It has now been alleged that she has already been threatened, as well. Other agents declared, they had been undermined, by, their own officials, and 'it was galling'! "She had been put in a very uncomfortable spot, her career was ended"! All agreed that Bush had a very bad week, 'bad several months', actually. There had been no White house official indicted over the tenure of numerous presidents, and it was inflicted on this one! And they admitted that there had always been a certain degree of defiance, in this particular White house. Not a good omen!

There was another shocking revelation described by Sister Joan Chittister; this involved a spokeswoman of the US administration who had tried to speak to women in Turkey, and Saudi Arabia, extolling the advantages of good relationships with the United States, and its democracy and lifestyle. *It came as no surprise (except for this administration!), that those women had no favorable reaction, no applause; and their reply was 'they did not need America to make their lives complete'!* What an eye opener, that was! They revealed more intelligence than the official, who tried to talk to them in that manner. Chittister met with a group of international religious leaders; "the Indian said that it was the US capitalism that was destroying India". The Korean added that "those who are the biggest criminals, are known to be great civilizers; they condemn terrorists, but Bush and Blair, who had killed thousands, are enshrined". Chittister added that what mattered most, was, that this, regrettably, was the perception, of many in our world, of the United States government. *"The whole world, really, does not want to be American"!* Most significantly, Chittister, concluded with the reaction of an imam from Sudan, when he suggested with sadness in his voice, that the US had missed an opportunity after 9/11. They could have decided, he said, not to react, by perpetrating more destruction, by the US itself. He further added that US authorities could have tried to learn the reasons, for what happened on 9/11, so it will not happen again, anywhere! And Chittister felt that the expressions, by members of that religious gathering, were sobering, and thought provoking.

Americans had supported president Bush on a war that has been called unjust, immoral, and illegal, and they did so by a significant majority according to polls; but now that majority has eroded dramatically. Some of us, and a vast majority of world citizens, did not support this war, with the excuses that were presented to the people of the world. Many innocent people have been killed, besides our own soldiers, passing a milestone in October 2005, as over 2000, of our men and women, had been killed. How many more are yet to come, before our politicians regain their autonomy? It has been stated that Americans need to take back the reigns of their government, to protect their fragile democracy, to get it back on the right track. Moreover we, all, have an urgent task, to protect planet earth, from the assaults we have heaped upon it.

In addition, we had a United Kingdom, ministry of defense report, in the Sunday Times, on the Internet. This revealed the serious concern in Britain, over the post war chaos in Iraq, as the violence there, continued to escalate. They avoided blaming Bush for the crisis, only because UK has been 'an ally' in this war. Most leaders in the world had, indeed, blamed both Bush, and Blair, for everything that has gone wrong. *Apparently, the British have been lamenting the fact that, in post war Iraq, Britain was forced to play the part of an occupying power,* and most Iraqis hated the presence of occupation forces in their country! Neither did the British relish the idea of continuing to play second fiddle to America, so to speak, 'the junior partner'! If pundits in the Blair regime are having second thoughts about this colossal misadventure, it is much too late, after the carnage. Shame on them!

As further proof that the Iraq war had caused more violence, than the help provided, as claimed by the US administration, we had the London bomb attacks, resulting in many killed, or injured, there, as well. Violence escalated in Afghanistan, and there were recent bombings at a seaside resort, in Egypt, where many Egyptians and tourists were killed. In August, several British tourists were still being listed as missing, as the search for victims had continued. Additional bombings have occurred in Bali. And, lest we forget, the violence, and instability, in the Israeli-Palestinian conflict, has not gone away! That saga of Israel, and Palestine, continues, as of this writing. The hand of some countries in the west, particularly the US, has been all over the face of that saga, *the good, and the bad.*

As readers might raise questions, about some of these views 'from outside', some direct quotes will follow. On a recent visit to Europe we reunited with some friends from Belgium, and Switzerland, and a few from Britain, and other areas. By and large, they detested what the Bush administration had forced on the world. The Belgian, and Swiss, couples, were familiar with this author's previous book, and seemed to agree with topics discussed therein. They wondered if criticism of the Bush, and Blair governments, and the war in Iraq, could cause trouble, for authors of such compositions, in America? The Swiss couple indicated that most around the world seemed to hold similar sentiments about the US, perhaps, much worse. They added, that, although they had been to the US several times, not many would be eager to visit the US, at this time, unless there were major changes in the attitudes of US officials.

A friend of theirs had a relative visit the United States. This individual was promptly arrested, at the port of entry, and jailed without warning. There were no charges, and access to lawyers was denied. After some time, without explanation, the individual was released, and sent back to the country of origin. To the end, no reasons were given, and the entire family was terrified by such treatment, at the hands of Americans. Thus, our Swiss friends reiterated that such behavior was unacceptable, and could not sit well, with the rest of the free world. This writer, has found it difficult to respond to such comments, there have been too many. I advised them that, surely, this would be a good test for freedom of speech, democracy, and basic human rights, in the US. They knew of the hundreds who were imprisoned by our justice department, without charges being filed, without due process, and who had found no democracy, or rights, in this country. Many, in our own government, had criticized these practices, and most Americans were in disagreement, with them, as well.

An interesting conversation was overheard in Europe, between two Americans, we can call them Jones, and Smith. Smith had completed a tour of duty in Iraq/Kuwait theatre of war- - -

Smith told Jones that the situation, in Iraq, was not at all what he had expected, from official government reports; and not what they were telling people, back home! He said there were many, very young marines sent there, in harm's way. And there were, too many American contractors, in Iraq, they were everywhere. Everybody was siphoning off, taxpayer money, as much as they could, and as fast as possible.

Jones said, is that so?

Smith: yes, these contractors can easily make $100,000 per head, per year, or more; and their accommodation, and transportation, and other perks, are usually paid for, by Uncle Sam! Most of that income is free of federal taxes, all, courtesy of US taxpayers.

Jones: is that so? What about the locals, the Iraqis? How do they feel?

Smith: oh, the Iraqis do not want us there, at all.

Jones; you mean, they want us out of Iraq?

Smith: absolutely, the Iraqis do not want us there. They are suspicious of, and dislike, Americans. They want us to leave Iraq as soon as possible. Other places in the Middle East may be different, only because we have had large military bases there, for some years.

These two men then discussed how, for some in the US military, the stop loss orders of the defense department, might not be applied across the board. Young soldiers had complained, and some, had, indeed, sued the government, over those stop loss orders, being used by military officials.

Readers will conclude that these comments by someone with military experience in Iraq, on the ground, are astounding, and most disturbing!

In October, news reports televised videos by an Australian journalist, shot in Afghanistan, showing US soldiers burning bodies of Taliban fighters who had been killed. It was alleged they did that, to taunt Taliban, and other extremist Muslims, and to force Taliban fighters to come out of hiding. By now, we are all familiar with capitalistic mumbo jumbo, in scandal situations, 'we will investigate'. Critics announced that it was yet, another, violation of the Geneva Convention, and it is bound to incite more anger, all over the world. In other words, honest people could not expect much from the US government, right? They would resort to damage control worldwide, *it seems they have had plenty of practice at damage control, in the past few years!* How would the Afghan government react? Most people have known that the puppet government, there, had been completely impotent, in dealing with the Americans. Many have called that, imperialism!

These reports, and those on the White house leak, induced correspondents to state that, this was the biggest mess, in our government, in 20 years, and this all happened with a republican controlled government in the US. They sensed that it had reached serious levels, for all of them. Americans well remember (or do they?), there were scandals in the Nixon administration, that had destroyed that presidency; scandals during the Reagan administration; scandals in the Clinton administration; and now, numerous scandals in this Bush administration, considered by most, more serious than any of the others, when taken together. With all this, another writer lamented (as we had many comments on Iran from US officials), that it was impossible to see, how present 'westernized', 'alcohol drenched', youth, in Iran, were any better than, the austere youth of post-revolution Iran. Once again, this was a reflection on the west, on our lifestyle, as if we needed more reminders!

On the questions of scandals in the US government, a writer to Time, magazine, was highly critical of the fanatical, political, right wing, in America, as they tried to legitimize everything they did; even if there was criminal involvement, such as during the Nixon, Watergate, disgrace. No doubt, such writers see many parallels, between recent scandals coming out of Washington, and those from the Nixon era. Another writer commented, how extremist ideologies were a leisure pastime pursuit, and those who were busy earning a living, did not have time, for such radicalism! Importantly, that writer emphasized, that, in the battle of ideas, with extremists, bullets do not win. And, as if we were not facing enough serious problems, Newsweek, carried a frightening headline, that the whole world was confronting Global warming, *except Washington- - -!*

There was another, CBS '60 Minutes Two', special report, on Afghanistan. Guest speakers discussed heroin production in that country, how it had grown to become the largest undertaking, of any country, greater even, than that of Colombia, a well-known drug trafficking country. They accused, that there was now, rampant corruption in government; and some local governors, and police members, were, themselves, actively involved in the drug industry. This is a terrible analysis of the status of Afghanistan, after 3 years of US domination! The US *has had major dictatorial powers over the Afghan government, according to critics.* But all we hear from C. Rice, and other US officials, is, how much progress has been achieved everywhere! *The above reports reject such statements, coming from our government, because unrest had actually increased, over there, and more US soldiers were being killed.* Then, there was the burning of those bodies of Taliban fighters. Surely, the above reports, say it all!

Over a period of months, we heard news reports, about, the US military failing to meet their quota of recruits, as required. Bad news from Iraq and Afghanistan, helped many young people decide they did not want to be in the military, even with all the financial incentives, often dangled before these youth. Other discussions referred to rural America, how in some small towns, entire families had strong military traditions, where seemingly, in several generations, young men and women, picked the military as a career of choice. But then, it was also emphasized that, in some of these towns, job opportunities were low, and farming had declined. *Therefore, young men and women stated, that, if they wanted to aim for college education, to enable them to seek job opportunities elsewhere, a start in the military was a necessity, for them. Many were well aware, that, in time of war, they might never come back- - -!* Furthermore, other critics alleged, that, some of the officials responsible for recruiting, *could have been responsible, for pressuring some of them into signing up, when these youth (often minorities), did not fully understand the implications of what they were signing, now that, America was at war!* Hearing such comments, certainly reflected, once again, on the state of our democracy---! And to those on the outside, it leaves a bad impression; such difficulties with recruiting, have been heard in news releases in UK, as well, where similar deficiencies had been encountered.

Certainly, we are bombarded with reports on many crises, but we cannot place all these, at the doorstep of the Bush administration. True, their policies had created much rancor, but some of the problems, and the animosity, go back to the early days of the Israeli-Palestinian upheavals, as many thinkers had maintained, for some time. The Muslim world was angered. A writer to the Florida Times Union, described how 'Palestinians were driven from land'. This was affirming what had been done to these people, by the US, UK, by some in the UN, and by Israel. Israel's arguments had been that, the land had been promised to them by God. Palestinians responded by claiming residence on that land for over 2000 years. The article referred to terrorism, which had been adopted by the Jews, in the early days of the struggle (the Stern gang, Irgun, Hadassah, and more); innocent people, were, murdered, by those groups, as well. The report referred to brutal actions by Ariel Sharon, Benjamin Netanyahu, and Avraham Stern, but there was no documentation of what type of brutal actions, they were writing about. That writer also condemned the suicide bombings by Palestinians, no matter how tragic their plight, and this echoed opinions by many experts, all over. No matter how grievous the reasons, were. They mentioned that 59% of Europeans believed that Israel was the biggest threat to peace in the Middle East, but there were many who disagreed with such assumptions. They also felt that the United States was alone, in its solid support for Israel, no matter what. That, once again, raised the specter of Mammon controlling every facet of US politics.

Consider for a moment how Muslims, how Arabs, how any group of people, how you, would feel, when you heard the following excerpt from one of the Encyclopedias. This referred to what happened to Palestine. *"More than 8000 square miles of Palestine now belong to Israel, and the rest to Lebanon, Jordan, and Syria"!* When we consider that, and what the US, UK, and the UN, had perpetrated, *then, perhaps, many will begin to understand the upheavals in the Middle East,* that led to anti-American, anti-Israeli, and also, anti-western, sentiments. The possibility of two independent nations, living in peace, side by side, was there from the beginning; but there were groups on each side of the divide, who were not willing to compromise, in the slightest. The existence of Palestine had been known for some 5000 years, and most of the events described in the bible, occurred in, and around, Palestine. It used to be considered sacred for Jews, Christians, and Muslims, alike. As in other parts of the world, through the ages, Palestine had a stormy history. In 1917, a Zionist movement was growing more powerful, and they persuaded the British to issue a statement of intent; that they favored the establishment of an independent Jewish nation in Palestine (Balfour Declaration), thus, essentially dividing Palestine into a Jewish and an Arab, state. The British continued to rule the country under a mandate, and thousands of Jews saw the opportunity of a lifetime, and began to resettle in formerly Palestinian territory. Conflicts between Arabs, and Jews resulted, and acts of terror by both Jews, and Arabs, were carried out. Jewish terrorist acts against both Arabs, and the British, soon escalated; and animosities intensified.

In 1947 the British government referred that crisis to the United Nations for resolution, and after deliberations, that organization declared, that, there would indeed, be, two independent states, and an international city of Jerusalem. The Jews accepted these plans, but the Arabs rejected them---that Arab move, turned the region upside, down, because the conflicts increased, terrorist acts became a daily occurrence, and many innocent people were killed, by both sides! The entire political game had become unraveled. Some condemned actions taken by the British, and the UN; but many condemned the rejection by the Arabs, as a unique opportunity that was missed.

Could these events have fanned the flames of anti-western anger, and the US, in particular, as that writer put it, because of 'its solid support for Israel'? It has been asserted that, those activities, also, pushed extremist groups, amongst those millions of angry Muslims, to form various terrorist movements. Thus, these changes in the Palestinian regions, over many decades, resulted in condemnable actions, by Jewish terrorist groups, and many, by Arab terrorist groups. But in the eyes of the world, terrorism, by any side, is always wrong, and must be condemned, equally. *It has been emphasized, by many, it bears repeating, there are many forms of 'terrorism'; some of it, regrettably, is at the hands of the State!* With too many crises in our world, it is too late to blame one, or two, groups, or individuals. Most foreign policies have been a disaster, because they failed to keep in focus, and analyze, the course, and causes, of many adverse events, throughout history.

Some recent headlines from the Independent (UK), newspaper, reflect on some of the discussions, in this book, how people see us, from the other side! 'Bush faces his Watergate; the White house has lost a key man, but the *whole chain of command may be engulfed, as lies, that led to war, are revealed'.* 'Bush picks Alito'; this was about a federal judge embraced by conservatives, nominated by Bush for the Supreme Court. Critics accused that Bush bowed down before the extreme right conservatives, and had set the stage for more divisiveness. 'Bush and Blair-the parallels are close. If Libby is found guilty, it could suggest a culture of *deceit in the White house, as in Downing Street'*. Many of these, dealt, with the White house leak revelations, and the widely held belief, that lies, and fabrications, were, used, by the two governments, to go to war against Iraq. Then there was an amazing piece on Italy's Berlusconi, 'I tried to talk Bush out of invading Iraq', he is alleged to have stated. This mediocre politician is a few months away from elections, and thus, he is claiming (now!) that he opposed the war, from the start. He is pathetic! His people have been highly critical, of his behavior, vis a vis the US, throughout the whole Iraq ordeal.

Others, looking in, from the outside, can view some aspects of US culture, and other western countries, and assume that significant segregation, and discrimination persist. It is fairly common to see schools, churches, country clubs, and other establishments, and residential neighborhoods, virtually segregated. Some, practically, all White; others, practically, all Black, and Hispanic, or other ethnic groups. Laws might state that it should not be so, but in reality, that is how it is! Then, we are well aware of persisting religious discrimination in many Muslim countries, against other religious beliefs, particularly Christian. Countries mentioned by writers have included, Saudi Arabia, Indonesia, Pakistan, India, Yemen, and others. Most often, such discrimination is at the hands of fundamentalist Muslims. Leaders, in all these countries, have tried to announce that it is, behavior that is against the law, and against the faith beliefs, in those countries.

A letter writer from Berlin in Time magazine, stated, that Bush's purpose in crawling back to Europe was to thwart the development of a United Europe, and to cajole, browbeat, scare, or even threaten, Europeans, into submission to America's global policies of vandalism, and institutionalized lawlessness. The writer concluded by saying that 'Bush should have been sent packing, and roundly rejected'. Of course these people realize what happened, in the US! But, are these not disturbing analyses by citizens of other countries? And another from Belgium went like this: 'Rather, it's a question of the Bush administration admitting, that in order to invade Iraq, and scare the American people into reelecting Bush, *it systematically distorted the truth, to dupe the American people into thinking S. Hussein was behind 9/11'*. As mentioned by many, such comments, probably have more truth than meets the eye, as there was the semblance of brainwashing, and constant propaganda, emanating from Washington! What has American policy degenerated into, that we have millions, around the world, who protest against US global policies; who express views as the above? The above quotations, are not ancient, they are all, in the past few months! US policies keep on generating more such sentiments, year, after, year. When will we show people everywhere, that we can speak the truth, that we can be trusted; that we do not always lie; that we have concluded that we must cease our posturing, and warmongering. They will see that, we can really lend a helping hand, around the world. When are we going to show the world that we have many men, and women, in America, who are capable, and considerate, who can lead, if need be; and they should come forth in large numbers, to play their part, for the good of people everywhere.

We have witnessed some acts of cooperation in the international arena, when tragedy strikes, in different regions, on our planet. The United States was seen playing its part, attempting to reach out to others. Not too long ago, a Russian mini, submarine, became ensnared, in tough, net lines, in the ocean depths. A crew of seven was trapped, unable to escape. To their credit, instead of hiding behind secrecy, as was customary, in the past, for all nations, Russian officials promptly contacted Japanese, British, and the American governments, seeking assistance. These countries responded, as all countries, should, in disaster situations. In the US, they started assembling the personnel, and necessary equipment, to send to the scene, for a rescue mission. Similar activities were also proceeding in the British, and Japanese, sectors. This is the type of behavior patterns, that this writer had strongly advocated, in "Mirror Reflections=Mirages", for prompt, no strings attached, assistance, in all humanitarian crises; not threatening language, or preparations for war, or aggression against states, without genuine reasons.

The team from Britain was first to reach the scene of this accident, and quickly, and efficiently, proceeded with rescue operations. The submarine was freed from its ensnaring lines, and it was then able to surface. All crew, members, were alive and well, and needless to stay, extremely grateful. This event brought several nations together, in a cooperative mission of mercy, to save lives. They are certainly worthy of praise from all over the world; and we can all hope, that we are beginning to see more efforts like these, in all types of emergencies. Indeed, in recent months, we have witnessed the Asian tsunami, the Pakistan earthquake, hurricanes in the US, floods in Europe, and many other parts of the world; and terrible mud slides in Guatemala, where villages were buried; and much, much, more. All this, besides health disasters, such as Aids, and other entities, already discussed. There is now the fear of the bird influenza in Asia, thousands of birds had been killed, and there have been human deaths as well. The fear, mainly, centers, around the virus mutating, to enable human, to human, transmission, which could result in a catastrophic pandemic.

'Doctors without borders', has had a remarkable history, setting an example for mankind. They have often been one of the first groups to respond to humanitarian crises around the world, no matter how poor the country, sometimes, under the harshest of conditions. Some descriptions of their experiences are heart wrenching. More governments need to continue on a similar path, for the benefit of all mankind; and to protect our fragile planet, as well.

American government officials have become regular targets, for much criticism, from around the world, not simply from, predominantly Muslim, countries. In October Spanish authorities again accused US soldiers of murdering a Spanish journalist, at a Baghdad hotel, and, allegedly, had issued worldwide requests for the arrest of those soldiers. But foreign country representatives have often accused the US of flaunting international laws; and when they ordered the arrest of members of the US armed forces for trial in those countries, the American government always denied those accusations, and rarely would any arrests be made, and then, for 'show' trials in the US, itself. But when US officials wanted a citizen of another country arrested, and sent to America, for trial, they issued all types of threats against those countries; and they kept it up. *Does that begin to sound like an imperial power issuing edicts?*

International media continued to hear commentaries on the US government, and the Halliburton companies, in the US; vice president Cheney was a former CEO of that company, and therefore they had attracted considerable attention. It appeared that lucrative contracts continued to be given to that company, for Iraq, without bidding; and there were many accusations of special treatment, nepotism, and so on. When critics stated that Halliburton had overcharged the government, in many areas, according to reports, US officials issued statements that, most of the charges made by that company, had been fair, and reasonable. It was also alleged, that any government employee, who complained of improprieties, was either demoted, or dismissed; is that amazing, or what; more imperialism? Because of these many scandals, a member of congress, talked before the House, of "this unbelievable waste, fraud, and abuse"! Later, similar accusations were made about special contracts being given, for the post-Katrina, hurricane, disasters; *and, it was implied, that, these, too, were often given to companies who were political supporters, of this administration, hence, why critics have been talking of so much cronyism, in this government, much more than usual.*

Others have watched in dismay, as the United States became mired in international intrigue, of sorts, in political corruption, and chicanery; this from a government, they hoped, would always remain a beacon for the rest of humanity. Not anymore! They saw politicians at great odds, a president who had caused division amongst his people. When events turned against the president, all he had to do, is, come up with something to distract the media, and the people. Thus, in early November, for the second time, he nominated another judge for the Supreme Court, just when the indictment was handed down on a senior White house official. The ruse succeeded for a short time, in diverting reporters' attention. Then, the democratic side challenged the republican majority, to produce results of the investigation into the reasons given for the Iraq war, as these were connected to the indictment just handed down, by the grand jury. Republicans had stalled that investigation for well over a year; and thus, the democratic move, shut down the senate, to go into secret session. It drew attention of all in the US, and the rest of the world, no doubt. It also allowed people to notice how, in America, with all branches of government under the control of one party, *it had become much more like a dictatorship, an oligarchy, had it not?*

In November 2005 there were also more news reports, of American CIA officials, holding so called 'terror suspects', for interrogation, in secret locations, in Asian, and eastern European countries, and elsewhere. A spokesman for Bush stated that, it was all done according to law, and no torture is ever used! We do not condone it, he said. If it is all according to law, why is it, that many US government, and military officials, from the president all the way down, *had been debating the Geneva Convention, and what exactly defined torture, and this, in the twenty first century, if you please- - - -? And why were there, so many reports of abuse, and torture, of prisoners, allegedly, resulting in several deaths, all at the hands of US authorities, in Iraq, in Afghanistan, and at the Cuban, Guantanamo, prisons? And we are still hearing of other secret, 'American', locations, in many other countries- - -!* Surely, all those reports were not fabricated? Where does hypocrisy end, in all this? Or does it ever end?

But then, people around the world, did hear, of a shining light, in America, in 2005; and that was in the image of Rosa Parks. It did not come from the White house, or Congress, or from any other halls of justice, but it came in Rosa Parks, herself. There were, well deserved, eulogies, for this great lady; and many politicians, seemed to want to be 'seen', at her funeral, and rightly so. This Afro-American lady, some 50 years ago, simply refused to give up her seat on a public bus, to Whites! It was not ancient history, but a mere 50 years, but the laws of these United States, then, *permitted brutal racial discrimination, and abuse of human, civil, rights. She had long wondered 'how America, her country, had come to this'!* But that act by Rosa Parks, lit the flame, and it led to a massive boycott of the transportation system, which then, impacted on the government. It gave birth to the great civil rights movements in America; and the long march for justice and freedom, of the Black community, and other minorities. But critics have claimed, that, even today, the proposals for the requirement of photo ID cards, for voting privileges, would adversely impact mostly minorities, once again. There have been too many accusations, of voting irregularities, in the last two presidential elections, in the US, and these were directed particularly at minorities. Why does it appear, that officials never seem to properly address those problems? Are we giving the impression, to the world, once again, that it is all, political?

MORE ON OUR WORLD

A list, of people, who were presumed to have influenced our lives, was published by Time magazine, in April 2005. It was not readily discernible, if that influence was always positive, or in some cases, possibly, negative. Did politics enter into the selection process? Yes, many would agree, that some of the people proposed, were noteworthy, and deserving; others somewhat questionable, and yet, others, some critics would maintain, should not be on such a list. The latter may also influence lives, but in the wrong direction. Apparently, president Jimmy Carter did not make that particular list (he deserves to be on every such list!), and that was noteworthy. He is a remarkable gentleman who has continued to do much good for humanity, everywhere; for peace, and justice, year, after year, *and he is still at it!* And, naturally, we would include Pope John Paul II, with his superb ministry in reaching out to all people of our world, truly, another man of peace!

Some of those selected had achieved much, the Dalai Lama, it was said, that 'nobody left his presence without feeling uplifted; and people came away more hopeful for a better world'. Nelson Mandela was well known for the struggles in South Africa, against Apartheid, injustice, and subjugation, of other human beings. Eliot Spitzer of New York was a tireless crusader, to end injustice, corruption, and criminal behavior, in the corporate world. Andrew Weil, a Harvard professor, and for millions of people, the face of alternative medicine in the healing arts, he pursued the combination of traditional, and alternative, medicine. There was the newly elected president of Ukraine, showing the power of ordinary people. Bill Gates, of, Microsoft fame, and 'Windows'; but who has done much good with his fortune. Mahmoud Abbas, who had emerged as the new leader of the Palestinian nation. Mary Robinson who was a writer from Ireland. Yes, also. Michael Moore, whose controversial movies at least provoked debate, and truth, to emerge, from the sleazy, political scenes, of the early twenty first century, in London, and Washington. Others with a positive impact, would be Bill Clinton, the Google guys, and Oprah Winfrey, with her truths of life, on our screens, week, after week. There were others on Time's list, those who spoke out against the abuse of Muslim women, those who had stimulated debate, on life, and ethics; and others, were from India, China, and more. 'Time' had an extensive list, but still, many would argue, if, the contributions, by some of these, personalities, was positive.

With regard to that G-8 summit in Scotland, the British newspaper, Independent, pointed out that authorities there, were concerned with Sir Bob Geldof, calling for a million protesters to descend on the site of the meetings, *to draw the world's attention to the tragedy of Africa.* The authorities worried about the potential for violence, and that the cities could not cope with such a large crowd. The 'Independent' also described how, the British health minister was organizing this meeting, in a super expensive locale (rooms were up to 900 pounds sterling per night), and costing British taxpayers huge amounts of money. The excuse by the minister was, that, the location had to do with security! What utter nonsense! Critics called it, a scandalous waste of money. The characters of the group of 8, have been meeting in lavish surroundings for years, it was no secret. They claimed to be discussing Africa, and world poverty, *amidst all that luxury. Is that, not a discordant note?*

We have read many critiques, about the group of 8, the World Bank, and the International Monetary Fund, *how little they had achieved, and they carried a stigma of shame, with reference to the world's poor.* At the 2005 economic forum in Davos, Switzerland, Ethics and Poverty, took center stage; global poverty, and disease, pushed 'America, and trade', off the front burner. News articles affirmed that Davos had been the meeting place, for some years, where, the, world's high, and mighty, would congregate, to talk about trade policy, the US dollar; to meet with corporate executives, and leading politicians. As discussed by many writers, the elite, and the powerful, do all this. It reflects on the corruption in the so-called capitalistic, free market, systems. They might give a glance at the plagues of poverty, hunger, and rampant disease, in our world, then do nothing, or very little, to provide solutions; and go on, to meet another day.

Why was it, that, France's Chirac, was quoted, by reporters, as saying, "It is time for Ethics"? Time, indeed! Where have all these world organizations been, all these decades, that it is now, that, they consider, ethics? Millions of our brothers, and sisters, have suffered so much, and many have died! How many years have we been told, of the danger of starvation, in sub-Sahara Africa, and other regions? To force home these points, that the wealthy nations should have done much better, years ago; and on the background of tragic reports, we hear, almost daily, we have recently received news, of remarkable feats, by NASA, of the United States. A probe that had been launched into Space, several years ago, had successfully reached the Comet, it was sent to meet, and penetrate; this, to study its composition, and gather as much information as possible, *perhaps, even, back to the creation of our Universe.* This revelation, after hearing of so many tragedies, and disasters, seemed to cry out, "We can achieve such remarkable feats, but man has not yet learned, how to solve the curse of poverty, and people, in our world, still dying from starvation, why- - -?

In a previous book, we had described, and it will be repeated here, the seemingly fragile 'democracy', in the US; and the call, by many, for electoral reform; that, it was badly needed. It now transpires that, there is a groundswell of complaints, in the UK as well, that democracy was in short supply, and people there, too, are clamoring, for electoral reforms. Imagine, *the two culprits in the Iraq tragedy, and they are having their own problems, with free and fair elections. Yet, they wanted to force their own ideas of democracy, on Iraq, and other countries, at the point of a gun, no less!* Are they teaching them electoral manipulation?

What about the environment, well, the reports on global warming, are directed, mostly, at the fully, industrialized, nations; and such reports, have been steadily increasing, as there have been forecasts of more violent weather (hurricanes), changes in rainfall, torrential downpours with flooding, mudslides, drought, earthquakes, and, more. A gradual melting of polar icecaps, and glaciers. All this could portend serious consequences, for planet earth. The United Kingdom has usually been blessed with plentiful rain, but is now facing water shortages, and unusually balmy weather. Europe has experienced numerous floods. Pollution has increased everywhere, and natural, habitats, are being destroyed, by man. Large tracts of forest, are still being bulldozed, in the US, and other countries. Business officials, and politicians, inform the public, that, more trees would be replanted. *But the truth is, that they cannot replace the echo, systems, that had existed in those forests.* This destruction is carried out to make way for malls, or factories, for, what is called, development, and progress. And, this travesty goes on, year, after, year, in small, or, large, countries, rich, or poor. As with the Amazon rainforests, when sister Dorothy Lang, was murdered in Brazil, for her defense of the poor; according to Time magazine, she wrote, "how the skies over Brazil, will soon be dark, by day, or by night- - -if the rain forests vanish, so will one million species "! Mankind had been given warnings, and people have lost their lives, to do what is right, as attested by the above; *but are governments, and politicians, listening? Are people taking any notice?*

Scientists have declared that thousands of animal, and plant, species, have already been wiped out, and our oceans are also dying. Perhaps, *this is the way we are to destroy planet earth,* not by some cataclysmic event, such as a nuclear holocaust, or massive meteors from outer space, colliding with earth; *but, by man's own evil traits, unbridled greed, greenhouse gases, these, will do in, planet earth.* People need to change attitudes, have we heard, that, before? And, now, because of that G-8 summit, in Scotland, we have been hearing of, *Africa dying;* it is dying indeed, and we can start doing something, about it, by protecting planet earth, all corners of it!

One recent example came with a report in the 'Independent' (UK), in June 2005, and that, should give all of us, pause, for deep, and sad, reflection. The article stated that a century ago, some 100,000, or more, Tigers, roamed our planet; and today, it was estimated, that a mere 3000 survived- - -! Most of the blame was attributed to poaching by criminals, and, indifference, on the part of government officials. The Tiger habitats, were mostly in third world countries, poor, often in turmoil, steeped in corruption, at all levels; and, perhaps, without any serious, constructive help, from 'the west'. Experts have also accused those governments of using unscientific methods, to estimate the number of certain species that survive. This might make the figures appear better, than they actually are!

According to reports, this Bush administration, had one of the worst environment records; they had consistently opposed any mandatory reductions in industry emissions (the economy, you know!). Thus, republicans, particularly in the present government, have often been accused of catering to big business, rather than the welfare of the people. They have been accused of ignoring, all evidence of serious pollution threats, to our planet. They try to deceive Americans into believing, that there was inadequate proof. In California, a study was started on volunteers, and this will measure the levels of various chemicals in their bodies. Thus, they hope to establish *levels of human exposure to industrial chemicals all around us, in the air we breathe, the food we eat, and the water we drink!* The next step would be, for researchers to decide, if such chemicals, and such levels in humans, were related to specific health problems. There were numerous studies, previously, linking tobacco to serious health problems, and it had become well recognized today, with appropriate warnings being issued, about that product. But it had taken many years, before the public saw any significant action by their government, or by the tobacco industry itself. In western societies the advertising of tobacco has now been curtailed, in some countries, more than others; but now, some companies are reaching out to those, living, in underdeveloped countries, to push advertising, and to sell their products. Therefore, it remains to be seen, how many other chemicals, are responsible for health problems, chemicals used regularly by industry, and by people. There are many who believe, that there is some relationship, between diseases, and the use of chemicals; one that has received considerable debate, is cancer. Absolute proof, so far, has not been found, but it may not be far behind.

Two populous, but poor, countries, India, and Pakistan, have also seen much violence across their borders, and within their own countries, for many years. In recent months, there has been more discourse between leaders of those countries, and other moves by officials, to defuse tension, and the dangerous impasse. They are both nuclear powers, hence, the danger for mankind. Disagreements have decreased, and until recently there was a relative calm. But, in the past few weeks, there was another 'terrorist', bombing attack, in India, with loss of life. Pakistan had often been implicated with terrorists attending radical Islamic schools, in that country. The dictator of Pakistan had ordered the registration of all religious schools, and the disclosure of their financing. But leaders, in those schools, have resisted, and protested. A guest, on BBC news, said, some Pakistani intelligence staff, had run a number of those schools, to train insurgents, to fight in India, over Kashmir! But, most of the other schools had never preached violence, and they were upset at the methods used by Musharraf, of Pakistan. But also dominating the news, over there, was the terrible earthquake, with its aftermath. Reports suggested that Pakistan was going to spend several billions of dollars, to purchase fighter aircraft, but the president shelved that idea, to help, instead, the thousands of victims, devastated by the earthquake. Most people will see that, as the right, humanitarian, thing, to do; quite a change, for some of these countries!

Also in Ireland, the problems, between north, and south, had persisted, but greatly diminished, and less violent, since moves had been taken, with America's help, to bring the parties, to the negotiating table. 'Time' magazine, had reported that Sinn Fein leader, Gerry Adams, announced that, it was time for the IRA to use politics, and a democratic process, to achieve the goal, of a united Ireland. But other reports suggested that the IRA was still recruiting, and training, new members, to maintain their status quo. However, in July 2005, the Irish Republican army (IRA), indeed, announced, publicly, that it would no longer use violence, to achieve the union of Ireland. This was welcomed by most citizens; and what another remarkable, change, that was, after many years of bitterness, violence, and yes, even, death.

There have been many discussions, and reports written, on ending world poverty, and hunger, on providing greater assistance for Aids, and more. President Carter, for many years, and now, also president Clinton, and Bill Gates, have all worked hard in that area; and there have been others. A recent quotation from Blair of UK, on helping Africa, went like this, 'It is now, or never'. In "Mirror Reflections=Mirages", we presented at length, many aspects of the global tragedies of poverty, and hunger, not only in Africa, but also in *Asia, Latin America, and other regions; the glaring chasm of the haves and the have not!* As if to highlight these points, Time magazine, featured a recent article on Abu Dhabi's new Emirates hotel. "Even by profligate standards of the Gulf", it begins. People are well aware of poverty, and suffering, in large sections of the Middle East, and yet, a few, there, continue to live it up to the hilt, they always have. There is this hotel, complete with crystal chandeliers (about a thousand of them), gold leaf, mosaic, columns, marble, and much more. A night's stay starts at $625! One question, the article goes on, to ask, "Do you arrive by yacht, or helicopter, or in one of a fleet of Rolls Royce"? One can easily conclude, that, as long as we continue to produce these obscene excesses, *the prospects for peace and justice, for all, in our world, seem far away, and out of reach.* What an amazing contrast that is, with some of the late Holy Father's (John Paul II), quotations in these pages, on peace and justice, and brotherly love.

We had previously outlined how the wealthier nations, the International Monetary Fund, could use their excesses, and direct their energies, for relief, and the good of mankind; not for war (as was done in Iraq). We emphasized, how, all nations should drastically reduce their expenditures, on the military, and on weapons of war, and apply all this, for the solutions, to world poverty, once, and for all! Critics had also pointed out that, because of prevalent corruption, in many of those countries, giving money alone, would only help a little, and had never provided, lasting remedies. Money is important, no doubt; but, besides charitable efforts, all countries, through the UN, should help with improving health care, such as, fighting Aids, Malaria, Tuberculosis, other infectious diseases; providing water supplies, and the availability of clean, safe, water. They should help improve education; farming and agriculture, in general; with utilities, and infrastructure, and more. Yes, all this would require money, lots of it, but the international community could plunge, right in, and do it; teach them to protect their forests, and their land, the overall environment. At the Carter Center, they have already been teaching them, principles on some of the above; *but what about all governments, stepping up, to the plate, and doing more, of their share, such as the US?* We need to start by nurturing, and protecting, nature, ourselves, as well. Then, we can teach!

We cannot do it quickly; neither should we try to force our ideas of 'democracy', by acts of aggression against others. Gradually, through education, old habits, certain aspects of old cultures, begin to fade, and change. Not all, old, native, cultures, are bad, or harmful, or must be replaced by western ideologies; far from it. Sometimes, we need to admit, that, it is our habits, or some aspects of our culture, that perhaps, should be changed, or modified. Thus, a slight alteration, the intermingling, and assimilation, of different cultures, might be the logical solution, in many instances. Indeed, there are disastrous, barbaric, acts, that some, presume to call, 'culture'. For instance, those who, for many years, defended Fox hunting, with dogs, chasing a terrified Fox, in the UK, and elsewhere. There, they called it, culture, as well. The hunters, in Malta, who shoot any bird that flies over the island, call it 'sport', or a 'tradition'. Nonsense! These are barbaric acts, and such habits ought to be changed. Today, you can 'hunt', or 'shoot', decoys, thus, leaving nature's creatures alone! In some countries we have also read of the terrible practice, of deliberate, physical injuries, inflicted by the State, on those convicted of crimes; this, apart from, the handing down of death sentences. The latter, remains the source of much debate, and disagreements, even in religious circles.

An article by Fred Burton, attempted to dissect the structure of Al Qaeda, and he looked at it, more, or less, as a pyramid. The apex represented their leaders, Bin Laden, and al Zawahiri; the middle sector consisted of tactical commanders, who were well trained; and the base, was made up of militants, and sympathizers, who were the ones going on many suicide missions. He concluded that although the attacks on Al Qaeda, by the Americans, had weakened it somewhat, it remained a serious threat. But, the article did not expand into the reasons, why these groups, target mainly the west, particularly Americans, and those cooperating with their policies. Most, experts, dismiss religion, as the primary reason for such attacks, but rather, the aggressive actions by America.

T. Dahlby, author of, 'Allah's Torch', was on a C-Span television program, and reported on his visit to Indonesia, to meet leaders of an Islamic, fundamentalist, front. He said, being an American, he expected to have a rough experience, with such an interview. He received a lot of criticism, but he was told that, at least, he was an American, who would listen. They said, as they could talk to him, perhaps, he should become president! After the dictatorship of Suharto, the country had remained in turmoil, and many claim that the government, there, continues to be very repressive. They suggested that, many of their problems, were caused by the policies of America, and Israel. Even after the Bali attacks, much terrorism had persisted. There was friction, with bouts of violence, between Christians, and Islamic fundamentalists. The author had traveled there, to assess the situation, at this time. Suharto was known to be heavy handed with his people, as he tried to hold the country together. He was definitely dictatorial, but the US, did not consider any attacks on that country. On the contrary, the US, Europe, Australia, and others, had dealings, with such a dictator.

Then there was a book by Jung Chang, featured in the Sunday Times (UK), and it presented a profile of China's former leader Mao; and the myths surrounding 'their man', were shattered. Mao was revealed as, 'a bloodthirsty egomaniac', who, was bent on promiscuity, mass murder, and self, gratification; that, he avoided fighting the Japanese, and was dependent on the Russians! Undoubtedly, millions, in mainland, China, will state that these are views of a writer, who was a bitter opponent, or dissident; and their views, on Mao, would be quite different. Now, economists extol the great progress China had achieved, with 9% growth, over a decade. Guest speakers, on the Jim Lehrer, news hour, pointed to the problems China was facing, a weak banking system, a stock market that faltered; there was a tremendous gap between the few who had been successful, in the major cities, and the masses of peasants in the rural areas, who remained amongst the poorest, in the world. They also said that, the Chinese, government, has been aware of increasing incidents of unrest, recently, over 70,000 incidents in one year. The communist party has had special meetings to try close the gap between the haves, and the, have not. They realize too well, that most of their economic growth had come from increased exports, because of their advantage, of a cheap labor force; but, most importantly, China held, vast amounts, of America's debt!

From the Netherlands, there were reports that the government had expelled imams for expressing support for Bin Laden; for preaching extremism, and for turning Muslims away from western values (was this done, at the insistence of the US authorities?). They announced that the government was attempting to train more moderate, Dutch speaking, Muslim preachers. Some critics might wonder, if that is a new thrust into indoctrination, by the Dutch government. It would be commendable, of leaders in that country, if they were dealing harshly with those imams, simply, because they were preaching violence, and not discriminating against the Muslim population, as many around the world have accused. However, why is it wrong for some preachers to encourage their flock, *to stay away from certain western values, such as nudity, debauchery, drugs, and alcohol, and prostitution? The ever present, me, me society!* Would the Dutch government also object to that? Or does the government hope to attract, and keep, those imams, who have nice words to say, about the west, expressing praise, and admiration?

There were other reports about a trial of murderers of a Dutch film, maker, in Holland. Allegedly, he had been brutally murdered because, Muslims claimed, he had insulted their Qu'ran over the mistreatment of women in Muslim society. But Muslims in Holland saw it as an attack, on their culture, and their religion. It was brought out that a Muslim conspiracy might have led to his murder. Anger in Holland became widespread, and the Muslim population, there, remained, largely, poorly educated, and they had high rates of unemployment. In spite of Holland's reputation, as a country of true assimilation, democracy, and freedom, Muslims in that country, felt they had been marginalized. The above topic has been discussed in many countries, and it points to a clash of cultures. It is obvious that discussions between differing ethnic groups is most important, in an effort to find a solution that is just for all. As opposed to the US, or UK, Holland was noted as a truly, open, society; therefore, it is regrettable that such events have taken place. Muslims are now claiming the same for many other countries, namely that they are discriminated against. Can they be proven wrong? Just this November, there were several days of rioting, by Muslims, in France, where there is a large Muslim population. There again, was great misunderstanding, and it has resulted in much violence. They claimed, once more, the same discrimination, and lack of access to a decent education, and jobs.

Holland had also been noted for tolerance, and independent thinking; but since the Iraq war it was seen as embracing the concept of aggression. Yes, we certainly need to protect ourselves from the preaching of violence, and incitement to terrorism; but should we not learn to reach out; to try to determine what the 'west' is doing, that, 'they feel is terribly wrong', and has caused so much resentment, and anger. On the other, side, of the impasse, Muslims must also understand, that, if it is the old question, of religion, 'that ours, is the only true religion', that particular issue had led to much violence, and suffering, in the history of this planet. We cannot go down that road, again. A 'one religion', philosophy, *will never be resolved by force, by wars, as evidenced by the past several hundred years!* But solutions may be possible, only, through frequent discussions, and a universal *search for the Truth.* We should all be free, to discuss, with individuals, any particular belief, of any religion, but there must be no trickery or coercion, and people should be free to accept, or reject, without further harassment.

In August 2005, the push by the Bush administration, for an Iraqi constitution, failed, and missed three separate date lines. The major factions, in the country, had considerable disagreement on many issues, Federalism, being one of them. But women were also concerned about "women's rights", and that was important. Because, Islamic laws were interpreted differently, by various clerics, and women were raising questions about 9 year old girls being forced into marriage; about men being permitted to take 3, 4, or more, wives. A man could repeat 3 times 'I divorce you', and the woman is then considered divorced, and is forced to leave the home, and it may be the only home she had known for many years. In other words, according to some opinions, men would have all the rights, and women, none! Now, by the culture, and the standards, that people in the west, have lived by, such policies would not go down well, and are bound to cause serious friction. These thoughts demonstrate why we need a powerful, United Nations, where views could be exchanged, where dialogue would be limitless, in an effort to achieve proper balance, and just solutions. If dictatorship tactics are prohibited, and countries with larger financial contributions are not allowed to bully their way around, to exercise any veto power; then, such a UN, could certainly open the road to solving some of our world's problems.

Another dilemma for many people, more serious for those living in western countries, is that of identity theft. In the US it has become commonplace; highly personal data, that should be treated in strict confidence, may be lost, or can be reported stolen, by corporations, or even, by, agencies of the government. The American government permits companies (and they can run a lucrative business), to collect all types of information on US citizens, and others; and they allow certain data to be sold, or, all that information is stored, on the websites of companies, allegedly, with security in place. Such information can include, financial data, credit card use, bank accounts, shopping habits, social security numbers, and much more. Health records are increasingly being computerized, in the cyberspace generation, and may be vulnerable to theft. All this, can be lost in shipping transit, or can be stolen outright. Millions of people have already been affected.

Well, you ask, are the corporations, or the US government, then, forced to make full restitution? Or pay penalties for causing anguish, and harm? In most cases, not much is resolved, and the victims are left holding the bag, and corporations go on their merry way. They may receive the customary, tap on the wrist. Does this go on, only in the US? No, certainly not, there have been complaints from the UK, and other countries. Such individuals, whose identity was stolen, and their data misused, in their name, had their credit ratings destroyed; and, huge financial charges were made against their cards, in their name. Others, had bank accounts, decimated. It can take years for some of these people, to clear up, the mess, when governments should be able to cooperate, and put a stop to it. Such thefts, and scams, can also be perpetrated from underdeveloped countries, such as Africa, via the Internet. And, the more business is transacted through the Internet, the greater the risk, although, companies are still trying to perfect their security measures. Confidential data have also been reported stolen from, mail boxes, in people's homes.

Then, we have the tragedies, to humanity, and to the environment, of chemical disasters, the dangers posed by nuclear plants, in so many countries; and we had already written about the many oil spills that have assaulted nature, over several years. One such chemical, disaster, drew a full page advertisement, recently, in the 'Independent' (UK), by the Bhopal Medical Appeal, about that accident, some years back, in Bhopal, India. Yes, this was a presentation, to attract donations; but some statements in this piece, went right to the heart, as many of us remember, how terrible it was, for the poor people, who lived, or worked, there. It was a massive black eye, for governments, and for corporations, in capitalistic, materialistic, societies, as they plunge deeper, and deeper, into an abyss, as they seek 'cheap labor', in foreign lands! This industrial disaster was responsible for the deaths, or serious injury, of literally, hundreds of people. This appeal called on Union Carbide owners, Dow Chemical, to clean the factory, and the underground water system, in the area. *Are they still begging for justice, many years after that disaster- - -?* A survivor commented, how people were crying, and screaming, as they were beaten, by, police, as they sought justice. Their outcry, 'my God, are we less than human!' struck a cord, because the Court had ordered the local government to provide clean water, but, allegedly, they had ignored those orders, why? Citizens had claimed that the police showed no mercy, not even on children.

Is that how much clout, gigantic, capitalistic, US, or multinational, corporations, have, with foreign governments? Yet again, what a sad day, for planet earth! Local citizens blamed all the problems in their community, on that Union Carbide factory; were they all wrong? Reporters said, "The people did not ask to be gassed, on that night of horrors". If this advertisement is correct, as it implies, it would be a travesty indeed, if the Indian government, with all its claims to democracy, had not dealt properly, and justly, with this calamity, on its people, on their own soil, by a foreign company. True, a caste system persists, to this day, in some of those nations, and that is another human tragedy. There is little doubt, that such factories created many jobs in those communities, and helped in the local economy; and therefore, politicians, would not undertake any harsh measures. Still, these corporations, usually, face rigid regulations, in their own countries, sometimes, depending, on which political party, is in power. But, *should leaders, not always put their people, first? From all, that has been presented, so far, does it seem like it?*

International policies can be a source of upheaval, and dismay. A website on the Internet, had reported that, a former White house official, had fingered, 'the Cheney-Rumsfeld Axis, to hijack US foreign policy, and *knowingly mislead congress, in order to get its support, for an unlawful war'*. There have been more cries in congress, for an expansion of the special investigations, by Fitzgerald, because of possible serious crimes committed, at the highest levels, of the US government. A government, in America, totally controlled by republicans, in a dictatorial, tyrannical, manner, has essentially forgotten its sworn duties, to the country, and to the people. But they find time to exchange uncomplimentary words on the international stage. North Korea's, leader, was called, a few nasty words, by US officials, at the highest levels; and, in return, the N. Korean leader, called Bush 'a half baked man, and a Philistine', (coincidentally, a clergyman, had labeled the US, a nation of Pharisees)! Cheney was called 'a cruel monster'; but previous reports on the N. Korean leader, had marked him, as, 'unstable, and bizarre'. But, what a state we have gotten into, that a powerful nation, and, a small, troubled nation, can now find the time, to engage in such insults, instead of seriously working towards, a lasting peace.

In the past, we had been accustomed to scenes from third world countries, of violent arguments, or even fist fights, amongst officials, inside government buildings. Presumably, we used to be told, that, such activities do not take place, in developed, 'more civilized' countries. No, they do not. In our more 'civilized societies', politicians call, one another, *my honorable friend, or, the honorable gentleman from the other side;* this, in the debating chambers. Then, behind the scenes, and on the campaign trail, or in advertisements, *they call one another, liars, or cheats, more, or less, dishonest, and all sorts of disparaging innuendos; in other words, insults, there, as well!* Are we that different? In some respects yes, in many others, not different at all. We simply adopt a change of color, like the, well known, Chameleon. In the recent past, there have been harsh words exchanged, also, between Britain, and Iran, between the US, and Venezuela, between Israel, and some other countries, and much more.

The European press also highlighted, the Arab-South American summit that had been scheduled, for May 2005. There was an interesting comment, that dealt with concerns, this, had caused, in government circles, in the US, and Israel. Was this, another reflection, on these countries, interfering, as they often do, in the internal affairs, of other sovereign States? These particular, summit meetings, were emphasizing, the rights of States, and people everywhere, to resist foreign occupation (a reference to the US, and to Israel). The days of colonialism are gone, or so we thought! Conferees, at the meetings, stated, that *terrorism in all its forms, must be combated, through international cooperation.* Some referred to the US and Israel, in that regard, as they had been condemned, in the past, by many human rights organizations. What can possibly be wrong with such a summit, amongst leaders of nations; why, was it, criticized, by 'our side'? Was it, because we did not control the agenda?

Also, in May 2005, Europe was celebrating the defeat of the Nazi regime. Some news outlets published photographs, of then, Italy's Mussolini, and his mistress; they had been murdered, disfigured, and left hanging, in full view. Again, that reminded us of actions, once used, by barbarians; but it was at the end of world war two, a hard war, where millions of people had suffered greatly. And now, just simply, count, how many 'wars', we have been involved in, since that greatest war, *and we are still at it, today!* In the old days, defeated enemies, and their leaders, were sometimes, treated with respect, even as they faced questioning, and trials. And in the remote past, there was mostly hand, to hand, combat, and the ugliness of wars, left a more lasting, searing, image, perhaps, than it does, today. It has become too impersonal!

As mentioned elsewhere, news from Iran, showed that a hard line mayor, had won a landslide victory, in their elections, and this was contrary to US expectations. The latter had hoped, a more moderate candidate, would emerge. It came as no surprise, that, Bush administration, and UK, officials, accused, that those elections, were unduly influenced by clerics; *but, these same politicians, never admit that, elections in the US, and UK, are also unduly influenced, by money, by power, and by corrupt practices, to suppress minority voting, as has been reported from the US, year, after, year!* You exclaim, so, what is the difference, between us, and them? Some, but not such a glaring difference, that we could teach others. In other areas of the Middle East, there were other elections, where, voting results, were not exactly what US officials, had hoped. Both in Lebanon, and in Palestinian territories, groups listed as 'terrorist organizations', by the US, and Israel, had gained significant political clout. All this shows, an amazing lack of positive influence, by the US, on our world, today. That is what some scholars, and reporters, have been suggesting; some influence yes, but not much. According to US reports, later on, the new Iranian leader was alleged, to have said, that Israel should be destroyed. A first reaction, would be, was that true? Was it, in response to, continued threats against Iran, from the US, Israel, and from UK? Such summarily issued, declarations, are to be condemned, as are, continued threats that are issued against countries.

Many, here, and abroad, have expressed concern at all the violence in our world. What is wrong with society? There are continuing reports, on atrocities, ethnic cleansing, repression, besides what we read, from past histories, of the US, and the colonial powers. There are names that continue to resound, Cambodia, Rwanda, India and Pakistan, Sudan, Latin American countries, the Balkans, and the Middle East, and more. In the US, and UN, officials have continued to debate, if they should have intervened, in some of these, to save thousands of innocent victims. During world war two, let us not forget, we had the slaughter by the Nazis, and from the atomic bomb attacks, and more. Quite a history, for mankind, to deal with! All this, is such a black mark on humanity!

The ethnic cleansing in the Balkans, is recent history as well, and we have heard many reports on the murders, and brutality, perpetrated, in that part of Europe. The trials at The Hague brought to light, some of this, and the Srebrenica massacres, were well documented; they were carried out, in spite of protection, under the UN. Videos have surfaced, at those trials, showing some of those dastardly acts. It was alleged that soldiers, under Serbian leader Mladic, executed large numbers of Muslims, in cold blood!

And now, several years after a negotiated peace, they are still uncovering graves, with hundreds of human remains. People there, and around the world, have cried out for justice. Those Serbian leaders, suspected of being responsible, for those atrocities, are still at large. One has to wonder, why, officials in the US, the UK, and UN, have not demanded sanctions, embargoes, and what have you, against those governments, until those responsible, are apprehended. It was officials, in the US, and UK, who tried to put out fabrications, for the purpose of going after S. Hussein, of Iraq. Well, what about those Serbian leaders? When will people in that region, see justice being applied, instead of more demonstrations of different standards!

From Israel, reporters alleged, that Israeli soldiers had come forward describing how they had participated in, 'officially ordered killings', of Palestinian police, hunting down unarmed Palestinians, and shooting them, point blank; how, these soldiers later confessed, 'enjoying' such activities. They suggested that, the idea was, to kill them, whether they were armed, or not! These commentaries were from writers in UK newspapers. Other, former soldiers, in Israel, have come out with criticism of their military, and of the Sharon government, in the occupied Palestinian territories. These, and many other blemishes, will long tarnish, the conscience of Israel

At a senate hearing in the US, in July, they again, discussed the abuse of prisoners, by Americans, at Guantanamo, Cuba. A US general was heard testifying, that, taken one, by one, those acts would perhaps, not be called, abuse; but taken together, they could present a problem for America! What poppycock, what awful gibberish, and this, coming from a US general- - -! Some of the senate republicans, in their amazing wisdom, still tried to justify the abuse (most decent people called it torture), because they claimed, it gave us information that *could* save US lives! The same type of reasoning, they used, for Hiroshima, and Nagasaki! Nothing seems to change, in our government! Many experts will consider this, trash, condoning the use of evil towards an end, and coming from the highest levels, in the US government. Many of these politicians, often give out information, to reporters, 'on condition, they do not divulge their names'. On a news program, they discussed how, a former government official, had alleged, that Cheney, and Rumsfeld, had hijacked much of the decisions about invading Iraq; they probably also *influenced the handling of post-war Iraq, and the handling of prisoners.* These people criticized their ineptitude, as they tried to use a specific excuse, 'of war on terror', to relax, long established, strict rules, on how to treat prisoners.

In November 2005, there were many news releases, both here, and abroad, on the US abuse, 'torture', of prisoners; but, Bush, and Cheney, continued to insist that torture was not used on detainees. However, when senator McCain tried to legislate precisely, what is allowed in, the treatment of detainees, both Bush, and Cheney, objected to that legislation. There was also talk of a veto, by the president. And they both asserted that *the CIA must not be restricted in its efforts to obtain, information that, could protect the American people!* The more one heard their reasoning, the more ridiculous, it sounded; how can such talk, be believed, when they add that, the US does not condone torture!

But, at the same time, they continue to refuse to define, what can, or cannot, be used, in the interrogation process, by American officials. It was alleged that Cheney visited the senate to 'persuade' republicans, to block the McCain amendment! McCain was once, a prisoner of war, and, much more than Cheney, knows first hand, what torture means. Whereas, all those, trying to oppose, the McCain effort, were mediocre politicians, and that, is putting it kindly. According to an editorial in America magazine, the effort by US officials, to have the CIA excluded, 'would be tantamount to condoning torture'. Agents of the FBI (US is chock full of secret agencies!), had reported on torture techniques at Guantanamo, mentioned elsewhere; and according to the editorial, one of them said that, we would not believe what he had seen, there- - -! The question was raised why a *truly independent commission*, had not already started, an investigation, into 'torture' methods, possibly used, by US personnel. And the editor concluded that, "we cannot win the war on terror, by becoming terrorists ourselves", quite true, indeed! *We are in the year of our Lord, 2005, and, are we, being told, by our highest officials, in America, that they are still trying to define, what constitutes, torture? That is another tragedy, for planet earth!*

There were additional reports on the much criticized activities, by the US, in sending suspects, captured illegally, to third world countries for 'rough interrogation'; but, *this time there were witnesses.* On the CBS '60 Minutes' program, they discussed how these activities had started under Clinton, but had increased dramatically under Bush. The destination of these, 'suspects', was always to countries where, torture was known to take place, during these so-called 'interrogations'. Witnesses claimed that secret service personnel used knives, to slit clothes, off prisoners, and they were forcefully, given, tranquillizers. All this was perpetrated without cause, in many cases, and without court procedure. *Several innocent people had been seized in this manner, and so treated. As mentioned above, such revelations suggested, that America too, behaved like a terrorist nation.* And, if we do such things, how can our magnanimous politicians criticize others? They alleged that some torture techniques, used *in Uzbekistan, were right out of, the middle ages! One of the destination countries to which these 'suspects' were sent!* A British agent alleged, that, America's CIA officials knew very well, that these captives would be tortured! And apparently these injustices were still going on, even though Bush had stated that harsh abuse must not be tolerated. Surely, methods of torture would no longer exist today, unless countries represented at the UN, were continuing to behave like puppets. They do not unite to resist, and forcefully condemn, these practices; and thus, they become impotent to act in a constructive manner. In essence, they become guilty by association, as well, all of them.

As if our world had not experienced enough calamities, we had many reports on the Pakistan massive earthquake, and what followed. More than ten days after the disaster, we heard that nobody had yet reached many remote mountain villages; and people there, had no tents for shelter, they were without food, or water. Many of those places could only be reached by helicopter, or by mule train. Neither had they seen any medical help. They had lost their homes; and the weather was terrible, with rain, and very cold night temperatures. It was estimated that thousands had been injured, many seriously, and many could die. We were told that some of those, who had been reached, needed surgery, without the use of an anaesthetic, without medicine, and without clean water. What a human tragedy! In other words, the US, UK, and other powerful countries, can send thousands of troops, fighter planes, transports, bombers, tanks, trucks, helicopters, ships, and mobile hospitals, half way around the world, in a few days, *all to be used for war; but for humanitarian assistance, we can never get there quickly, to provide merciful help! Or, we claim, we cannot come up with the funds!* The humanitarian representative for the UN, was a guest, on the PBS Jim Lehrer, news hour. He discussed the crisis in the Pakistan-Kashmir mountain region, struck by the disaster. It was emphasized how the international community, especially the wealthier nations, had not properly stepped up to the plate. The discussants showed that, whereas for the Tsunami relief, they had about 1000 helicopters; for Pakistan, they had a tenth of that, or less. They had many fewer tents, than was actually needed, to provide some shelter. Extremely cold weather was expected in the mountains in 3-5 weeks, and thousands of people had not been reached, as yet. Many villages were at 5000 feet elevation, or above, and therefore the weather can be very harsh. Again, it was reasserted that many children, and those injured, would suffer, and die, without immediate assistance, from the outside world.

On Iraq, eventful news, reports, are always on the airwaves. But, experts had warned, that, what was done, to Iraq, could spark much unrest, elsewhere, sooner, or later. For over ten days in October-November, 2005, hundreds of Muslim youth, rioted in the suburbs of Paris, France, and soon spread to over 200 cities, around the country. Two youths thought police were chasing them (which was denied), and as they attempted to run, they were accidentally electrocuted, and died. That started the violence, in the streets of France. Thousands of cars were torched, and many buildings were set on fire; soon, curfews were declared for many cities. Police were forced to use tear gas, as more violence continued. We heard of the despair of Muslim youth, how they were discriminated against; one young man stated that, he had papers that declared him a French citizen. But when he went to the police, he was not treated like Frenchmen; and most of those young people had little chance, of getting a decent job. Similar situations existed in other European countries, perhaps, not as severe as in France. Before long, some of that violence had spread to UK, Netherlands, Belgium, and Germany. It was emphasized, that Europe might yet face a bigger crisis, because they lagged behind, in assimilating Muslims, into the local society; and they still needed to drastically reduce all aspects of discrimination. Those reports seemed to reflect, on what happened, in the US, in the past, regarding discrimination, against the Black population, in America.

Why do we continue to face so many overwhelming problems, in our world? Well, serious acts, of injustice, still persist, everywhere; especially as they relate, to third world countries. A Time magazine, notation, stated that, wealthy nations gave a billion $ yearly, for overseas help; *but, those same countries subsidized their own farmers, one billion $, each, and every, day! Yes, more injustice!* Therefore, with so many crises, all around us, it seemed appropriate for ElBaradei, head of the International Atomic Energy Agency, (and the IAEA), to be awarded the Nobel Peace prize, for 2005. It was well deserved!

TRENDS IN MODERN SOCIETY

Over the years Hollywood, California, in the US, has had its critics, who declared that, some undesirable trends in society, had emerged from that enclave. Before the advent of television, or when that technology was still in its infancy, (there were no computers, or Internet, or videos), the motion picture industry, and radio, provided entertainment, and exerted significant influence, on people's lives. *A picture was as good as, a thousand words!* Back, then, a larger percentage of the population visited the cinema regularly, more than they do today. But in recent years, there were increasing comments about the industry not being properly policed, as to what type, of subject matter they are permitted to project, on the screen. Others, protested, equally loud, that we must preserve freedom of speech, and freedom of expression, in the arts. But, many continued to assert that, Hollywood, had not assumed responsibility, and was spreading its influence, often, in the wrong direction.

Then, television came on the world scene, soon to be followed by computers, videos, and the ubiquitous, Internet. Within a few years, these, too, began to exert major influence, not always, a good influence. These brought their presentations, directly into the homes, into living rooms, and bedrooms, or in the study; therefore, the effect on the public, and especially, on young people, was immense! A speaker, at a church service, pointed out that television, and now, the Internet, could present views on lifestyles, that were still controversial; but, present them, in a way, 'that everything was now permissible', in our lives. He emphasized how, for years, media had depicted divorce, as easy, and relatively harmless, and desirable; that it was alright, for anybody, to live with a companion, outside of marriage; and many more topics, such as homosexuality, that have been the cause, of much debate, and disagreement. We were later bombarded with the cell phone, on whose tiny screens, many of the things on computers, could now be transmitted, and that gadget is with us, wherever we go!

Early in 2005, American news media featured senate committee hearings, on important changes that were being proposed, by the government. The Bush administration had zeroed in, on Public Broadcasting, because they received some government funding; thus, certain republicans, wanted those in charge of Public Broadcasting, to appear more pro-right wing, and pro-republican, in their programming. They wanted to see fewer programs criticizing Bush and his associates, and their many failures; and one would assume, they wanted to see more programs, complimenting Bush, and his successes. Such a ploy, focused once more, on the decline of America's freedoms, and democracy. The pro-right groups had disagreed with features like, 'Now', on PBS, because, these, never hesitated to take on issues, no matter how controversial, or how embarrassing, for political pundits! Therefore, they forced the cutting back of such a program, from one hour, to half an hour, *'so that the other time could be devoted to more conservative issues'. Quite pathetic, really! Is that control, and dictatorship, or what?*

Public Broadcasting, in any country, was meant to remain completely independent; but, now, politicians had placed a director on the corporation board, who could lean towards the Bush administration. Is that not called, corruption? At that senate hearing, a speaker, Boaz, said that, anyone who had watched Bill Moyers (retired), on the 'Now' program, would have concluded that it was liberal, and biased. What is wrong with that, Mr. Boaz, if it tells the truth? However, few people would agree with Boaz, on that description! He kept on, attacking the Public broadcasting system, *but he had no harsh words for Fox media, including television, that many critics had called, a perfect mouthpiece for Bush!* At that hearing, Boaz gave the impression that he was living in the clouds; the only excuse he could come up with, to defend Fox officials, was, that they received no government funding, and thus, they could do what they wished. In other words, if government agencies provide any funds, they must also dictate what they want. Yes, we have had many examples of government funds, from the 'west', with regard to third world countries. The above, reveals another influence, not necessarily a good trend - - - the power of politics, controlling freedom of expression, in our media. Most would agree that, some controls would not be out of place, in extreme situations; but the case against Public broadcasting was purely, cheap, politics. Incidentally since these lines were written, that director who had been forced on to the board, had to resign, it had created so much discord! If there are controls, they should come from a multi-faceted, completely independent, agency, not the government!

Feature stories in motion pictures, often tackled controversial topics, perhaps, they started as a Hollywood 'creation', so to speak; these included, relationships between men, and women; men, and men; women, and women. According to producers, these subjects were important enough to explore on the screen, as long as people paid to see them. It was only a matter of time, before we saw partial, or total, nudity, on the screen, "because it was important for the story", said the producers. What nonsense! Next, we reached a point where a man, and a woman, had barely met, for the first time, when one, or the other, would ask, if they could go up to the residence, for a drink, may be? The scene would then move to the couple in bed! In this manner, serious, marital relationships, (till death do us, part), became trivialized, and morals were relaxed, even more, the slippery slope, to depravity. In the old days of the cinema, the couple, were either, already married; or, after a long period of courtship, you saw them enter the bedroom, the door closed behind them. *The rest was left to the viewer's imagination!* It soon came about, that, from Hollywood, amongst those in the world of art, and the elite, it became commonplace to hear, 'so, and so, was her partner, or his partner', no mention of husband, or wife. Another one was, 'they had one child, or two children, by their partner'! What a society, we have become. There were many cultures, wherein, polygamy was embraced; we used to look down, on such practices, and rejected them. But, have we done much better, in recent decades?

Teachers, psychologists, and church affiliated officials, had long maintained, that unstable home environments, such as, the two worker families, so prevalent in western society; single parent homes, divorce, unmarried couples, living together, and more; all these, had contributed to young children, developing, many problems, that could stay with them, for life. Some had also made a connection, with children from dysfunctional homes, going into drug habits, alcohol, crime, and suicide; and they themselves, could end up in unstable home environments, when they are fully grown, and independent. This writer had also discussed similar topics, in "Mirror Reflections=Mirages". It was therefore good news, for a change, to hear a '60 Minutes' program, on CBS, dealing with a study on an increasing number of women, in the US, who had decided to leave successful, well paying, jobs, to become 'stay at home mums'. According to researchers this trend is catching on, in America, and that is a good thing. Previous studies had shown that in 2 parent, worker, families, not enough attention was being given to the children, and they suffered. *Such a move, for women to return to the home, to look after the family, can only have, very positive results.* This, indeed, is one trend that the United States could export, to other countries, knowing that it could produce remarkably good results.

Also on the positive side, motion pictures, have tackled, topics, that might be hard, to sit through, but that could also impact our value system, as a society. Such topics included, stories from the bible, others, on wars, and those, on life experiences in prisons, and more. Many stories from the bible have been portrayed, over the years; a recent one, from 2004-'05, 'The Passion of Christ', created much debate and controversy, even before it was released for world viewing. Many in the Jewish community, launched protests, to try block its release, as they had raised objections, but the movie was very well received, worldwide. There were several movies, intended to stimulate social debate, on the harshness of prison life, on death row inmates, and on stories of those accused, and sentenced, but who were innocent of those crimes. Of war movies, there were many, on world war one, world war two, Korea, Vietnam; and many of these were not meant to glamorize wars; but rather, to drive home, the horrors, and tragedy, of war. One such movie, that had been highly acclaimed, was, "Saving Private Ryan", poignant, and graphic. *If it was hoped, with some of these movies, to awaken politicians, and governments everywhere, to the violence, and the evils, of wars, it had not succeeded, because we are still in the trenches, so to speak!*

Experiments have shown that, animals can be conditioned to some extent, and so can many individuals. One can then, extend that, by saying, that, if you feed animals 'garbage', a steady diet of it, they soon learn to like nothing, but garbage. Yes, call it, indoctrination, and, brain manipulation. Over a number of years, we have seen the rape of music, and dance, in so-called, 'modern entertainment'. There is nothing wrong with change, with innovation, but here, we are talking of extremes, of everybody trying to be like somebody else. How can producers of this stuff, call it entertainment? Alleged professionals have taken old, precious, melodies, ballet, musicals, and opera, and then, tried to adulterate them into swing, pop etc., it could be called, the rape of the musical score.

What has become of the lovely melodies, the lyrics, of bygone days? Composers have tried to produce modern ballet, and opera, but they were nowhere as well received, as the classics of golden years, the works of masters! Even in the era of the Beatles, and Elvis

Presley, they had plenty of hip swinging, rock-type, musical scores, but they also produced melodies with lovely rhythms, and lyrics that made sense, that fit in, very well. Whereas today, we hear substantial amounts of rap, and rave, hip-hop, with raunchy lyrics, and gyrations to match, *and, should these things, be honored with the title, music?* Many doubt that it is entertainment, either. It is true, modern society, has been indoctrinated, into that style, and laps it up. Our youth want more of it, and may bring the house down, with their shouting, and applause. Older people, as a rule, tend to lament those lost, golden, years, of music, and the theatre. So they try to make the transition, to present day charades, but it is a poor transition, at best, an imitation, of sorts.

Take an example of a modern live show in a theatre, or even on a much touted cruise ship, one run by a well, known, company. What do you get? One, and a half, hours, or more, of ear shattering sound (noise), flashing lights, banging, smoke, laser beams, and people shouting, arms flailing wildly, or punching the air, and legs kicking, necks jerking, in all directions; people on stage, jumping, and falling, with all joints, and other appendages, bending, and twisting, in all dimensions, in rapid, jerky, motion- - -and yes, screaming at all decibel levels! *This is, what is now called, 'a show, entertainment'; it is an insult to the arts, to call it, music, singing, and dance.* It is a travesty, perhaps, to also call it, entertainment. In the old days, ordinary singers, tenors, sopranos, baritones, all types, tried hard to have their voices project, to most of the audience. They used simple technology, to produce modest amplification, in larger theatres; in small, more intimate, theatres, you mostly heard their natural voices. It worked nicely, it was well received, it was art. That, was called, entertainment.

We call our present trend, progress, but, is it? We use all types of technology, to amplify the singers' voices, ten fold, a hundred fold, or more, and you no longer distinguish, what their natural voices, sound like. Add to this, a character, who sits, or stands, by a synthesizer, and you have produced, an ear drum damaging, brain shattering, deafening, mayhem. Yes, teens seem to love it all, because they buy the tapes, CDs, and videos, and keep companies in a lucrative business. Otherwise, the producers of such mediocre 'art' would quickly disappear, from the 'entertainment' scenario. Are staff workers in such theatres, deaf? Do customers, who constantly indulge in this stuff, damage the hearing apparatus? Indeed, some experts have answered in the affirmative.

What about the quality of sound? Many of us have sat through a long performance, where you get mostly, extremely loud notes, from various instruments. Again, is it 'music'? Nowadays, compositions must have a repetitious, monotonous, loud, drum, beat, more, or less, continuous; every other note must be a drum, beat; and, of course, there is no distinction, from one act, to the next! These monstrosities are advertised as music. It is a degradation of society, just as we have seen, degradation, in the entertainment industry. If that industry did what is right, it would not need to fear the government, imposing controls. They also insist on producing shows, containing extreme violence, or semi-nude, or nude, scenes; we have seen raunchy, suggestive, gestures; *and, of course, that ubiquitous, vulgarity, and four letter words, galore, and, even blasphemy!* All this, whether it is in movies, in live theatre, in videos, or on our television screens. In the US, and likely, elsewhere, in the west, it is now common to have sitcoms, the so-called 'soaps', on television, where, during periods in the conversation, you hear more 'beeps', than actual words. By law, the beeps replace vulgarities, to some degree. *Thus, most of the words, in some sentences, are now replaced by beeps, instead.* What purpose, does such extreme vulgarity, serve? How much worse will it get, before we do something about it? Again, it would be an insult, to call such depravity, entertainment, would it not? Do producers believe, that, it is the only way to attract an audience? If that is what audiences want, then, it is as has been stated, already, if you get accustomed to trash, all you will want is, trash!

A substantial percentage of the public, seem to approve, and legal authorities do not care much, or clamp down hard enough, on such behavior, because of the ideology of freedom of speech, and freedom of expression. If politicians want to make it a crime, (not freedom of expression), to insult, or to burn, a national flag, why is it not a much greater crime, to insult the religious beliefs of a group of people? Yet, we have seen such insults on screen, on stage, and in magazines, and recently, allegedly, in the military. *The paltry excuse, was, that it became expressive art!* It is true that, freedom of speech and freedom of expression, are highly desirable, and they are very precious; there are millions who do not enjoy them, today. *But, with that freedom, also comes, responsibility.* When these are carried to the wrong extremes, they must obviously be curtailed, to some extent. Moralists, theologians, religious ministers, and religious rights groups, do not condone, or welcome, these trends in behavior patterns; and, as a rule, they have a more conservative approach, to lifestyles. Many had concluded that, it was only the extremes, on the right, or on the left, that had caused problems for our society.

These trends in human behavior have often started in America, or other developed nations, the cultural, revolution, as it was called. Sociologists have long maintained that affluence, tended to lean towards gradual degradation, in many instances. Sometimes, the process started in other, less affluent, countries; but whatever the source, these practices soon influenced places like, the US, UK, Italy, Germany, France, Scandinavian countries, Australia, Canada; and, yes, even places, like, Russia, China, and Japan, traditionally, much more conservative nations. Even much smaller nations, like Malta, had been influenced. It is only a question of time, before such trends, spread even further, and it could produce a clash of cultures, indeed. It bears repeating, again, it is that important, if you expose our young people, to a steady diet of trash, they soon learn to appreciate, only trash; the downward spiral in social deterioration. Sociologists also blamed some of this, on one's environment, on parents, on teachers, on so-called, role model personalities. Some had assumed role model status, when they did not deserve it. Television, movies, radio, magazines, other media, and now, the ubiquitous, Internet, have all contributed to this disastrous malady.

Even the quality of service, in developed countries, has greatly deteriorated. Customers in places like US, UK, and others, had complained for years, that the quality of service had gone to pot. You can call a business, an appliance dealer, an automobile dealer, a manufacturer's warranty offices, insurance companies, financial institutions, anyone, and what do you get? Nowadays, you almost never hear a human voice answering, at the end of the line, no, you get a recording; and what does 'it' say? The voice says, 'they are very busy', *and all their professionals (may be one, or two?) are attending to other customers, to please stay on the line.* Then you are presented with an array of advertisements, and rotten music. With auto dealers, they inform you about how good they are; what a terrific car they can offer you; that, their sales staff, and their service, are the best. Then comes the clincher, they can diagnose all the problems with your car, and they recommend only what service is needed; and they only use genuine new parts (not rebuilt parts?). They add that, they would never tell you a part needs replacing, if it is not defective! *After all that, they add, that you will not have long to wait! Imagine!* The message repeats itself, and you wait, 10, 15, 20 minutes, or longer. You either hang up, or if you are endowed with patience, you listen to more trash.

Perhaps some are better than that, but why do they have to present you with such nonsense, to start with, and waste your precious time, if they are good, and honest? There have been many reports, in the US, and elsewhere, of businesses cheating, and deceiving their customers. It is amazing that governments, in developed countries, have allowed citizens to go through all that, to be taken for a ride, so to speak. As expected, during political campaigns, these businesses are quick with their financial contributions. How about, those corporate officials, who promote their products in advertisements, showing how well, their companies protect our environment, air, land, and water? The photography is grand, as are the comments, and before it is over, the viewer is almost convinced, that these companies had actually, improved considerably, on Mother Nature, since the early days of creation. Most of us have enough common sense, to realize that all the above are mostly, untrue; but then, why do politicians everywhere allow such fraud, and corruption, to go on? Is it the cozy relationship, between the corporate world, and politics?

Does anyone call what is described here, service, honesty, and integrity? Hardly, it is corruption in business, to the maximum. They also talk about corporate, and business, conventions, where many suspect, that a lot of discussion takes place, on how best to improve, the bottom line; perhaps, even if the rules need to be bent a little, here, or there.

Some years ago, there was an undercover, surveillance operation, on certain food markets; it was presented on television programs, and presumably, in newspapers as well. These reports alleged, that pieces of chicken, or meat, that fell on the floor, were promptly picked up by employees, and returned to the tray, as is, for the display case. Employees were watched, as they checked various items, on the shelves, in supermarkets, and they replaced labels with expired dates, with newer ones! Some salads in display cases, had contents that had changed color, and texture, and so on, after a period of time, were all these promptly discarded? No, on occasions, they apparently witnessed, fresh material brought in, to be mixed with the older product, and trays were then embellished, with fresh layers, on top. Most readers know quite well, how these industries work. Some businesses, if they have produce that is obviously rotting, do not immediately, throw it all out, but instead, they sometimes reduce the price, and try to sell some, or, most of it; and consumers may then feel, they are getting a bargain. That is alright, **if** you are properly advised, of what you are getting. We trust, not many companies do such things.

These activities can go on, even as government officials, inform the public that, the food industry is well regulated, and inspected, for the safety of their citizens. Regulated perhaps, *but is it well, regulated, and inspected?* From the above incidents, and they could represent, a drop in the bucket, does it sound like it is? Some companies may be very well run, but for many others, judging by such reports, there is a lot of improvement that is needed, on behalf of the people. This is another example of progressive, market capitalism, in our modern society.

As we are on the topic of food, society underwent a major switch some years back, with the advent of the fast food industry; and that, was to usher in, tremendous changes in the eating habits of many people, across the world. This type of degeneration also, started mainly in America, and was gradually exported to most parts of the world. It was, embraced, at first, by young people, but then, more, and, more, people, took to it. In a similar manner, the use of hot peppers, highly spiced foods, sushi, and other products, were exported from other countries, to the US; and they also caught on. We have seen companies grow remarkably well, such as, McDonald's, of hamburger fame; Wendy's, Burger King, Burger Queen, Taco Bell, Long John Silver, Subway, and many more. Then came different establishments, but still 'fast food' in style, Kentucky fried Chicken, Ponderosa Steak House, Pizza Hut, Sizzler Steak House, Steak and Shake, and dozens more, depending, often, on location. It was not long, before those eating places, became very popular with the younger generation, and later, with older generations; and also, with the poorer segments of society, as it afforded them the opportunity to eat out, and be able to afford it. The latter could seldom afford, the luxury, of more formal restaurants. The usual question of the haves, and the have not, the choice of establishment, we can afford; its influence on social patterns, and on life structures.

In the years following the invasion by the fast food industry, such eating places, were soon springing up, in Europe, Australia, Canada, Latin America, Japan, and many other parts of the world. The fast food, industry, also began to receive serious criticism, as a generally unhealthy, type of diet, especially when combined with inadequate exercise; too much fat, too much carbohydrate, too many calories! In Britain, they soon began, to experience obesity, which was unusual for that country, even amongst young people; and British critics, immediately, blamed, fast food, habits, imported from the United States. Over a number of years, in America, the percentage of overweight, and markedly obese individuals, rose sharply. This development, resulted in the emergence, of, many types of diet fads; and the number of persons needing stomach bypass surgery, was increasing. By 2004-2005, obesity, in America, was labeled an epidemic, by health authorities; and it soon led to serious health problems, resulting in a huge, health related, financial drain. .

We had long been accused, in the US, of being a litigious society; thus, before long, law suits were filed, against fast food companies, for enticing young people, to eat unhealthy foods. In spite of all that information, bad diet habits persisted, amongst our youth, and the poor, both in America, and elsewhere. Numerous books, and videos, on diet and exercise, and good health habits, appeared over the last several years. These had enriched, those who had produced, and, marketed them. But, for this group of people, who became enamored with this food, genuine solutions seemed out of reach. It required considerable dieting, and exercise, and much discipline, to succeed!

Eye opening, trends, in society, descended also, on the fashion industry. Over past decades, enormous changes came on the scene, some of them, hard to conceive. Ages ago, women were decked in large, hoop, skirts, and super tight corsets, to produce an appealing figure? Men displayed three quarter length coats, with long sleeved shirts, and fanciful cuffs, at the wrists; and colorful waistcoats. Yes, they had head wigs, in the past, both for men, and women; and these were worn regularly in 'social circles'. Whereas, today, wigs, are still in use, but only for specific purposes. There were, knee length, or ankle length, coats; knee high, or thigh high boots; ankle length boots; top hats, bowler hats, and more. Then, let us fast forward, to the 'mod' fashions, unleashed, on society; such as, decorative hose, or panty hose; mini skirts, they became shorter, and shorter; designer socks; sneakers of all types, color, material, air cushions, air holes, some even glowed in the dark, others, lit up, with each step taken! Shops had blouses with ever more, plunging necklines, some semi transparent; backs were even more plunging, towards the lumbar region.

What about the beach? There, we witnessed the transition, from, long sleeved, long legged, suits, to striped suits, to a shorter variety, but still, a full swimsuit. Then came the two piece swimsuit, which became shorter, and then very brief,, when it was called, the Bikini, because of the effect, it allegedly had, on the male sex. Some bikinis became so tiny, that they were nicknamed, postage stamp suits. Next, women were presented with the thongs; then came the topless; and soon, some women, did not bother, with any suit, at all, and went to swim, naked. Some countries were known to have beaches for nude bathers; where allowed by law; other countries were even more liberal, and had no specific assigned beaches.

In modern times, we also had the Jeans craze, some were decent, new, looking; others, appeared partially, or, completely, faded, as if they had been salvaged from the trash heap. On one occasion, we also saw a display window with a special sale 'washed out Jeans', and there was the sample, on view! Some specimens came with tears in the seat, or the knee, cap, region; others had frayed ends. All these, *were considered in style, and therefore quite pricey.* Then we saw shorts, or skirts, in similar styles, with faded areas, or holes, or frayed edges. Shoes began to assume a variety of colors, some were rounded, or pointed; for women, we had high heels, or short, or pedestal heels, broad heels, or stiletto types, often very pointed, risking, toe injury. Just when we thought we had seen it all, came the flip-flop fashions. Can they be called footwear? Yes, and these have been worn to all types of functions, apparently, even, where they were not supposed to, and were not welcomed. Before leaving the fashion mood, we must mention a more, recent, entry, in pants; in the past, we had baggy pants legs, and baggy pants derrière; then came, the baggy crotch, hanging down to the knees, with baggy thighs, and legs. Soon, thousands of the male youth were seen, wearing these, 'as suitable attire', even for school! Naturally, fashion creators could not care less, *because as fast as they changed styles, young, old, and, in between, mostly the young, rushed, to buy.* Inventors raked in, lots of money, in due course, they dreamt up another shocking style, and the cycle repeated itself!

Other trends, not always beneficial, for citizens in various countries, dealt with industry, with specific businesses, yet again, and of course, with governments, sometimes in collusion. In the so-called insurance sector, warranties are sometimes worthless, both in the US, and elsewhere. Business owners can brazenly cheat, by tempting customers with, *'lifetime warranty'! What does that mean?* They muddy the water even more, by not being specific, whether it is the 'life' of the product, the life of the buyer; surely it cannot be forever, because they would be out of business, but that is what is implied. Much of the time, when you try to have these cheats, for a necessary inspection, or repairs, of their 'warranty' product, you either do not hear from them; or you are given the run around; or it could take weeks, or months. Then they add, that they may be forced to charge fees, for the visit, or for labor, or both! Moreover, many of these companies who grant 'lifetime warranty', are found to have gone out of business. Because of ineptness in government circles, and the corruption of money, in politics, these practices are allowed to go on.

In years past, when many of us were much younger, advertising was perhaps, much more, honest. It was considered unethical, unprofessional, for members of the medical profession, to advertise to the public at large. Now, in newspapers, magazines, and even on television, you see ads, by doctors, and other professionals, that they can do such, and such, *implying that they are better, and very good, at it!* That is wrong, and likely, it has hurt the standing of the profession. Should it not be discontinued? There is also the pharmaceutical industry, often, with many politicians, in their pockets, so to speak! *The amount of advertising this industry carries out, in all media sources, has long been a scandal.* Besides praising their product, as if it was the ultimate remedy, for particular health problems, they never miss, suggesting to consumers, *that they should promptly talk with their doctors, about those products; are they suitable for them?* This is considered unprofessional, by many, and should be stopped. Moreover, all the advertising by these companies, likely costs, hundreds of millions of dollars. That cost, surely, is passed on to patients, in the scandalous cost of medicine, in the United States. When the industry is criticized, for maintaining high drug prices, they turn it around, and state, *they need it, to recover the cost of research, and development!* But, to some extent, is it not also corruption, unfortunately, with the backing of many, in government? *People at all levels, and the medical profession, will be served well, if the pharmaceutical industry, is kept in check; if all corporations, are kept, properly, in check.*

There was a recent report on California, in the US, on an initiative, that the drug companies wanted to have legislation passed, that would be much more favorable to them! Critics alleged, that they had spent over 100 million dollars, to have that initiative succeed, but voters there, soundly rejected the move. What is amazing is, that the US government, sees the above tactics, and many more, like them, and yet, *politicians permit these pharmaceutical companies, to charge obscene prices, for much needed medication.* In many cases, people cannot afford them. And, the drug industry is allowed, by uncertain legal principles, by the government, *to keep on claiming, that those prices are justified, because of their huge investments into research, and development! Is the above money, spent to have an initiative passed, by voters, is that, called, research, and development- - -?* These weaknesses in government agencies can be found anywhere. In recent months we had also witnessed, a great signing, photo, opportunity, for some of our politicians, when the prescription drug benefit bill, was forcefully legislated, for seniors, in America. By November 15, Medicare recipients were asked to start signing up for that program; but at the same time, news reports *showed that fully 60%, or more, of America's seniors, did not know what to do about that prescription drug program, they did not understand it, at all!* Is that not typical of government bureaucracy, they had their signing, and photo, opportunities, but the people did not matter, apparently.

In our media as well, some trends have been deplorable, and not in the interest of the public. We had referred to reports of the government, in the US, trying to influence, and control, public broadcasting, normally considered, completely independent, in the rest of the developed world. We had mentioned that a pro Bush administration director had been forced, on the board, of public broadcasting, but had since resigned, as he had created much controversy. However, he had already appointed another official to that board, who allegedly, had been very close to the Bush administration; *would they still call that, independent broadcasting?* During a discussion on C-Span television, the question of balance in the media was brought up. It was shown that most radio talk shows, in the US, were extreme right wing. There were hardly any, on the other side of the spectrum, to provide the opposite point of view. To the average listener, this did not sound much, like freedom of speech, freedom of expression. As if to emphasize the existing problems, with media, a headline on the Internet went like this, "How American media sell wars, spin elections, and destroy democracy". Sad, but how true, that is.

We have also seen the cell phone industry explode on the world market. In the US consumers were protected to some extent, by certain laws, for credit card fraud, For example, if large sums of money were charged to a stolen credit card, the owner was only responsible for a specified, small sum. Whereas, similar laws, for cell phone fraud, were non-existent. Thus, a cell phone owner could be responsible for thousands of dollars, if a cell phone was lost, or stolen, and was fraudulently used. A spokesman for citizen protection, said that the lucrative cell phone industry, wants to keep similar restrictive legislation, off the books, and therefore they donate generously to politicians, to keep such legislation from being presented, and they get what they want! Is that called corruption, or is it 'free market economy', as dictated, by pundits?

Other social habits that were declared injurious, to health, were addictions to alcohol, and tobacco, use. With time, these led to significant disease, cancer, stomach, and liver problems, bleeding, heart, and artery disease, lung disease, and more. Their impact on society is beyond comprehension. At first, there was immense denial from industry, and some politicians, on the harmful effects of tobacco; there were many special interest groups, involved, and people paid a terrible price. For many years now, alcohol addiction has been considered, a disease. But attitude, to tobacco, had many film stars, in the old days, always appearing with cigarettes in their mouth, or lighting one. Many of them died of cancer. Famed anchor newsman Peter Jennings, recently died of lung cancer, after a brief illness. He announced his illness, and reminded everybody of his past smoking habit, many years previously.

Society was also beset by an epidemic of drug abuse, and addiction, to both prescription drugs, and others, that were illegal. Many had died of overdose. Some of our youth also experimented with dangerous chemicals, to get a 'high'. This tragedy gradually spread to most parts of the world; but of the developed countries, the US with its vast population, was a major consumer of drugs. Thus, some drug lords, in poorer countries, were eager to increase production, for illegal export, to the US. The financial rewards, for these drug lords, were huge. In the west the drug habit had mushroomed a long time ago, but soon spread to countries, large, or small, rich, or poor, developed, or underdeveloped. In America, government bureaucracy created drug agencies, drug czars, with budgets running into the hundreds of millions of dollars. *Such sound bites, in speeches, might have made politicians, feel good, but they had little impact on the use of drugs!* Policies were directed at other countries, to get them to cease production of this contraband, for export. It was well known, that, for some of those countries, drug production and sales, were the only source of income for those people, and through corruption, some of that income, reached officials at all levels of their government. In the US itself, thousands of users were jailed, most often, from minority groups. But our government did a very poor job of educating young people, to try and convince them, that the habit could destroy their lives; to learn to 'say no, to drugs'. Therefore, as we were trying to force others to cease production, they, in turn, accused, that we were not doing a great job, in decreasing demand, amongst our own people!

These drugs came by injection, by inhalers, by tablets or capsules, of all sizes and colors; such names as Speed, LSD, Cocaine, Heroin, Uppers and Downers, Amphetamines, Marihuana, Oxycontin, Ecstasy, Codeine, and many more. Other types were concocted in basements, and other, makeshift laboratories. As time passed many young people were getting seriously ill, and addicted, and many died prematurely. In America politicians responded by declaring drug use illegal; and certain drugs were only permitted by a doctor's prescription, for specific purposes. Drug users, and pushers, were hit with harsh jail sentences. But according to critics of this system, those with power, connections, and money, did not receive similar harsh treatment by the government. In the entertainment industry, rumors were common, that some of them, 'kept going', by day, and by night, because of drugs in their system. Some other countries were as harsh as the US, or worse;

yet, others, were more lenient, providing clean, safe, syringes, and needles, to users; many had free clinics, to provide medical assistance, and supervision, to help addicts stay off drugs. Others, made Marihuana legal, and a few others legalized the use of certain drugs, for cancer sufferers. Most countries tried to improve their campaign against drug use, but in spite of all efforts, this tragedy persists in our society.

It has been obvious for some time, that for most nations, the control of drug abuse, has been a lost battle, partly because corruption thrived at all levels, in some governments, as drug pushers, and traffickers, became multimillionaires, almost overnight, at the expense of others. They were thus able to influence politicians, in some countries. In the US, an ominous wall grew up, out of the paranoia, over security of borders; this, to control the crossing of illegal immigrants; the illegal importation of drugs, and other contraband; and to stop those entering, with intentions of acts of terrorism. But in the eyes of critics, this separation wall, between the US, and Mexico, projected ugly connotations, of the dividing wall between East, and West, Berlin; of the wall Israel has built, to shut in, the Palestinian people; and of the Apartheid philosophy of the old South Africa, No, the US wall had nothing attractive to justify its progress; but some of the right wing, extreme groups, were clamoring for a higher, and a longer wall! Some citizens apparently, had nothing better to do, and decided to behave like vigilantes themselves, along that wall! A logical question would be, to ask why authorities would permit such behavior? These people patrolled that border, and more, or less, would take the law into their own hands. Regrettably, some politicians were in agreement with these people; whilst, most experts doubted if such a wall, could have any impact on the drug crisis in the US.

The drug abuse, crisis, has obviously generated, extensive work, for the legal profession, and the justice system. We have touched upon advertising, and we cannot leave the section of trends in society, without reminding readers, of the extensive advertising business that attorneys get involved in. The legal profession as well, has been very active in marketing their profession, to the public, their special expertise in the field of law, and so on. They come at you, in telephone books, by the dozen, and frequently on television, and other media. You hear the advice that you should never settle a particular case, 'before talking to us'; if you have been injured in an accident; if you have been wronged, 'do not say, or sign, anything, before calling us; the first consultation is free'; and much, much, more. We had already mentioned, that, the US had long been considered, the most litigious country in the world, and therefore, large numbers of people embrace law, as their chosen profession. Some critics have accused certain lawyers of being 'ambulance chasers', implying that they were perhaps encouraging, and, seeking persons, they can persuade, to file law suits, after accidents; after an untoward medical outcome; and many other types of wrongdoing, or even corporate mishaps. Following the securities scandals, in the United States, hundreds of lawsuits were filed. A tense atmosphere had developed between the medical, and legal, professions, because of the perception that, medical malpractice lawsuits had mushroomed, because of aggressive, and perhaps unethical, lawyers, encouraging patients to file suits, on the slightest excuse. Some critics even accused lawyers of directly, or indirectly, soliciting business, from prospective clients.

An example that is often, quoted, is that, of childbirth; but there are many others, in different fields, as well. If there is a congenital anomaly, a birth defect, of any type, it has been alleged, that sometimes, lawsuits are filed against doctors, and hospitals, even though there was no act of malpractice, but simply, a natural phenomenon. Physicians have tended to blame frivolous lawsuits, and skyrocketing, malpractice, awards, for the often, unaffordable, malpractice insurance premiums, physicians have been forced to pay. So much so, that many had retired from the medical field prematurely; others, had decided 'to go bare', that is, carry no malpractice insurance. It has been debated many times, that these events, had rendered medical care in the US, the most expensive in the world; millions of our citizens, have been unable to afford decent care; there is inequality in the accessibility of medical care; and many have also claimed, that it has made, health care in America, inferior, when compared to some other, developed, countries. *What have we done, to that once noble profession, Medicine?*

Readers must think for a moment, as they go through this section, on social trends, does it not mirror a serious decline, in the values of our society, of a nation, or nations? No, *we are not talking of 'values', as mouthed by government officials, and extreme right wing groups, when they verbalize 'values'; when they give them, only lip service; but then, they demonstrate their true colors, by what they say, or by their actions!* We had previously referred to the decline, and fall, of empires; that America had been behaving like an empire, not a welcome one, at that. It was bishop Fulton Sheen who, in one of his programs, had compared the civilizations, of the 'west', and the 'east'. He put it succinctly, and in a way, it could explain many of the problems facing society; current problems between 'east', and 'west', often aggravated by inept politicians, on both sides. He said, in the west, we have *love, but without sacrifice, without mortification, without self, denial, (do we really, know, what that, is, sacrifice, and self, denial?); he continued, but in the east, they have a culture of sacrifice, without love.* That may be an oversimplification, but when we consider the mess in our world, some of its truths, may become self, evident!

The future cannot look particularly bright, unless we are prepared to make the right choices, make hard decisions, and start acting, appropriately. Leaders, wherever they are, cannot possibly be, on the right track, when they say 'we believe we are right', 'we feel right about our actions'; but then, they proceed to do terrible things! We need stronger efforts to stamp out corruption, at all levels of government, in all nations, wherever it exists. *Not an easy task, but a worthwhile goal to aim for, and to achieve.* It had never been accomplished, that is why humanity had suffered, to such a degree, as our planet had continued, on the path of one crisis, after another. Simply consider these, all the wars, all the violence, natural disasters; hunger, poverty, disease; rivalries, and hate, frictions of all sorts; rampant corruption, and dishonesty, and much more! There has been tangible progress in some areas, but in others, what we have called 'progress', had turned into a mirage, a disaster! *We must set higher standards for everybody, and try to abide by them, and do better; learn from past mistakes.*

VALUES IN OUR SOCIETY

A humanitarian disaster in Niger, Africa, was featured on a CNN television program, when reporters pointed out, that, bureaucracy in many African countries, was very complex, and the infrastructure in some of those countries, most inadequate. Many of their children were dying. A woman had walked from her village, to obtain some free grain, which was being distributed in a nearby village; one of her three children had already died from starvation, and its complications. Guest speakers stated that for some of those people, such walks could be several miles long, and they would be in no condition for such a journey, At first, this woman was told *she did not belong to that particular village community, she should await her turn, in her own village.* But, as she continued to plead her case, before the cameras, officials relented, and she received her portion of grain.

Some months before this, warnings had been issued by the United Nations, that a crisis in Niger, was on the horizon; and that this, was not the only African country, facing such disasters. A few were able to publicize their plight, because of photographs appearing in western media; but many others had no such publicity. One of the comments was, that in spite of such dire warnings, from the UN, no major assistance had been rushed to those needy people, especially from western countries. Should we not all question, why some western governments, had not stepped up, to the plate, not as much as they could have? This, to save lives, lost needlessly from malnutrition; but at the same time, those governments *had billions of dollars to waste on weapons of death and destruction, and on immoral wars!* The reports continued that, some three and a half million people were in danger of dying; and 800,000 of them, were children. Previously cattle had thrived, but because of the famine, their herds were dying as well; and many of the local people could not remember when the last meal was! There was lack of rain, as is often the case, in those regions, and, doctors without borders, responded early, but could not do enough by themselves. The population was mostly Muslim, and it was a former French colony. Many felt that the Niger government was at least partially responsible. One particularly telling, heading, read, 'Starving, in plain sight', by Anderson Cooper. Reporters showed that, as their government was distributing a little food, they were also demanding payment, to show the degree of corruption in some of those politicians!

A PBS news hour report was even more disturbing, because those people were desperately poor; and even if food was available, for sale, in a nearby market, they could not afford to buy anything! What would be the moral thing to do, *give those persons the food they needed, or watch them die, because they could not pay for it?* Local citizens apparently, did not care enough, and neither did those, who were well off. Another expert, on that same program said, that only 300 million dollars, a year, had recently been provided to help out; and of that, *the US contributed about 15 million!* America, please note, they said 15 million, *to help these desperately poor people; when we spend well over 450 billion dollars, per year, on weapons, on the military, and much more, on wars!* That point, cannot be emphasized often enough! It is surely, a glaring question of values, and of morality; of how that word, values, has often been misused, in western countries, by people, both in, and out of, government.

These crises, in parts of Africa, had been recurring for some years, famine, drought, locust infestations, or other calamities. They had suffered under their colonial rulers; then, citizens in those countries had passed, from one corrupt dictator, to another. They suffer now, because richer nations were often too slow, to respond, when disasters strike. The people of Niger were considered amongst the poorest in the world, with a high illiteracy rate; and therefore, they do not understand how to handle bureaucracy. In their culture, *they also tend to believe, that they are being punished, for the sins of their forefathers.*

As if to shock us out of our complacency, about the happenings in our world, there was another contrasting piece of news, on Malibu beach, California, in the US. It appeared that, the extremely wealthy people, with their mansions, by the sea, had tried to keep the beach all to themselves; they tried to keep the public from getting there, by blocking access lanes passing by their properties. People kept up the fight, and the courts, in California, sided with the public, on this one; that, those beaches, were there, for everybody, they were not private beaches! In other areas, the wealthy would likely get away with such schemes. Another commentary was that, the police tended to use rough tactics, when dealing with rowdy teenagers in poorer neighborhoods; whereas when it happened in rich, upper class, neighborhoods, the police used a more lenient approach. These are examples in glaring contrasts, between recent reports on the tragedies of Africa, 'the have not'; and the excesses, that can come out of wealthy sectors, 'the have too much', around our world.

When travelers visit third world countries, they soon learn that, most of the people living there, love their country, just as those in the west, love theirs. Yes, there is much deprivation, but those people learn to live without the excesses, and the waste, found in western society. At the same time, we might discover that third world countries have their own groups, of the elite, with more wealth, and power, just as is found in wealthier nations. Even, as the vast majority of their citizens, live under appalling conditions. Whenever church groups visit sister parishes, in these poor countries, on mission work, they invariably report, that they themselves, gained much more, from the experience, of being with those poor people, than any benefits they were able to give.

Similar trends could be found in ancient cultures as well, such as the temple people. Their social structures allowed for a group of the elite, to be better off, and thus, exercised more power, than the rest. Some of them also felt the need to live at a higher altitude, than the rest of the community, as had been deduced from archaeological findings, on the Mayan civilization; the rich, and the poor, the powerful, and those not so powerful. Like distributions in social status, were found in other ancient civilizations, such as Egypt, and before them, the temple people of Malta, 2000 to 4000 years B.C. Thus, the culture of the 'elite', lording it, over peons, is as old as history itself! A similar system, of sorts, existed probably, during the different stages of development, in human beings, on this earth; when various tribes roamed a sparsely populated planet, even back to the cavemen period.

Thus, those with the capacity to exert influence, or acquire crude weapons, (status symbols, for them), were considered the 'important ones'. They had clubs fashioned from animal skeletons, or some type of sharp instrument, made into the prototype of the spear; some used rocks; the early weapons of injury, and death. Some of it was obviously meant for hunting, or for protection from marauding animals. But, soon, they were being used for combat. The history of violence, uprisings, murder, betrayal, is as old, as humans, on this earth.

In Europe, and other regions, so-called centers of civilization, one group, or clan, pitted themselves against another, the barbarians from the north, against those, 'more, civilized' from the south. Once more, the great example, of the downfall, of the Roman Empire, comes to mind. This trend continued to develop, when later through history, clans, or the elite, and powerful, owned most of the land; they built their own army of fighters; and they enclosed themselves inside towers, or castles, or small hamlets surrounded by fortifications. These overlords virtually 'owned' all the people under them. The mentality then, was, to fight off a usurper, an invader; are we not still doing the same today? Different methodology, but the purpose remains the same, conquer, and subdue, and change boundaries. An old example, of the clash of civilizations, the east, and the west, was the Crusades, famous, or infamous, for its time. Then, sometimes misguided, Christian leaders of Europe, walled themselves in, behind fortifications, bastions, scattered over the Mediterranean regions. This, to fight off, equally misguided leaders, and their armies, of the Ottoman Empire. Many such bastions have been preserved, in Rhodes, Cyprus, Malta, and elsewhere; the purported romantic story, of the Knights of St. John of Jerusalem, Knights of Malta. There again, regrettably, stories have been told, of acts of brutality, by both sides.

Elsewhere in this book, we have written about persisting tiers, in the social ladder, today, in most countries, east, or west, developed, or underdeveloped. As if to confirm that point, a communication arrived recently, from the Columban Fathers, who support missions in several countries. It referred to Pakistan where, in spite of social progress made, Catholics there, remained relegated, to a minority social group, traditionally found employed in the lowest jobs, such as street sweeping. *They lived with a certain stigma, and so, children could easily pick up prejudices.* Building bridges between social groups had become an important part of mission work! Missionaries had unfortunately, also been murdered, because of their efforts, and guidance, provided. They pointed out how missionary schools in Pakistan, did not restrict enrollment to Christian students alone; but a significant number of Muslim students also attended, the building of bridges! However, it was reported that even in Pakistan, Christian schools must offer courses on Islam, by government decree. They also emphasized that religious intolerance was prevalent in Pakistan society; it was also experienced, in India; and it was a growing problem for our world. For many years, we had heard of a lack of religious freedom in places, like oil rich, Saudi Arabia, although it had remained friendly with the west; and, at the other extreme, we had the warring factions, of protestants, and Catholics, in Northern Ireland.

When describing morals, and values, some people state that they believe in certain actions, that they are doing the right thing. But that does not necessarily mean that those actions were right, that it was moral, no matter how many times they repeat such statements. Sometimes people, knowingly, adopt evil, as a means to a good ending; and though they might feel good about the ending, we have often heard that it is not moral, to use evil, as a means to a good end. Is it not still wrong, no matter how one tried to disguise it? Bush, and Blair, had often stated that what they did in Iraq was right, because they wanted to bring freedom, and democracy (the end) to the region, although that was only their excuse, right? But, they used evil, an immoral, unjust, war, with death and destruction, to achieve that 'good end'. Therefore, it was wrong, as Iraq was not attacking, or threatening, the US, and UK. What was done, *can never be called right or moral, no matter how many people said, they believed it!* And propaganda, and distortions, will not change that fact!

Another significant, controversial issue is the question of abortion, when we discuss morals, and values. Prima facie, the taking of a life is never 'good', never moral; and in that regard, arguments have also been extended, and debated, on the taking of innocent life in war; and the taking of life in prisons. So much so, that most civilized nations have done away with death penalties, in their judicial system, but the US is not one of them! Author Sister Helen Prejean, in a "A Voice for the Forgotten", in the St. Augustine Catholic magazine, had some inspiring words for all of us; and she had recently published a new book, "The Death of Innocents". She described how she had become spiritual advisor to two condemned men, and accompanied them to their executions. It was striking that, from her contact experience with them, she firmly believed they were innocent. And she called the inequality of the American judicial system, **the machinery of death.** Powerful! She discussed how Pope John Paul II, viewed the death penalty 'in the same light as the other life issues, such as abortion, assisted suicide-'. Another stunning statement she made was, that, only *a deeply violent society, following a morally bankrupt policy, would tell a victim's family 'we are going to kill the one who killed your loved one, and you get to sit in the front row and watch it'! Again, these are most thought provoking words.* Leaders in government, everywhere, should take such words as these, by Sister Prejean, debate them with a clear conscience, and attempt to change the course of mankind, for the better.

Those on the extreme right seem to pick, and choose, what suits them, when it comes to talk on morals, and values. Thus, they come out against abortion (pro life), which is correct; but where were they, when it came to the Iraq war, and nuclear weapons proliferation, and the use of biochemical weapons, the saving of thousands of lives, by choosing peace, instead of war? Why were they not marching in the streets by the millions, as they did in the rest of the world? And what about their voices, being heard, loud, and clear, on the death penalty; and on the injustices that persist, here at home, and around the world. The pro-abortion group, euphemistically, called, pro-choice, provide many reasons for their standing, the health of the mother; this is not the right time; we cannot afford another child; that there was a rape; that this pregnancy was not planned; and many of them even question if, at the earliest stages, a foetus, should be called 'life', a person. Most of these reasons have been around for years. There is no 'choice' here, that is a terrible word to use; the choice of these people should have been about protections against an unwanted pregnancy, if that was the path they wanted to follow. Surely, there are many opportunities, and methods, of contraception, that they should have been familiar with. But even contraception, presents a moral dilemma, because in some faiths, it is considered immoral, a sin. However, in the modern era of two worker families, nobody considers the large families of old, with 6, 8, or more, children. Today, one to four children, is considered sufficient, for a family. Hence, there is family planning, according to natural cycles in the female. It does involve self, discipline, and denial of self, something western society has forgotten a long time ago. Thus, the facilitation of abortion has played into the hands *of the 'me society', and materialism, they take precedence, most of the time, in decisions people make.*

The choice of the pro-abortion group, should therefore, have been, about the lifestyle they wanted to adopt. If there were instances of abortion, for discussion, where it is still a serious, and a hard decision, from a humanitarian point of view, these would be, pregnancies as a result of rape; or if a pregnancy is actually endangering the life of the mother, and two persons, instead of one, would die. However, from a moral, theological, viewpoint, that is still the taking of a life, and therefore, for many, unacceptable. As long as human beings are, as they are, debates about when life, actually begins, will go on; but for some faiths, the start of life, has been accepted as the time of conception. Now, that modern technology has made possible, the concept of test tube fertilization, *it has muddied the issue even more, since that is not the natural environment of the mother's womb, and therefore, debates are likely to intensify, amongst scientists, and theologians.* Mankind, as we know, only too well, has interfered with nature too many times, not only in the assaults on our environment!

On another 'Now' program, with David Broncaccio, on Public broadcasting, guests discussed the increasing frustration expressed, by Americans, with journalism, or our lack of journalism. They blamed it on politicians, and media owners, *striking deals behind closed doors, in Washington; but, obviously, it goes on in other countries, as well. Is that called, democracy?* They said, this was not a conservative, or a liberal issue, *it was an American issue, and democracy was at stake!* These topics have been discussed often, both within this country, and abroad, that is, the poor caliber of reporting, in the US. They pointed out how, over here, most people claimed that, 'reporting in their particular region', was the worst, in the whole country. *In that case, it must be pretty bad, everywhere, right?* They reemphasized how when overseas media had forcefully questioned the Bush arguments for the Iraq war, for example, media in the US, were fully pushing the Bush-republican agenda; why, because media owners were, more or less, in the pockets of the republican hierarchy. All, that, is so disconnected, from the true meaning of freedom of the press, and democracy; from the way they are supposed to be!

One cannot talk of values in societies, without commenting again, on corruptions in governments at all levels; and in businesses and corporations. Some of these have been covered in other sections of this book; and some, in a previous publication, "Mirror Reflections = Mirages". But corruption has been ubiquitous, and therefore is encountered everywhere. However, lest we conclude that it has only been a recent phenomenon, Harry Caudill, from the US, referred to it, in "Night Comes to the Cumberlands". He described quite vividly, the status of the haves, and the have not; and the flagrant corruption in government, and amongst officials in corporations - - - *and these reports were about events in the early 1900's!*

What other assaults on social values have we faced in recent times? Tattoos came on the scene- - tattoo parlors had sprung up, everywhere, in many parts of America, and elsewhere. The practice of tattooing had been around since most of us were kids, many years ago. And in native cultures, the aborigines of Australia, the native, American Indians, and others, in the old days, were already using derivatives extracted from nature, to paint faces, and other parts of their bodies. This was usually done in preparation for certain rituals, or in preparation for combat. White, and red (ochre), were commonly used colors, but there were others. Such colors have also been found in primitive paintings, in caves, and in pre-historic temples from ancient times.

In our younger days, it was often said that, the lower sectors of society resorted to the practice of 'tattoos'. Indeed, tattoo parlors were not prevalent then; and it was more often seen in the armed forces, around many parts of the world, and particularly in sailors. In recent years, this 'tattoo expression' had increased dramatically; and not to be outdone, women too, adopted this 'fashion', or fad. Although it had expanded across all segments of society, by the late twentieth century, it had remained primarily a function of the lesser educated, segments, of society. And now, it is not applied only to arms and legs; in the old days, it was predominantly the arms. Today, they have used all areas of the chest, abdomen, back, buttocks, *and places in between. That is a sad statistic, but true;* are they all really, making an expression, of some type? Sad, because many of these modern applications, unlike in ancient times, are more permanent. Now, there are also 'applicable' tattoos that can easily be removed. But the former technique of tattoos had rendered them, almost impossible to remove, except perhaps, by certain types of skin surgery. Then, there was always the risk of disease transmission, such as Hepatitis, and other serious illnesses, through needles, instruments, and so on.

We have also witnessed bizarre hairstyles, 'skin heads', 'razor heads', 'blockheads', heads suggesting, that they had been struck, by a bolt of lightning, and more. Hair coloring as well, came on the scene, no, not the customary blonde, brunette, or redhead; but yellow, green, blue, orange, multicolor, etc. Many believe, that, when people talk of values, such fads must also be considered. Next, another onslaught hit society, that of body piercing, again this appeared mostly, in the poorer, lesser educated, sectors, of the communities. It was not simply the standard pierced ears, for earrings. Historically, in certain native cultures, they had also adopted the custom of body piercing, many years ago, nose, tongue, ears, etc. But the craze that took over western society, in recent history, was, again, an expression of sorts, by the youth in our society. It rendered possible, multiple, ear piercing, some being quite large, not simply, tiny holes; piercing of the tongue, nose, chin, navel, eyebrows, breasts, and other areas. *Reading all this, some are bound to ask, had society lost it? Readers will have to judge for themselves, as they go through some of these pages, because society has certainly been buffeted by too many storms, in recent years.*

Also, many years ago, a wave of immorality, became entangled in the social fabric of some countries, perhaps mainly from the 'west'. That was orgies, with multiple couples, exchanging sex partners. Oh, yes, some will no doubt exclaim that, it is old stuff, because they had similar activities, in ancient Rome! *Yes, but the point here, is, that in its final years, Rome had become decadent, and it ushered in, the downfall of that once glorious empire!* Have we seen the writing on the wall? Have we looked at the mirror lately? Some claimed that it was the upper crust of society, that had decided to experiment with such dubious behavior, and again, Hollywood, became a target, as being a terrible example, for society to emulate. Obviously, in those days, people had not yet heard of that word AIDS, and therefore, we cannot but wonder, even though some people had poor concepts of 'values', and morality, would the fear of AIDS have induced them to reject such lifestyles? They might not have heard of AIDS, but the presence of other sexually transmitted diseases, was already, common knowledge, back then.

With regard to social attitudes, and behavior, a pastoral letter of 1986, by US Catholic Bishops, was entitled "Economic Justice for All". It was comprehensive, thought provoking, and an excellent guide, for all of us, to work for the common good, for the nation, and for our world. Now, twenty years later, *we sadly realize that most of the problems outlined in that letter, are still with us today,* **some had worsened considerably!** Twenty years, and we had made such little progress?

That letter outlined, how the American experiment had involved conflict, suffering, the injustices to Native Americans, a revolution, slavery, a violent civil war, and more! And gradually came the attempts to change the structures in this country, both political, and economic. They reminded us how the US was now in a global economy, and we all shared a common environment, an environment that had been under serious attack. Amongst the unemployed, a larger percentage was from the Black, and Hispanic, communities; and poverty was already on the increase. And we now realize that these had only grown worse! 'Harsh poverty had persisted in spite of our great wealth', they said; and, they added, *'for a people believing in progress, this should be cause for alarm'. Yes, it was the late Pope John Paul II, who had always spoken on behalf of the poor- - -!*

The Bishops focused our attention on the disparity between income, and consumption, by some, when many others, have so little to live on; how, exclusion from social life, can result, eventually, in restriction of freedom of speech, greater power in the hands of, just a few, *and repression by the state.* Surely, these specters, mentioned in that pastoral letter, are with us now, as outlined in this book! Again, Pope John Paul II, in one of his talks in Canada, in 1984, had reiterated *that the needs of the poor should be considered before the desires of the wealthy - - - -!*

To drive home the serious problem of poverty, these Bishops showed, that, the number of children, living under poor circumstances, had increased substantially, and that, Black youth, were three times more likely, to grow up in poverty, than White youth. And again, such statistics, twenty years later, were the same, or actually worse! We have been shown how homelessness had been affecting more women, and children, as well. Where is all the progress, so glibly flaunted by some politicians on the right, usually republican? *They have obviously looked at life through rose, colored, glasses; or they go around with blinders on.*

Another disturbing item in that pastoral letter, was that in the US, we had lagged behind most industrialized nations, in providing resources for development assistance, to third world countries; and that we cared less than before, about such causes! How often have we heard such announcements? In 2005, we have been hearing more of the same, *that, we were practically at the bottom of the heap, in the percentage of GDP that we provide for global aid!* We readily announce that we are the world's richest, and strongest economy, but we do not care, to do enough, to help our brethren! Yet, another challenge, was, that recent Popes, had strongly supported the United Nations, as an important step, in the formation of the global community; and our republican side of the aisle, with some democrats, had often been outspoken **against the United Nations.** They noted how, the US had taken steps to weaken, rather than strengthen, multinational approaches. Our fellow Americans must consider, that, these statements were uttered 20 years ago, and look at where we are today; look at what America did in Iraq! *No, nothing has really changed, but in some respects, it has worsened - - -!*

The Bishops also pointed out that, as our world had become so complex, we might be tempted to find self-centered solutions, the 'me society'. They warned that rising military expenditures, everywhere in the world, *should engender fears for the future of our planet.* If this was stated twenty years ago, can readers imagine, how much larger military expenditures, we have wasted, on the military machine, since then? Yes, indeed, and what about the impact, of that increased military spending, on our economy, on our culture, on the stability to our fragile, and uncertain, peace?

Economy: The economies of many nations have been stagnant, at best; for the United States, it had been in terrible shape for a few years. Only recently had it shown some signs of life; but for the majority of Americans, it had remained in the doldrums. Oil prices continued to climb, our citizens continued to accumulate more, and more, debt; and more Americans were experiencing difficulties, with paying bills on time. The Bush administration had been claiming progress on the economic front; yes, jobs had been created, but they were mostly service sector jobs, and most economists said these were low paying jobs, replacing higher paying jobs that had been lost! The US dollar had plunged significantly in value, against the Euro and the yen. In October 2005, an economist had a circular on the Internet, where, he pointed out that the US role as a world leader, would soon be challenged, by the rest of the world; that other countries would soon replace the US, as purchasers of oil from the Middle East; and that the dollar would be voted out of office, and currencies linked to the dollar, would become unacceptable. As many would agree, this is a very bleak picture, for the US, if it came to pass.

The deficits of the United States are enormous, and have been steadily climbing in recent years. Economists are seeing danger signals, as foreigners start investing less in US equities, and treasuries; and more Americans are seeking investments overseas; and gold prices had continued to climb! The stock market had never recovered the heights of the late 1990's; and the Federal Reserve in the US, had a difficult period trying to keep the economy stimulated. It has been suggested often enough, that, as global economies are intertwined, if it remains stagnant in the US, it will act on the rest of the world. As economies had recovered mildly, the cost of living in much of Europe, and Japan, was quite high, and gasoline prices in the US had reached over $3 a gallon, and those same prices in Europe, had been at least twice as high.

Some major companies had continued to plan in late 2005, to lay off more workers. In the US, General Motors announced the lay off, of some 30,000 workers, and the closure of some of its plants. This was ominous, for such a major company. Japan reported that it would consider raising prices on its cars in America, to help these US companies, lest they go under. *Imagine that, Japan, coming to the rescue of US companies. The world had certainly changed!* Many corporations were having serious difficulties with their pension plans that were not properly funded; and on 'Now', a PBS television program, guests discussed precisely such a topic; that, many American companies do not put aside, funds, as required by law. When employees are ready to retire, they get the run around, from their bosses; people face many hurdles, and then they get, much less, than what was promised them, or what they thought they were going to get, in their pension checks. Many corporations also wanted to change their health care commitments, to their employees, signs of more trouble in the US economy! Regrettably, a republican controlled congress, and administration, in the US, usually sided with corporations, in these matters, not with 'we the people'! Thus, when our officials, at the highest levels, talk of values, or morals, these are the factors that Americans need to consider, and hold up, before them. And, when officials, or corporate executives, state that a war (as they did for Iraq) *might stimulate an economy, that was in poor shape, where are the 'values', or 'morals', in such a statement?* Yes, indeed, we have tremendous corruption!

US, airlines, faced their own crises as well, some of them losing large sums of money, because of soaring gasoline prices, and going into bankruptcy; oil, at well over $60 a barrel, had hit them hard. Here, too, executives were asking congress to allow them to cut back, on employee health care benefits, and to make changes in pension plans as well. Corporate executives always try to solve problems through their workers. In other words, they wanted to cut back on employee benefits, but there was little talk of scaling back, on, obscenely huge, salaries, and benefits, of CEOs, and on all their perks. This seemed to be acceptable with the present government, in America. It is likely that in 2005, many corporations, in different countries, found themselves in the situation, where they had promised their employees a certain level of retirement, but then the workers found themselves with fewer benefits than they had anticipated, because of shaky economies. Some officials in the US, and others, amongst the elite, including Greenspan, according to reports, had been applauding the strong economy, just as jobs continued to be cut, and outsourcing of work to other countries, was increasing. Do, those, elite, wherever they are, talk to the average Americans, those in the trenches, to see if they felt that their economic situation was strong? They are not likely to seek views from ordinary folk, because they prefer to propagate half truths, and exaggerations.

An economics professor, appearing on a program, said that Americans had embraced *materialism,* they spend more than they earn; and therefore many of them are living with negative cash flows, with their debts increasing. A well, known, TV personality, Suze Orman, with her program on economics, was always advising young Americans to tighten their belts, *to strive harder to live only within their means, and get out of debt,* if necessary, by tearing up their credit cards! Many now talk of a housing bubble, getting ready to burst, similar to the stock market bubble of a few years ago. Matthew Biggs, in the correspondence section of 'America' magazine, dealt with 'truths', something that could apply to many aspects of society, including our presentations, within these pages. He said 'on the right, a growing number of thinkers, and activists, *privately conceded the absence of truth'! The absence of truth - - - in how many facets, of our political sphere, have we been witnessing that, the absence of truth?* How about that, America? Have we not been running into that malady, both here, and abroad?

Our magnanimous US government under the Bush administration, in November 2005, struggled, with, budget reconciliation activities. We said magnanimous, because this government is unbelievable; republicans wanted cuts in social programs, such as food stamps, education, healthcare; at the same time, they wanted more tax cuts for the wealthiest Americans, as well as making those cuts, permanent! This is scandalous, it is immoral, and it confirms the absence of true 'values', in present government circles. Surely, some of these people need to look up the definition of 'values'. We are not condoning the practice of permanent government give away, to foster a section of society behaving like parasites, wanting things, for nothing. We have promoted all along, equal opportunity for all, especially in education, and job availability; and a helping hand to all who are down, to help them, when they are really in need, to get back on their feet. All we need to do is look at the aftermath of Katrina, to realize what we mean!

On the PBS 'Now' program, with David Broncaccio, more scandals emerged on storm ravaged New Orleans, after the hurricanes, and the reconstruction that would be needed.

A law had been set aside by the administration; according to that law, certain workers had to be paid $28 per hour, but the law was suspended because of the aftermath of hurricane, Katrina. This gave cover, for contractors not hiring local workers, in New Orleans, because they would have to be paid those higher wages. Instead, they hired illegal immigrants, and paid them about half the legally required pay, and the companies could pocket the difference! It was reported that these 'undocumented workers', were bussed to their jobs, and they were housed in camps that were run like a prison, with guards! What was a greater evil was, when workers stated, *that, even the paltry checks, they had been promised, were often short! Many of the workers were made to sleep in large trailers, with layers of bunks in them, and no windows!*

Did the Bush administration realize what evils were unleashed, for post Katrina work, by this gross abuse of human beings, the undocumented immigrant? Once again discussants reported how Halliburton (Cheney's former company) had received lucrative contracts for work in New Orleans! Why, was not Iraq, lucrative enough, for Halliburton- - -? One Latino worker lamented the fact, that, they were treated in such a manner; as all they had done was, to offer their labor, for the reconstruction of New Orleans. Thus, they could earn some money, to send to families, that they were forced to leave behind. On this, an Afro-American commented how these poor people were being abused again, just like the black population had been abused, for years, in America's past!

Those on the right, find it easy, and indeed, quite cheap, to talk of values, and morals. But, as is often stated, when you have to place your actions, where your mouth is, that is a different story. In August 2005 members of the Afro-American community, planned street marches, to commemorate advances they had gained through civil rights struggles. Several thousand marched in Atlanta, Georgia, and other places. They pointed out that *some of the voting rights they had gained, in the 1960's legislation, were due to expire soon. And they feared that the right leaning government, in Washington, would weaken those rights even more.* Now, why would politicians of this great country, grant civil rights to the black population, in the 1960's, rights they had deserved all along, and include provisions, that some aspects of those rights, would expire within a number of years? What sort of deceit, and corruption, would that be? *Instead they should have been debating how to strengthen those rights, all along!* It was only 40-50 years ago, or so, that citizens, mostly in the black population, risked their lives to try get an equal right to vote; and others, mainly whites, fought bitterly to try to stop them from getting those rights- - -no, this was not in that distant, third world, country; *this was the United States of America, not that long ago!*

Recent public surveys, in the US, showed that almost 70%, of Americans, did not feel good about the economy, about their job prospects; and they were not better off, than they were, a few years ago. They were not better off than their parents were; and similar poll numbers, might well be found in other developed countries, as well. Two thirds of working, women, did not feel the economy was good, for them, as they had continued to struggle. These were impressive statistics, as the republican administration, and Wall

Street, tycoons, had continued to praise the strong US, economy, that so many of our citizens, did not experience. Critics claimed that these were the customary manipulations of figures, by official sources.

A recent Sprott report, outlined some evidence of Central Bank manipulation of gold prices; and they had also concluded, *that the US government had been intervening, to support the stock market, surreptitiously, too many times.* This was carried out under various administrations, and not only, in an emergency situation! If true, these are most disturbing reports on US government activities, in a supposed 'democracy'! *It is one thing to do this, in an emergency, critics, continued, it is a different story, when it is* done *on a regular basis, and without public knowledge!* They suggested that such government, behavior, exposed the elite, those on the inside, to certain knowledge, about the stock market, that average citizens did not possess; and therefore, they could not compete fairly. As readers digest all this, and other items in this book, they might start to see, why, so many people, in the US, lost small fortunes, in the recent stock market crash. If these scandals were verifiable, it would be amazing that, many, Americans, did not start to protest, and demand justice. Does the above, confirm what many have asserted, that, people get the government they deserve, because they had not learned hard lessons, and because, they did not care enough? These revelations were astounding, to say the least!

Education, and Healthcare: Many, including this writer, have pointed out that education, healthcare, and economics, are often intertwined, as one, impacts, on the other. The economic status, affects how much education one is likely to achieve, or the quality of healthcare obtained, or lack of any significant healthcare. The level of education affects our capacity to seek, and hold, jobs, with good financial rewards. And experts have often stated, that, the financial standing of people, and the type of job, will dictate what type of healthcare program, they get enrolled in; and how good they feel about themselves. In the US, members of congress have often debated healthcare, and many of them announce, that, the American people, deserve as good a system, as government officials had. Undoubtedly, this applied also, to other countries, in the 'west'. In the lesser, developed nations, we know too well, that the elite get superior care, anywhere in the world, whereas the rest of their citizens, have to do without! Thus, poor financial conditions, can lead to inadequate education, insufficient job opportunities, and inadequate healthcare, a mighty hurdle, to surmount! This, can also lead to a depressed state of mind, that further aggravates the other parameters, a vicious cycle, that is very difficult to escape.

The British newspaper, 'Independent', featured an article on an interview with poet Seamus Heaney, when he was asked, if young people had lost interest in poetry, because they preferred to write rap lyrics, or pop music. He replied that, the young could still be talented. They might enjoy going to a disco, or to a rave, but they might also be quite capable of writing poetry! He said that, *much depended on teachers and parents, of those young people;* and it would be related to their upbringing, and the quality of education, in general. Let us consider also, modern attitudes towards sports activities- - nowadays, rowdyism, brawls, and violence, are taken for granted, they are part of the game; and they have become commonplace on the playing fields, in many countries, including the US, and UK. In our younger years, the quality of sportsmanship was of a much higher caliber, and not many, can dispute that fact. Now, there are some, who have advocated serious legal action, with punishment, for such renegades, both, on the field, or in the stands. Some players associations, levee hefty fines, against players guilty of such misconduct, and often, also exclude them, from a number of games. Such actions have been taken, against players, who had been unnecessarily rough, to the point of deliberately, injuring, opposing players. It seemed that winning, always winning, had become the rule of the game, but also winning, at any cost! That is wrong, that is not sportsmanship!

Another discussion, on '60 Minutes', on CBS television station, dealt with career colleges, in the US, that had access to, government guaranteed, student loans; and thus, in their curriculum, they included courses in the culinary arts, in paramedical fields, in the fashion industry, and so on. That was not wrong; but it was alleged that, college officials hired employees, *to tempt large numbers of young people to enroll, any warm body would do!* This guaranteed, that, those government funds would keep rolling in! They claimed that such colleges, and certain companies, were even listed on the stock exchange, and had done well for investors! Students were told that, after graduation from these schools, they would find jobs readily, and salaries could start at 30-50 thousand dollars per year, and climb from there.

Graduate students were interviewed for this TV program, they stated that they could not find any jobs; and what they found, only paid a fraction of what they had been told. Lawsuits had been filed against some of those colleges, and investigations by the government had begun; and by officials at the stock exchange. It was found that graduation, and attendance, records, had been falsified as well; but a representative for some of these colleges said, that such, allegations, are not necessarily true. However, it was also discovered that, many of those colleges, *gave large campaign donations, to members of congress, on the committee for education! Interesting, is that how they received such large, guaranteed, student loans, from the government? You have to wonder.*

There were other reports on the New Orleans school system, some of their buildings were 50-100 years old; and, they said, some of them needed to be demolished, and then be rebuilt. Corruption, was prevalent, there was theft, and abuse, of funds, that had been provided for education. They found a worker who had not worked in years, but had received 'sick pay', checks, for over 30 years. Other employees claimed, and received, overtime of, close to 50 hours per week, for a whole year! Just imagine, an employee, working 40 hours per week, then, also claiming an additional 50 hours of overtime! *Were they cooking, eating, and sleeping, at the school?* Cheating in the grading system was found as well, because the majority of, seventh grade students, were not proficient at mathematics, and the English language, but they received passing grades. Such scandals are, no doubt, found elsewhere, both in the US, and other countries. Another serious injustice, in America, is the fact that millions, pay taxes to the government for public school support; when they send their own children to private, parochial, and other schools. The government uses that tax money for public schools, and for other causes, but contributes little, or nothing, towards the running of the private school system. And yet, leaders understand, only too well, that if suddenly, private schools were to close down, the public school system did not have the capacity to absorb, the tens of thousands of pupils, who attend private schools. If the government claimed, separation of, church, and state, why do government officials, force citizens, to support public schools, when they do not plan to send the children there? Where is the freedom of choice? There is no question that, all should pay their fair share of taxes, based on income; but not everyone should be forced, to contribute, to a particular public school system, should they?

In 2005, we also had reports, on the standards of education, of children in members, of the European Union. It was alarming to hear, that, in a number of member states, a good percentage of the children did not even finish grade school education. Previously we had discussed gaps in the education system in the US, and now, the finger is pointing at Europe, with flaws in their own education programs. In the UK, they were debating how to improve the British system, as they needed to substantially, increase spending, on their education departments. Some countries reported that an increasing number, in the labor force, had fallen behind in their standard of education, and thus, had become less competitive, in the world's labor markets.

At the Group of 8 meeting, in Scotland, there were the usual discussions, back, and forth, about the plight of most third world countries; the education standards, the lack of cohesive health care, and in many cases, the lack of a financial structure, to organize these. Many had continued to criticize the G-8 gatherings, because of their photo opportunities, and propaganda, but that they seldom provided any real, lasting, solutions. President Bill Clinton was appointed as a United Nations, representative, to coordinate efforts, aimed at combating AIDS crises, in many of those, poor, countries.

In "Mirror Reflections=Mirages", we discussed mounting problems within the US health care system, as well (the haves, and the have not). As if to prove our point, recent reports, in the New England Journal of Medicine, showed that in America, there was a marked disparity, in health care, between whites, and colored folk; that blacks, had received inferior health care for many years; but, it was disturbing to note, that, instead of the situation getting better, it had actually grown much worse. And now, we are hearing about problems with health care, in some of the European countries, as well, a larger country, the UK, a small one, Malta, and others. Those countries, with a single payer system, were doing remarkably well, at one time, delivering, good, universal health service, to all their citizens. However, many weaknesses had sprung up, with incompetence, delays, long waiting lists, for patient care, restricted health care, for some treatment modalities, and more. Those advocating a single payer program, for the US, do not want a mediocre system, for this country, but rather, to learn from mistakes of others.

For example, in Canada, in Australia, and in the Scandinavian countries, they have done much better, for their people, with healthcare, than in the US. Perhaps, they also managed to avoid many of the pitfalls, experienced in UK, and in other healthcare systems, and they were better financed, through an equitable tax program. I had worked under the National Health system, in UK, soon after it was launched. The public, physicians, hospitals, and other paramedical groups, found it a very good system, as a rule, in those earlier years. But in recent years, according to reports, some difficulties had been encountered; although, UK has a reputation for excellent, medical care.

Then again, we must contrast the fact that, if difficulties are encountered, in the wealthier nations, like the US, and UK, how much worse, are the crises, that beset underdeveloped, third world, countries, when their resources are so meager? It has been stated often, that, for many of them to be able to resolve their problems, *corruption must first be eliminated, both within the government, and in corporations. This would apply to most other, countries, as well.* In June 2005, there were reports, that Canada would no longer be a ready source, of cheaper drugs, for the US market; and therefore, would institute a ban on such exports. Reporters, and other critics, reiterated, that, *it was payback time, for the pharmaceutical industry, in America, allegedly, for their steady support of the Bush administration, and the republican machines.* Experts, often refer to this type of corruption, *the influence of money everywhere, in politics. And some corrupt, politicians, attempt to tell citizens, in America, that there never was, a quid pro quo, in these matters! Who are they kidding?*

In our global society, it is not possible to talk of values, without always placing it in the context of education, healthcare, the economy, the environment, and more. Our environment affects all of us; the other parameters, impact mostly, the poorer segments of society. In 'America' magazine, professor Kenneth R. Hines, discussed aspects of the social teachings, of the Catholic Church. He wrote how "any vision of a good society, must have as its foundation, the correct view of the human person, and the nature of the good life, for people". That, human beings should not be considered, only, in their economic, and political, dimensions. And Fr. Thomas Massaro, S.J., discussed some of those same teachings; but he emphasized an important section, when he said, 'reminding entrepreneurs, and investors, that the proper end of economic activity, *is the progress of the entire community, especially, of its poorest members'.*

On a PBS program, 'Now', with David Broncaccio, they commented on an upcoming film on the company, Enron, and on corporate abuses. The director pointed to *the culture of greed, in major corporations, in America;* how employees were encouraged, to compete harshly, against each other, to go out, into the market, and get very aggressive, *capitalism, at its worst! Have we heard that, before?* What was their philosophy? 'If anyone stands in your way, rip them apart. If you need to stand, on, your grandma's, neck, do so, go ahead'! They alluded to sloppy behavior of banks; to Wall Street lawyers, and government agencies, as they encouraged the, alleged, illegalities that had been going on, at some of those companies, such as, Enron. Amazingly, they showed an audio of an

Enron official, shouting, "Wow, burn baby, burn", as he watched a wildfire, in California, threatening, their power grids (because Enron could sell them electricity, at outrageous rates). The program guests said, *'it says something pretty damning, about human culture'*, that permitted such things, to go on. It was alleged that, the republican dominated government, in Washington, did not want to charge right in, and stop such behavior, 'not to disturb the markets'! There it is, again, a government doing its best, to protect business companies, and 'to hell', with the people, who are being abused. *Presumably, it matters little, which political party is in control?*

These are American companies, although many, are also, multinational; their executive officials, often, earn, millions of dollars, in salaries, benefits, and other perks. When these companies crash, as they sometimes do, those executives are reasonably protected, and do very well, for themselves. The people, and the employees, suffer tremendous losses, in case, after, case. Some, critics, have sensed that, churches, today, do not emphasize some of these points, on social teaching, often enough. And therefore, leaders of nations, various officials, in government, and in business, and people, themselves, tend to stray away, from such teachings, on social, and moral, issues; and on the dignity of the human person. They do not find them appealing. In most instances, they prefer to go, whichever way suits them.

Environment: Recently, Chinese scientists reported that, a large glacier on the Tibet side, of Mount Everest, had melted, significantly; and likewise, on the mountain, side, of Nepal. They suggested that, this had ominous implications, for the future global supply, of fresh water. US government officials, and others, have tended to downplay, any talk of global warming, for many years, as they had done, on talk of, environmental, damage, as a whole. Usually, this posturing, was meant to favor, and appease, industry tycoons, the source of most of our pollution problems. The precarious state of the environment, also featured prominently, in EU policies, as they tried to bring in, other nations, new, and old, into some degree of conformity, with plans, to improve, and protect, the environment--water, air, and land. Spain has recorded the worst drought in its history, and they had many serious fires, and changes in climate. Portugal, too, had experienced many fires, after severe periods of drought, with destruction of forests, homes, and loss of life. Fires had struck Portugal, in 2003, as well. Other parts of Europe, such as, Germany, Romania, Switzerland, and others, had disastrous floods. *Whereas, US officials, keep repeating, that, they see no evidence of significant climate changes! They do not want to face up to the causes, pollution, everywhere.*

Western governments have often accused, those, in third world countries, of being short sighted, and irresponsible, when they clear cut, large areas of forest. This would cause soil erosion, and the land could be rendered useless; and if more forests were destroyed, it could increase the risk, of additional climate change. However, in western countries, as well, we regularly see clear, cutting, of large tracts of forest, for commercial buildings, for parking lots, for residential communities, and more. And, the US is a leader, in this area of development. It is true, that they will plant a certain number of trees, according to government regulations, along streets, park areas, and near, newly constructed homes. But, let us not deceive ourselves, the newly planted, young, trees, could never restore, the interaction, with nature, and the grandeur, of large areas of forest, that had been bulldozed in this manner. As you travel around the country, you witness, this assault on nature, wherever you go.

You cannot bulldoze, and destroy, 20, 30, 50, 70, year old trees, or more, and replace only some of them, with young trees, and not expect adverse effects, on our environment. Although our politicians continue to insist, that there is no serious danger, to our climate, they cannot fool, all the people, all the time. Just recently, the US senate rejected mandatory reductions, in greenhouse gases emissions; but instead, voted only, for some controls, by the companies, themselves! A group of scientists recently, again, issued harsh criticism, of the Bush administration attitudes, on the environment, on climate change, in our world, today, *and called it, seriously misguided!*

At the start of, and during, world war two, some forests in the US, were already being decimated, as brought out, by Harry M. Caudill, in "Night Comes to the Cumberlands". What a surprisingly appropriate title, that was, for such a book! Even then, people were crusading, for their state, and federal, governments, to preserve some of the majestic woodlands; *but governors, and other legislators, had scoffed at their request.* Then, the author described how, a few years after the Pearl Harbor attacks, "magnificent virgin timber", became history. He described clear cutting operations, by lumber companies, so that some hills, were nearly made bare. Then, he said, *"almost overnight, they were transformed, from primeval, and incredibly beautiful, forests, to desolate wastelands".* Yes, we are trying to tell, third world countries, what they cannot do; but, we have done it, before them, and what is worse, we are still at it!

The indiscriminate destruction of forests, in the US, had annihilated that beautiful bird, the Ivory-billed Woodpecker, 'The Lord God bird', as it was once called. Its forest habitats had been wiped out, years ago. Now, there are reports that, this bird, once thought to be extinct, might have been spotted, in a southern State. Given the history of mankind, how destructive man had been, on this planet, news media should not have publicized this discovery. They even referred to the forests, where this extremely rare bird, might have been spotted. It is a bad idea to put such information, before the public. And, if indeed, some specimens of this bird, are still in existence, they might have already, sentenced them, to be wiped out, yet again.

In August 2005, a PBS television program, presented the plight of coral reefs; how, 50% of the reefs were gone, dead; *and the remaining reefs were in serious danger.* Our lackadaisical policies, and those, in other countries, need to awaken world leaders, from their deep slumber. *Most scientists had concluded that, the destruction, of our reefs, was caused by, over-fishing, pollution from land, and global warming.* They warned, that so much depended on the reefs, in nature, that, if they died, so would the oceans, and man's survival would become precarious. They had studied the world famous Great Barrier

Reef, in Australia, and reefs, off the Florida coast, in the US. Florida had been overwhelmed with development, and pollution run off, from farmland. But the problems, with the Australian reef, were not from over development, *and therefore, global warming was probably responsible, for any damage done, to that reef.* And, it is, this global warming, that US officials, and American corporations, had tried to downplay, all along.

What were some of the first announcements, by president Bush, after the devastation of Katrina? *Why, that the government should relax anti-pollution, regulations, for the oil industry, to encourage the availability of fuel.* It is true that there was a disaster, but sometimes, such relaxed regulations, are never put back, in force. An experiment, in Australia, clearly showed, that, if a section of reef was strictly protected, 'no fishing, no touching', that particular reef remained perfectly healthy. An American biologist said that, we had no significant protections, for American reefs; and that, the attitude, of Americans, usually was, 'it is mine, I'll take whatever I can, don't worry about tomorrow'. All this points to man's intrusion, yet again, as the cause of destruction, of our reefs. Commissions had been set up, to study these disasters, around the world, and they urged world governments, *to adopt good ocean policies!*

An article in Smithsonian, dealt with the plight of National parks, in the United States. These are large tracts of wilderness, in beautiful, pristine, areas of the country, a heritage for future generations. Apparently, there too, pollution in those parks had got out of hand. They pointed to, the quality of the air, that had deteriorated, considerably; but they could not be certain, what had caused that. Some parks had started limiting the number of visitors, and the number of cars, to see if that would alleviate the problems. But, we must conclude, that if the air was badly polluted in those pristine parks, can we possibly fathom, what we had done, to the rest of nature, in those areas; *and what about the air, in the rest of America? Are we slowly, but surely, poisoning ourselves?* And if the US is so polluted, what about other countries, *what about the rest of planet earth- - -?*

In a Columban Mission magazine, Fr. Paul McCartin, wrote about Japan's garbage crisis, that it was one of the world's worst, environmental, dilemmas; and how, some of their garbage, had to be shipped out of the country, because of shortage, of disposal sites. Because of this garbage problem, Japan had eight, to nine times, the number of waste incinerators, that the US had; and they discovered that, many of those incinerators, were pouring high levels of dangerous Dioxin, into the air. *One newspaper reported that, the amount of Dioxin found in breast milk, was twenty six times, the allowable limit!* This article concluded, with this noteworthy statement, "No matter where, or how, we dispose of something, it will have an effect, on us, and on the rest of the earth"! Right! That goes right, to the point that, the world community, under the UN, must deal with threats from pollution, just as they must deal with, threats from weapons proliferation. This is, where, humanity, has been crying out, for justice, and for peace, in all aspects of our lives.

We cannot talk of values, without referring to a recent '60 Minutes' program, on CBS television station. This, dealt with the obscene size, of some private homes, in many parts of America, today. Yes, some of our citizens, had seen these scandalous structures, or mansions, in many parts of Europe; but these Americans, forgot that, most of those monstrous homes, were built in the older days of Europe- - -they were the decadent times, of 'old Europe'; and those decadent times, had given rise to violent revolutions. Guests on this program, showed a few of the areas, where, people were buying average size houses, only, to have them torn down, to build newer homes of, 6000 to 9000 square feet; or even, 40,000 to nearly 60,000 square feet! They emphasized that, the average size American family, these days, was only 3.6 persons; and yet, they seemed to want, at least 5 bathrooms, and umpteen bedrooms, living rooms, play rooms, and much more. During this program, they interviewed some of the owners, of these monstrosities; and looking at all this, one had to wonder about the priorities in life, for some of them. They still wanted larger, and larger, homes, to put more, and more, of their stuff, in them!

We, as a society, need to direct a few questions, to some of these people. Do they remember the stories, behind the book, 'The Ugly American'? Have we done enough, since those far away days, to no longer project, such an image? Judging by the widespread, anti-American sentiment, around our world, one has to wonder? And, the most important question, would be, have they looked, lately, at faces of starving children, and adults, in Africa, India, Latin America, and many other parts of the world? Have they looked, at the faces of people, who had been devastated, by major disasters, in many parts of the world, as well as, here, in America? Some of these disasters were, hurricanes, such as, Charlie, Ivan, Katrina, Rita, and Wilma; then, there were also, massive floods, the tsunami in Asia, tornadoes, earthquakes, fires, mudslides- - -and, much more, both in the US, and especially, in many other countries, such as the recent earthquake in Pakistan. We can only hope that, if the people, featured in the above TV program, could afford so much, on self gratification, that perhaps, they had also lent a good, helping, hand, to the poorest, of the poor, around the world.

For many of the crises, on our planet, including the serious one, of pollution, there is plenty of blame, to spread around; to the governments of poor, underdeveloped, countries; those, of the rich, fully, developed, countries; large ones, and others, quite small. All had contributed to these crises, and, of pollution, in particular. This section on values, and the environment, will include, quite appropriately, a National Geographic correspondence, by Rob Hofer, from Canada. This, dealt with species of animals, and plants, that may be alien to a particular region, and he wrote thus, "Homo Sapiens is a species that has spread like cancer, around the world, causing the extinction of millions of other species"! That was right, to the subject, when talking about mankind's troubles, on this fragile planet; and it should provide us with much food, for thought.

And a contrast, in values, comes to us from a Navajo, indigenous, American, as he was featured on one of our news programs. He became an avid photographer, and loved his native, western US, the red rocks region, the Navajo lived on a large reservation in the area. His photographs brought out the beauty of canyons, and desert landscapes, like no other. He taught his art to other young people, because, as he said, he wanted to pass on the beauty of nature, that surrounds us; he did not want to forget the history of his people, their way of life, their culture. He hoped that, others, amongst his people, who come after them, would keep it going; would preserve some of the Navajo traditions.

Politicians, and others, should not talk, of 'values', as a sound bite, for their convenience, to gain political, or other, advantages, at any particular moment. They must first learn, and understand, the true meaning, of 'values'.

HOMELAND (IN)SECURITY IN THE U.S.

American politicians, had come up with an idea, to advance security, to create a new bureaucracy, called 'homeland security', and it was to be run by a 'big chief'; and presumably, all other secret agencies (of which America had many) would come under one umbrella, or, so they said. Perhaps then, acts of terror could be prevented, as it had been alleged that, some important clues leading up to 9/11, had been botched up. We need to remember that all political parties, campaign on promises to cut Big Government, down to size, to reduce the number of federal employees, to avoid wasting money, and to reduce government bureaucracy. You know the story, only too well. *As soon as they get elected, it is business as usual, new cabinet positions, thousands more, employees, and more money wasted than ever before, billions more!* Then, what happened? After hurricane Katrina (and more on that later), the whole world saw vividly, in shocking picture, after picture, that the Bush administration had actually created a department of 'homeland insecurity'.

There is no talk of, the buck stops here with me; and many in the disaster areas, voiced their opinions that, this Washington government had a terrible track record! News media repeatedly showed a video, where Bush tells one of the agency directors, after the utter devastation from the storm, "you did a heck of a job". Some said that this guy showed he was not prepared for a disaster; but he stated that he had given his superiors, and the White house, ample warning of what was coming! Allegedly, he was fired soon after. Media should show that news bite, over, and over, again, perhaps we will learn some lessons. Americans, and others in the west, often accuse other governments, of an absence of true 'democracy', of corruption, nepotism, and favoritism. Well, now, are we not doing the same, in the 'west'? Undoubtedly, the British must have dreamt up, similar security bureaucracies. In the former austere state, of the Soviet Union, they had the KGB; in Israel they had their own 'alphabet soup', and so had other countries, some, much more ruthless, than others. But, are we not competing in that department, of ruthlessness, as well, judging by the news, of our detainees in foreign prisons, and of torture? No sensible person believes that, such behavior, gives anyone, more security!

We have all seen many reports, of people traveling to the US, and encountering great difficulty. The republican administration had demanded, that, all countries *should provide much advance information, all types of personal details, on their citizens, before they depart for the US.* Most countries, especially some in Europe, and Muslim nations, protested, at this assault on freedoms, and basic human rights, at the hands of America, the displayer of the famed statue of Liberty! American officials responded that perhaps, this would avoid planes being diverted, or turned back, when already in the air. Early in June, a flight from Britain was in the news, as it was diverted to Canada; a hijack warning signal, had been accidentally triggered, and the Americans had gone on the offensive. Other planes had already been diverted to Maine; yet others, had been kept on the tarmac, at the airport of departure, as in France. There were many other incidents, such as people being yanked off planes, sometimes personalities, who were perfectly innocent, because they were mistakenly identified. In "Mirror Reflections=Mirages", we discussed this façade of homeland security, and the patriot act, in the US; with the heavy boot of the federal government stomping on people, everywhere, in the world. The innocent, the suspect, and the obviously guilty, are all lumped together.

The Times of Malta, and there were similar reports from other sources, had a letter writer protest, because the US government had refused her an entry visa, to the country. She simply wanted to visit family members. Officials, through their embassy, stated that everyone was welcome, to visit America (welcome?), but firstly, they needed to subject people, to all sorts of screening, the third degree, if you will! The embassy explained that, they must make sure that, those requesting a traveling visa, for the US, *had solid reasons, beyond doubt, to want to return to their country of origin.* They must have family members left behind, a steady job, home ownership, (a small fortune in the bank?), etc. In other words, if you had no family left, if you were retired, and the only one left, if you were not wealthy, and could not own a home, but simply rented your place, why would you want to travel to the US? There might be some logic in that, and you would likely be rejected, even if, all you wanted to do, was, to visit, family, or friends, living in another country. This writer happens to know a few people who love to do, just that. With so much rigmarole going on, why would anyone from any part of the world, simply 'want to visit the US'? Or, for that matter, why would anyone want to travel to another country, under similar circumstances? Is all this confusion, called, *security?*

It should come as no surprise that, with a new department bureaucracy, in Washington, with cabinet positions, and hundreds of new employees, we would soon face money scandals. On a '60 Minutes' television program, on CBS, reporters, and guests, discussed, *the hundreds of millions, of our tax dollars, devoted to homeland security!* And how it was being allocated to local government politicians, **for ludicrous, and scandalous projects, nothing to do with security!** Such projects, costing huge amounts of money, included, *rap music, roads, bullet proof vests for dogs, some funds were for the North pole, Alaska; and some items were so ridiculous, that readers would not believe them, in America!* Are these the responsible officials in Washington, who are supposed to be running this country? Is it any wonder that, a recent poll asked citizens if their representatives, in congress, were working for the genuine interests of the people? *A full 97% responded that they were not! But the people elected them, right?*

A congressman admitted that all the above revelations, constituted what they called 'pork barrel', distribution of money that, was allocated, after 9/11, on advice from a special commission. The funds were supposed to be distributed, according to the likelihood that, a city would be the target of a serious attack. They call this 'pork barrel', in Washington, a nicer phrase that, *in most other countries is called, corruption!* When such things go on, in other countries, our politicians call those governments, all types of names, corrupt, tyrants, dictators, and more. But when these things are carried on, in our government, why, that is normal behavior, it is called, 'governing in a democracy'! Do readers see the spins, in such double talk? Does it matter that, we call it by nice sounding names? For example, if some in congress were to say, I will not vote with you, unless, such, and such, is also included in that bill, for my district, what is that? In plain English, it used to be called blackmail, and corruption. In the progressive, capitalistic system, of the 'west', we call it 'striking a deal', bargaining, accommodation, pork- - -! Who are we kidding? Here, we are dealing with enormous waste of taxpayer money, are we not? If there is abuse of power, and dishonesty, nobody should be above the law.

A lot of the hanky, panky, that goes on in Washington, does it improve our sense of security? Is that what some of our leaders think? Most of us, understand only too well, that it goes on, in most government circles; and that is partly the reason, for so much trouble, in our world. The war, the lies, the abuse or torture, of detainees, the killing of many people, and the destruction, most experts believe that, none, of those, had improved our security. And now, in late November 2005, we heard of another enormous scandal on the part of the US government. Many feel that the secrecy within US government agencies, is probably, worse than in any other country, we may even put the former Soviet Union to shame! Los Angeles Times, reporters, broke the story about this newest corruption, and deceit, in the US government. They uncovered a long time plot, of agencies in the Bush administration, who were *secretly paying* middle men, in Iraq, *to print articles in Iraqi papers, and in other media, that were very favorable to the US, and its military activities, in Iraq;* and about the "progress" going on, in Iraq. Allegedly, even newspapers, had been paid, to accept, and print, this propaganda junk! America, when will you wake up, and exercise your rights to protest, with your votes? Do you realize how your taxes are being squandered? To force a sham of a democracy, with the gun, and the force of the military, on another sovereign nation! Then, we allegedly, have to use propaganda, corruption, undercover activities, *and lies, to convince the people of Iraq, that what America did to Iraq, was all good, and above board.* Many experts, and thinkers, will wonder, what type of warped democracy the US, had connived, to teach people of the Middle East, and to the Iraqis, themselves! They consider this, an outrage by the American government, against the Iraqi people, and against our citizens.

If we continue to perpetrate lies, and deceit, and teach these, how can we ever achieve real security? On his wonderful program, 'Hardball', on MSNBC television station, Chris Matthews asked, **'how far will America go, to sell the Iraq war'?** Right! With his guests, they tore into, the above signs of decadence. They pointed out how we are now in the business of peddling news to the Iraqis; and at the same time, Rumsfeld insulted the world *by praising the 'Iraqi free media'!* Many Americans will not appreciate that, this Washington clique, was spending one hundred million dollars, or more, to do this! Do people understand, that, we ridiculed the Russians, Germans, Chinese, and Japanese, when they did these things? Do Americans care anymore? *Then, on this program, they showed Bush announcing that, we were teaching Iraqis how to run their democracy! My, my!* Naturally, our government, and the pentagon, will state that they knew nothing of these activities. Give us a break! Pat Buchanan, a former presidential candidate, appeared on the program, and his idiotic comments indicated that, all this was normal procedure, in war, and the only misfortune was, that it was uncovered. This guy is something else!

It was like a farce, to hear government officials in the US, talking of freedom of the press in Iraq; they had already suppressed free media before, in that country, because they mostly criticized, America! Chris Matthews jumped in, and said, 'if you want good press, just buy it'! These revelations, truly showed, the horrendous foreign policies of the US, which had caused upheavals, in the world, and animosity towards our country.

When aircraft were first hijacked, people had their political, reasons; they were escaping from massive oppression, and seeking asylum. The methods they used were illegal, though for a good purpose; as was mentioned previously, the use by some, of evil means, to achieve something better. Later on, hijacking became a tool for criminal behavior, and for terrorism; and some of it, was related to the long standing, Israeli-Palestinian conflict, and discrimination. Soon after these events had begun, we already had some type of airport passenger screening, this was not new, for guns, knives, bombs, and so on. Then, came, the 'shoe bomber'; guess what happened next, in the US? Why, of course, most of us got to remove our shoes, as if we were going to become shoe bombers. If someone had tried to use a lighter, for illegal purposes, these were no longer allowed; and that was fine, as most airlines had become smoke free, why allow lighters, or matches? Regrettably, some airports still had 'smoking sections', in their non-smoking buildings, so those afflicted with that malady, could still have their puffs, before boarding their next flight.

Then, we had the use of box cutters, by those criminals, who committed the 9/11 attacks, in the US; so, these, and scissors, and razors, and other sharp objects, were added to the 'no-no', list. Did anyone in government, in western countries, ever consider that, these 'terrorists', might not use the same modus operandi, twice? As we proceed, readers can best judge, if some of this was excessive paranoia, because as we move along, we begin to understand, that there are better, and, *more rewarding ways, to cope with the roots of terrorism, we had not yet, adopted, the correct approach.*

Although this 'security', or now, 'homeland security', has been ever mounting, officials in government, refused to agree, with their critics, that Big Brother, had been assaulting our freedoms, and basic human rights, by harsher, and harsher, measures! Look at the 'open society' in the UK, once a bulwark of freedom, and democracy; now, they have thousands of cameras everywhere, snooping, on everyone, when they least expected it. Some will say, if it can stop major crime, it was worth it, perhaps, but at what cost- -? And, what comes next? Why, some people found their luggage broken into, perhaps damage was perpetrated, and personal items began to disappear, as well; and the traveler may find a note that, such, and such, needed to be inspected, 'for security'. Or, they did not even find such a note. What type of illegal behavior, do we call that? Could authorities devise a plan, *to open, and inspect luggage, in front of the owners?* No, they say, it would create an impossible logjam, at our airports. Other countries have done that, why not, the US? In Israel, people are briefly, but, efficiently, interviewed, and their luggage is inspected in front of the traveler; there are other, measures, aimed at preserving security. And, incidentally, Israel has had the reputation, of marketing, the safest airline. That country has other 'not so admirable' problems, but for airline safety, it scores high marks. And the airport transit time, runs at about 2 to 3 hours, not more than is required for US, and other, airports.

What else could happen at our airports? If someone is suspected of hiding a forbidden object in a jacket, or coat, or in a hat, why, besides shoes, we get to remove hats, and jackets, and coats. Some might ask, do we get to undress, next? Not yet, but critics had already accused 'security' officials, of getting too 'intimate' with frisking of female passengers! There was a barrage, of criticism, even though in most cases, female officials were used. For many years, your purses, your cameras, and your hand luggage, items from your pockets, and so on, had always been X-ray screened, before entry to the secure areas of airports. But many of these screeners had been found poorly trained. Even more disturbing, were reports that, cargo packages going on these same passenger aircraft, were *poorly screened, or not at all.* We ask readers, what sense does it make, to put citizens through hell, 'to protect the people of America', when, at the same time, you fail to protect them from potentially dangerous cargo, on that same aircraft?

As if that was not enough, we heard horror stories from critics of the government, that, hundreds of huge containers, arrived daily, at the nation's seaports, and most of those were seldom thoroughly screened. Others had accused, that, those containers, could indeed, hide, a plethora of weapons of destruction that, could pose a threat, to millions of Americans. There were many reports on these topics, in the months leading to the last presidential elections, the usual sound bites, by some politicians. With all this information coming at you, the reader can best judge, the effectiveness of this 'homeland security', or paranoia, if you will.

Whilst we are on the subject of airport security checks, some slapstick humor, with tongue in cheek, would be appropriate; simply, to point out the ridiculous, if we are always playing catch up, with those who have criminal intent. What if a passenger hid a forbidden device in denture prostheses? Why, we would find an army of dentists at our airports, to give us all a dental exam, before we board the aircraft. We can carry that, one further, what if someone hid a device, up, the rear end? Why, the traveling public would then encounter, an army of proctologists, *to do you know what, to you, before you can embark! Thus, you may have aged quite a few years, before you start on your adventure! You may no longer be able to make it!* Readers will appreciate that, this is serious matter, and that, our government, had not always approached these problems correctly.

At most airports, we had all become accustomed, to passing through metal detectors, before getting frisked, if an alarm was triggered, or because of 'profile' discrimination. Now, at US airports, you are also subjected to blasts of air, that scatter your few wisps of hair, your curls, or your toupee, hither, and thither. At some US airports, critics have already accused our government, of using technology, bordering on pornography. This referred to machines, used to screen the human anatomy, to show in some detail, the nooks, and crevices, and bumps, and protrusions, of the male, and female, forms. Some, had facetiously, commented, that long lines would form, as screeners took longer 'to do a good job', as they studied these images, on their screens, (ha, ha!), for 'homeland security', of course. Give us another break! We can do much better than that, can we at least try?

This could produce a few chuckles, here, or there, if it was not such a serious matter. Just like the political talk, by the president, and others, on the Mexican border, and illegal aliens. Americans, and many officials, in Washington, tend to shift all the blame, on to the Mexicans, themselves! The main problem is, as some critics have stated so well, that US corporations *want to keep these illegal 'aliens' coming, so they can pay them 4 dollars an hour, or less, when otherwise, they would have to pay, 8 or 9 dollars, an hour. The companies keep the difference, to inflate their bottom line!* That is closer to the truth. Yes, these Mexicans come for work, and they pay their taxes; but they also do hard work, such as, roadwork, or roof work, or picking fruits, and vegetables, that, nobody else would do, for that same amount of money! Who would perform those jobs, if the illegal immigrants, suddenly stopped coming?

As we said before, in these pages, and in "Mirror Reflections=Mirages", instead of all this mumbo, jumbo, we need to concentrate more effort, in removing the scourges of poverty, and injustices, that give rise to despair, and then, to terrorism. *We must offer hope, and people everywhere, could then reap enormous rewards.* Again, in the case of the London bombings, security staff, there, after the attacks, began inspecting backpacks. Soon after, it was tried over here as well, in the transportation system, they called it random checking; or, could it also have been, discriminatory profiling, once again? As already mentioned, our officials, had to play catch up, for lack of anything else to do, they have missed the point.

A US congressman, in July 2005, was discussing a bill, to promote free trade, between us, and Central American countries. The Bush, clique, had used political muscle, to force passage of that bill. Democrats were mostly dubious, of the benefits of such a bill, as were, many others. There, again, republicans announced that, it would help our border security, as it would stop some of their young people, from coming over, illegally, looking for work! But, we had pointed out that, it would do none of that, and instead, the bill could cost Americans, some of the jobs, they already enjoyed. Why? Because, it would encourage US, companies, to 'do business', in poor, Central American countries, because of the low wages. Those people may be poor, 'but they are not stupid', was one interesting comment! US corporations would pay such cheap labor, at about 50 cents an hour, to increase their profits, much of which, go to executive salaries, and perks. Those countries had no just labor laws, no controls for worker safety, and no environmental regulations. *In short, we would use, and, abuse, those people, purely for the benefit of US corporations, not to help the Central American countries!* If all this, is true, America has been employing, amazingly deceitful, practices, towards other, poorer, nations. Would such actions then, foster despair that lends itself to terrorism? Do such actions help our homeland security, or do they make things much worse, for their people, and for ours?

What about the thousands of cameras spying all over London? It so happens, that they proved most valuable, to officials, in their investigations. Is it also happening, all over the US? We have been shown spying satellites, up in the sky, revealing some neighborhoods in significant detail. Britain claims to be an open society, and so do we, in America, but, are we really an, 'open', society? Many, in the richer countries of the west, had the affront, to criticize Russians, Germans, Chinese, North Koreans, Iranians, Arab countries, everybody, for spying, and exercising control, over their people. *Well, what are we, doing?*

We cannot talk of homeland 'insecurity', without reference, in this chapter, to hurricanes. When Katrina had struck, the government, as usual, had announced, that help was on the way. Well, it was not; as many had criticized, they did not see any of that help, for 4, 6, or even 8 days. All governments at the local, state, or federal levels, should have had their staff, and all equipment, ready, close by, to assist, and save lives. They had ample warning about the location, and time, of the landfall of Katrina, but they flunked the test, just when the people needed them! A republican governor, naturally, said that federal government help was right there, on the ground; but most others had denied that. Once more, we must point out, that, if CNN, and other major news outlets, could be right there, on the ground, with directors, crews, and equipment, soon after the hurricane struck, to survey damage, and give out information, and assist; *if they could move that quickly, what was wrong with the republican administration, in Washington?* Some harsher critics asked, if they thought less, of our black, fellow citizens, than they thought of, animals? Some of the victims announced that, Bush, and other officials, should stop talking, and reading figures, from notes, and instead, show some compassion!

The US government collects scores of billions, in taxes, and boasts of numerous military bases, aircraft, helicopters, stores, ships of all types, land transportation, and boats; with all that, how was it that, the government failed to mount a massive effort, for Katrina, ready for a real emergency (not an imaginary one, this time). That is how, a decent, caring, competent, government, would react. A mediocre politician was shown stating, that if we had sent 10,000 troops beforehand, and they were not needed, we would have been accused of overreacting! *And, this guy was previously, in homeland security!* Comments from the trenches, of the destruction, from Katrina, continued on the 8th day; many charity groups were there, on the ground, or in the water, providing help, meals, and clothing, to groups that, federal government agencies, had not yet discovered! *All sang the same tune, that the Bush administration had proved itself incapable of handling a real emergency, the security of our people.*

Later, much too late, according to the majority of those, polled, Bush announced that the federal government would rebuild New Orleans, better than before. Costs were bandied about, as high as 200 billion dollars; but everything the government states, often misses the mark, and therefore, that figure would double, at least. There were other reports, from Europe, that several countries had plenty of aid, ready to be flown in, to help the victims. But, they felt that, because of petty attitudes, of some US government officials, reporters alleged, they were not given permission to enter the US. If Americans had access to most reports, from overseas, they would be amazed at such actions, by their 'leaders' in Washington. Was all, that, going on, because of 'security'? Or, had it turned into Schizophrenia, as some had already suggested?

We have had politicians, talking about homeland security, for some years, about czars, and cabinet positions, about secretaries of defense, about allocating lots of funds, for this, or that, project. All of it, was cheap talk, because when the federal government faced its first, massive, widespread test, it flunked badly; and experts in the field, had rated it an 'F', even below that! Many kept comparing the scene of devastation, to a nuclear Armageddon, and others, kept on, repeating, that such scenes, are usually witnessed in, third world, very poor countries, not in America. Yet, others, kept asking why, the tsunami efforts for Asia, were so much better organized, than for Katrina. Many agreed that the catastrophe was overwhelming, and government was caught badly unprepared, in spite of their talk, and the commissions, and committees, they had set up, and previous rehearsals. Many had died, who would otherwise, be alive.

The suffering, for some of them, must have been beyond comprehension; to repeat, we can only imagine, situations, without food, or water, without medical care, without power of any type, without sanitation facilities, in extreme, hot and humid conditions, in some areas, terrible overcrowding, and without any help, coming, from anyone! On top of all that, many, were injured, or ill, in hospitals, or nursing homes. *Some, had quickly, accused the Bush administration, of playing the race, and class, cards, because the victims were, overwhelmingly black, and poor.* Others claimed, that dirty politics entered the picture, because states with republican governors, had received faster assistance, than Louisiana, had. In many of these events, the truth often lies, somewhere, in between. It should not come as a shock, that, in such extreme situations, some had committed crimes; a few allegedly, might have committed suicide. No, there is no excuse for any of that, but historically, man's behavior, has left much, to be desired. Then, there were many predictions that, thousands might have died, that thousands, might still be trapped in their homes, that living conditions in New Orleans, had become unsafe, and the city could be uninhabitable, for many months.

Some of those reporters, there on the ground, were obviously moved, at what they had witnessed, and their experience; and they wondered, in a loud voice, why these poor people, had been left, so helpless! Many black people were shown, on a highway, they had been left there, in extremely hot conditions, and a few had died there, on the spot. One woman had a dead husband at her feet; another man said they pulled a dead person, from a home, and two days later, the body was still there, in the street; another had died in the wheelchair, and was left there, for all to see. Through all this, a republican politician was quoted as saying, that perhaps, the city of New Orleans should never be rebuilt. That created a furor. And there were others, who accused the Bush administration, of lack of help, because he had diverted so many resources, in personnel, and finances, to Iraq. Then, most importantly, scientists had long warned, that, the destruction of the wetlands, had left the gulf region, open, for a disaster. Previously, there had been discussions, to restore the marshlands, and to strengthen the levees, *but, critics claimed, the Bush administration, had eliminated 90% of the funds for those projects.* And, there had been much criticism that, the president, had not immediately left, his vacation home, to direct relief operations, with the different agencies of the government.

Eventually, thousands of people were bussed to Houston, Texas, and the facilities, there, were quickly overwhelmed, and many had to be transported again, to other facilities, in different cities, or even, different states. That is how enormous, this chaotic situation, had become. Those poor victims had been through hell, but the authorities in Texas, had come forward with genuine efforts for massive assistance. And as pointed out, already, offers started coming in, from other states, and from around the world. It was reported that, even Fidel Castro, of Cuba, so shabbily treated by several US administrations, came through, with an offer to send teams of doctors, with medical supplies, so badly needed in such a disaster. The editor of 'Nation', criticized the Bush circle, for getting ready, with additional tax breaks, for the richest in the country, when we are surrounded with all that suffering, and so much poverty; and at the same time, *republicans continued to refuse, to raise the minimum wage, for our poorest workers, so they could make a decent living.* One particular headline read, 'clearly, a nation failed its poorest'! To compound the tragedy, officials announced that, besides Bush, many other senior officials would also visit the stricken areas, to try repair the damage done, to the administration, and attempt to project a more positive image.

A highly qualified scientist, appeared on a program, and he said that, within the past year, they had met with federal agencies, and many government officials, including some from the White house; and they had discussed a scenario of what would happen to New Orleans, and the Gulf region, with a category 5 hurricane! He said that, at that meeting, they had laid out plans, how to act promptly to help the people, and to mitigate the effects of the disaster. Then he accused, that the disaster had struck the area, precisely as they had predicted, *but the government still failed in its reaction.* Seven days after the strike by Katrina, they were still finding many people in their homes, on roofs, etc. Wolf Blitzer, on CNN, showed a distraught man, sobbing, in tears. He said an old lady from a nursing home had been calling government officials, to come help them, because of rising water levels. They told her 'they were coming, Tuesday; then they told her Wednesday. She kept calling; they told her, Thursday; she told them they were not able to hang on much longer, then, they said they would get to them, on Friday. *When, at last, they got there, some had already drowned! There were, hundreds, of heart wrenching stories, like this one, where the government, at federal, state, or local, levels, had badly failed its citizens!*

And in the chaos, and confusion, of the evacuation, officials bungled things so badly, that even then, numerous family members were separated from each other, children from parents, siblings from each other, wives from husbands, and on, and on, went these horrendous stories. How on earth, could so many government agencies, prove to be so utterly incompetent? Many in the media, tried to help, showing pictures, of some of these 'lost' family members, to try discover which city, and state they might have ended up in, or which building facility, or which hospital! It was mind boggling, that they showed, how little, citizens could depend, on their government, in emergency situations. Ever since the tragedy, finger pointing, and blame, allocation, have been rampant, directed especially, at the White house, and at the governor of Louisiana. According to experts, we are making decisions, in this country, that were guaranteed to produce bigger, and more costly, disasters. Not because of the hurricanes, themselves, but because governments were permitting huge expenditures, on development, right in the path of natural disasters, and therefore, prone to destruction. Thus, the federal government would spend billions, in repairs, and reconstruction, ready for the next devastation! They suggested that, governments should not be in the business of encouraging development, in disaster prone areas, over, and over, again.

A resident of New Orleans, made an appropriate comment, when she said that, their troubles were not only from Katrina, but rather, from hurricane FEMA, that is, the federal emergency management administration. They, alluded to the fact, that, federal governments kept making the same irresponsible, decisions, and never learnt. Three months after the disaster, we were hearing about people, who had been placed in hotels, or other rented units, who were about ready to be evicted; and many who had rented property, in New Orleans, or had mortgage property they were buying, that was damaged or destroyed, had to come up with rental, or mortgage, payments, or find themselves evicted as well, with no home, to return to, in due course! And, in many cases, where people had insurance, some of them were discovering, that their insurance companies were not recognizing, all their losses, as legitimate claims. But, as we had mentioned before, insurance companies often dodge the bullet, at any opportunity they get! In such a colossal failure, the citizens were thus, receiving one blow, after another.

In the US, authorities had quickly, and perhaps humbly (humility is so rare in government circles), learned that, being rich, and powerful, and vast, matters little, when faced with massive disasters, natural, or, caused by man. The pathetic performance of governments, after Katrina, was commented upon, extensively, both in US media, and overseas. Thus, with hurricane Rita, following soon after, the Bush administration rushed out ahead. With its various departments, they organized all types of assistance, to be close by, this time, where the disaster would strike, to be able to provide immediate help. State, and local, governments similarly, learned, from Katrina, and were better prepared, ahead of the storm. However, authorities have yet to understand, and try to solve, the hardships, of another form of disaster; that is, they ordered mass evacuation; and thousands of people, ended up on expressways, and other roads, going nowhere. They were jammed to a standstill, or going at 3 to 5 miles per hour, so that, cars ran out of fuel, overheated, and tempers flared. Hundreds, abandoned their cars, and moved to the side of the road, or tried to seek some type of shelter, still in the path of the approaching hurricane! America has faced many hurricanes, but we have yet to find solutions, to make proper preparations, to move people quickly, but efficiently, to safety, to save lives. Before

Katrina, president Bush was on vacation, and remained there, at first; but with hurricane Rita, he was already planning to be in Texas, where the storm was forecast to make landfall. And reporters announced that this time, he was trying to show that he would not be caught unprepared, again.

On the program, 'Now', on PBS, guest speakers directed more criticism at both, the Bush, administration, and 'homeland security'. They said that he had inherited a great organization (FEMA) that, had been developed under Clinton; but under Bush, it had been gutted, and crippled, with personnel cuts, and money being shifted elsewhere. What was more disturbing was that, critics maintained that, qualified staff had been removed, and inexperienced people were put on the job, friends, of friends, in high places, *cronyism!* Administration officials were also accused of, focusing too much on terrorism, and not enough, on natural disasters, here at home.

Critics said that, audit reports of the government agency, FEMA, showed that, in 2004, they had spent millions of dollars in Florida (the governor a brother of Bush), and Florida was very important, in the 2004 elections! They had things ready in that state before the hurricanes hit, and those, were nowhere as severe, as Katrina, or Rita. There were no such rapid responses for Louisiana or Mississippi, this time, but perhaps, we may see better action, in future, after all the intense criticism, and worldwide dissemination, of news reports 'from the trenches'. Just consider this, if this is how a government responds, to an emergency, when they are handed, on a silver platter, 3 to 4 days' warning of an impending catastrophe, when it would reach land, and where it would strike; *what would such a government do, when those who would launch an attack, do so in secret, without warning, and you do not know when, or where, they are coming?* Perhaps the American people are beginning to realize how much can go wrong, when any government begins to act like an oligarchy, not a democracy.

Will changes, in our attitudes, improve aspects of homeland security? Many believe that they would, indeed. Bush administration officials had begun to refrain from using the word 'terrorist', indiscriminately; in our previous book we had written at length, about US double standards, in foreign policy. Reports suggested that they are now using 'global struggle against extremists', or words like that! News media suddenly, showed several people using similar phrases, just like puppets on a string. 'I say this, you do the same'! Before this, they were all intoning the same tune, 'we will take the fight to the terrorists'; 'it is war, on the terrorists'; 'bring it on', etc.

It has been obvious to many intelligent, sensible, people, that such talk had made matters much worse; it had escalated violence; and yes, experts have repeatedly claimed that, it had actually increased recruits for 'their cause', against US occupation forces, and their allies. True, American, British, and Australian, officials, had denied that; but what else would they say? They would never admit to gross misjudgment, and errors. *They had been at odds with the vast majority of people, on our planet! What is to come next, if we are to safeguard our security, and hopefully, not only that, but world peace- - -?*

"VIVA IL PAPA"

The following arrived via the Internet from a cousin, in Malta, and it reflects on the philosophy, and life, of Karol Wojtyla, Poland's future Pope John Paul II.
Chief Maquinna saw a large house, and because he was curious about it, he was told that it was a bank. That, white people, put money there, and later they got it back with interest. He replied that, they were Indian, and had no such banks. If they had money, or blankets, to spare, they gave them to others; and by, and by, these were returned to them, and their hearts felt good. He said 'our way of giving, is our bank'!

Karol Wojtyla was born in 1920, and as a young man, he had many friends, some of whom remained very close, even during his papacy. He was said to have had close contacts with the Jewish community, in that region of Poland, and some of his closest friends were Jewish. As young men, and women, these youth had experienced oppression under a Nazi occupation, and later, a difficult life, under communism. Karol was a writer, an actor, and also tried his hand at singing. His friends could not believe it, at first, when he announced his intention to enter the priesthood. He started his religious training in the underground seminary, and was ordained priest in 1946. He was nominated Bishop at a young age, and was elected cardinal in 1967. He continued to speak out for justice, and for peace. He soon became a thorn in the side of the communist regime, in his native Poland. And when rumors spread that he might become the next pope, a communist official said that, it was a great idea, as they would get rid of him, as pope, in Rome! Another official replied, 'Be careful what you wish for, because it may come to pass, and it will be worse for us'.

He was elected pope in 1978, and was to occupy the papacy for almost 27 years. "VIVA IL PAPA", was the cry, the acclamation that went up, from thousands of people gathered in St. Peter's square, when he was elected Pope, and appeared at that famous window, at the Vatican. When the announcement was made, the acclamation, 'VIVA', was uttered by, religious, by ordinary folk, by visitors, and by the curious, alike. They all joined in. He knew that millions of people, around the world, never had an opportunity to see 'their pope', in Rome. Therefore he believed that he should travel, far, and wide, to as many countries as possible, to give an opportunity to many, in other countries, to be 'with their pope', close by! For world youth day, hundreds of thousands of youth traveled to see him, wherever he went. It had become an annual event, at his request. He visited over 100 countries, sometimes visiting 3 or 4 countries in one trip; and he continued his overseas ministry, even when his infirmities were beginning to take their toll. He was fluent in many languages, and he soon gained in popularity, across a broad spectrum of people, throughout the world. He is said to have canonized more departed souls, than all previous popes, put together.

Many of our popes have been outspoken, in their writings, and the spoken word, on the sanctity of life, and on injustices; and on violence, and the horrors of war; and in particular, John Paul II, who had first hand experience in world war two, and the aftermath of the influence, by the communist regime, in his native Poland. The late pope preached incessantly for peace, and against war; and, till the very end, he tried to prevent the most recent war in Iraq. He was most concerned with its consequences on many innocent people, and on the whole world. An article in 'America', magazine, featured a gathering of Muslim, Christian, and other religious leaders, and various scholars. The participants agreed that, "the possession of nuclear weapons *was an unacceptable risk for the human community in these times, and was a continuing threat to the entire planet, and to its fragile echo-system*". It continued that, "the risks of theft, or an accident, made even the possession of nuclear weapons, a danger, to God's creation"! Yet, we have had reports on the US, Russia, China, India, Pakistan, UK, France, Israel, and others, possessing numerous nuclear weapons, of all types. By far the most heavily armed, are presumed to be, the US, and the former Soviet Union. Other governments keep trying to acquire these weapons as well. But, with the extreme secrecy of governments, from the east, or from the west, *nobody knows for certain, what numbers we are dealing with.* We know that many nations have encountered serious difficulties, with the safe storage, or disposal, of radioactive materials, whether from weapons, or from industrial sources, and with safeguarding nuclear products, from criminals.

Pope John Paul II prayerfully yearned for a new millennium, in peace and justice for all. It must have been disappointing, and heartbreaking, for him, to realize that this would be a most difficult task, as the Americans launched their new war on Iraq; and considering man's history of constant conflicts. He had witnessed the many uprisings, sometimes violent, in many parts of the world, Rwanda, the Balkans, Iraq and Iran, the Jewish and Palestinian, prolonged confrontation, and killing, of innocent people, and more; and then, he witnessed the attacks of 9/11, on the World trade center, in New York, followed by the US attacks on Afghanistan; and later, by the fabrications, by the US, and UK, for the Iraq war. Besides his passion for peace, and justice, the pope also looked forward to a millennium, where humanity would see more religious harmony. He reached out to the Jewish people, to bring the two great religions, Christianity, and Judaism, closer together, than ever before, as they had such common, ancient, roots. Towards these goals, he worked for a papal visit to the Holy lands of the Middle East, to pray at so many sites, intimately connected, with these religions. This visit, he achieved, before his death.

Many articles in 'America', magazine, have dealt with, social issues, with war, and peace, and with religious issues, in general; and with questions raised within the Catholic church. Pope John Paul II had emphasized that he was not a pacifist, *but he kept on harping on the evils of war, devastation of lives, killing of the innocent, and even the terrible, lasting effects, on the 'victors', on those who actually do the killing. Many of these lives are destroyed often, both physically, and, psychologically.* Then, solutions become even more difficult, to achieve. Although tradition had upheld the 'just war' theory, *many theologians, philosophers, and thinkers, have emphasized our responsibility to favor, and promote, peace.* It also raised the question for debates, on abandoning the just war theory altogether, because the innocent are so seldom protected; and other forms of solution should be sought out. Ah, if Bush, and Blair, and their groups, had even bothered to listen, to such words of wisdom! These articles also included a Memorial Day reflection, by Rev. Fr. Drew Christiansen, which ended with the hope that, "the church would lead the way to a less violent world order", because Iraq was an excellent example of the consequences, of 'a resort to arms', attitude. Many critics have asserted that in the US, Christian churches were conspicuously absent, in their vocal opposition to this war. Others had wondered if they had shirked their duty. As for world war two, historians will delve into that one, as well.

An editorial in that same magazine, continued to quote popes, on social issues. Blessed pope John XXIII, preached that, *the richness of a nation was not in all the money, and things, it possessed, but rather,* "in the equitable division, and distribution, of that wealth". Then, this editorial continued, with the Gospels pointing out that, we are responsible for our brothers, and sisters, wherever they are, in rich, or in poor, countries; and, the writer warned us, 'unless our country degenerates into two classes, those who have everything, and those who have nothing'. Have we not been rushing headlong in that direction, for some time? Pope John Paul II, in one of his earlier sermons, invited all those who might have felt powerful, to accept Christ in their lives; not to worry that, He would ever take anything from them. Christ indeed, would take something, away from them, but only those evil qualities, such as, corruption, manipulation of laws, and the 'do as you please' psychology. He would not take away desirable things, like freedom, dignity, or, anything to do with a just society! With so many of the popes, their teachings have been most relevant, and right, for humanity. A recent news heading read, 'some say Europe is no longer Christian', but that Christian principles seemed alive, and well, in Germany. Others, might profess they are Christian, but only give lip service, to the meaning 'of being Christian'. Certain beliefs they embrace, others, they reject intensely. In modern society, any religion, must, at times, present, many aspects that are open to debate, and controversy,

There were reports on the ongoing studies of ancient documents, books, and letters, in the vaults of the Catholic Church in Rome, going back to the reformation, and the inquisition. Those were some of the dark days in the church's history, whereby church authorities, through a special commission, banned many books, even if they simply disagreed with some of the positions of the church; others, for what was then perceived, as, downright heresy. Once the ban was placed, it applied to all church members, who were forbidden to read, or own that material, under penalty of excommunication. Many agreed that such cavalier attitudes were not the proper way, to teach the faithful; it was more like an absolute autocracy. But, we have come a long way, since those dark days, of Christianity. The late pope worked hard, and reached out to all groups; he dumbfounded many, when he visited in prison, the man who had tried to kill him. However, some critics continue to maintain that the Catholic Church still imposes, excessive restrictions, and controls. More recently, there was an outpouring of letters, and commentaries, on the resignation, of Fr. Reese, S.J., recent past editor, of 'America' magazine. Reports alleged that, there were persistent criticisms, and pressure, from Vatican sources, to have him replaced. Apparently, some in Vatican circles, had objected to the way 'America', had continued to highlight, and open for discussion, many of the controversial issues facing the church. But many people, catholic, and non catholic, alike, had felt that intense discussion of such issues, were most important for the health of the church. Why should we fear debate of different viewpoints?

In "Mirror Reflections=Mirages", we commented on some of the writings, and comments, of Pope John Paul II. Since then, the pope had died, after a prolonged battle with ill health; towards the end, he had rejected an offer to return to hospital, for more intensive care, knowing that the time had come. His last public appearance was in the latter part of March 2005. He died April 2, at about 9.37pm. That evening St. Peter's piazza was packed with people, in a vigil of prayer; and when his death was announced, the vast crowd broke out in applause, by clapping, an expression of love, and respect, for "their Papa"!

After much speculation in the media, cardinal Ratzinger was elected the new pope, taking the name, Benedict XVI. The outpouring of grief, and praises bestowed on the deceased Holy Father, were beyond description. It was not long, before there were calls, for him to receive early nomination, for sainthood. Indeed, here was a man who, in spite of an attempt on his life, when he was seriously wounded; in spite of crippling arthritis, Parkinsonism, a fractured hip, surgical procedures, and more, managed to achieve greatness, with immense humility, for the church, and for a troubled world. More than any other pope, he traveled outside Italy, extensively, to so many countries, even with his failing health. Wherever he went, he gave opportunity to hundreds of thousands, to see, and hear him. He was especially adept, at attracting the youth, the future church, the future of the world.

Thus, it came as no surprise, after his death, to see enormous crowds, from all over, millions of people, converging on Rome, and on Vatican City. An estimate of hundreds of thousands, from his native Poland, were said to have left their homes, their towns, to be 'with their Pope', at the end! This whole episode was covered extensively in all media, and especially on television, in the US, and most parts of the world. *He truly belonged to all people, to the whole world. To say that it was moving, and magnificent, was putting it mildly-----!* Reports also suggested that hundreds of millions across the world, tuned in to their TV sets, or to radios, to listen in, to those proceedings, as they were given extensive coverage. One felt mesmerized. Three American presidents attended the funeral services. There was also speculation early on, in the media, about the Pope's successor, if perhaps there was inside string pulling, going on, in the political world of the Vatican, that might have resulted in the election of cardinal Ratzinger. The vast majority, however, realized that he was well qualified, was duly elected through the usual process; and, even though he was different from John Paul II, he deserved a chance, before critics started on their attacks.

Much was projected on worldwide news outlets, both before, and after, the late pope's death. An article in 'Time' magazine, highlighted the fact that heads of state, friends, and perhaps, also those considered enemies, were in Rome, together, in liturgy, sharing at least, for a moment, *a sign of peace!* How amazing, and wonderful, that was! If only such an outpouring of sentiment, were universally deep seated, and directed towards all mankind; and if only, *we made it a policy of each, and every day.* Pope John Paul II would so love to witness that, from the heavens beyond. But humanity being as fickle as it is, we soon heard predictions about his potential successor; would he be young, or old; liberal, or stoically conservative; from Italy, or another nation; from Europe, or from poorer countries such as, Africa, Latin America, or beyond. And when Ratzinger became Pope Benedict XVI, lo and behold, we started hearing comments about his past, his adherence to rigid church doctrine; whether he would be able to reach out as much, or travel as much, as his predecessor. Some were critical of the selection of Ratzinger, even certain insiders, within the Catholic Church. Why could not people, the so-called experts, simply give the new pope a chance? Yes, John Paul II, left enormous shoes, for someone to fit into, true enough. The new pope will undoubtedly do the very best he can, in a very disturbed world.

In connection with the late Pope's pleas, on behalf of the poor, and the hungry, a pastor at a church service, had some heart wrenching comments, when he said, 'Africa is dying'. He said that, we should all care that three bishops were going to meet the Group of Eight, at their summit in Scotland. The bishops would tell that group that, the 'dream of Africa', was 'children without Aids'! Then he pointed out how 30,000 children, died each day, in Africa, from hunger, malnutrition, and other treatable diseases, besides those facing Aids. He said that most of us were very well off, and had excesses. Again, in the book, "Mirror Reflections=Mirages", this writer attempted to plea, not only, for the poor, and hungry, of Africa, but also, for all those over Latin America, Asia, the Middle East, and more.

Catholics, and other Christians, and those from other religious faiths, attended the late pope's funeral, often sitting side, by side, or, across from each other. There were leaders from most nations, kings, princes, queens, prime ministers, presidents, ambassadors, other politicians, besides hundreds of thousands of people, from all walks of life, jammed into St. Peter's square, and on the outside. In "The Pope Answers", John Paul II, stated that there are millions, who never get the chance to hear the Gospel of the church. They received a special gift, from Jesus, because he died for them, as well as, for us. The pope went on to say that, the church was glad that there were many true, and holy, things, in other religions as, Buddhism, Hinduism, Islam, and others. On those issues of poverty, hunger, and disease, John Paul II emphasized how, it had always been important for the church, to do its work through missionaries; that, they also carried out their work by building schools, hospitals, universities, printing presses, training farms, workshops, etc. He reminded us that the poor of the world were also hungry for God. Pope John Paul II knew this, only too well, as he traveled the corners of the globe, even in the last infirm, and frail, years, of his life's ministry. And we were also reminded, in his book, lest we tend to forget, that in 1990 alone, several missionaries doing work in various countries, had been murdered. They are often helping people, in dangerous areas of the world, in countries, with a great deal of unrest, amongst 'the poorest of the poor'.

The late pope had repeatedly emphasized that human development, cannot exclude respect for the natural world, and cannot forever 'exploit the animals, and plants, and the natural elements'. He also reminded all of us, *that mankind had a moral responsibility, in the use, or misuse, of nature.* Judging by what has gone on, in our world, even in developed countries, perhaps, especially in those very countries, how many have heeded such teachings? It is amazing how many, of John Paul the second's, writings, had direct bearing on human behavior, and on what people had done to this fragile planet. *His comments continued to reiterate the need to look after the poor, the hungry, the sick, and the oppressed; but nowhere did they mention, that, we could do this through aggression, through wars, by destruction, and by violent death.*

One of the doctors, who consulted on Pope John Paul II, in his struggle for survival, after the assassination attempt, in 1981, was American, Dr. Kevin M. Cahill. He described, in 'America' magazine, how this pope was a cooperative, and obedient, patient; and how, in his lifetime of practice, as a physician, he had not seen a better example of a seriously ill patient, "who combined humility, and inherent nobility"! This doctor soon became impressed with the pope's wide range of interests, that reflected on the pope's qualities that, made him such "an influence in a shallow, and fickle, world".

An editorial in that same magazine, presented many challenges that remained for the new Pope, Benedict XVI, besides, moulding, and guiding, the church, into the twenty first century. To repeat some of them, those challenges included, the existence of numerous nuclear weapons, economic inequalities, consequences of globalization (good, or bad), wars, environmental damage and destruction; and the changes in our climate discussed so often, by scientists. This article emphasized how it was most important for members of all religions, to work together, to live in peace. As for the Catholic Church, challenges included, divorce, abortion, contraception, the requirement of celibacy for the priesthood, homosexuality, the decrease in the number of priests, and importantly, the role of women in the church.

The editor pointed out that discussions on the ordination of women needed to continue; that, "it was most often women, who passed on the faith, as educators, and mothers". It emphasized how, "a church that cannot openly discuss such matters", would be considered, a church in retreat. There are many thinkers who agree with such statements. Allegedly, theologians had been silenced, and reprimanded, for openly discussing some of these issues. Some writers to "America" have already complained that the magazine had adopted a 'more conservative' approach, since the resignation of its previous editor. The forced manipulation, or indoctrination, of people, in any church, is not a good sign; surely, we had many hard lessons from ancient church history. There were many reports, in the past, of suppression, of lack of democracy, in the church, so to speak; although, democracy in its true meaning, might not be applicable to the totality of the church. But then, how else will any church, be able to delve into, and try to resolve, such questions, as outlined above? How can it make progress? How will it survive, and grow? Let us recall that the Catholic Church has championed freedoms all over the world.

Another piece, in 'America', magazine, was edited by Fr. E. Martin, S.J., and it dealt with responses from prominent Catholics in the US, as to what the next pope should do. There were many and varied suggestions. One hoped that the new pope *would require Curia officials to do missionary work in inner city parishes, to experience life there; he went on, that, when one lived well, had regular meals, all the comforts of life, and received VIP treatment, it helped muddy theological values!* Those who have lived missionary lives, in third world countries, under enormous hardships, will no doubt, agree with that writer. Some said that the new pope should be like John Paul II; others, that he should not be like any of the previous popes, but rather, his own pastoral leader. Another believed that, the pope needed to hear the cries of the poor, because they were being silenced by all the media hype. Then, there were some, who thought that the pope should invite, past, vocal critics, of the church, for sharing of the bread. Others again reiterated, that the pope should remove restrictions on the priesthood, presently limited to celibate males. And some felt, that, greater authority, should be given, to local bishops, and to local parishes.

According to some of these reports, Pope Benedict XVI, gave reasons for his choice of a name, to align himself with Pope Benedict XV, who demonstrated courage, and had tried hard, to prevent world war one; and later tried to limit its dangerous consequences. This is very much in line, with the late John Paul II, trying to prevent the war in Iraq, because of unforeseen consequences (and his fear of consequences, has already come to pass, in Iraq). Some of our, politicians, thought they were smarter, than our late pope, and now, they would never admit, how terribly wrong they were. As far as an apology from American officials, critics have maintained that, it had rarely happened, in the past, because of extreme arrogance. Commentators have also wondered if, Benedict XVI would also be a traveling pope, like his predecessor. The answer soon came, when the Vatican announced that, he would travel to Germany in August, for world youth day! And as in previous youth day gatherings, tens of thousands of young men, and women, were expected to be there, for the new pope.

The book, "The Pope Answers", (St. Paul Publications), is an adaptation, by Sr. Juliette Baker, from John Paul the second's encyclical, 'Redemptoris Missio', and is in a format of questions, and answers. We are reminded how Christianity is multifaceted, and it refers to many other religions, besides Christianity; but there were some 230 million people, in the world, who still called themselves, Atheist. There were a billion, or a little above that, who professed to be Roman Catholic; and then, in the Christian faiths, there were also, protestants, Anglicans, Orthodox, and many others. Muslims numbered under a billion people; then there were Buddhists, Hindus; many, in various Chinese religions; and smaller groups included Jews, Sikhs, Shintoists, and many others. Others went by the name 'New' religionists.

Readers will conclude that, that is quite a mix of religions, scattered around the globe. There is, and has been, controversy, within the Catholic Church, itself, within other Christian communities; and there have been longstanding disagreements, between Catholics, and other Christians. It is no wonder then, that there have been disagreements, between Christians, and, those of other religions; and between those belonging to many different religions, amongst themselves. Even in the Muslim religion, we have recently heard more, and more, that imams lament the fact, that, different groups of Muslims, around the world, have interpreted some of the teachings in the Qu'ran, in many different ways, such as, the questions of violence, wars, the role of women, etc. It was this great divide between Christianity, and other faiths, that, Pope John Paul II tried hard to bridge over. Regrettably, we see, in history, religions used as a pretext, for violence, and many of our wars; and we find it also in our recent past. It has reared its ugly head again, with America's wars in Afghanistan, and now, Iraq. Muslims, especially, those with strong fundamental views, had been hurt, and angered, by this, and called 'for holy war'. They had long claimed they were being marginalized, and discriminated against; and that word, 'crusade', had reappeared several times, in speeches, by our side, or by theirs; and our side had been referred to as 'infidels', which was another relic from the past, of inter-religious, wars. Thus, we find humanity repeating past mistakes, over, and over. And yet, there remains a great deal of goodness, in many people, everywhere; this needs to be brought out, to be nurtured continuously, to overcome so many evil traits.

One of the questions in the pope's book, dealt with members of the Catholic, Christian, or other faiths, trying to persuade others, to change their religious beliefs; that most people would likely resent such an approach. This topic had often given rise to misconceptions, in the past. Yes, serious misdeeds, had been committed in ancient times, 'to achieve conversion', in an attempt to force people, to change their religious beliefs, for example, to force them to recognize Christianity, as the one, true, faith. Many lost their lives in these awful, misinterpretations, of "religion". In more recent history, however, the attitude of churches has been quite different; and the old methods, were not the ways, recent popes, had referred to, when they used the word, 'Mission'. In "The Pope Answers", John Paul II emphasized that, the church does not tell anyone, to change their religion; rather, they are invited to listen to the 'Good News', as listed in the Gospels. Each person was free to accept, or reject, such an offer.

A pastor discussed how bishops, priests, and other ministers, of the church, had opinions on peace, on wars, and on killing of innocent people, and so on; but they were not permitted to preach about such matters to their 'flock', or urge people what to do, how to vote, because of that 'famous' separation of church, and state. They might have a strong opinion, beliefs, on some of those questions, but they had to keep them to themselves, as far as their official capacity, in the church, was concerned. Thus, they said, we were supposed to have 'free speech', in America, *but in this country, church officials, were not free, to say, what they believed in!* If the church stepped out of line, certain corrupt politicians would have those churches investigated, and threaten their 'tax free status'. My, my, is that the sound of *Mammon*, jingling again, in the US, even interfering, in the running of our churches? *There is another good example of a 'fragile democracy', in a 'free society'!* On the other hand, in many churches around the world, church officials have spoken out against evil, against oppression, for the poor, indigenous people, and had been victimized for it, as we know, only too well, from our neighbors in Latin America.

Extreme religious rights groups, talk a great deal about values, and morals, and this goes on in many countries, but was especially prevalent in the last republican, presidential, campaigns, in America. They talk of the bible, and of scripture, but do they really meditate, on the subjects they talk about, do they believe them? Or, is it simply idle talk, and shady politics, as usual? Such idle talk would be difficult to come across, in the late pope's writings, he was usually succinct, and to the point. There are many examples, for such groups of people to ponder. Are we not told, 'Thou shall not kill', and all religious groups, refer to this teaching? It does not only say, 'thou shall not kill babies, or the elderly, or the infirm', *it also included prisoners, all types of violence with murder, the innocent in Iraq, or in Afghanistan, the innocent of world war two, those in the Balkans, in Ireland, in Israel or Palestine, in Asia, in Africa, and Latin America, wherever- - -!* **'Thou shall not kill', we were told.**

Religious teachings also spelled out, for us, 'Love your neighbor, as yourself'. They did not say, to, only, 'love your friends, or those you like, or of a certain color, or creed, or the rich, or those who give you gifts, or rewards'! Your neighbors could be total strangers; white, or of color; rich, or poor; healthy, or sick; they could be living in distant lands. And the hardest teaching of Jesus, that baffled all those around him, *'Love your enemies'!* It did not say that, you could bomb Baghdad, or Hiroshima, or Nagasaki, or Tokyo, or Berlin, or Cologne, or London, or Coventry, or Malta, or New York, or so many other cities, or countries, back into the Middle Ages. Ah, how very difficult, almost impossible, many of these teachings, had proved, for humanity, to follow! As we have witnessed in speeches, in campaign slogans, and in writings, there is mainly, a great deal of talk, because talk is cheap, it comes easy- - -!

Pope John Paul II, throughout his life, expressed great devotion to the Blessed Virgin Mary; and a few lines in a particular church hymn, are so appropriate to some of the above thoughts in this section, "Gentle Mother, peaceful dove, teach us wisdom, teach us love". Yes, indeed, Pope John Paul II wanted to usher in, he yearned for, a *new millennium* of justice for all (and there is no justice, without love); and of lasting peace. No doubt, his successors will work hard, towards those same goals.

AND THE JOURNEY GOES ON

Pope John Paul II was a staunch promoter of peace on our planet, and he had looked on the approach of a new millennium, as an opportunity for mankind to change course, and live in peace. It must have been most disheartening for him, to see another major war, in the Middle East, and in Afghanistan, so early in the twenty first century.

Our journey goes on, but, because most international affairs thinkers, believe that, this US administration had become seriously mired in Iraq, that journey cannot continue, without updated reports on Iraq; and, perhaps, additional reactions from other parts of the world. Recently, a blip arrived via the Internet. This implied that authorities in Saudi Arabia (and these are alleged friends of the US), had assessed the chaotic situation in Iraq, and they had warned British, and American, officials, that Iraq was disintegrating; that the upcoming elections, though a good sign, might not stem the tide of danger on the ground, in Iraq. December 2005 was supposed to bring an elected Iraqi government; but there again, experts had maintained that Iraq had a quasi government of sorts, that was a puppet of the US, and nothing would change. They had an election, under the gun, and accusations of much corruption in the electoral process, all under the control of the American military. *There is much corruption in elections in the US, why not in Iraq, right?* The so-called Iraqi constitution, had the disapproval of a significant percentage of the population; inter-ethnic strife was prevalent; Sunnis were murdering Shiites, and Shiites were murdering, or torturing, Sunnis. They might have assumed that 'if our American liberators' do some of these things, we could do likewise.

Towards the latter part of 2005, most polls in the US were certainly not promising for Bush, and reporters in the US, and overseas, continued to dissect the drop in popularity for this president, down to around 35%; and Cheney's numbers were even more dismal, at 19%! Critics seemed to agree that the most important factor, in those polls, was that Americans had lost confidence in Bush's handling of the country's problems; they no longer believed his reasons for the war (some of us did not believe them, before the war started)! A substantial number of those polled, no longer believed that he was truthful, or caring, and even questioned his integrity, according to some of those polls. Other leaders around the western world, unless they were tyrannical, or dictatorial, would have asked for a vote of confidence, *and if it turned against them, they resigned!* If democracy had become a sham, as some had feared for the US, then there seldom is any resignation by senior officials, and then only for fear of impeachment. And because of political cronyism, resignation, in the US government, had become quite rare in recent years, no matter what the accusations. Some critics had fingered this republican administration, as one of the most corrupt; a commentator put it succinctly when he said, *absolute power corrupts absolutely!* No doubt, this referred to the many scandals in this US government, with republican domination in the Senate, House, and White house; and some also maintain, a republican leaning Supreme Court. *Yes, absolute power corrupts absolutely!*

A November poll showed that 57% of Americans believed that Bush deliberately misled them on Iraq, to make the case for war; 60% of those polled, wanted to see congressional hearings begin. They reported that both republicans, and democrats, had a net negative rating with the public, that is, "a pox on both your houses", as one commentator put it. That is a sad state of affairs in US politics, that is why there is an increasing belief, the issue of true democracy, has been on the edge, it had turned into an imitation of one. And, as many as 79% of Americans, were of the opinion, that, the Libby indictment (Cheney's right hand man), was indeed, a very serious matter for this republican administration.

Experts had alleged that an Iraqi expatriate, Chalabi, had duped the Bush administration, on weapons of mass destruction in Iraq, and the administration knew it. US officials had tried to stir up trouble for the man, in Iraq, but they were rebuffed, because Chalabi had gained in popularity over there, and had even been elected to the provisional government. What does that say for American policy? How did US officials react? Why, in November 2005, Chalabi was of course, invited to Washington, 'because there were important matters to discuss with him'! As the Bush administration, by most reports, was in trouble on Iraq, possibly they felt the need to talk to this guy, after all; the same man they had tried to criminalize just a few months before. Thus Chalabi, wealthy, and influential, returned to Washington, in spite of his alleged trickery against US authorities. A reporter on a Chris Matthews program, on MSNBC, said that Chalabi would tell you anything, whether it is about Iraq, or Iran, or Syria, or Israel. Therefore, these speakers said, as a shrewd politician, *he sensed that the Americans were looking for an excuse, any excuse, to invade Iraq!* It was alleged that, Chalabi fed them highly questionable data on Iraq, and Saddam's plots; and our US government believed all that trash, and plunged into their propaganda on the American people, *about the mushroom cloud that will come upon us from Iraq- - - -!*

On Veterans' day, 2005, critics accused that Bush gave a speech, sounding more like campaign slogans, and rhetoric, still trying to justify his war on Iraq. He continued to paint certain democratic congressmen as unpatriotic, for continuing to criticize the war. Bush himself, had been totally out of touch with the rest of the world, and now, even the American people, belatedly, believed that Bush deliberately misled them. Many others had claimed that, the US had imperialistic notions on Iraq, and the oil, rich, Middle East! Here, we need to recall that some half a century ago, American officials had warned the British, and the French, to get out of the Suez Canal region, 'or else'! Many politicians then, had questioned that aggressive stance by the US government, but could they have had well laid plans, all along? Thus, critics said, Bush talked about *leaving Iraq in due course, but they sensed that, it was all just talk.*

As proof, they cited claims that the Americans were busy, building large military bases in Iraq, naturally, for US forces, 'because the new Iraqi government would almost certainly ask us to stay'! Oh, give us a break. Such disgraceful policies, had caused the US much trouble around the world, and citizens of the world understood that, only too well. Again, on the program 'Hardball', with Chris Matthews, guests discussed how the

American government aimed to keep forces, in Iraq, for an indefinite period, and they would not leave any time soon; and that, America wanted to keep on, exerting its influence, in the region- - - - imperialism?

Another reporter, who had been embedded with US forces, was discussing Iraq. He said it was clear that US forces had become the target, every time they ventured out; and this was precisely what congressman Murtha had been saying in December 2005! But some American officers were announcing that by going out, and attacking, they were making some streets safer. Most Iraqis disagreed, because the Americans were making lives more dangerous for everybody. Army officers, in Iraq, told this reporter that, wherever they saw a package, or an object, or a parked car, they assumed it was a bomb. *Every young man on the streets was considered a suspect; they even had to consider women, and children, as suspects, sometimes.* This was a sad commentary, and an eye opener. Is that what America's policies had done, to Iraq? Such reports were diametrically opposed to statements put out by US officials, that, they were spreading freedom, and democracy. Do the above statements *correlate with freedom, and democracy, for the average Iraqis, in the street? Readers will be, the judge, of that.*

Also in November 2005, we had reports that US forces had entered a facility in Iraq (under Iraqi control), and they found a substantial number of Sunni Iraqis, who had been held captive; some had been starved, and tortured, some had died. Are we to assume that the 'new democratic' Iraqis, had decided they could behave like that, because they had seen, or heard of, actions against prisoners, by American forces, in Iraq, or in Afghanistan, and at Guantanamo, Cuba? As is typical of some US government officials, when any illegal behavior was uncovered in Iraq, they promptly announced that they were not aware of such a facility, under Iraqi security. They did not know who authorized it. Allegedly, Shiites had perpetrated those acts against the Sunnis. Sunni officials demanded an independent investigation, not one run by the Americans. Soon after these regrettable revelations, came reports *that US forces had used white phosphorus, a chemical weapon, during the American attacks on Fallujah!*

White phosphorus had been declared illegal, internationally; but as critics had stated before, American governments had often ignored international laws. To try to deflect the ugly implications of this news release, *US officials announced that it was used only on the insurgents- - - -! Are we admitting now, to chemical, and perhaps, biological, warfare, the United States of America?* How far into the depths had we descended? But, as we all know, many pathetic, officials, had not been able to distinguish between an insurgent, and an innocent Iraqi civilian; most of them were called insurgents; notice the above statements. Surely, people everywhere, remember that, Bush, and Blair, and their cliques, went to Iraq to remove Saddam Hussein because of weapons of mass destruction, that is, an ongoing nuclear program, and chemical, and biological, weapons, which the Iraqis did not possess; but the US did! With a 'holier than thou' attitude, some American politicians attempt to convince the world, that US forces never use chemical weapons. When will the US government learn that the rest of the world, had long ago, stopped believing much of what came out of Washington?

Towards the end of 2005, the International Red Cross had again demanded *that it gets free access to all detainees in US custody, wherever they were.* That agency had not been allowed (as had happened in iron curtain countries in the past) to visit some of the detainees. Most sensible persons, on this earth, would immediately ask, why? And, the only plausible answer would be, because US authorities might have 'abused, or tortured', some of those detainees, and therefore, the Red Cross did not gain access to them. With all this news out there, Bush administration officials continued to state that, *they handled their detainees according to the Geneva Convention (not true, according to world critics);* and they claimed that the US did not abuse its prisoners (not true either, according to those same critics). A high CIA official then, allegedly said, that, *torture was in the eye of the beholder.* With such depraved talk, one has to wonder how those people would like to be subjected to the same treatment, as some of those detainees were? Critics had indeed, been quite vocal, but they did not need anything else, to understand what had been going on, in America, besides statements, as the above!

Professor Mark J. Allman, wrote on 'Post war Justice', in 'America' magazine, and highlighted the glaring difference between US assessments, and those coming from other countries. The question was, on the serious danger posed to innocent people, from the use of depleted uranium ammunitions, the US military had deployed for some years, in its various confrontations. Readers will recall that, there are those who had asserted that there was no conscience left, in some of our world's leaders. This article showed that US army studies, had concluded that, depleted uranium posed no serious risks. *Surprised? Was it not the pentagon that years ago, had denied that, Agent Orange had caused untold harm to US personnel, and Vietnamese civilians?* They had been proved wrong. On the other hand, the UK atomic energy commission estimated that, *about 500,000 people in Kuwait, and Iraq, could die from the use of these weapons, in the first Gulf war, alone!* Who is telling the truth, and who is not?

This article also pointed out the hypocrisy of US officials, launching a war against Iraq, because of prohibited weapons, whereas US forces had used their own weapons of mass destruction in Iraq, depleted uranium ammunitions (and we also had white phosphorus)! The professor reminded us how Pope John Paul II, and nearly all, major religious leaders, in the world, had criticized the US invasion, as unjust. Thus, now, *after nearly three years of this war, Bush admitted in recent speeches, that they went to war on the basis of 'faulty intelligence', and he assumed responsibility for deciding on the war!* Prior to this, we had heard from White house spokespersons, that Bush could not recall any mistakes that he had made, during his administration. Critics attacked, that, his speeches, now, were an attempt to improve his dismal poll numbers. The professor also discussed how, Americans, now, had the responsibility for reconstruction, and reparations, in Iraq (as we had done most of the destruction). He said that sacrifices had to be made by Americans, *because it was our penance, for committing the sins of war- - -!* Powerful words those, that should penetrate the conscience, even, of the tough, skinned!

In October 2005, the trial of Saddam Hussein was well publicized in Iraq, and the US, many assumed, for propaganda purposes. The first criminal charges against him were that, in a village, there was an attempt on his life. Instead of trying to apprehend the culprits, to bring them to justice, the Hussein regime allegedly took revenge, and murdered a large number of villagers. Accordingly he had been charged in an Iraqi 'court of law', as people all over the world, and justice, would expect; that the trial be fair, and completely impartial, which would be difficult in Iraq. For that tyrannical act, Hussein is facing trial, as he should, and perhaps, for other acts, as well.

Experts had accused the US of dragging its feet, on this trial, *because it feared what would come out, about the 'cozy' relationship of US officials with Saddam, in the past. They also raised the question whether the US might have given the go ahead, for Iraq to invade Kuwait.* However, recently, reporters talked with ordinary folk in the streets of Jordan, as they had closely followed the Hussein trial proceedings. Almost unanimously, those people, in Jordan, ridiculed the court, the trial,, and the domineering control by the US, according to these reports. Then, they added, if this is not a farce, for show, why is Hussein not at the Hague World Court, like Milosevic? That was an important question, coming from Jordan, for the Bush administration to ponder. The trial was muddied, further, when Hussein accused at his trial, that for months, US forces had abused him, in prison, and beat him

But for fairness, and justice, let us consider certain incidents 'by our side', some of those, in the 'west'. In parts of Iraq, or Afghanistan, shots, or rockets, or improvised bombs, were used against US forces mostly, sometimes, British, rarely, another nationality, as they had so few personnel, there. Most often, the US military did not know who the culprits were, either; it had been common knowledge that 'intelligence', in Iraq, was abysmal. Thus, US forces retaliated with heavy air power, and bombed sections of those villages, or towns. Reporters usually claimed that, in those attacks, innocent civilians were killed; but US officials called this, *collateral damage, are those, clean sounding words, for murder?* Critics would obviously, have a right to ask if any of this, had any resemblance, even remotely, to the above charges, against Hussein?

Again, historically, Israeli authorities had usually bombed Palestinian territories, suspected of launching shots against Israelis, or into Israel itself. Or, because, they simply believed, terrorists were in a particular area, or building. Israelis would bomb those locations, or fired missiles into them, and critics had often claimed, that many innocent people had also been killed, or maimed, perhaps, with the guilty parties. We were seldom told the truth on such matters, and US officials were usually conspicuously silent, free from much criticism. Once again, do these activities bear any resemblance to the above trial? *This topic could lead to immense ethical, and theological, discussions, on war, on retaliation, on revenge; on those who believed in hitting back, with more savage force than was used against us, because 'we had the power'.* Or simply, to hold discussions on values, such as, what is right; what is wrong? Yet, we have much to learn- - -!

A guest speaker appeared on CNN in November, and stated that Bush had declared victory in Afghanistan, and yet, in 2005 attacks against the US, and coalition forces, had increased over there; and regrettably, more American personnel had been killed. Reporters claimed that, even the president of Afghanistan could not go anywhere without United States forces guarding him. <u>What type of victory can be claimed there, as well</u>? It had been alleged that the US was once again, supporting war, lords, as we had done in the past, and these, were engaged in the largest, illegal, lucrative, drug trade, ever! *If true, how does that, portray America, before the whole world?*

With the quagmire of Iraq, and other trouble spots, and so much still going on in Afghanistan, members of congress in the US, were calling for our forces to start coming back home, to save American lives. And increasingly, Americans were declaring at the polls, lack of trust in their leadership; and in the handling of the war by Bush, and Cheney, and their clique. How did the president, and vice president, react? As expected, they launched a verbal attack on democrats, because initially, they had also supported this war! But, it was common knowledge that, when congress supported the war, *it was not true that they had full access to the intelligence, that Bush, and Cheney, already had- - -!*

In "Mirror Reflections=Mirages", as well as, in this book, we have quoted reports on how US officials usually extend help, often, with many strings attached. In December 2005, new reports revealed that many schools, in America, that had received government funds, resented the presence of US military officials, in their schools, to recruit young men and women, for the armed forces. *Critics had alleged that, US officials used questionable tactics, and false information, in their recruiting procedures.* Thus, school authorities hoped to continue to receive funds for education, but at the same time, be able to prevent the military from recruiting on their premises. The American government attitude was such, that, recruiting had to proceed, or school funds would be removed. These arguments ended up, before the Supreme Court, for their legal deliberations.

On the PBS program 'Now', with David Broncaccio, critics claimed that US recruiting in this way, enticed kids under 18, to sign up for the military----they were enticed *with promises of money, the good life, and recruiters pretended they were their good friends! Of course, they never mentioned war, or Iraq!* It was also alleged that the 'no child left behind' ploy, by president Bush, meant that, if schools did not open their doors for the military, they would indeed forfeit their funding. Such behavior by the government, and by the military was referred to, as corrupt, yet again! And, was it by accident that *recruiters were notably active in schools of economically depressed areas?* No, because it was the poorer communities that were more likely to respond, and have kids sign up, because of the promised benefits, by government officials.

A former recruiter was on a news program, and stated that for him, *the job was a nightmare;* that, they went into these deprived areas, *and some recruiters used deception.* As many potential recruits, had problems of one type, or another, those offers by the military sounded quite attractive to them. This ex-army official said that recruiters were expected to meet their 'quota of victims'. *They used what was called 'frauding', to trap prospective candidates.* The military was said to spend about 4 billion dollars a year, in this practice, of recruiting; but they were also working on secretive, computerized, data systems, of all US high schools, *to pinpoint those, that were most likely to yield recruits for the armed forces.* What was equally disturbing, were reports by a pastor, that the Bush administration had (more, or less) muzzled church authorities, not to say anything political; no comments against the government, or Iraq, because of a threat that, those who did that, would likely be investigated by the Internal Revenue service (IRS). America must be the only "free" country, in the world, where church pastors are not allowed to criticize the government; just as they are not allowed to do so, in tyrannical, dictatorship, states. How much more evidence of incipient, home style, dictatorship, are we about to discover?

How desperate can a situation become, in the US, for the military, for the pentagon? On a Wolf Blitzer program, on CNN, reports showed that, a single mother had been out of the armed forces some twenty years, she thought she was done with that part of her life; but she had just been called up by the US military, for service in Iraq! Thus, it came to pass that military officials were falling short, in the number of military recruits, needed. These were more signs of trouble, reflecting on the chaos in Iraq; similar to the troubles Bush had been experiencing, in his rapid decline at the polls.

That is how political pundits, and the elite, had dreamed up the series of 'information' speeches, to be given by him, in December 2005. *Why only 'inform the public', after the polls for Bush had crashed?* In the speeches he apparently kept on associating Iraq with Al Qaeda, as an excuse for his going to war; that Al Qaeda was intent on building an empire, all the way to Indonesia! What about the growing 'American Empire' across this globe, developed under various administrations, including this one? It seemed that, wherever US forces went, there, they often remained. According to speedy news reports, Bush ratings allegedly improved, ever so slightly, after those speeches. If that held true, it would only confirm the opinions of world critics, that Americans tended to be quite fickle, and showed no real interest in international implications.

And, as if the problems American foreign policy had unleashed, on Iraq, were not serious enough, US politicians had engendered an international nightmare; amongst 'friendly' nations, and others, not quite so friendly, America had become a pariah. In his speeches Bush tried to explain his Iraq policies, as critics had stated he had none; and most of his talks had been before captive audiences, strictly controlled, military crowds, or a 'yes', highly screened, audience. Supposedly he would try to explain how, or when, US forces would begin to wind down in Iraq. Critics promptly accused, that Bush gave no new details, just a rehash of his old positions, no timetable for withdrawal, nothing. The same day, of one of the Bush speeches, a reporter was shown talking *with Iraqi forces and their commanders, because Bush had announced that as many as 30 Iraqi brigades were ready, to take over from US forces.* Whereas experts had stated that perhaps 1 brigade was actually prepared, and the Iraqi forces interviewed, seemed to agree. They said that they were not ready, they had no body protection, antiquated weapons; and the insurgents were better armed. They claimed that they needed American forces with them, because they never knew who was in charge in Iraq!

This year had brought many crises across our world, with many disasters hitting various countries. In the US, besides the tragedies of war, natural disasters were becoming more numerous, and more severe. Hurricanes were quite powerful in 2004, and they were even worse in 2005. Many months after the Katrina hurricane, thousands of people had remained devastated, and more details were emerging. As often happens, in catastrophes of this magnitude, a criminal element takes advantage of the chaos and tries to make money, out of the misfortunes of others. US government agencies were investigating, and prosecuting, those who proved to be so callous.

They referred to a man who alleged he used a private plane to fly victims out of the area, including those injured, and children. He received thousands of dollars in donations. Others, applied for government cash relief, 'after they had lost everything', but they were nowhere near the storm affected areas. Others had been accused of defrauding the Red Cross in its humanitarian efforts. There was a report on the CBS '60 Minutes' program, showing a major bridge, that could permit people to escape from the storm ravaged areas, of New Orleans. But apparently, police, from a town, on the other side had blocked that bridge; because they wanted to stop residents of New Orleans from crossing over. Shots were fired to turn the crowd back, and it was pointed out that those people were 95% black. The mayor and police, from the town across the bridge, were accused of racism, but they responded, that they were only protecting their town from chaos, and anarchy, as they too, had suffered from Katrina.

There were also congressional hearings in Washington, and one, after another, the hurricane evacuees, reported that they had seen little, or none, of the help that had been promised, by the federal government. They had faced nothing but obstruction, and hassles, from officials of the federal emergency management agency (FEMA). One lady said that they had ruined her health, and she was now being treated for high blood pressure! *They complained that the officials even suggested what answers to write on their government forms.* Most of the evacuees agreed that the only genuine help they had seen came from church, or other, voluntary organizations.

There were also intermittent reports of persisting difficulties in the US economy, and with the education, and health care, systems. In December 2005, news reports alleged that, *about 5% of 'advanced' students, in the US, were actually 'illiterate'; and now, even at college levels, only 31% of students could read at a proficient level.* And amongst Hispanics, only 30% were doing reasonably well in English. As education, and economy, impact on each other, it was no surprise to hear adverse reports on the economic front, as well. Credit card debt had increased from about 30 billion dollars in the early 1990's, to a staggering figure of over 800 billion in 2005! Such a level of debt is disastrous for the people themselves, but also for the US economy, because experts have long asserted that there will be a day of reckoning. Coupled with this, two major US companies, General Motors, and Ford, announced plans to lay off tens of thousands of workers, and close several plants, over the next few months. Andy Rooney of the CBS '60 Minutes' program, discussed how consumer ratings on automobiles, with a decent reputation for performance, listed only two that were American, and they were in the lower section of the list; all the others were from foreign companies, predominantly, Japan. And amongst those autos with very poor ratings, the majority were, regrettably, American cars. Andy humorously suggested that, American company officials could spend less time dreaming up fancy names for their cars, and more time on trying to build better cars!

Guests on the program 'Now', on PBS, with David Broncaccio, discussed certain manipulations by the oil industry; and how the Bush administration, instead of pursuing legislation, against their officials, rammed through congress, laws, to give the oil industry a gift of billions of dollars in tax breaks, and other perks! *They showed how the Bush clique granted this largesse, even as oil prices had soared, and remained sky high; and oil companies had declared record profits, in the tens of billions of dollars, and their CEOs raked in a bonanza, in options, bonuses, etc.* At a news conference, senators claimed that republicans had refused to insist on sworn testimony, by oil executives, at government hearings! Why is it that whenever we hear of oil company investigations, we also hear that republicans are firmly on the side of "OIL"? Food, for thought, is there, for everyone!

Critics had alleged that *oil tycoons manipulated the closure of refineries, to create the appearance, of a shortage of gasoline, and thus, they forced prices up, at the pump. It was all smoke, and mirrors, they said!* Critics also reiterated that American citizens needed to learn that, in a way, American democracy had become a sham; that is why, a whistle blower against these oil giants 'can only grant an interview, with a complete disguise'. People with a little common sense, would certainly assume that, if we were *truly a free, democratic, society, such whistle blowers should be able to talk openly, and report unlawful practices, without fear of persecutions, or worse!* What type of dictatorial government members, have we been sending to Washington? Senators also accused the Bush people of wanting to force oil drilling in the Alaska refuge, on the American people. Once again, it had been alleged that lawmakers, slipped many shady appropriations (pork), in the defense budget bills. *This is a customary ploy in American style, democracy- - -manipulation.*

Other commentators had pointed to the republican controlled administration, as the culture of corruption. A top democrat then called the Bush administration, 'a culture of corruption, and cronyism'. Are these not descriptions of perfect statesmen? There have been reports on numerous scandals in this administration, with investigations on members of congress, and some highly placed officials, even those close to Bush, and Cheney. In typical fashion, a republican, accused the democrats that, they previously had their own scandals, but now, they blamed everything on republicans, tit, for tat! But, a political analyst said that, these republican scandals were much more serious. News reports continued to suggest that Rove, the right hand man of Bush, remained under investigation by the special prosecutor, in the White house leak scandal.

In November 2005, yet another scandal broke out, when an influential republican congressman, publicly admitted to accepting bribes. He soon resigned. It was alleged that he had received the free use of a large yacht, a mansion, a Rolls Royce, and more. It was said that in exchange for his 'rewards', he had been instrumental, in specific companies receiving lucrative defense contracts. And, harsh critics are always clamoring that this is one that was caught; what about all the others? The same had been stated about the corporate scandals in America. In a speech before congress, senator John McCain berated the revolving door practice, in US politics; how members of congress felt beholden to corporations; that there were allegations that some members received payment for 'services rendered', whilst still holding office! This is not really new, as many critics have been making similar allegations for years. *But the depth of apparent corruption, and fickle conscience, in some politicians, here, and elsewhere, is difficult to comprehend.*

When Libby, the right hand man of Cheney, was indicted by the grand jury, for the special prosecutor, critics said that another reporter, Woodward, had testified that, he had learned about the White house leak, from a high official, at least one month before Libby. They alleged that, as Woodward was not free to reveal his source, *his coming forward could be some form of legal mumbo jumbo, to provide some cover for Libby.* The world of politics is an absolute maze of deals, trickery, manipulations, and confabulation, and therefore, we may never learn the absolute truth, in such matters! They also said that Woodward had not provided any new information, through which the special prosecutor could indict, **the real culprit!** Thus, Woodward's intentions became subject to criticism as well, and other reporters chastised him. He, of course, had been writing books concerning the politics of Iraq. Readers of such jargon, would conclude, that some US politicians must spend nights, and days, all at taxpayers' expense, trying to dream up ways, of thwarting the law. These same officials *often announce, with tongue in cheek, that they are working for the American people. Oh, give us another break!*

News commentator, Olbermann, on MSNBC station, featured comments by John Dean, a former Nixon high official, who theorized that perhaps, Libby, could have been covering up, for vice president Cheney, in this enormous White house scandal. These guest speakers implied that, if democrats won handily in the 2006 elections in the US, then Cheney's health *could suddenly appear to deteriorate, as an excuse for him to step down, and leave!* Some November polls showed that, *on integrity, Cheney was only given 29% approval, and that the majority of Americans believed he deliberately misled the people, on Iraq!* Apparently later, John Dean had also commented on the December story, about Bush authorizing spying on American citizens, without consulting congress, and the courts. Allegedly, Dean said that, *if Bush admitted to willfully doing this, he probably broke the laws of the land. Dean had first hand experience of abuse of power, under Nixon! He should know what abuse is, surely.* Coincidentally, in December, some European papers quoted Internet reports on impeachment that, 57% were now in favor.

Senior administration officials, including the president, have sometimes been criticized because their so-called 'impromptu' interviews are rare, and that, perhaps, they are given advance notice of the subject matter, and questions that would be asked of them. This likely goes on with leaders all over the world, so much for 'impromptu', interviews! For example, the 'town hall meetings' politicians hold in the US, are they really free, and open? Are the topics not discussed ahead of time, with the speakers; and the audience, are they not strictly screened, and selected? On an MSNBC program, listeners were submitting emails, on actions by president Bush, concerning some of these discussions. One viewer said that in the US, *presidential prerogative had come to mean abuse of power!*

Early in November, most news stations featured the summit of the Americas, in Mar del Plata, Argentina. As had been the case at many of these summits, there were demonstrations, and soon, it turned violent---violent, mostly anti-American protests, with the burning of US flags, and buildings, and cars, were torched. Police used force, and hurled tear gas. Critics alleged that Bush, and company, had attracted bigger, and more violent protests. News clips showed Bush during a speech, admitting that it was not easy for the host government, to have these meetings, especially if he (Bush) was attending. This seemed to confirm world opinion that, increasingly, America's administration policies had generated more intense anti-Americanism.

These, often misguided, policies of the US, and others, became clearer when we learned that the recent United Nations summit was disappointing to many, in its results. There was failure to agree on a nuclear non-proliferation treaty, which the UN secretary general, had pressed for. *And the consequences of that failure would be laid at the doorstep of the US military-industrial complex.* An 'America' magazine editorial was most appropriate, and to the point, when it stated, "How can *non-nuclear states like Iran, be expected to refrain from developing nuclear weapons, when nuclear armed states renege on their commitments to disarm*". It went on, "This is especially the case when the pentagon is floating a plan to employ nuclear weapons, to deter, and preemptively destroy, non-nuclear threats". Thinkers, worldwide, had known this for years, as it pertained to the US. The editorial suggested that the US conspired with thugs from underdeveloped countries, to keep up a business that resulted in thousands of deaths every year, in poor countries. This, of course, referred to the scandalous weapons industry.

Another troubling report came in December 2005. The US government had imprisoned a man for about three years as 'an enemy combatant', a ruse devised by the Bush administration. But they had court authorization, this time, to do this. However, when the administration found that they had no solid proof on this man, to try him in a military court, they changed tactics, and asked the courts to transfer him into the civil system, on a different charge. Apparently, *the appellate courts rebuked the Bush people, by refusing to do so, after they had held him for over 3 years as an enemy combatant!* Reporters alleged that the courts sensed that, perhaps, Bush *wanted to avoid review of this case by the US Supreme Court, fearing they would lose their argument there, as well!* Why do we keep hearing of so many shady manoeuvres, under this republican regime, over, and over, and over, again?

Our world is unstable indeed, and reportedly, it had been made worse, not only, by persisting dictatorships in many countries, but also by powerful countries, like America; and other highly developed countries from the 'west', through corruption, and chicanery. When we, in the 'know-better' regions, behave like that, developing, or underdeveloped, nations, tend to do much worse. A recent report on PBS, television station, featured two women, one from Zimbabwe, the other, from Uzbekistan; and they described tyrannical acts by the governments in those countries. These two ladies visited news organizations in Europe, and in America, describing what was going on 'back home', in their countries, oppression, detention, seizure and destruction, of homes, closure of newspapers, severe control on all news reporting; and, in the case of Uzbekistan, forces recently firing on groups of civilians, who were demonstrating peacefully, in city streets, killing hundreds. We had referred briefly to such news reports, which the Uzbek government had denied; but here, now, was a witness account from one of their own, courageous, citizens. Officials, in the US, had allegedly, also developed cozy relationships, with this particular government.

In December 2005, news outlets exploded with the leaking of yet another, super scandal, *that the national security agency, in the US, was given authority, by the Bush regime, to spy, and secretly eavesdrop, on citizens in America, and others overseas, without court authorization.* Many of us suspected all along, that such intense spying was going on, that perhaps, US agencies had acted outside the law. And an attorney general, would excuse it all by stating that, if we are to fight terrorism, we must do what it takes. We are, burdened by people, in high office, who, in their official capacity, can act, in an irresponsible, and incomprehensible, manner. They ramrod in, the patriot act, on the American people, and they use it profusely, to hide their actions. In that patriot act, critics asserted that, they had instilled attacks on civil liberties, on civil rights, and on all types of freedoms. *They accused that, this once shining beacon of a democracy, had turned into a dark, sinister, unrecognizable, bully!* Some, had long questioned, if America's actions, brought to light over a period of a few years, were any different from the SS, the KGB, or so many other, super secret, tyrannical, agencies, in so many countries. Apparently, the Bush administration had given police, and secret agencies, as much leeway as they wanted. John Q. public was stabbed in the back, so to speak. Does it fit in, at all, with that label that, 'Americans got the government they deserved'? How disturbing, a label, that was.

What was even more condemnable in this 'democracy' was that, *a major news outlet allegedly knew all this was going on, at least a year before, and chose to keep such explosive news, under wraps.* This, was done, in cahoots with the US government, guess why? *For national security, of course!* People all over the world will be laughing their heads off --- now, besides a dubious democracy, they can also point to a lack of freedom of the press, in America. With all that going on, US officials pontificate that, they are the 'experts' who, can spread democracies, and freedoms, to other countries. Well, is that amazing, or what?

Whenever extreme, and dangerous, secrecy, was not uncovered by some brave souls, those journalists, who were truly trying to protect the interests of Americans, then, the Bush administration remained completely silent, and secretive. However, when such dastardly acts came to light, the president was then compelled, at times, to come out in the open, to try to preserve some standing with the American public. Thus, with this spying leak scandal, *Bush was forced to admit that he had authorized the spying; then came the clincher, 'to protect the American people, and to fight terrorism'!* These had become the collection basket, for all sorts of activities, by this government. Has this administration, so quickly, forgotten the nasty actions of the past, by US politicians, on the pretense of fighting communism? How people's freedoms, rights, and lives, in the US, were all destroyed? Are our fellow Americans, not any wiser? Have they not understood, the constant spins coming out of Washington? Why, all they need to do is, consider the following, emanating in profusion, from government officials.

We attacked Afghanistan—to protect the American people, to fight terrorism.
We attacked Iraq—to protect the American people, to fight terrorism (amongst many other, paltry, excuses).
We forced the patriot act on Americans—to protect Americans, to fight terrorism.
Government spies everywhere at will—to protect Americans, to fight terrorism.
We assault people's civil rights—to protect the American people, to fight terrorism.
We trash liberties, democracies—to protect Americans, to fight terrorism.
We condone abuse and torture of prisoners—to protect Americans, to fight terrorism.
We break, and ridicule, international laws—to protect Americans, to fight terrorism.
We trample on 'free' media rights—to protect the American people, to fight terrorism.
We assault the environment—to protect the American people, to fight terrorism.
We spy on our own citizens at will—to protect the American people, to fight terrorism.
We have also abused or tortured prisoners—to protect Americans, to fight terrorism.

Is it possible that, all those, advising president Bush, are so blinded, that they do not feel disgust, at this broken record? Are most Americans, so thoroughly brainwashed, that they do not recognize propaganda, misinformation, and lies, even if they stared them, in the face? Where was the extreme right wing, in all this? Surely, our citizens remember that, a great deal of corrupt activity was going on, not that long ago, under the Nixon administration? Has this, now become, the standard fare, of doing business, in these United States?

To add insult, to injury, Bush associates claimed that, those who had leaked, sensitive, corrupt, possibly illegal, activities, by this government, spying on its citizens, *were themselves, unpatriotic, and threatened the security of the country.* What utter poppycock, that is! *As a congressman put it, quite succinctly, referring to Bush, 'he was elected president, not king'!* Yes, indeed, we need to keep that, always in focus, because critics have reminded us that, many of the things that have been going on, in America, were activities often seen in dictatorships. That had long been suggested by thinkers, as well as, by ordinary folk, both in this country, and overseas.

How do true, decent, democracies, work, in practice? Let us take the example of the US, for as long as many can remember- - - spy on everybody, everywhere, if you can get away with it, even on your own citizens. Now, do not even bother with getting congressional, or court, approval; simply do it, like an oligarchy, and absolute monarchy, a veritable Big Brother! The US is overwhelmed with security, and spy, agencies, involving thousands of employees, and hundreds of millions of dollars, one can only guess. Such groups include CIA, FBI, NSA, NSC; and surely, there are other letters in this alphabet soup of agencies, some that, we had not even heard of. There is no doubt that other countries do the same, democracies, or absolute monarchies, or dictator states. This indeed, is Big Brother philosophy, at its worst.

And as we saw in the previous paragraphs, the cheap, pathetic excuse, by our officials, is always, 'because we are fighting terrorism, to protect Americans from attack'. It is as low as you can get, in politics. At the end of December, the Bush justice department started investigations on who, leaked the spying practices, by this administration; some would add, to strike fear into reporters, and the freedoms of our citizens. *Since this scandal broke out, experts had been stating that Bush could easily, have obtained, his authorization, without hassle, if he had gone through proper, legal, channels, but he chose not to do so! They claimed that he was trying to grant his presidency, unlimited powers, that, the constitution did not permit!* Thus, it becomes an irony that, the administration has been calling the leak 'illegal', but the actual clandestine spying, on US citizens, why, it was all, legal!

A senior democrat, in congress, responded to Bush criticism by announcing that Bush had circumvented both congress, and the courts, with his ploy, to spy on Americans. Now we can add eavesdropping, to the other government practices, of corruption, spying, snooping, break-in, kidnapping, and more. These continue to be justified 'for national security', of course. How many hundreds of times, have we heard these words, these excuses, from Bush administration officials, as their vocabulary had become so limited? On Olbermann's program, at year's end, on MSNBC, they commented thus, "since when could a White house press secretary survive a whole year, without saying anything"?

Commentators were also amazed that Bush alleged, he was upset, because the senate had held up reauthorization of his infamous patriot act, accusing them of endangering the American people. Americans, by now, know much better, than that! And critics quickly, added, if the president believed he could do what he liked, and spy without proper authorization, he did not need the patriot act, did he? There may be many gentlemen in our government, who take pride in the fact that, US officials, through a myriad of spying techniques, had intercepted millions of messages a second! Will Americans continue to support such actions by an erratic administration? That is an important question for 2006!

Have the American people forgotten so soon, and so completely, that there have been many examples in our world's past, where leaders had adopted somewhat similar tactics; much harsher ones, were those, under Stalin, and Hitler; but then, we also had the dictatorships of Asia, Africa, Latin America, and more.

For many months, reports seemed to reflect no end in sight, to all forms of corruption both within governments, and corporations. For the US, the national security agency, involved in the recent spying scandals, should appropriately be renamed, *'national spying agency', 'a national disgrace', an Albatross.* According to news reports, government officials had struck a deal with telecommunications companies, to intercept, and store, phone calls, and pass them on to government agencies, to be scrutinized; and also *to route as many calls as possible, from foreign countries, through US switches, so that the US government could spy at leisure, on everybody, everywhere.* Do government experts call this 'honorable conduct'? Or is it ugly, and degenerate, behavior? And, what about US corporate executives, who agree to collaborate in such dirty work, without court authorization, or due legislation by congress. There were also previous reports on Internet companies passing on emails, to government, for spying purposes; thus, now, we are hearing about many telecommunication companies, allegedly, doing some of the same dirty work. **What comes next?**

Sixty years ago, or so, *the United States spearheaded international tribunals to place Nazi leaders on trial before those courts.* But now, according to a law professor, writing in the UK, Sunday Times, *the system of international criminal justice, is coming back to haunt American officials!* This is because the Bush administration had not recognized the international criminal court. Critics announced that, there was concern, in Washington, that, a *permanent international criminal court, could turn against United States military adventures.* What is wrong with that, if we are aspiring towards international justice for all, with freedom, and democracy? Should anyone suspected of crimes in the US military, or elsewhere, not face such tribunals, like everybody else?

Our international relationships, and policies, have not fared much better. Surely, it serves no purpose if, allegedly, corrupt, American, administrations, secure the 'friendship' of equally corrupt administrations, in other countries, when the people in those same countries are anti-US policies. What US governments need, and should strive for, is the full support, and trust, of the people themselves, the people of the world. For example, a new leader in Germany, announced closer ties with Washington, but most of the German citizens were anti-Bush administration, policies. The same goes for Canada, Australia, and the United Kingdom. But these people are never against the general public, in the US.

Since the major, prolonged wars (and those were truly prolonged, lasting some 27 years), between the powerful, ancient empire, of Athens, and Sparta, man's thin veil of civilization, if we ever possessed one, had been shed; and we had blundered along blindly, ever since. We have referred to the constant strife, and wars, since man first started walking on planet earth. As a result, we had wandered far from the ideal of lasting peace. Pope John Paul II, many of the previous popes, and Pope Benedict XVI, coming after him, have always strived for lasting, universal, peace. Lisa Hepner, in the magazine 'Natural Awakenings', wrote an interesting article about the top ten things, we could all do, to create world peace. Those comments were quite relevant to some of the subjects covered in this book. She postulated that the effects would be individual, to start with, but would soon become collective. Her ten suggestions, were- - -pray, meditate, forgive, listen, seek to understand, smile, give, release judgment, speak gently, and play. *Not many could argue with these suggestions! And, most significantly, love and, justice, for all, would surely, follow.* With the contents presented in these pages, and polemics abounding, all around us, some of the above 'ideals', presented by Hepner, could produce remarkable, unforeseen, changes, in most of us, on this planet; changes, that would become important enough, for us, to absolutely, want to *strive for lasting, universal, peace- - -!*

Maintaining peace, within ourselves, in our families, in our community, in our country, in our world, is bound to be a constant struggle, because of man's nature. But we need to reemphasize that, many of the writings of the Popes, have urged, that it be done, that we must keep on trying. That, when we *strive to become enlightened in **Truth, then, we are already on the path to peace!***

IS THERE AN END, IN SIGHT?

Some of the material, in these pages, could induce readers to conclude that there is no end to all the corruption and deceit around our world. But it can all end, through hard work, and cooperation, amongst people, everywhere.

A jarring Thanksgiving (2005) reminder of democracy and freedom, and civil rights, came to America, when protesters were arrested, again, because they wanted to demonstrate near the ranch of president Bush, in Texas. If dictators in other countries do that, they are called tyrants, and oppressors of liberties of the people; if we do it, why, it is always the correct thing to do. This president must not see that there is dissent, in the US, with too many of his policies.

Ellsberg, a former defense department official, stated that it might have been his 70th arrest. It was reported that in the past, he had released secret documents showing that, the US government had deceived Americans, on whether the Vietnam, war, could be won, and on the number of casualties from that war. He stated that "they saw through that war, and they saw through this war (Iraq)----that the American people would get us out of this". Thus, here again, we see US government deceit on the Vietnam, war, and how much greater deceit have we heard on the Iraq war? How much deceit have we also had in other areas?

US congressman J. Murtha, himself, a decorated, Vietnam era veteran, had indeed stirred up a hornet's nest, when he proposed that the Bush administration should announce a timetable for redeployment of US forces out of Iraq. Murtha suggested 6 months, so that Iraqis would shape up, and assume more responsibility for their own affairs. Some critics felt that it was a betrayal of sorts that, most democrats in congress, did not immediately fully support, Murtha. Amazingly, a neophyte congresswoman took issue with Murtha, and stated in chambers, that, 'only cowards cut and run, not marines'. She was immediately, and deservedly, booed, and there were catcalls from the floor; and she was soon forced to erase her comments from the congressional record! If members in congress are so polarized, we can just imagine how divided, is, the American public.

Journalist Bill Moyers spoke at the anniversary of the National Security Archives. He took up the important question, of whether journalism, in the US, *could ever regain its independence*. He noted that serious journalism could be expensive, as it did not generate a great deal of money. He pointed out that, as various media in America, were bought out, journalism lost more of its independence. Since the beginning of the Iraq war, we have had numerous comments, both in the US, and from overseas, that American news organizations, by and large, had failed the people very badly. There was a lack of genuine, and forceful, critique, of actions by the Bush administration. When it came, it was much too late. A speaker on 'Hardball', on MSNBC, said that neither the president, nor the vice-president, were the type who would ever apologize, for any mistakes they had made! *Is that acceptable, nowadays?*

In October 2005, a memo arrived via the Internet, entitled 'A vision to buy gold'. An American writer zeroed in, on a speech by president Bush, before the UN, in September 2004. The writer highlighted the fact that, for Bush, there were absolutely no applause interruptions, to that speech; and he said, *that was in sharp contrast to virtually all other speakers, by world leaders, before that body!* He stated that the same day, he had decided to buy gold. He had been stationed overseas for many years, and he summarized world opinion, on the US, from that perspective, and his personal experience. He said that people in countries considered "friendly" to the US, did not particularly care for America, because of arrogance, and a lack of morals or integrity; and now, *people in countries not considered friendly, 'hate our guts'.*

That writer claimed he had not been overseas since Bush took office, but he concluded that, people would care even less, for America now, than they did before; hence, his 'vision to buy gold'! He understood that although America was rich, and had the biggest economy, it still depended on the full support of governments in other countries; it needed oil, and world trade, to keep the economy from collapsing. He was watching the enormous growth of OPEC, and China, India, and others; and he also pointed to the vulnerability of rulers, like those of Saudi Arabia, and Kuwait. He criticized that, forcing a perverse democracy in Iraq, might encourage Muslims from several countries, to unite against the 'American Satan'. Has that already happened, since our misadventure, in Iraq? The writer concluded that all the above events could haunt the American economy!

Readers will recall, that we have heard often enough, how the US, economy, and, the global economy, were interconnected. However, the international community did not enjoy an even playing field, in its economic life. Governments, in the 'west', had been criticized, because *most of the trade negotiations, around the world, ended up favoring western, developed, countries.* The group of eight, the World Bank, the international monetary fund, had all been frequently targeted for criticism, because for underdeveloped countries, there had been little progress!

An article by Jeffrey Gangemi, in Business Week magazine, was striking, as he discussed the remarkable social, and economic, efforts, by a professor Muhammad Yunus, in Bangladesh. Striking, because, Yunus was quoted thus, referring to that country, 'where nothing works, and there is no electricity'! Hearing such an assertion, one could rightly assume, in 2005, that they were describing the barren, lunar landscape; or the arid, inhospitable, deserts of Mars. No, this was planet earth, he was talking about; these were human beings, in one of the poorest countries, around us.

But, the professor's humanitarian efforts, were contrary to western practices, wherein, the loan industry sought out customers who could repay their loans, or had other types of collateral; and they would repay that loan, with hefty interest rates, and also, penalties, provided for. Professor Yunus, of Bangladesh, *launched village based, enterprises, whereby, even small loans, to poor people, had yielded remarkably good results.* His programs resulted in rather small, credit institutions, becoming available all over his country. He tried to demonstrate that, his system might be the only way to offer help, to many of the world's 1.2 billion poor, 'who lacked access to basic necessities'. His group also dealt *extensively with helping women, as well as, having a program for the poor. His aspirations were to turn the norms of the banking industry, on their head.*

His amazing philosophy that had proved successful thus far, was that, 'poor people could be both reliable borrowers, and avid entrepreneurs'. Critics, in the west, might be quick to point out that, these are desperately poor people, who had nothing; whereas those, in the west, were different. *Ah, yes, perhaps that is at the root of many of our problems, 'we are always different'!* And yet, there are lessons to be learned here, that must also be considered.

Some pundits, such as the securities elite, in the US, state that all the bad news in America, the war, the long periods of 'down markets', rates of unemployment, energy prices, the hurricanes, all that, had not slowed down consumer come back, and spending. Apparently true, but what these pundits failed to emphasize was that, *consumers, by and large, were spending money they did not have, and both personal, and national debts, in America, were at record highs!* Do these characters sense that there will be a day of reckoning? Beginning in 2006, financial institutions began requiring a higher minimum monthly payment, on credit card debt, than was ever required in the past. That, will, no doubt, hit consumers, badly.

A Harvard professor, David Cutler, said that in a survey, only 20% of Americans claimed they were happy with their health care system. He said that, was too small a number, for something as important as, their lives. He felt that the US health care system should pay more for quality care; *and particularly, spend more on preventive care.* America remains the only industrialized nation without universal health care; with many gaps in its health care system, gaps between the 'have', and the 'have not'. He referred to the Bush administration, Medicare, prescription drug program, 'as silly'. Although it would help some people, it had many deficiencies (who would dream up a program with a huge 'doughnut hole' in it, the deficiencies, but an American administration).

There was another report about some 10% of America's teens suffering from depression; and how depressed teens, were much more likely to smoke, use alcohol, and abuse drugs. In the New England Journal of Medicine, a report from the "Institute of Medicine" indicated that, *the American health care system was functioning at far lower levels, than it could, and should.* That was from a 2001 report. Thus, we have highlighted many tragic health deficiencies in third world countries, in many cases, absence of care. But even in the richer, western countries, where there is more than plenty, to go around, there are glaring disparities as well, that should be remedied.

On another front, on 'Now' with David Broncaccio, on PBS, guests discussed how a senator *who received most of his campaign donations, from oil giants, went around pontificating that talk of 'global warming' was a huge hoax!* President Bush pushed for, and signed, laws, *that gave huge tax breaks to energy companies*. Allegedly, such companies were also responsible for most of the damaging emissions, in the US. It appeared that they had received a nice gift from Bush. Meanwhile, most level headed scientists, believed that human activity, with enhanced green house gases, emissions, had indeed produced warming, with slow melting of our glaciers; *and they emphasized, that the time to do something, was now!* They questioned the senator referred to above, who waved around his book, favoring the 'hoax theory'. Referring to that, one scientist called it *a campaign of disinformation, and deceit, by the energy industry.* The latter had reportedly, paid certain scientists, to side with the industry. They showed how the Bush White house received memos from the energy bosses, on climate change, that there was no sound science to many of those reports. "They put words in the mouth of Bush". But, in recent months, some energy leaders had broken ranks, and also called for swift action on global warming!

Although corporate, and government, officials, often repeat that there is no assault on the environment, a recent report in National Geographic, raised more alarms. Studies showed that a large number of species of frogs, and other amphibians, had become extinct; many others were seriously threatened. The causes were thought to be depletion of their habitat (man's intrusion); and a fungus infection, a consequence of global warming, was also killing many of them. In the past we had other reports that, numerous specimens of amphibians had been seen, with many types of birth deformities.

And on the Internet there were more disturbing headlines, towards the end of 2005. One would call them amazing.
"Beyond the imperial presidency"
"Bush drags newspaper editors in, to give them their marching orders". One could respond to that, 'hurrah, for freedom and democracy, in the US' (if what we have been reading is all factual).
"Impeachment Buzz"; "The I-word is gaining ground".
"What did they say when they were impeaching Clinton"? This referred to Delay from Texas, who had faced indictment in that state, talking of 'rule of law'; 'the path of truth and justice'; '---no man is above the law'. Allegedly, Delay had been after Clinton's hide; but now, would he still be quoted in such a manner, with those words?

Other headlines included:
"Iraqis want US out as soon as possible"
"The ultimate quagmire"
"Bombs, protests, as Iraq election mood sours"
"US air strikes kill civilians"
All that, in December 2005, as Bush, Cheney, Rumsfeld, and, others, were talking of 'so much progress', in Iraq. And then we had this: "US opposes a litany of global treaties in 2005"! My, what a year that was! And early in 2006, there were Internet news items on the question of "Impeaching Blair, over Iraq"! Surprise, surprise! Now, if we reflected on all that, for a moment, we would be compelled to ask, if those were characteristics, to

look for, in decent, honorable, superpowers, with the hand of justice, and friendship, extended to all.

It was quite educational, to see an assessment of Iraq after 1000 days, in the journal 'Editor and publisher', that is, after one thousand days of war, and occupation, mainly by the United States. Some of the statistics were listed as follows:
70% of Iraqis had a sewage system that, more often, than not, did not work.
25 to 50% was a rough estimate of unemployment in Iraq; it might be much higher.
67% of Iraqis did not feel secure, and blamed it on the occupation.
Some 251 foreigners, in Iraq, had been kidnapped, and it was still going on.
After the progress cited by the Bush administration, in November 2005, there were 90 attacks daily; and this was compared to June 2003, when there were 8 attacks daily!

Americans had been bombarded by Washington propaganda that did not correlate well, with the above figures. Patrick Cockburn, added a BBC poll that showed only 28% of Iraqis *thought that democracy was a priority; whereas, half of all Iraqis, stated that Iraq needed a strong leader.* That writer added, rather dramatically, *a new Iraq is emerging and it is already drenched in blood!*

Another article by Colin Brown featured an American ambassador having to correct embarrassing denials, or statements, he had issued, at least twice, in recent weeks alone. Was that more evidence of honesty, and integrity, all the way around? And in that same vein, there was a troublesome article, with the headline, "Half truths that cloak a lawless world of depravity"! This described rather well, *the horrific practice of rendition by America's secret agencies, presently with the blessing of the Bush administration; and regrettably, with some collusion by the Blair government, and British secret agencies.* Britain once, had an honorable reputation, had it not? Not any more.

As democracy in the US, had been buffeted so badly, various government officials continued to utter similar words, or phrases, in a monotonous, parrot like, fashion. These were switched from 'spreading freedom and democracy, in the Middle East', and, by December 2005, in time for the Iraqi elections, they were talking about 'achieving victory'. Iraq already had several so-called elections; but these officials seemed to mimic each other's statements, rather well. What type of "victory" was the US administration referring to? Experts had agreed that, recruits for 'terrorism' had increased substantially. Although US officials continued to talk of 'liberating' Iraq, they could not walk in the streets there, without heavy armor protection; they were living, shut in, behind massively fortified zones. When government personnel visited Iraq, they often did so under cover of darkness, and only for very brief periods, and then, mostly inside military compounds.

A recent Chris Matthews, 'Hardball' program, on MSNBC, also reviewed statements by this US administration, on Iraq. Part of the discussion went on like this:
'They told the American people Iraq had weapons of mass destruction'- -not true!
'They said that S. Hussein was connected to 9/11- - not true!

'They said the war would be completely paid for with Iraqi oil'- -not true.
'They said Iraqis would welcome US forces with open arms'- -not true.
And there was much more- -! Now, our fellow Americans should judge the tragic consequences of all the above misinformation, and miscalculations, and many more, both for our young people in the armed forces, for our country; and for Iraq, as a nation.

In December 2005, the London Sunday Times had a report by a writer, who had just been secretly taken to Fallujah, in Iraq, to assess the results "of the ferocious US attacks against that city", *to destroy the enemy.* This was a disturbing, frightening report, for most decent, truth loving people, to see. It claimed that 4000 to 6000 people had been killed during that US operation, 'Phantom Fury'; and most of those were reported to have been civilians, but undoubtedly, our officials give a different story. There were 36,000 homes reportedly destroyed, or heavily damaged; and 60 nurseries, and 66 mosques, or other religious structures, had been hit. The writer was shocked to see such devastation, with huge areas having been flattened, with rubble as far as the eye could see. We must consider that, in the context of American reports on how terrible things were under Saddam Hussein, and how much better they were, under the US occupation! The reporter saw *only sporadic signs of reconstruction, mostly in the wealthier sections!* A mother of five children was seen sifting through the ruins of her home, as she reported that she had not even been provided with a tent; and all she had received was $700! On seeing Fallujah in such a state of destruction, the writer at first recalled an American officer in Vietnam, saying that, they had to destroy a village, in order to save it! *Except, the writer added, nobody they met in Fallujah, thought they had been saved!*

Reporters had long claimed that, the so-called compensation for thousands of victims of those, attacks, was slow in coming. And Fallujah citizens claimed that, when they received compensation, some of them, were stopped by Iraqi forces working with, the Americans, and their money was stolen. Another Iraqi described how he had lost 4 children during those attacks. The writer of this article described a clandestine meeting with some of the insurgents in Fallujah, as they talked of a new form of resistance, against US forces, that was being developed. One commander said that, *they planned revenge, and 'would settle scores for crimes committed against our people'.* Another insurgent said that clerics had advised them not to carry out indiscriminate, suicide missions, but instead to use their energies against Americans.

Another young Iraqi alleged that, he had been taken by Americans, and was accused of killings he had participated in; and he said that he was abused and tortured. When he was found to be innocent, he said he was released; but he told reporters, 'if the Americans think it is over, they do not know what is coming'. He had now become sympathetic towards the insurgents; he apparently was not, before that. The reporter, retorted, that, those actions by American, and Iraqi, forces, had re-ignited the insurgency. The article continued that, there was hate, rage, and mistrust of America, deeper than ever before. Now, should we consider all the above reports, in the context of a January 2006, article, by a highly, placed, British armed forces, official, who had actually served in Iraq?

News reports implied that, the British official had leveled stinging criticism of US military operations, in Iraq, how the US military so readily sought out confrontation. But his was not the first, as similar critiques had come from different parts of the world. Predictably, American military officials rejected "such British snobbery".

After the December 2005, Iraq elections, so intensely touted by Bush and his officials, 35 Iraqi political groups, who had competed in those elections, called them fraudulent! This took place under the domination of the US military. They demanded that the electoral commission be disbanded; and complaints were pouring in, from both Sunnis, and secular Shiites, including Allawi's group. Thousands marched in the streets, in protest; and United Nations supervisors continued to investigate allegations of fraud. On top of that election instability, were more reports that, Shiites had engaged in abuse, and torture, and killing, of Sunnis, in prisons under Iraqi control. This continued to be an embarrassment to Americans, who launched more investigations.

Steve Colecchi, in 'America', magazine, wrote this: "The many reports of prisoner abuse, by members of the US armed forces, tarnish the reputation of this country". This discussion dealt with the support by US bishops, for the condemnation of torture, and in support of the McCain amendment, in congress, against torture. Are Iraqis abusing other Iraqis, to settle old scores? And perhaps, did they feel encouraged to do so, because of so many reports of prisoner abuse, in Iraq, and elsewhere, by the Americans? Those are important questions to delve into. A guest speaker on PBS news, stated that, unfortunately, many of the world's dictators had used, harsh behaving, police forces, trained by the United States! Then they also referred to this torture, and killing, by extreme Shiites, in the Iraqi police forces, also trained primarily by the Americans, and by a few members from other countries.

More disturbing headlines, were still emerging, towards the end of 2005, and early in 2006. These dealt with the US, as well as, other countries, as one would expect. On the 'Katrina' hurricane disaster, in America, we had the following:
From Newsweek, "We show the world, the rich, and powerful, America, now they see us as we really are- -totally uncaring, of our most needy people, poor, helpless, and caught in harm's way". Many would take exception at such broad statements. Another wrote that he could not believe it, when aides to president Bush, *had nervously debated if they should ask him to cut short, his 5 weeks of vacation, after Katrina struck!* Then we had these, "Poverty in our backyard"; "The other America"; "Mother Nature's wake up call". From US News and World Report, we had comments as, "I have lived long enough to expect such incompetent response from government, all levels of government, to an emergency"; and "In the blame game, on who screwed up, after Katrina, you should also include the people, who voted in, this administration". Right!

More reports, critical of the Bush administration, dealt with the US government spying on Americans, illegally according to many, and probably without cause; and increasing reports of corruption, within the republican dominated congress, in connection with the justice department investigations, into the alleged, Abramoff, influence peddling, scandals, in the halls of congress! Those conspiracies were still unfolding, when reporters announced that he had pleaded guilty to certain activities, and agreed to fully 'cooperate', with the justice department, perhaps in exchange for a more lenient sentence, as is often the case; and it appeared that, justice officials would carry out a thorough investigation. On the spying scandals, initially, reporters alleged that, even justice officials had reservations about the legality of Bush embarking on spying activities, on Americans, without proper authorization. On an Olbermann program, on MSNBC, it was also pointed out that, as *there was a republican controlled congress, in Washington, they were not likely to seriously investigate their own, republican, White house.* Therefore, it was more likely, that nothing would be achieved; and, as had been stated previously, some had tarnished this government, with the label of, "a pox on both your houses"!

Journalists, and other critics, had long been writing on these numerous scandals surrounding this Bush administration. But, besides these, the dastardly 'rendition' practices, by the United States government, had also received a great deal of attention from media in the US, and many critics overseas. The peculiar, US foreign policies, and international relationships, were in disarray, more than ever before, and most of the blame had been placed squarely on the republican leadership.

In the UK, the 'Daily Telegraph', had interesting, but critical, articles by Alec Russell, on the transatlantic row, over the US government agencies, illegally kidnapping 'suspects', in other countries, and secretly delivering them to third world countries, *for the purpose of interrogation, by abuse, and torture, according to world opinion.* Officials in the United States kept on denying it. What was even worse, it had been alleged that, America had illegally used European airspace, and actual airfields, for these nefarious activities. These writers discussed how, American state official, C. Rice, would travel to Europe *in an attempt to repair bridges; but she would defend America's actions (as usual)!* These comments, and criticisms, about US officials, coming from all over the world, but especially from Europe, our friends, must be experienced, to realize, *how terrible were the things that, had been going on, under such flawed US foreign policies.*

The arguments put forward by critics have been that, if the United States claimed that this so-called 'rendition', was legal, and not for purposes of torture, fine, *'let the Americans handle those kidnapped in this manner, within their own justice system'!* Who could possibly argue with that? They pointed to innocent people who had been so kidnapped, and mistreated, in error! The newspaper articles detailed the erroneous 'rendition', by US officials, of Khaled Masri, a German citizen; as CIA agents had allegedly, taken him to Afghanistan in 2004, and kept him for 5 months. Then suddenly, 'the Americans released him in the streets of Albania'. Reporters asked Masri if he was afraid, and he told them *he feared he would be shot in the back.* Seeing all this, readers could rightly assume that, it was all fiction, but, regrettably, such occurrences, had allegedly taken place. Once again, like a bunch of puppets, members of the German administration remained fairly silent, on this scandal, on one of their citizens; another disgraceful spectacle by a German government that, seemingly, had lost its way, allowing others to stomp all over them. It was also reported that the number of kidnappings, 'in error', had increased; and they fingered the 'hazards of giving the CIA, a free hand'! Reports also showed that there were 437 such incursions over Germany, what a black eye for that nation. It is no wonder that critics had alleged that, former German chancellor Schroeder, did not care much for the administration in Washington. Now, they have the new chancellor, Merkel, who had not obtained a solid majority in their elections, and therefore, heads a coalition government, of sorts. In January 2006, she undertook her first visit to the US, to try patch up serious differences between Bush, and German officials over the Iraq war, and other international issues. The Bush administration now, needs Europe, very badly, once more, over the disputes with Iran.

Other countries listed with such 'illegal', intrusions, over their air space, were, Britain, Holland, Spain, Italy, Poland, Romania, etc. Are their government members, wimps, or what? Or, did they truly agree beforehand, to all the shenanigans about these 'rendition' kidnappings? Many felt it was a stab in the back, for the European Union. If those government officials had what it took, if they had integrity, not simply, ideas of grandeur, self aggrandizement, selfishness, and corruption, they would have demanded that the US stop these practices immediately; or else they could have closed all embassies of the US government in protest, and repatriated all their staff. In such situations, behind the scenes diplomatic protests, had never worked too well, look at the prelude to world war one, and world war two! Such actions, in protest, could have been continued until US officials asked for negotiations, and offered appropriate restitution, as well as adhering strictly to international laws. European governments could also have refused to welcome, to their countries, C. Rice, or any other US official, when these scandalous reports broke out. When serious offenses were committed, against nations, that, is how people of integrity, used to behave. Perhaps we should not be amazed that the European Union, as an important body, had reached nowhere, thus far; no muscle, no real power, no stature of major significance.

If members of the EU *provided assistance, and access to their airports, to transfer detainees, to third world countries, for abuse and torture, that is an abomination. If European countries actually accepted such detainees, for harsh interrogation, to bypass regular courts, that is an even greater abomination!* No country outside the EU, engaging in such practices, should be considered for EU membership. Reports in UK papers suggested that British secret agency MI5, had colluded with the CIA in America, over suspects sent to torture jails in Afghanistan, and Guantanamo (Cuba). A suspect alleged that, American interrogators threatened to, *"send you to Jordan, where electric cables would be used on you"*. And American officials (corrupt?) had tried to claim that, torture was not used, in those countries, where they sent these detainees. **Were those, more lies, from such officials, both here, and abroad?** In the UK, the head of MI5, refused comment, and in the US, the state department said that, when they acted, they did so 'lawfully'! Oh, is that so? How come the US government had been awash, in scandals, half truths, or worse, all over the place? Officials like to indulge in decent sounding words, but what about their actions? Those actions were laid bare, for the whole world to view. Attorneys were working with some of these suspects, who claimed to have been abused, or tortured, in that manner. If it is proved to be true, should not officials in both the UK, and US, be brought to justice, and if found guilty, be forced to make appropriate restitution, out of their personal assets, not out of government general funds. There might be additional sentences handed down as well. *Is that not the only type of justice, which would be likely to induce such people to change their behavior, perhaps, the only way to stamp out illegal behavior, by officials, anywhere in the world?*

Another Daily Telegraph article revealed the embarrassment of America's, C. Rice, when she met the new German chancellor, Merkel. They showed Rice with a facial grimace, fidgeting, and playing around with her hands, and fingers; and the facial expression on Merkel, matched Rice's, and spoke volumes. That goes for 'our allies', all because of the Bush administration tactics. Merkel was pleased *that Rice admitted that America had made mistakes! Eureka!* Mistakes? More than likely, they were all colossal blunders, and failures. And they reported that Merkel seemed to be trying hard, not to make eye contact with Rice; and they reiterated how American officials had a lot of explaining to do, in Europe. The same reporter also stated that, "America was more excoriated, and isolated, than in decades"! These were some of the repercussions of the Bush missteps. Other references they made, were, 'such insults are flying between America, and its European allies'; and there were references to past memories of CIA shenanigans, about their bad, old days, in Latin America; many critics had often pointed to America's rotten policies towards those regions, long before this. My, my, what have we come to, some of us, in the 'glorious west'?

If all the above referenced foreign governments, knew precisely, what was being concocted, on their territory, by the secret CIA agency, and other US officials, it would indeed, be a terrible omen, for those countries themselves, that they took no action to stop it, and for planet earth! And obviously, it would not portend much promise, for the future of mankind.

A former CIA official was interviewed on CBS, '60 Minutes' program, and he admitted that, "rendition, was finding somebody to do your dirty work, for you"! If the United States government, and its many secret agencies, were doing nothing that was inherently evil, *why were they using secret planes, with coded numbers, without markings, or other identification, contrary to requirements for all aircraft; and why were they not listed under a company headquarters, but listed instead, only 'shadow companies'?* Mr. Clinton, Mr. Bush, why were those people, thus kidnapped, sent only to countries where, according to critics, torture methods were known to be used; and to countries without reliable, strong, justice systems? *All these, are very important questions!* Masri, was also interviewed on '60 Minutes', and he stated that he was beaten, and intensely interrogated, for 5 months.

A British diplomat said that these planes were also flown to Uzbekistan, where barbaric torture was known to be used; and that America's CIA, was well aware of it! *A former CIA official also stated, rather shockingly, that, torture was acceptable to him, if the interrogators got what they were after!* What type of 'righteous ' people, were these, who were able to access important positions, in the US government, and why? The detainee, Masri, also reported that, he felt compelled to discuss with his 7 year old, son, what the Americans had done to him. If many detainees had told their children similar stories, and they too were innocent, and if these children related all those stories to their school friends, *can anyone, can our famous politicians, just imagine, what that would do to America's image abroad?* Whilst on this topic, it was then announced that Masri had filed lawsuits against certain United States officials. Will the citizens ever learn the truth, on those issues litigated, as yet another test, of our fragile democracy?

Another Bush administration scandal came out in January 2006 (scandals have been commonplace within this US administration). Senator John McCain, who had personal experience as a prisoner of war (when neither Bush, nor Cheney, had ever served in the active forces), and other lawmakers, overwhelmingly passed a bill forbidding torture of prisoners, or 'detainees', as another word chosen by the Bush people, to hide behind. On an MSNBC program, speakers said that, Bush reluctantly signed that legislation (some had presumed he did not wish to look obstructionist, on that issue). But then, *it was alleged that Bush added a rider of his own, to that legislation, stating that, because of his presidential powers, he alone would decide, when he needed to bypass such a law!* Well, well, what are laws for, in such a 'democracy'? It was suggested that many republicans in the president's own party, who had voted for that law, were incensed that he would still act behind their backs, so to speak; that Bush seemed to ignore the authority, and power, vested in congress, by the constitution of these United States. But why should these politicians be surprised? Many, well known, personalities around the world, had made similar criticism against Bush, because of his arrogance, they said, his pride, and his go it alone, 'Texan', strategy; that, it had brought us the tragedy of Iraq, an increase in world terrorism, and had fueled an increase in global anti-Americanism.

But, as with the heading of this section, is there an end in sight? Yes, there is. Bush, Blair, Sharon, Mubarak, will pass, as will many others. Arafat had passed; Hussein of Iraq was forced out, and is facing trial, as is Milosevic of Serbia. Other dictators, had come, and are gone. It is postulated that greater leaders will emerge, who will know right, from wrong; who will value the true meaning of 'humanitarian aid', of being 'my brother's keeper'; *the true meaning of justice; and who will treasure, and respect, peace on earth, and goodwill, towards humanity!*

We had witnessed an outpouring of generosity by people worldwide, much of it in the past few years alone, in the many calamities that had befallen mankind, on this planet; in the earthquakes of Iran, and now, in the mountain region of Pakistan; in the hurricanes, floods, and mudslides, of Central America; the tsunami along some of the coasts of the Indian ocean, in Indonesia, Thailand, India, Sri Lanka; the hurricanes, particularly the devastation of Katrina, in the US; floods in many parts of Europe; and more, disasters!

Citizens, everywhere, had pitched in with cash donations, food, and clothing, and more; and in poorer countries, they often pitched in, by assisting with their bare hands, as had been shown on news media. From the United States, and other countries, including Cuba, teams of doctors, and other helpers, went into the harsh climate of the Pakistan mountains, to provide desperately needed help, medical care, food, and so on. As already mentioned, the Katrina disasters, in the US, uncovered so much weakness, and inefficiency, within the government, but many towns, and organizations, and individuals, opened up their doors, and their wallets, there as well; and many other countries were not short, in their generosity, even towards a wealthy nation.

Some changes are already on the move, and much more is needed. Some politicians have sent mixed messages around our world. Yes, we have assisted in the tsunami devastated, regions, and in Pakistan, and elsewhere. But then, in January 2006, there were worldwide reports of an air attack by the United States, in those mountain regions of Pakistan, on 'alleged terrorist targets'. Pakistani, and other world reports, stated that the person, who had been targeted, by the Americans, was never even in the area, when the attacks were launched. *But they accused that the Americans had also killed 18 people, including a number of women and children. Others raised the question, if the Americans had been duped, once more, in their 'intelligence' operations!*

Predictably, US officials announced that terrorists had been killed; but the world had long been assaulted by such doubletalk, from Washington propagandists. On Olbermann news reports, on MSNBC, they also discussed how they had heard such claims from Bush officials many times before. They asked how the United States had been authorized to launch attacks inside Pakistan. Bush administration officials alleged that perhaps, there was an implied consent from the Pakistani president. Soon, the streets of many cities, in Pakistan, teemed with tens of thousands of citizens, protesting against the American government. Critics of Bush said that, his administration was further undermining the standing of the Pakistani president, with his own people; and the latter, had certainly, not been known, for the democratic governing, of his country. Even if some terrorists had been among those victims, what about the innocent, the women, and children, who were also killed? *Was that the killing of the innocent, by the State? Or was that 'collateral' damage, as US officials always referred to them?* In the discussions on the 'just war' theories, many theologians, and thinkers, have come to believe that, the conditions under which one could use a 'just war' excuse, are now extremely rare! *Therefore, by inference, one could state that, the killing of the innocent, in such attacks, is a crime against humanity; and how many such killings have we seen?*

There was another change, this one in Chile, early in 2006, a democratically elected woman president, a social democrat, reportedly. We had previously referred to former, tyrannical dictators, in many parts of Latin America, including Chile, often with support from the west, especially the United States. A reporter on PBS news pointed to the positive atmosphere, that those elections would produce great changes, for the better; that the people were now able to talk freely, about the suffering, and torture, under Pinochet, their former dictator. They also reported that many former government officials, in Chile, were now facing tribunals, to achieve reconciliation. Reconciliation, yes, but in those countries, where so many thousands had suffered, and died, usually the poor peasants, the people need to see the hand of justice as well, as justice had been a scarce commodity in those regions.

In these pages, we have also referred to crises facing our environment, and there have been movements for change in those areas, as well. There is pessimism in some quarters that some of those changes have been in the wrong direction, and we must alter course, or else. Some scientists now believe that, for the protection of planet earth, *we may have reached the point of no return.* An article in the 'Independent' (UK), outlined how professor Lovelock, and other scientists, had considered earth system science, 'as a planetary control system', wherein chemically, and atmospherically, living, organisms, interacted with their environment, to perpetuate life on earth. But, how many thoughts have we expressed, in this area, here, and elsewhere, on how intensely we had assailed our environment, and thus, *interrupted the chain of that interaction, to preserve life?* Scientists postulated that global warming, caused by man's activities, was real; but it was often denied by many, especially by those in American industry, and by politicians. But these scientists believed that environmental degradation had tipped the balance, that the polar ice caps had already started melting, at an alarming rate; and the first casualty would be the extinction of the polar bears, as they depended so much, on that ice, for their survival. We have heard that the number of polar bears was already in decline; and we have had many other warning signals, of man's damage to the environment. If the above theories are close to the truth, of what is happening to planet earth, then we must closely observe this animal, as another barometer, of serious environmental destruction.

In the world of politics, the numerous scandals, of corruption, bribery, lies, and dishonesty, that have come to light within the United States government, in Britain, and in many other countries, had spawned movements by citizens, and by some politicians, to demand a change in direction, towards a better world. That, we should no longer, tolerate, 'business as usual', in many of the world's capitals. How often, in the past, had we heard harsh criticism of members in governments, with the cry, 'throw all the bums out'? But nothing was ever achieved. Perhaps, this time, changes around the world are indeed genuine, perhaps they had already started, and they would include America, Britain, the European Union, and many other nations, and gather speed! Corrupt politicians, must, of necessity, be prevented from attaining positions of power in governments.

We need to see intensified efforts, through hard work, and perseverance, to bring those extreme factions, on the right, and, on the left, towards the center. We need to facilitate honest dialogue between those of different faiths, and between various ethnic groups. Ideally, we need serious, and drastic, curtailment, of the waste of huge expenditures, on the military industrial machine, by rich, and poor, countries, alike. We must solve the many problems described in these chapters, work harder, at it.
Then, yes, indeed, *we can truly say, "there is an end, in sight"!*

IS ANYONE LISTENING? FINAL THOUGHTS

Ancient Athens, had remained a source of Greek, intellectual life, even through upheavals, and wars. It had been described as a society that was 'aggressively democratic'. How could we compare, such thoughts on democracy, uttered about a civilization that, existed such a long time ago, to what we observe today? Here are a couple of related definitions recently found on the Internet: "a politician is one who shakes your hand before the elections, and your confidence afterwards"; "a diplomat is a person who tells you to go to hell, in such a way, that you actually look forward to the trip"! Truly, these are a dig at the political world, of today; but are all the recent attacks on politics, because we have been awash in deceit, lack of integrity, lack of truth, and more? And, if we look around, and observe, since the major prolonged wars, outlined throughout history, man's journey on Planet earth has indeed been stormy. We had embarked on a path of more wars and upheavals; ever more destructive weapons of death and destruction; *and, importantly, a loss of caring, and of morality.*

This country, America, once had a welcoming history, and had provided tremendous opportunity, to many who arrived on these shores, with nothing to their name, from very poor, or very unstable, countries. But when things began to change, America had become somewhat of an isolationist, and insular; many of its politicians were of superior caliber, others, regrettably, had led the country, down a terrible path. Other large, and young, countries, such as Australia, and Canada, had also extended a welcoming mat, and thousands of immigrants sought them out, and other regions as well, in search of a better life, especially after the war of the early 1940's.

Throughout the ages, we had thinkers, on planet earth, who theorized on various beliefs about the existence of a Supreme Being; and they wondered about the extent, and composition, of the Universe. Later, humans began to delve into the purpose of man on this earth, man's behavior, the function of the mind, man's attitudes, and unfathomable reactions. They marveled at the ocean realm, the skies, and the world around them. As science advanced, humans learned that the earth was round, not flat, that there were millions of stellar bodies, and other planets, 'up there', comprising our entire universe. As studies in plant, and animal life, progressed, we eventually explored the function of atoms, and molecules, that of cells, and nuclei, biochemistry, and genetics. Whole new worlds, unfolded, before us!

There were (and still are) those, who professed to be, agnostics, and they did not believe in a God. There were existentialists, and creationists; and there were evolutionists, who believed that life evolved over millennia; and that the existence of water, and organic molecules, meant the origin of life. But there are many who also believe that creation, and evolution, can be considered in union. One, does not necessarily negate, the other. There were credible, scientific studies, showing that terrestrial animals, evolved from the ocean depths. Others refined it even more, with a potpourri of quantum physics, magnetic fields, chemical particles, and biogenetics, in an attempt to explain life. Then, there were those who talked about two parallel universes, one a mirror image, of the other, in belief, or in fiction? In this final section, an attempt will be made, to revisit relevant events, in some of the countries already reported upon, such as, America, the United Kingdom, the European Union, regions in the Middle east, and others; and yes, even back, to the island of Malta.

In the international press, and the Internet, news headlines were coming out, fast, and furious, and some of them dealt with US government attitudes, and mistakes. In the UK Sunday Times, we read, "Iraqi worshippers risk their lives to celebrate Christmas in church". Many wondered if this would be typical of the type of freedom, and democracy, that US, and UK, forces, had brought to Iraq, at least as of the end of 2005. Early in January 2006, was one of the most violent days in Iraq, from attacks, and suicide, bombs. In one of the worst days yet recorded, some 130 Iraqis had been killed, and about 200 wounded, and at least 5 Americans had been reported, dead. All this, even as they had hoped that elections would bring change; but many had already fingered those same elections, as fraudulent, and tainted. In January, a commentator, on CNN, stated that, unfortunately, this war in Iraq, had indeed, re-energized Al Qaeda, and increased recruits for their cause, against the United States, because of the war. And many of those recruits came from other countries, including some, from the west.

On the Middle East, headlines read, "Today's Joseph and Mary, would face 15 check points", referring to the Israeli military road blocks, and mobile check points, that now controlled passage along the roads from Nazareth, to Bethlehem. The struggles between the Palestinian people, and Israel, had remained precarious, but Sharon had changed direction, leaving his extreme right wing party, forming a new party, to proceed with the peace efforts. However, early in 2006, Sharon suffered a major stroke, with hemorrhage in the brain; and before that, he had suffered a minor stroke as well. Reporters were already stating that his political career was finished, moreover, would he even survive? Others wondered what omen that, might portend for the region, as a whole, for the Palestinian crisis, as they had wondered, after Arafat's death. As of this writing, Sharon was still in a coma, and listed as critical, but in stable condition.

Another headline from the UK, Sunday Times, read, "Godalming geek made millions running the pentagon's war in Iraq"- -*this dealt with yet, another, Bush administration, sea of scandals.* This one, in particular, *about US government agencies, paying news media, to plant false reports in Iraqi newspapers, presumably, talking of America's enormous progress in Iraq! Except, nobody had believed any stories, coming from US officials!* How about that, as a pattern, to demonstrate true democracy, to third world countries? Other news, referred to problems with administrations across the Atlantic ocean, in Europe, "French army faces inquiry into genocide in Rwanda"; Rwanda had been the source of terrible stories, on the turmoil in that region, events that had not yet been resolved, in justice. Then, there was this, "Aftermath of EU deal turns ugly", and "Blair deflects EU fire, with attacks on reactionaries"- -these dealt with ongoing struggles, within the European Union, and lack of apparent strong leadership roles. Each country's leaders jostling for power to exert influence, on other leaders. They had been negotiating about legislation on the EU budget (eventually resolved), and subsidies on agriculture, amongst the different nations, and much more.

Had Blair, of Britain, been blundering along, for some time? According to his critics, he certainly had, not the least of his blunders, being, reports on his alleged dishonesty on Iraq. A Sunday Times article, also alleged that, he had embraced leaders on the African continent, calling them, 'enlightened'. They quoted, how Blair, had picked out an Ethiopian prime minister, even though, in Ethiopia, some government opponents were being summarily shot, others were being imprisoned, including children. They also referred to leaders in Uganda, and Eritrea, in similar terms. Not a good omen for the African continent, if Blair, had truly called, some of these characters, 'enlightened'! And how can we possibly understand, such chaos, in that continent, when it had been under so many different colonial powers, for so many years? *Had so little, of value, been achieved, under those colonial masters?*

Towards the close of 2005, we had some headlines from the 'Independent', UK, "Iraq factor returns to haunt Blair"; indeed, Iraq, should continue to haunt him, if the news media had any sense, any freedom of action, in UK, until he resigned. "Sleeze watchdog stalls Blair's 'crony' peer list", went another; we have had a few months, to also learn of the sleeze, hidden, in actions by republicans, in the Bush administration, in the US; but there is plenty of sleeze, left, for the Blair clique, and for others. Other comments encountered were, "Beginning of the end (for Blair)"? This was the aftermath of Blair adversities, at the polls. "Wounded Blair knows rebels will be back for more blood", critics felt that Blair's dreams of reform were in doubt; and suggestions persisted, that he should resign! He said he would not do so. Thus, they shook hands, across the Atlantic--!

In the meantime, Gordon Brown, in UK, had already been mentioned as a replacement, for Blair. In the 'Independent', Brown announced his own plans for reforms within his government. He said, "If we are serious about a new kind of politics, we must be serious about *the undemocratic nature of some of our institutions*". And, he included the issue of the House of Lords. They also brought out the question of a written constitution, which America has had, since its inception. Is, it, not amazing, how many things had gone wrong, and their similarities, both under Bush, and under Blair, on both sides of the ocean?

There were more news comments on Blair's missteps, and other aspects, on the European Union difficulties. One article alleged that Greek authorities had tortured a Pakistani, terror suspect, with collusion from Britain's spy cliques, in Athens. Investigations were in progress. We have heard so much, on spying, that it begins to sound like, unbelievable fiction! Then, there was the ongoing dispute, between Russia, and Ukraine, on gas supplies from Russia, as Russia tried to raise the gas prices, it charged. Ukraine blamed Russia, and Russia blamed Ukraine, for the impasse! Russia had become a most reliable source of energy supplies; and Russia wanted to regain its stature in the world, as a major supplier of energy. Accusations were leveled at Putin, because of his increasing state controls; but, we have recently seen examples of 'state controls', in both the US, and UK, as well, have we not? Europeans expressed concern over this Russia-Ukraine dispute, as a good portion of their gas supplies flowed from Russia, through Ukraine, to the rest of Europe.

Other reports dealt with specific members of the EU. Former German chancellor, Kohl, allegedly, had written that, Thatcher, a past, UK, prime minister, had been determined to keep the two Germanys, apart; the east, and west, from reuniting, into one Germany. She wanted to keep East Germany out of NATO. Kohl wrote that Thatcher had greatly miscalculated, world interest, in a united Germany. On Turkey, a country, whose politicians had been fighting long, and, hard, for membership in the European Union, there was a tragic headline, even towards the close of 2005, "Customers help stamp out Turkey's sex slaves", this, in 2005! It referred to victims, mostly young women from former Soviet Union countries, who were forced into prostitution, in Turkey; and how officials at the United Nations, with the help of Turkish clients, were able to free many of those young women, trapped in the sex slave industry. After all these years, we had not yet eliminated sex slavery, in our society!

Then, there was an interesting report from Britain, alleging that after midnight, almost all their emergency room visits, to hospitals, *were alcohol related. That was amazing, once again.* They blamed it on the early closing of pubs, in London, resulting in immense binge drinking, before closure, with a lot of drunkenness, and misbehavior, even by women, with brawls, and accidents, and numerous injuries, needing medical care. Thus, they had decided to experiment, by keeping the pubs open, much of the night, to avoid the binging scourge. Critics claimed that this would make Britain's alcohol problems, much worse.

And from France, there were reports of major riots, in many cities across the country, apparently, mostly, by the Muslim communities, living there. This generated such headlines as, "Social divide, and unrest"; "French footballers condemn handling of riots"; "Two years to sort out human rights". Two years, surely they could move much faster than that? There was also this, "Go home, in the name of Allah, order the imams- -to the rioters". This, as they tried to help bring some order, and, stability, to the mayhem, that had been created by rioters.

What about America? Did we witness any redeeming features, in 2005, in the midst of all the terrible news, that hit the airwaves? An awful reminder of America's racial past, came, when Rosa Parks died, in 2005. She had made history when, in the ugliness of racial discrimination, in the US, she had refused to give up her seat on a bus, in 1955, to a white person. We saw many (white) officials, vying, with many others, to pay their respects. In those dark days of America, Blacks, were treated badly, they could not enter many eating establishments, or hotels, or cinemas; on highways, they could not stop at many of the rest areas; they could only ride in backs of buses. They had job opportunities, closed to them; they could not rent, or live, wherever they desired, and on, and on. And it was amazing that in the late 1950's, and early 1960's. racial discrimination, was alive, and well, in the US; and many critics claim that, a great deal persists to this day, not in such a glaringly, open, fashion, as in the past. Other critics, in recent years, have also pointed to racial discrimination, going on, in many parts of the world, as well.

American efforts to send aid to the stricken areas hit by the tsunami, were prompt, and much appreciated; that assistance came from government, and private, institutions. An American student was on a sabbatical in Asia, to experience different cultures. When the tsunami struck, he immediately pitched in to help, in any way he could. He said that the suffering he witnessed, and working with those victims, had impacted his life in a way, that, it had changed his focus completely! Now, he spent every vacation, and any opportunity he got, on humanitarian aid, wherever he could go, he valued that experience so much. What wonderful testimonials, those were, by that young man! Unfortunately, as often happens in such cases, one year after the tsunami, most of the victims were still living in tents (at least they had tents). They had nowhere else to live, no fresh water, and no electricity. Although the aid response to this disaster was most generous, by all estimates, and it came from all over the world, actual help for many of the victims, had been little, and late, in coming. Experts asserted that one major consolation was the fact that, no lives were lost *after the tsunami, because of massive relief efforts. Whereas in many disasters, as many lives had been lost afterwards, as had been lost during the actual disasters.*

We have likewise seen help pouring into Pakistan's mountain regions, for humanitarian aid, for victims of severe earthquakes that had impacted that area, as commented before. But even in January, 2006, we are seeing reports on news correspondents traveling to those mountains to see for themselves, and tell the world what was going on. The harsh winter weather had descended on those mountain villages, many of them completely isolated. Television reports showed the villagers with tents that did not keep away the extreme cold; at night large groups, as many as twelve would huddle in a tent to try keep warm, and make it through the night. Some of the tents were not even waterproof, and people said that family members were dying under those extreme conditions. Children were very ill, some with serious eye infections, quite dangerous, in themselves, without proper treatment, which was not available in many of their locations. There were inadequate medical supplies, scarce food, and only frigid water for bathing of any sort. A Pakistani representative said that those people should decide to leave their villages, and move lower down, the mountains, where help could reach them faster, and also, more help was available.

A '60 Minutes' program, on CBS, featured a small group of paramedics, from New York, who got together after the earthquakes, and headed out for Pakistan, to offer any help they could! One of them reported that, *it was not complicated, that when they cleaned a wound, or applied a band-aid, the amount of good generated with the people, was immeasurable! Right!* There were, also, MASH hospital units from the US, and other medical units, from different countries, including Cuba! Most governments knew very well that, with the approaching winter weather, in those mountains, the need of those villages was urgent, and great. Many had considered the Pakistani president a dictator, but he was trying to muster help in his own country, and from other governments. The mountain people were known to be highly individualistic, under normal circumstances, and attached to their tribal customs.

On another front, on a PBS program, we heard of truly, global, efforts, to combat Malaria, in parts of Africa; that is, a preventable disease, through the control of infections transmitted by mosquitoes. Many of their victims suffered repeated attacks of Malaria. The reporters demonstrated how this global, humanitarian, effort, was working, with the provision of special nets for the people. The fiber, the chemicals for the nets, the labor, and cash, all came from different sources, a truly combined effort. They also commented how many governments in Africa, talked a great deal about Malaria, but they seldom demonstrated serious commitment, to fighting the disease.

President Jimmy Carter has enjoyed a remarkable career. Since his presidency, Carter has been a ray of hope, an extended hand, a caring personality, for millions, of the most needy people, on planet, earth. He appeared on the 'Now' program, on MSNBC, and discussed America's humanitarian aid to poor nations. Presently, the US government was giving 16 cents, *out of every hundred dollars, donated by the international community*. What was more disgusting, most of that '16 cents', America donated, *went mostly to poor countries allied with the US; or those that agreed to have military bases on their land!* Others received practically nothing, from the United States. Do we begin to realize, how our foreign policy had generated so much anti-Americanism? The discussion continued that, during the cold war, if certain poor countries were not given assistance, the Soviet Union would pitch in and help. Thus American aid funds were made available. But with the end of the cold war, US government authorities had become stingy, and donations for the world's poor remained low.

These speakers also cited Uganda, where, with assistance from the Carter center, and Gates' foundation, an AIDS incidence of 16%, considered very high, had been reduced to 6%! Carter center affiliates, they said, taught people, the A, B, C. A, for abstinence; B, for being faithful; and C, for condoms, and education. But then, the present administration, in Washington, developed their misguided policies, against condom use. US officials had pressured the Uganda government to stop distributing condoms, and the result was that, the incidence of AIDS shot back up to 9%. A group of fundamentalist, right, Christians, opposed condom use, on any account, reportedly. That was wrong according to many critics. It had been emphasized that, a program designed to control epidemics, to save lives, hopefully to reduce the number of orphans, in the poorest of countries, surely, under those circumstances, the use of condoms, and proper education, should be debated with greater impartiality.

In a 2005 communication, president Carter also outlined other projects of the Carter center, with its affiliates. He referred to progress that was made, against Guinea worm disease; against River blindness, against Trachoma, and much more. Specifically, this memorandum contained, rather poignant, descriptions, on Guinea worm disease. President Carter recalled how he, and Mrs. Carter, witnessed, first hand, the terrible effects of this disease, many times. One day, in a village, in Ghana, *"virtually the entire population, men, women, and children, lay sprawled in the streets, unable to walk"*, let *alone care for themselves, or the needs of their families.* As for River blindness, they emphasized how Merck pharmaceutical company, had generously provided much free medicine. It would be wonderful if all companies did this, to solve some of the problems, and misery, of the poor around the world.

It has long been recognized that president Carter, and his group, have been strong champions for human rights, for freedoms, and democracy. Through the Carter center, they had monitored negotiations on voting rights, and the elections themselves, in several third world countries, in many unstable regions. Carter also championed justice for all.

We know that debates have raged in the US, on and off, over the perception of a two tier justice system, here, as well. Perhaps, in the wake of corporate scandals, and indictments handed down, that no longer holds true? But there have been critics who still believed that, those in positions, of power, did not always answer to the same laws. Other debates were concerned with the type of justice served, by the death penalty, instituted by the state; some had called it, an equivalent to 'murder by the state'. America is an exception amongst western nations, in the existing application of the death penalty. Regrettably, there were many reports, in different parts of the US, *where innocent victims were put to death, by the state, and they were proved innocent, or significant doubts had been raised, after the fact!*

Experts have also commented on the dramatic changes in government policies, in Central and, South American, countries. United States administrations had long been criticized, for popping up, and supporting tyrannical leaders in that part of the world. The poor people of the regions had suffered years of oppression, and thousands had reportedly been murdered. On the other hand, our Washington politicians had reviled Castro, of Cuba, for over 30 years; but was he really, any worse, than some of those other tyrants, who had the support of the US, and who had committed so many alleged atrocities? Most of us have read numerous reports on this, and usually, where there is smoke, there is fire! Thus, the political pendulum in many of those countries continues to swing, away from the United States- - you might say, the results of our seriously flawed, foreign policy!

Public Broadcasting featured a report on Guatemala where 2% of the population owned 70% of the land! *Is there, not, something wrong, with such bizarre, lopsided, figures?* There, enormous poverty still persisted, and people were forced to cut down trees, to build shelters for their families, and to provide fuel. That deforestation resulted in major flooding, and huge mudslides, following hurricanes, causing a lot of devastation, and the death of hundreds. Reporters also showed the ongoing excavation of many skeletal remains; this, according to critics, from the butchery by previous Guatemala officials. Surely, this must remain a shame, with America, and other countries. *It had been said that thousands simply disappeared!* A Catholic church was shown, still displaying hundreds of names of people who had been killed; and along some streets, were photos of many persons who had disappeared. Investigative reporters confirmed that seldom were any of the culprits brought to justice, in Guatemala. Some of the professionals who were carrying out excavations, and doing forensic examinations to identify victims, had also continued to receive various threats.

Why was it that the United States, the UN, and the EU, had not taken strong steps, to see to it that, the Guatemala government must act promptly, and bring any culprits to justice? Is it because of old reports that, officials knew what was going on, but decided to turn a blind eye, as a matter of convenience?

We had other recent reports on Latin American countries. Elections, in Bolivia, in 2005, saw politicians who were 'moderate' towards the US, being thrown out; and instead, elected leaders, who were vocally opposed to policies of America, calling the Bush administration 'a dictatorship', but they were not the only ones, to do so. A journalist on PBS news said that Bolivia had joined an enlarging group of Latin American countries, at great odds with US foreign policy. *All these countries had suffered economic collapse, in spite of so-called, help from the US!* A major criticism was that trade was one sided, from their countries, towards the US! Such groups of nations now included, Ecuador, Brazil, Argentina, Venezuela, and others, whose people were against United States policies; and, of course, there is Cuba. *The only US posturing towards Latin America, had been, drugs, and terrorism; and that had failed miserably!* Bolivia authorities had just invited China to develop that country's energy sources, and the US government continued to be pushed aside, even more.

Regrettably, even today, some suppression of freedoms, and democracy, are being perpetrated, in too many countries, including developed nations; in some, suppression becomes much more violent, and tyrannical. In December 2005, the World Trade organization, gathered in Hong Kong. Predictably, wherever the WTO, or group of eight, meet, there are also many protests, and sometimes riots. Groups of activists, try to let the world understand that, these organizations seldom conclude any discussions that result in solutions for some of the world's major problems, the poor, and the terrible plight of third world countries. Yes, those meetings generated violence in Hong Kong, as they had done, in the US, UK, in Italy, in Switzerland, anywhere they met. Unfortunately, that violence in Hong Kong, led to authorities suppressing those demonstrations, using tear gas, and some 900 were arrested. The position taken by the small island of Malta, at the WTO, stemmed from a sense of solidarity with poorer, developing, nations, *whose agriculture was being hampered by current practices, favored by richer, developed, countries.*

From the regions of Asia, we also had a different type of report, dealing with Okinawa; apparently the region was noted for longevity amongst its citizens, the largest percentage of its people, anywhere, who lived to be 100 years old, or longer. Some of the reasons quoted, were, people worked hard in the fields, or in the case of men, fishing; a lot of the work was out of doors. They grew their own fruits and vegetables, and so on; and therefore they ate freely, of their own, home, grown, produce, and the fish they caught in their own, cleaner, waters. Most likely, a major difference, to their advantage, was the lack of chemicals, pesticides, etc., in the products they consumed. They also had one of the lowest rates of cancer, and of cardiovascular disease. Their social structure continued to value all generations, including the elderly, who were still part of the family. It seemed that family, socially close, contacts, and even romance, were, for them, conducive to good health.

Returning to the Middle East, there, many troubling uncertainties had persisted, besides the Israeli-Palestinian quagmire. There were more harsh exchanges between officials from the US, and from Syria. Guests, on a PBS, news program, included reports by some Americans, who had lived in Syria for many years. They seemed to be unanimous in their disagreements with US policies. They believed that *America was not in the region to help those people, but rather, to help itself.* A Syrian minister commented that if the US administration truly wanted a genuine democracy for the region, they would be dealing with their president, instead of demonizing him. It shows yet again, that in the world of very dirty politics, it is hard to know, who to believe, or even trust, to tell the truth.

There were reports of instability in Lebanon. Then, Jordan, according to critics, became a casualty of the Bush war, on Iraq. On November 9, 2005, three international hotels were bombed, in Amman, Jordan; and these were frequented by westerners, and contractors working in Iraq. Initial estimates showed that 60 had been killed, and many more had suffered significant injuries. They knew of three bombers, but several days after the bombing, Jordan officials 'announced' that a fourth bomber, a woman, 'had confessed' to planning to join in those attacks, but her detonation device had failed; or did she change her mind? She was shown on worldwide television with bombs strapped to her body. Critics rightly raised the question if she was telling the truth, or whether she was really cooperating; or, was she responding to pressure, or perhaps torture, at the hands of Jordanian officials? In our present propaganda wars, on all sides, these were legitimate questions.

There was also the situation in Iran, with the new leader of that country. Commentators have alleged that officials in the US, UK, and Israel, had been urging action against Iran for some time; perhaps sanctions through the UN security, council. Others had also suggested that perhaps there would be a 'secret' attack against suspected nuclear facilities, in Iran, by Israel, or by the US; but this could result in a global nightmare. There have been many debates in western countries, about Iran attempting to develop nuclear technology. The Iranian authorities had maintained their right to do so, for peaceful purposes; whereas they believed Israel already had nuclear weapons, as well as, other, well known countries, such as, US, UK, Russia, France, India, Pakistan, and others. The Iranian leader had continued to pronounce dangerous comments about Israel, and that had muddied the water, even more. Perhaps, it was simple rhetoric, as politicians often do, in this case, to counteract statements coming out of Tel Aviv, London, and out of Washington.

The crisis of nuclear proliferation has been haunting our planet, since world war two, and many policies, developed, at the United Nations, have not been taken seriously, not even, by countries, in the west. No major efforts had been undertaken, at a total ban, and at nuclear disarmament. We often find ourselves in a state of confrontation, or uttering many dictatorial demands; seldom, using proper and decent dialogue, and the art of rapprochement. The late pope John Paul II had been a tireless, strong, advocate, for disarmament. During the height of the cold war, the secrecy, and rivalry, between the United States, and the Soviet Union, had intensified considerably, with regard to the development, and possession, of nuclear weapons. And certain events had come close to precipitating a crisis.

Russia has also been experiencing turmoil of its own, with attacks by separatist groups, within its borders. It is no longer as isolated as it was once, in the days of the harsher Soviet Union. It has increasingly participated in global commerce, with investments from the 'west', and now it is also an active participant in the group of eight activities. It has strived to regain some of the stature it had attained, in the post world war two, era. It has also maintained a position of influence at the United Nations.

China, even under the influence of a longstanding communist regime, had continued to grow more powerful; it, too, did not remain as isolated as in the past, and had become a major trade partner, in many parts of the world, with large amounts of exports to the west. It had achieved such remarkable growth, that it started carrying a significant portion of the debt of the United States. It had also made great strides in the fields of science, industry, and also, space exploration. It had long been a major military power, and was now a nuclear power as well.

We have already referred to some of the empires in history that, have come, and gone. There were the dynasties of old, in parts of Asia. The Spanish empire at one time extended to most of the Americas. The once powerful British Empire was no more, But as mentioned, it was replaced by, a loosely, knit, group, as the 'Commonwealth of nations'. For the 2005 gathering of the 'Commonwealth of nations', many of the dignitaries from those countries assembled in Malta, and these included Queen Elizabeth the second, of England, and her husband, the Duke of Edinburgh. It was quite a feat for such a small island to carry out. It was reported that, of necessity, security had to be very tight, having such a large number of leaders of nations, together, in a small country. For the occasion, the British navy also dispatched the aircraft carrier, 'Illustrious', famous during Malta's epic struggles in world war two.

Undoubtedly, the topics to be discussed by the group would be many, and varied; and there would be those who hoped that, members at that gathering, would be vocal, and push hard for peace, and justice, in our troubled world.

It would not be an easy task, as Britain had supported Bush in an illegal, unjust, war, with the consequences that have been unfolding; and many of those countries, at the gathering, had opposed the war, and some of the policies of America. About this same time, in November, the major holiday of 'Thanksgiving', was being celebrated in the US, a holiday, that had reached the stature of Christmas, in importance and popularity; and the enormous number of people who travel to be with family, or friends, for the occasion. We can only hope, and pray, that if we begin to solve our problems, with a true formula for greater tolerance, for charity, for friendships, and understanding, and for peace and justice, on out planet, *then, we will have reached an important goal, and have good reason to celebrate our Thanksgiving!*

As of early 2006 the European Union had not yet found its proper niche, on the world stage, not on Iraq, not in the Israeli-Palestinian impasse, not on the confrontations with North Korea, or Iran, with the United States.. The EU had continued to grow in number of member states, but numerous questions besetting that group of nations, had remained unresolved, and contentious. Positions taken by Britain, or France, or Germany, were, not infrequently, at odds with positions of other member countries.

On another continent, in Africa, the turbulent years of Liberia, appeared to have turned, dramatically, for the better, after the former leader of that country had been forced into exile; and United Nations forces encouraged, and monitored, peaceful negotiations amongst the various factions. Supervised, 'democratic', elections had taken place, with the election of a female president. Amongst her qualifications, American news media listed her 'Harvard' enhanced, education. But, commentators were quick to add, it remained to be seen what course Liberia would follow; could it act as a beacon for other young African nations? If it turned into a success story, then, perhaps other politicians, in many parts of troubled Africa would be inclined to follow in her footsteps.

For a change of scenario we also had this, in January 2006. CNN featured a news story on a 2 year old, Hippopotamus, and a Tortoise, said to be about 130 years old. It turned into a most interesting report, because scientists were amazed, and quite baffled, at the close, friendly, relationship, between these two, wonderful creatures. It emphasized how much there is in nature that, humans still, cannot fully understand. They showed this Hippopotamus, and Tortoise, 'playing' together; and snoozing, with one's head, close to, or actually on, the other. They were also emitting certain sounds at each other! Was that communication? The video photography that was televised on these events, was superb, to say the least; and certainly enough, to provoke more intense study of nature, all around us. Another remarkable feat for the US, also in January, was the safe return to earth, of the probe that was launched a few years ago, to penetrate a comet, to collect interstellar particles, and return it to earth for research. It was a successful venture, and study results are pending. Other probes launched into our universe for research, used nuclear fuel, and *are bound to cause much debate, again, as to what is right, or what is wrong, in our acts!*

Another country we have touched upon is North Korea. It is generally believed to already possess nuclear weapons, and has one of the largest military on earth. The rhetoric flying between officials of the US and N. Korea, and some other countries, had continued, unless the US happened to be 'distracted' by Syria, or Iran, or Venezuela, or Iraq! In January 2006, investigative reporter Dan Rather presented a feature, on '60 Minutes', on CBS. He spent about one week in North Korea, and met with some of their officials. He emphasized how they were still obsessed by the threats, they perceived, were being transmitted, by American officials. Dan explained to his viewers that wherever he went, it was understood that, his 'controller' would be with him; and he could only visit where they wanted him to go.

Here, it is fair to state that many visitors to America, from certain countries, would encounter similar problems; they would also be under constant surveillance, without them knowing it; and there would be many places they would not be permitted to visit, is that not right? And now, we know that the Bush administration has allegedly been spying extensively, both at home, and abroad! *What is the difference, we ask our readers?* Except that, this White house prefers to hide its actions behind nicer sounding terminology (they are trying to call it something else, besides spying); and they like to hide behind the 'war' word, and 'fighting terrorism'; everything, is justified, on that account. What was striking about North Korea, were the 'shows', and military parades, that, Dan Rather was able to show, his viewers. Many reports on that country had been so negative, with regard to the extreme poverty of the masses, lack of adequate food, constant oppression, etc. With all that, one has to wonder how the North Koreans could possibly afford such a large military; and how did they always manage to gather such huge crowds in their streets, or their arena (hundreds of thousands), for a proud, military, parade, or for a celebration of their leader? More food, for thought!

In the United States, the year 2005, and early 2006, were teeming with news releases, on the many scandals surrounding this Bush administration, and the republican controlled congress. Not the least of those was the manner in which America was taken to war in Iraq. Recently, reporters noted how, veterans, returning from Iraq, were entering politics, and campaigning against the Iraq war, and the way that war is being conducted! Olbermann, and guests, on MSNBC news, commented, on all that, *how in Washington, politicians had tried to root out corruption, in congress, for one hundred years; and it appeared that they had not succeeded!* On the Bush spying scandals, many reporters, and experts, had asserted that the nation's laws were very specific; that, for the president to start spying on American citizens, he needed authorization by congress, or by the courts. Guests on PBS, 'Now', program, stated that *the president deliberately acted outside the law; and it was so secretive that, they used another nice sounding term for it, calling it "The Program"!* The president's man, Gonzales, appeared on the Jim Lehrer news hour, on PBS, and in parrot like fashion, he kept repeating that the spying was extremely limited, and no laws were broken. Critics have strongly disagreed with him. And Americans were further insulted, when, Gonzales announced that, now, congress was kept fully informed; *only, after they got caught?*

However, a woman who had worked under Reagan, understandably, stated that, Bush had acted within the law; he had decided he had the powers to work outside present regulations on spying by the government, in a state of war. Many experts have disagreed with that reasoning.

On the question of a tendency to abuse, or corruption, in government in America, for the year 2004 alone, reporters estimated there were some 250 former lawmakers, in Washington, in the "lobbying business"! *That year, about 3.6 billion dollars had been spent on lobbying activities;* that is, trying to inform, and influence (as we all know, too well) lawmakers in their decisions. *Is that what goes for freedom, and democracy, these days; what we want to demonstrate to developing countries?* Or is, it, once more, a question of the 'have', and the 'have not', one government for the elite, and a totally different one, for all other Americans? Is there, also, a justice system for the elite, and powerful, and a different one for the rest of America? On these lobbying scandals, and possible bribery, in Washington, reporters alleged that the wife of a congressman had received at least 150,000 dollars 'for work and services'.

We have also been shown in news releases, how, numerous politicians, republican, and democrat, but mostly republican, were falling all over themselves, trying to return large sums of money, their campaigns had received, *donating most of it to various charities.* This included money that was returned from Bush's campaign funds! They added that some other politicians had money they did not return as they felt there was no wrongdoing. Most commentators agreed that, the Abramoff scandals in the US government, were so serious, and so pervasive, and extreme, that perhaps, good things would come of it, in the end; such as, 'cleaning out sleaze, corruption, and disgraceful behavior, from the halls of congress'.

In the above scandals, names, had already been spewed out, by reporters, such as, Delay, a leader in congress; Ralph Reed, a right wing advocate on 'morals', who had his own political ambitions, and once campaigned for high office; and there were many other names, they are still coming out! On the Chris Matthews news reports, on MSNBC, they commented how, only now, *did these politicians see the 'need' to return all that money, only after the scandal broke out, in the open! Does that tell us something?* They also referred to the lobbying system in the US government, 'as a nasty, dirty, business'. What else can one add! That is how business was conducted in America, and lobbyists "quickly figured out who could be bought"! That is a black eye, on our system of government. Many sensible politicians rushed with proposals to bring back honesty, and reform government; but surely they had all known what was going on, in Washington, all these years! Is there a risk that, they might end up solving nothing, yet again?

After all these scandals were uncovered, and splashed on our news media, reporters alleged that, White house sources issued a statement that, 'they looked forward to working with the republicans in congress, to build on the achievements they had made on behalf of the American people'. Critics are bound to ask, what achievements? Those tax breaks, that were enacted, for the wealthiest 1%, in the country; and, of course, for corporate America? Can they boast of an economy that had improved mainly for the wealthy, and for business; as the majority of the middle class, and the poor, were left far behind? Do we need more examples? When Ford motor company, in January, announced the laying off, of some 25,000 workers, or more, and the closing of several plants, many of the workers who would be affected were devastated. Ford was forced to do that because of a poor business climate, and loss of revenues; but in spite of that, and the hardships for the people, the stock market on Wall Street, applauded the news, and rose higher, for that day! *That is the tremendous disconnect between business executives, and the average citizen.* And, had America's stature in the world improved, in the past few years? A correspondent wrote to National Geographic magazine, as he had read about oil related contracts in Chad, going to their government cronies; and there was widespread waste, and inefficiency. He made the point, that, he was saddened, *because it sounded so much like my country, the United States!*

On the other major scandal of prisoner abuse at the hands of Americans, a former US interrogator appeared on 'Hardball', with Chris Matthews, on MSNBC. He said that in their experience, some 90% of captured prisoners were found to be innocent! But US *officials had told them that everyone was guilty, until they proved their innocence; a standard of justice, directly opposite, to that in the US!* This came from an American who actually worked as an interrogator in Iraq. Do we believe him, or do we believe shady pundits in Washington? What type of democracy had the Bush administration. exported, to teach the people of a new Iraq? An example they quoted on the program was, if a car was stopped, at a checkpoint, and a shovel was found inside the car, the driver, and occupants, were immediately, suspected, by US officials, of planning, to plant bombs! Thus, they were arrested.

The guest on this program also stated that, when they had completed their interrogation, the prisoners were moved somewhere else, and they could not tell what had happened to them, after that! In these discussions we also heard about US marines entering homes, subduing 'suspects', they asked them questions over, and over, again, and also punched, and kicked them. This was yet, another news report, about abuse, from someone, who claimed to have worked closely with the American armed forces. Some of our top officials in Washington had the gall to state that our forces were now battle hardened, because of the war in Iraq? Is that what you call all these nasty reports on America? The day after the above feature had aired, Matthews received, and read, a letter from military officials denying that they ever authorized abuse of prisoners! *Does anyone, in their right mind, expect them to admit to it? Come, now, give us credit for some common sense!*

What of the Supreme Being, referred to earlier in this section? Throughout man's journey, on this planet, the concept, on who God was, had continued to evolve. God was seen in the sky, in the sun, and in the moon; in comets streaking through the sky; and in a myriad stars. An awesome God was seen in the phenomenon of an eclipse; God was seen in the earth, all around, and the elements. He was in the magnificent forests, in other plant or, animal life; in lightning storms; and an 'angry' God was seen in the sounds of thunder, and yes, in the eruption of volcanoes. He was seen in the unfathomable depths of oceans, and in the richness of life therein- - -pantheism! Cultures existed, where people, not knowing who God was, or what He looked like, or where to search, created images, 'idols', various statues of animals, mythological subjects, or any imaginary figures, and venerated them as their 'actual' deities. In a recent movie, a scientist expressed it well when he said, *I do not know what God is, but I sense, God is.* In a way, that explains much of the above, 'God is'; but they did not know, who, 'God was'. Indeed, mankind has been on a long journey in search of God, since the beginning of time. *And we are still trying to figure out, when that, beginning was!*

It is quite a jolt to move from the philosophical, and theological, debates, on the existence of God, who God is, from creation, and evolution, to our struggles, here on earth; to turmoil, and conflicts; to disasters and diseases; to poverty and starvation; to oppression and discrimination; to dishonesty, and corruption, in governments, and corporations, and in the relationships between human beings. *Thus, we are jolted to the present, to try to do something about it!* But is, there also, the serene, the sublime, and decency, in our midst, mixed in, with a tendency to evil? *Yes, of course, there is.* If we persist, and look, that too, we can discover, all around us, the good, and beautiful, sometimes, where, and when, we least expect it. We have touched upon just a few decent acts by individuals in all walks of life. There are many more.

Much of the beauty in nature has been depicted often, in literature, and in movies. In the National Geographic society, "Ocean Realm", the authors discussed the awesome beauty in the oceans, even in the darkness of their depths. Scientists have long shown that, even at extreme ocean depths, where no light, or energy, from the sun, ever, penetrate, there is abundant life around volcanic, chimney, vents, *in spite of the lack of sunlight, the extreme temperatures, either very hot, or very cold, and the intense water pressures at those depths.* In the IMAX movie, "Aliens of the Deep", they captured amazing photography of areas around such volcanic discharges, absolutely teeming with shrimp, with crab and fish, and other ocean life forms. Absolutely wonderful!

But as part of the human assault on the environment, they also pointed out how humanity had imperiled the seas, as well. The authors referred to some people who looked upon the ocean *'as a safe place to deposit their nuclear waste'. Safe place? Did those people ever consider the safety of future generations?* Much of our climate, our very lives, depended on the health of the oceans; and we had already touched on some of the destruction heaped upon it, the plight of the coral reefs, and the species of fish that are disappearing, or becoming toxic. Why? There is global, warming, scientists seem to have agreed on that. There had been an increase in the number of oil spills; oil discarded from ships; garbage and chemicals that are being dumped into the sea, everywhere. Yes, the health of our whole environment is intimately tied to the health of our oceans. *What next?*

The Mediterranean sea has been increasingly encroached upon, over the years; it has been labeled a 'sheltered sea', with an increasing population, and industry, over the years, along its shores; and therefore the sea was most vulnerable. Many scientists had considered the Mediterranean already, adversely affected, perhaps to the point of no return? International agreements have been important, to do something about its plight, but discussions are still in progress amongst the many nations, involved. Those same authors also commented on how canals had connected oceans, where no such connections existed before, thus altering the environment. Wetlands had been reclaimed for dry land development, and in some countries, parts of the coastal areas were also reclaimed from the sea! Do we really believe that, *if humans continue on this path, that, we will not feel the impact of the destructive forces of nature?* Have we not seen enough evidence in the last few years? *Were the Asian tsunami, the destructive US hurricanes, and many other natural disasters, our warning signals?*

In these last pages, we have revisited developments in different areas of the globe. At this point, we will revisit Malta, as well. According to Sir Harry Luke, in his book, 'Malta', Queen Elizabeth the first, reigning, in the latter half of the 1500's, had expressed it very well, on the great Siege of Malta, in 1565. She was quoted, thus, *"If the Turks should prevail against the Isle of Malta, it is uncertain, what further peril might follow the rest of Christendom"!* The Turks did not prevail against Malta in 1565; and the German, Italian, axis, did not prevail against Malta, during the 3-year siege, of world war two, in the early 1940's.

In 1989, National Geographic, magazine, published an article, 'The Passion of Freedom', by William S. Ellis. He quoted author Raymond Massey, who said, of the Maltese people, "We were deprived of our rights, for many centuries; that is one of the reasons we are so obsessed with politics". The article continued that, down through the centuries Malta had been put to the survival test, time, and time, again. The islands had been under the control of outsiders for hundreds of years. They were bartered or sold, to one nobleman, or another, *without regard to the wishes of the people.* The islanders were not too numerous, they had no military, they were not rich; and thus, *they were at the mercy of European powers, a good example of the 'have', and the 'have not', in our past.* Some of the noblemen, who 'bought' Malta, exercised harsh control over the population. Those who protested, and protest they did, were exiled, or imprisoned, or were put to death. According to Laspina, those periods were referred to as *The Times of the Tyrants,* for Maltese historians. However, for the first time, in the early 1960's, it gained its independence from Britain. *Malta became master of its own destiny.*

Discussions on the Knights of Malta (also, Knights of St. John of Jerusalem, Knights of Rhodes), evoke thoughts of romance, aristocracy, and valor. The knights were originally 'hospitallers', charged with service to Christians, stricken during pilgrimages to Holy places, in Jerusalem. Later, in defense of Christianity, the Order became a military might, and also a naval power. The Knights of Malta ruled over the islands for over 250 years.

These knights were grouped into Langues (Tongues), such as, Provence, Auvergne,

France, Germany, Italy, England, Castile-Portugal, and so on. They came from all over Europe, and from some of their most aristocratic, titled, families. As Malta was a very small island, like many other islands, it had become a pawn, in the hands of the mighty, of Europe. Therefore, in its past, it had passed from one ruler, to another. St. John's co-cathedral, in Valletta, has several chapels dedicated to the above different Langues, or countries of origin. Reading some of the names of the Grandmasters associated with Malta, is like a 'who's who', record, of those early times; and it reveals quite readily, the source, from some of the long established, families, of Europe. These are some of the names: de Lisle Adam; di Ponte, de Sainte Jalle, D'Omedes, de la Sengle, de la Valette, del Monte, de la Cassiere, de Verdalle, Garzes, de Wignacourt, de Vasconcellos, de Paule, de Lascaris Castellar, de Redin, Cotoner, Carafa, Perellos y Rocaful, Zondadari, de Vilhena, Despuig, Pinto de Fonseca, Ximenes de Texada, de Rohan Polduc, von Hompesch.

As would be expected, the islands carry many names of towns, or regions, or monuments, etc., reflecting on these Grandmasters, or the countries of origin; or certain events of that period. Similarly, names of streets, but these had been changed, according to the winds of politics. They were mostly in English, during British rule; and following the islands' accession, to independence, many names were changed to Maltese, in line with winds of nationalism, at the time. It was said that, some of the Grandmasters were greatly disturbed by the attitude of some of their knights, who were apt not to adhere to the strict requirements of their Christian faith. They were not willing to do that, but they were willing to die in defense of Christianity. In time, some of the Grandmasters, themselves, and the knights, did not get on well, with church authorities, in Rome.

During the second, world war, the magnificent opera house, in Valletta, was destroyed, but was never rebuilt. The capital city was left with the Manoel theatre, a gem in its own right, built by the Grandmasters, in 1731. It is well preserved to this day, and used regularly for performances. The typical Maltese fishing boat is seen in fishing villages; and is called 'Luzzu'. They are painted in lovely, bright, colors, and on the bow, is usually found the design of an 'eye of Osiris'; traditionally that was supposed to ward off tragedy at sea.

In recent years Malta's number of tourists had reached around a million each year, mostly from Europe. For the size of the island, that is a significant tourist trade. The past 10 to 20 years had also seen the development of several 4, and 5 star, hotels, to provide amenities for the tourism industry, which had become the single, largest industry, in the islands. The ready availability, of plentiful fresh water, had become a problem, because of very short periods of rainfall. Therefore, the surrounding, Mediterranean sea provided the solution towards reclaiming more fresh water, out of the oceans.

The social structure is quite good; education is mostly free, and so is most of the health care; but for some aspects of the latter there are means tests. There are government pension schemes, and subsidized housing; and there are children allowances, and aid for the elderly, and the handicapped, besides the poor. Church, and other, charity, organizations have assisted, in many of these projects. These days, widespread, mass, poverty, is unknown in Malta, and corner street begging had become a thing of the past. But as mentioned earlier, the substantial increase of illegal immigrants, from N. Africa, and drug trafficking, had created new social problems.

Malta's destiny has been tied closely to Europe's; but since it's independence, most of the government's policies have leaned towards non-alignment, and the preservation of peace in our world.

Singer Jennifer Berezan was searching for answers, for something different, because, as she put it, *she lived in a culture of violence, injustice, and alienation.* Surely, from many of the reports in these chapters, we begin to realize that, such a description is close to the truth, even today. She journeyed to the Mediterranean region, to research ancient Neolithic cultures; and she discovered that in ages past, certain people *"lived in harmony, in highly artistic, egalitarian, peaceful, societies, organized around the Mother goddess".* She decided that, in Malta, *she had found the pinnacle of her discovery, the famous Hypogeum, with its 6000 year old, history.* This is one of the oldest temples in the world, not built out of massive, rock blocks, like other surface, temples, but entirely carved out of solid rock, deep, underground. In this magnificent relic of ancient times, Berezan, and her group, recorded a 'healing' chant on CD, in the ancient Oracle chambers, created for sound, by those earliest of architects!

She had obtained the permission, and cooperation, of Malta's archeological department. This CD, entitled 'Returning', is a beautiful melody that evokes periods of calm, inner peace, solace, and moods, for meditation. Joan Marler said that, in those chambers, "the extraordinary sounds were heard throughout the sacred darkness; echoes, as the voice of ancestors, who had returned to the mother of us all". We can only hope that, this Hypogeum, will remain open for limited access, by the public, with advance reservation only; a step in the right direction, to preserve, and protect, such an ancient marvel.

Sadly, since those far, far away, times, how much have we strayed from solace, from justice, from love, from peaceful coexistence? A writer to National Geographic, magazine, referred to humanity, when he commented, on the Pygmies of the forests, of the Congo, thus, "If the Congo's poorest people, are also the happiest, *what does this say, about the so-called blessings, of civilization"? Right!*

CONCLUSION

What can we, all of humanity, do, to place ourselves firmly, on the path of justice, and peace? We have often debated the need for greater tolerance, and understanding, more dialogue amongst human beings, and much less confrontation. Historically, wealthier, more developed, nations, have taken advantage of less developed, nations; that has always been part of our problem. Trying to help us get on the right track, in his first encyclical, Pope Benedict XVI followed the cause of many previous popes, and emphasized the need for more love and charity in our world. That would also go hand, in hand, with justice and peace, for all.

In 'Night Comes to the Cumberlands', by Caudill, mentioned earlier, we read of the destruction of nature, and the environment, in that particular region of America, to extract coal; *and that was 50 to 60 years ago! Now, we are witnessing more of the same (destruction) in Alberta, Canada.* Do we ever learn anything? This time it is to extract oil from dirt. Yes, we need fuel, lots of it, because of our excesses, but large areas of pristine wilderness are being destroyed, to achieve that purpose. Business tycoons, and corrupt individuals, usually, pontificate that, the beauty of nature would be restored, and reinvigorated; but, as we all know, it is never restored the way it once, was, and it is never accomplished in a timely manner. In the process of extracting oil from dirt, a large amount of pollutants were being released into the atmosphere. Once again, many experts had, long, maintained that, we need to find other, renewable, sources of energy that are also, more environmental, friendly. That is the only, sane, way to proceed, in order to protect our planet! Regrettably, politicians, and business leaders, do not listen too well.

Recent reports confirmed that, this winter, unusually cold weather had gripped most of Europe. Many scientists have become concerned that our climate changes, caused by man, might have already reached a point, where they cannot be reversed. This, as America, according to critics, has had one of the worst anti-environment administrations ever. They are the only ones who have been so blind, *as to claim that, there is no proof of climate change; they wanted more study!* Always the same pathetic reasoning, let us have another commission, let us do further study!

If we needed lessons from history, we have had many groups of people, entire civilizations *who, simply, ceased to exist, and vanished.* To mention just one example, the ancient civilization of Nubia, was powerful, and remarkable, for its time, with many magnificent structures. It was reported that, Nubia, was once, surrounded by forests and lush vegetation. However, as the people continued to cut down their trees, for fuel and other uses, the forests were soon, decimated. Following that, there obviously was, climate change, the desert sands moved in, and their magnificent buildings became ghost towns; and the people vanished, as many other civilizations had done, before, and after, them, often leaving no clues, as to what had actually happened to them..

We must find ways to foster greater justice, in the sharing of the world's riches, and resources; and we need to demonstrate more acceptance of ethnic, and religious, freedoms, and diversity. We had heard often enough, in the past, and it has been repeated here, that we need to practice 'being our brother's keeper'; for those who have plenty, to share with those who have little, or none. Those who have too many comforts, and luxuries, and enjoy stability in their countries, also need to help the less fortunate, in many, areas- - -in agriculture, in the ready availability of clean water; in education, and health care; in democracy, and human rights; in the creation of job opportunities; in the building of living accommodations; a tall order, indeed. This applies to government entities, to individuals, and corporations, and charitable organizations. We have referred to president Jimmy Carter, and his center, who has done these very things for many years; but we need many more, like Carter, in all developed, and lesser, developed, nations, doing the same!

As a possible solution to some of the difficulties facing humanity, we look upon the United Nations; many personalities, have expressed the view that, our present world needs a powerful, well organized, well functioning, but trustworthy, international body, much more than it needs, a single, powerful, country, a super-power. It is recognized that such a revitalized, UN, must also have a larger group of representative countries, to act as the 'security council'; and no single nation would be permitted to hold veto, powers. Then, things would most likely change for the better. There must also be strong efforts, to resolve, and eliminate, all allegations of corruption. There have been too many such allegations- -no United Nations could possibly function well, if corruption is not rooted out, from whichever source.

For another major solution, we must revisit the military-industrial complex. Nobody, as far as we know, has tried to come up with a reasonable figure (and publicize it well, worldwide) *of all the money spent on the military, and on weapons, and armaments of all types, around the world, each year.* It is a very difficult task because the military juntas, governments, and the weapons industry, are much more likely to lie, than to tell the truth, about such precise expenditures, on instruments of death, and devastation. But even so, if we were to come up with a rough estimate, most people would be astounded. For the US alone, it is probably *in the range of 500 billion dollars, or much more, yearly. A former pentagon analyst was on PBS news, and confirmed how America spent about half a trillion dollars per year, on the military, and we did not get a lot for that money; "we are certainly not getting what we pay for",* he said! But then the former Soviet Union had also spent huge amounts. Then there is all of Europe, China, India and Pakistan; and all other countries, large, or small. There is South Africa, Israel, and the Middle East, Canada, Australia, and Japan, and more. We must keep in mind that, even poor countries spend heavily on weapons, and some type of a military- - -there is Indonesia, N. Korea, and S. Korea, Vietnam, Philippines, all countries in Africa, and many more.

If men, and women, on planet earth, had a reasonably accurate figure, of all expenditures thus squandered, by the above countries, *they would be utterly shocked. Shocked, because everyone would soon realize, that, all those sums would add up to trillions of dollars (yes, with a T)!* Then, they would also experience 'a vision', and understand how such a fortune, would likely solve most of humanity's urgent needs, and even more than that. Because, we must remember that, such an obscene amount of money, is spent year, after, year, on the same disillusionment, that weapons, and power are the answer.

If the above reasoning is close to the truth, why is it that, we do not have a sufficient number of leaders, in all those countries, with enough common sense, to do what is right? That is the face of national leaders, as it is portrayed on the world's stage- -a paralysis, where they seldom manage to solve any serious problems. A guest, on PBS, 'Now', with David Broncaccio, stated that, the conglomerate that has interests in "weapons, and in war", *would never act to try to curtail the military-industrial machine. These groups include the weapons industry, the military, and congress!* They discussed how the weapons, and military equipment corporations, have branch industries in practically every state, in America. Thus, most congressmen have an axe to grind, when they want federal money for their district, to keep factories open, and to provide jobs. But what types of jobs are those, producing what? That is the way the vicious cycle keeps on, perpetuating itself, in country, after, country.

Consider some recent upheavals. We had accusations by the west, that leaders, in Russia, were implementing more state controls. But in January, British newspapers reported on Russian authorities arresting more British spies, as the Blair government continued to muddle along. But Russians have had other problems, in dealing with Chechen rebel groups, carrying out terrorist acts within Russia; the most serious one, was perhaps, the seizure of a school, resulting in the death of large numbers of innocent, school children. Chechnya wanted a separate state, but, once more, killing innocent people is not the way to achieve that goal.

We had comments from the world community directed at the US, for numerous unfolding scandals in the Bush administration, as they kept on stonewalling investigations, into many of them. The usual motto that power is might, and we do what we want! Some of those scandals included: *the White house leak; torture of prisoners; the illegal practice of 'rendition'; spying on the international community at will; spying on American citizens—* stung by heavy criticism, the Bush clique tried to change the focus from 'domestic spying', to 'international spying', the excuse of course, being "terrorism", they use all types of tricks. There were more scandals: *lobbyists in Washington; bribery and corruption; the failure of the administration in the Katrina disaster over Louisiana-* reporters have shown that of the grand promises by Bush, immediately after 'Katrina' had struck, most of them had not been fulfilled! Talk is cheap. More scandals were, *what was known by White house staff, before the attacks of 9/11; there were tax breaks for the wealthiest Americans; the lies, and/or, fabrications, on Iraq, and much more!* Of course, we cannot forget the alleged voting scandals, of the last two presidential elections. On Iraq, criticism is still being leveled in the UK that, Blair, and Bush, had decided to attack Iraq, irrespective of any UN decisions; but then, many people had always believed that. Some would call the above, a plethora of scandals!

Then there is China; it had continued to grow rapidly, both as an economic power, and in its stature on the world stage. World politics had reached a point where, certain actions that might be entertained by the US, or Europe, now, had to take into consideration opinions from Russia or China, as well. That is the way political winds are blowing these days. In the same region, we had reports from Nepal, on an ongoing Maoist rebellion; they claim that the uprising is against a capitalistic system, full of abuse, and corruption. Here too, there are those who call them terrorists, and others say they are simply freedom fighters, depending on which side you lean towards.

What can we add, on the stature of the United States, on the world stage? We have had several major international events that *have reflected on the increasing weakness, of the American government's influence, with citizens of too many countries, including those we call 'our friends'!* Towards the end of January 2006, elections were held in the Palestinian territories. Prior to these elections, pundits in Washington had already announced that the current ruling party (with whom the Bush people had been negotiating), would likely win, although, perhaps, not with an absolute majority. Were our Washington officials wrong? Did they have to eat humble pie? You bet! When results of those elections were announced, those officials were devastated, although they tried to put a mild spin on it all, as usual. *It showed once more, how little, US government officials understood, of what is developing in the rest of the world!* A high official in Latin America rightly put it this way, *"the trouble with the American government is that, they think the rest of the world is backward, and all the people live in huts".* Right!

Not only did the ruling party in the Palestinian territories not win, but, the Hamas faction had scored a landslide victory that, perhaps, even took them, by surprise. Experts had been wondering, if we were beginning to witness, the consequences, of flawed, US policies, towards the Middle East, and the rest of the world. President Carter confirmed that the elections had been fair, and democratic, and the people had expressed their feelings at the polls. Bush, on the other hand, was already announcing that they would not deal with Hamas, 'a terrorist organization'; and he was also suggesting that aid funds, to the Palestinians, would be cut; and Washington pundits were trying to rally support for their policies. *We had more of the same, actions of confrontation, and threats.* After the numerous reports, on the suffering of the Palestinian people, how can politicians, how can anyone, be amazed at the results? Most thinkers had not been surprised at the Hamas election victory.

In the typical, pathetic, performance, on international policies, this US administration, and Israel, were quickly seeking support from western governments, not to recognize Hamas, unless they made concessions. No talk of dialogue, with each side conceding something! There is no question that Hamas leaders should renounce their calls for the destruction of Israel, and offer to live in peace with their neighbors. But western countries, led by the US, had again demonstrated to all nations that, yes, democracy, and free elections, are urged for all citizens everywhere, *but only if the results go the way we want them to go- - -! Otherwise, we do not recognize those elections, amazing, or what?*

On this background, we cannot forget the events that had befallen the Israeli leader, Sharon, who had remained critically ill, in a coma. There are no longer frequent reports, about 'his medically induced coma'. It has become obvious that Sharon's strokes were much more critical, than Israeli officials first reported. Although it was going nowhere, fast, at least, Sharon had started dialogue with the Palestinians. Bush, rightly, admitted that, if you give people a chance to express themselves democratically, they will tell you, how they feel. The Palestinian people had high rates of unemployment, budget deficits, so that, the salaries of government employees could not be paid; garbage can be seen everywhere, in the streets, for lack of sanitation programs; and they continue to live under a military occupation; and on top of that, Israel withheld taxes that they keep from Arab employees, that should be paid to the Palestinian authority. These are only some, of the American, and Israeli, policies that spell, failure.

The lesson from this was that, our amazing, Washington officials, had expressed surprise at those election results; but many of us were not in the least, surprised, why? Because we try to understand the feelings of the masses, and they reveal them, when they are free to express their views. We also understand how the poor, truly, feel, about those who try to help them, in their desperate needs; and about those, who only 'pretend' to help them, through ulterior motives.

A report in January showed that the US military in Iraq, had, on occasion, jailed wives of suspected terrorists, to force those terrorists to surrender. American officials have denied it. But, if it has been carried out, it is, as terrible an act, as those tyrants, we had accused of using innocent people, as human shields. How many times had we leveled, such accusations? There were also reports from the EU about their investigations into America's *rendition program. They concluded that American officials had transferred over 100 detainees to other countries, where torture was likely to be used!* And the European Union itself, was staggering under accusations, that, they probably knew about the illegal transport of those prisoners, 'for interrogation and torture', in other countries. Critics in Europe *accused the US of 'gangster tactics'! Was the EU, in collusion- - -?*

At the end of January, CNN also featured a story about a British woman, whose son went to war in Iraq, and was killed within three weeks. She was expressing anger, and rallying support all across Britain, where anti-Bush, and anti-Blair, sentiments were rapidly escalating. The British were calling *those 'leaders', criminals, and the Iraq war, 'illegal'. That, too, we had heard before.*

A writer to National Geographic, magazine, commented on the continent of Africa, and one might add, it could apply to many parts of the world, today. He said that most of their problems had been related to- -colonialism, communism, capitalism, socialism, tribalism, paganism, and nepotism, "all the -isms". Perhaps that was a little simplistic, but then came the punch line, *"some had been imported, others, were home grown. They gave rise to violence, corruption, and incompetence". Right!* In 'America', magazine, there were comments on statements by Canadian Catholic bishops, on the attitudes of the US, and

Canadian, governments, towards racial profiling, especially as it pertains to Arabs, and Muslims. Regrettably, such profiling seems to be getting worse, in many countries. Archbishop Ebacher, of Gatineau, Quebec, was urging Canadians to combat their prejudices. Then, he had this to say, *"It is a fundamental inversion of values, when laws, and politics, place national interests before human dignity"*. Such a pronouncement applies equally well to the Bush administration, and to the Blair regime, as they have found it so easy to pontificate on values, especially here, in the US. It also applies to all governments, if we wish to stay focused on *what is right, and what is wrong, and live by those principles!*

On the same train of thought, on values, professor J.F.Kavanagh, wrote in 'America' magazine, on torture, *"Is there any evil you would not do, in the name of defeating evil"*? *A powerful question*- - that topic should be a required study for all government officials, particularly in western countries, simply because, we claim to be above all others, *to be more civilized.* When we do that, we are held to, much higher standards, right? But, truthfully, it should be debated, and meditated upon, by all people, everywhere. Kavanagh quoted attorney A. Dershowitz (with a certain reputation, in the field of law), who seemed to excuse 'authorized torture' under highly controlled conditions- -for example, the case of a captured terrorist who knows of a hidden bomb, or an impending attack; in other words, to save lives. Most thinkers are likely to disagree with Dershowitz, that he was terribly wrong, in that belief. Unfortunately, this article also stated, that a small majority of Americans believed that, *'rendition' of captives to countries with a shady reputation, was acceptable. But, allegedly, the vast majority of Americans did not believe Bush when he said that, the US government did not use torture!*

Kavanagh concluded thus, "- - is there any evil we would not do, to be victorious over evil"? But then comes a most important caveat, *"If we cannot think of one we have paid a terrible price for our victory. **The evil ones will have succeeded in conquering, not our lands, but our souls"**!* These are indeed powerful, philosophical, thoughts, but in our present state of mind, of excusing preemptive wars; excusing the killing of innocents, 'because it happens in war'; excusing the abuse, or torture, of prisoners, and it was only perpetrated by, a few low level rascals; excusing 'rendition'; excusing so many other despicable acts, by people who should know better- - -yes, with such a state of mind, we must focus, and debate, such thoughts, such actions, otherwise, *we have truly lost our souls.*

On peace, Dr. Vinod D. Deshmukh, wrote a remarkable poem in his book, "A Poet's Vision". He suggested how a peaceful life was possible, not only that, but, *it was urgently needed in this confused, fearful, greedy, and violent, world!* That is a most appropriate description, of the state of our present world. The author then urged that, each one of us should consider the choices we make, because we can make a difference, *"by making peace with our own body, mind, self, and nature"*.

Patriarch Michel Sabbah, of Jerusalem, was also quoted, in 'America' magazine, when he stated that, *demolition, death, and fighting, would never produce anything, but more of the same.* Would our leaders, and most world leaders, understand that? He added, *"when injustice, the cause of violence, ceases, violence will stop, and security will reign"!* That is simple enough, but, once again, will those same leaders, understand, that? Although he was referring to the turmoil in the Middle East, such an assertion would apply, equally well, to all regions on earth, where conditions of turmoil, and deprivation, persist, for tens of millions of people.

Yes, if we wish to foster Justice, and Peace, on planet earth, there are many ideas, and suggestions, presented, in these pages. Are we good enough to do something about it? Can we muster enough courage, to get politicians, everywhere, to change course, before it is much too late? *These thoughts have come from experts, and thinkers, but also, from ordinary, men, and women, in all walks of life, just like you, and, you- - - -!*

Addendum- - -1

On a recent visit to Europe we had the opportunity to reassess some of the topics discussed in this book. Therefore, we will, once again, also touch upon, briefly, some of the countries already mentioned in these pages.

On the question of homeland security (or insecurity- - -?), we noted that at a London airport you did not face as big a hassle as at some US airports, where some Europeans, and others, had felt that, they were humiliated, at the hands of the Americans. In London, you did not get to remove your shoe, but you did remove your jacket or coat; and if the security alarm was triggered, you were subjected to frisking procedures there as well. A certain character was interested in the contents of one's pockets! He felt the need to poke his nose into credit cards, travelers' checks, cash, and so on! *How many dangerous devices could there be on such items?* Unbelievably, at some US airports you were forced to pick up your luggage, go through a form of screening, then hand in your luggage for security, all over again; and then you picked up your luggage again, at 'baggage arrivals'! How many visitors need such a hassle after a particularly strenuous trip?

Considering that both in the US, and UK, authorities had been harping on airline security, something amazing was noted on a British flight. Certain drinks, including some alcoholic beverage, were complimentary. In that context we must remember past comments about the Brits being excessive drinkers, when the laws were changed to allow pubs in the UK, to stay open late into the night. Well, half way across the trip on this flight, a stewardess announced that they had already run out of beer, but other beverage was still available! The laughter and loud voices, were, in direct proportion, to the amount of booze consumed- - -! The British people need to challenge the Blair regime, to see if the above is a good way to maintain security in the air.

In May 2006, news reports on the Internet, suggested that a Washington think-tank, spearheaded by business leaders, was searching for answers on how to stem the alarming rise of anti-Americanism around the world, as most of that rise had reportedly, occurred under this Bush administration watch, in the US. In this book, and a previous one (Mirror Reflections- Mirages), this author presented many possible causes for such anti-American sentiments, and proposed a number of solutions.

Early in May, regional elections were held in parts of Britain, and news headlines screamed of the possibility that *Blair would be defeated again at the polls.* Sure enough, Blair's labor party lost well over 200 seats in those elections, and members of his party were proclaiming that *Blair should announce a date for his departure "sooner, rather than, later"!* That, right there, said a great deal about Blair, as some headlines referred to 'Butcher Blair', just as some Europeans had previously referred to 'Butchers Blair, and Bush'. Other commentators alleged that Blair, like Bush, would steadfastly resist being pushed aside. Soon after all this he was seen on a BBC program, looking quite awful.

In the UK there were also signs that the economy was not doing well, and problems with health care, and education, had persisted. There were elements of racial discrimination, and people felt that Blair had trashed their civil rights, and freedoms. There were increasing reports of scandals within his cabinet, as well. Thus, after another defeat at the polls, the prime minister, like Bush in the US, went on another reshuffling game, in an attempt to save his own skin.

The status of the European Union as a whole remained shaky, as a larger percentage of Europeans had concluded that, membership in such a union, would not necessarily enhance the living standards of their people. In France, massive protests occurred over new labor laws, which forced some changes, but the political situation remained uncertain. In Italy, Berlusconi, who had allied himself with Bush, on Iraq, was defeated at elections held there, in April. He, too, tried to claim fraud at the polls, but the courts soon ruled against him, and he was forced to resign. He had been a controversial figure all along, and the majority of Italians opposed him when he sided with Bush on the Iraq war. However, news media claimed that he, and other politicians, managed to attend funerals of Italians, who had been killed in Iraq, or Afghanistan; and why was it that Blair, and Bush, did not have the courage to do the same for their own soldiers, who likewise, had lost their lives in those wars?

What about tiny Malta? Reports continued to show some political uncertainty there as well, and the population allegiance was fairly equally divided amongst the two major parties, labor, and nationalist. Economy problems had persisted, with a high cost of living, and scarcity of good paying jobs. Their health care system was uneven, and perhaps had become somewhat erratic. A much, needed, new hospital, had been in the construction phase for many years with cost overruns, and no certain date for opening. Over-development of limited land space had persisted, without responsible government controls. Many of their cities, and towns, now simply merged one, right into the other, without any 'open' country in between! And there were ongoing debates as to whether membership in the EU would indeed, produce any benefits there, as well.

In the US, as in UK, it was suggested that Bush planned to re-shuffle members in his government, in an effort to stop the precipitous slide at the polls, for the Bush regime. Their fortunes had certainly been reversed over a period of many months. Scandals continued to plague his administration, and a guest on 'Hardball', with Chris Matthews, on MSNBC television, concluded that Washington, under this administration, was setting a record for government scandals! Most experts around the world, except the Bush clique, continued to state that the US misadventure in Iraq was a disaster; and the Internet was besieged with comments on that point. Afghanistan was not much better, as troubling reports of violence from that region, had increased. Had much, changed, in America, since material for this book was gathered, about 14 months ago? Not much, judging by numerous worldwide reports. Not much had changed in the rest of the world either, as evidenced by continued, adverse reports, from the Middle East, Nepal, Pakistan, India, North Korea, Iran, Somalia, many parts of Africa, and much more.

A '60 Minutes' television program, on CBS, dealt with alleged corruption in the student loan system in the United states; and this was costing taxpayers millions of dollars, with substantial amounts going to company executives, it was reported. On the other hand, many students had accumulated large debts, and many of them were forced to default on those loans, often, because of unforeseen emergencies, which loan companies refused to take into consideration! Does all this sound like a country whose economy has heated up, and is doing very well? Why has the dollar continued to do so poorly, against some major currencies?

Also, in the US, there was much talk of numerous military, and so-called, security agencies, so that some pointed to the attacks of 9/11, and the ravages of 'Katrina', as colossal failures of those agencies, within the US government! In May 2006, there was intense furor over the Bush administration having secret pacts with US companies to collect data of phone and email records, on tens of millions of Americans, for the government; in short, a fishing expedition of spying, by the Bush administration, which, of course, they denied. New calls for an impartial investigation were made! This information had been leaked in the past, but it is a disgrace that a republican controlled congress, in the US, has permitted such destruction of the rights, and liberties, of the people! *Thus, when the Bush clique talks of the NSA agency, are they referring to a national security agency, or, more likely, **a national spying agency (NSA)?***

Once again people worldwide, witnessed a republican controlled, dictatorial, congress, in America, as they steamrolled another tax cut bill, giving a break to the wealthiest Americans, in May 2006. Tax breaks on dividends and capital gains- - *and these characters pontificate that they did it for all Americans! Do they really believe that the poor, and most of the middle class, can afford anything that produces dividends, and capital gains? Who are they kidding?* Do these government officials, mostly republican, live on planet earth, or are they on a distant planet, out there? It was immediately reported that with such a republican bill, the wealthy could save $42,000 per year, compared to $45 for the poorer segment of our community! *Amazing, only in America- - -!* Thus, we perpetuate the scourge of the rich, getting much richer, as the poor and lower middle class, get much poorer. On the economic front, America had lost stature as it continued to be a debtor nation, whereas India, and China, had continued to gain stature!

Polls in the US continued to show abysmal, low, approval ratings, for both Cheney and Bush; and there were discussions as to whether they could ever bounce back; or whether Cheney's worldwide unpopularity had dragged Bush, down, as well. There were also talks of candidates for the November elections raising, once again, huge amounts of money- - - more proof of money controlling politics in America; Mammon, always ruling over the United States.

Reporters had targeted Cheney, as he launched more criticism of Putin, and Russia, "on democracy". Putin had criticisms of his own, about the US; and Gorbachev, reportedly, called Cheney's remarks, 'interference in Russia's internal affairs'. How can the US, in 2006, criticize other sovereign nations, after the accusations leveled against it, around the world, over a number of years? Then, there was the highest legal figure in UK, who, in May 2006, suggested that Guantanamo (Cuba), had become a symbol of gross injustice, and more, for the United States; that the prison should be closed! Allegedly, about the same time, the International Red Cross *had issued another scathing criticism of the US government, on the handling of detainees!*

In upheavals of old Europe, the Church and the Papacy, were at times, at odds with corrupt politics of monarchs. The relationship between Church and Royal Courts was often one of tolerance, and rapprochement. A sad example was the greed of colonial powers from Europe, vying for tyrannical control of lands, and their booty, in South America, where, indigenous people, were often, treated savagely, even by those who professed to be Christian. Apparently Church authorities could not favorably influence those colonial rulers, at times. There again, members of the Jesuit Society appeared at odds, as they often worked with the native people to improve their lives, and show them the path to God. Thus some of the European Courts criticized the Jesuit fathers, and for a time, their priests were not welcome in parts of Europe. Has history changed so little?

Because of election politics in America, the question of 'legal', or 'illegal', immigrants, had surfaced with a vengeance; and in April/May 2006, there were massive protests in many cities across the country. Illegal immigration from parts of Africa had also impacted Europe; and the problems there escalated even more, whether these people were legal, or illegal, because of serious failure by the communities to help the newcomers 'assimilate'. For tiny Malta, as well, the problem of illegal immigrants from Africa, had fomented, and had become a cause for racial prejudice. Historically, the Jesuit Fathers, wherever they were, had always championed the cause for justice, for peace, and for the poor. Thus, in Malta, Jesuit priests were giving talks, to encourage charity, tolerance, and acceptance. Within a short time of such talks, several cars belonging to the Jesuit Fathers were torched! For these "Christian" islands these were tragic events, indeed.

US politicians attempted to force the UN security, council, to vote sanctions on Iran. However, Russia, and China, allegedly, resisted such plans by the Bush administration. The Russian representative had an interesting comment, saying that, *they talk of carrots, and sticks; but, as we all know, a large carrot can become a stick.* The rhetoric between the Bush administration, and the Iranian regime had escalated; but in early 2006, on the Internet, polls showed that the majority of Americans (at least those with common sense) stated that Iran had a right to pursue its own peaceful, nuclear, technology, why not? America, Russia, China, Israel, UK, and others, had pursued their own, all along, not only for peaceful purposes, but also for war! US politicians had not threatened sanctions, or bombing, against any of those countries.

On the Olbermann program, on MSNBC television, a critic suggested that, on the scandal of spying on US citizens, the Bush administration had seemingly broken the law. Yet, he said, during the state of the union speech, 'lawmakers' gave Bush a standing ovation, when he stated that he would continue the spying program "to protect the nation". He added that, during this Bush presidency, people who had pushed the line to the edge of the legal limit, *or beyond it, to achieve something the president believed in, seemed to rapidly advance their careers- - -something, he said, so bizarre, that he had not seen in his legal career!* They also showed that in Washington politics, everyone seemed to get a medal, or a pat on the back, no matter how good, or how terrible, the job performed. *How about that, for a true, and tested, democracy, US style? And, in how many other countries, is the same encountered?*

On Iraq, in the spring of 2006, many politicians, and journalists, were stating, loud, and clear, that it was a mistake, for America, to go to war in Iraq; better late, than never, what? Then, they add, 'but here we are, we must move forward'. What these characters do not tell the American people, and the people of the world, is, why many heads had not rolled, because a country was taken into such a war, the manner it was accomplished; and causing the deaths of well over 2400, US armed forces personnel, and many, many, others, including tens of thousands of innocent civilians. There were additional reports in 2006, *that the Bush administration allegedly had good intelligence that Iraq did not possess weapons of mass destruction, long before America launched its attack- - -! My, my, what a world we find ourselves in!*

Indeed, not only for Iraq, or Afghanistan, or the US, or UK, many difficulties continued to face mankind, in many areas on planet Earth. Some thinkers had wondered, perhaps not loudly enough, if most of the problems faced by so many developing countries, were not *direct consequences of misguided, corrupt, policies, of past imperial powers from Europe, and elsewhere, and now, from the United states.*

In Nepal, there were more violent demonstrations against a monarchy perceived as corrupt, by the people. Parliament, there, had been dissolved, and harsh military tactics had been employed. However, in 2006, the monarch had been forced to relent somewhat, as pictures of violence were splashed all over the world. In the Sudan, the crisis between the North, and the South, had persisted; and in particular, the tragedy of Darfur. Both the United States, and the United Nations had been involved, and Christian leaders, and others, as attempts at a negotiated peace of sorts, had been rekindled. In the Western Sahara, as well, large numbers of refugees had been leading lives of misery, feeling victimized by the monarchy in Morocco. This is one of the countries with which the US had maintained 'friendly relations'; and where, reportedly, unfortunate victims of US rendition practices, had been sent for harsh interrogation methods. On the illegal immigration of Africans, Morocco had been perceived as doing the dirty work for Europe! In Somalia, violence had again intensified between Islamic groups, and warlords. In typical opportunistic fashion, the US government had reportedly been supporting those warlords!

In the Middle East, the crisis between the Israelis, and Palestinians, had continued; and in May, the US government announced a grant of 10 million dollars for the Palestinian people, in their desperate need. It did not appear to amount to much considering their plight. Some church members who, seemingly, rarely issue political comments, in the US, stated that Bethlehem had been encircled by the Israelis, causing untold hardships for the people, for commerce, for the exercise of their daily needs, simply to survive.

On the Pope, and the Church, the popularity of, and love for, John Paul II, had not decreased any, since his death about a year earlier; and many continued to push for his beatification as soon as feasible. Pope Benedict XVI had surprised critics by not assuming an ultra rigid, conservative, role, as some had predicted. In the spring of 2006, news reports suggested that the Catholic Church might relax the laws on contraception (the use of condoms), in special situations, such as the widespread epidemic of AIDS in some of the poorest countries of Africa. Many had been calling for changes in the church, it remained to be seen, how changes might be brought about, if at all.

The pedophile accusations against some of the priesthood continued to generate some headlines, in spite of the fact that there were many more crises facing our entire world, day, by day. In the US a number of parochial schools had been closed because of attendance, and perhaps also, some financial constraints, as more families sent children to public schools because of the economy. It had been another difficult period for the Catholic Church, especially in America, but elsewhere as well. Vocations to the priesthood, and religious life, remained very low, in the US, and the rest of the western nations. To many, this suggested a direct impact of materialism, on western society, particularly, as vocations in poorer, so-called, third world countries, had increased. In other sections of the book, we have referred to the effects of materialism, of Mammon, on society as a whole; its influence on our social values.

On the question of faith, and religion, it had been reported that Jacob Lorber (1800-1864), had received a calling as 'God's scribe'; and that he had listened to that calling till the end of his life. During 24 years he completed some 24 volumes, the result of his "Divine inspiration", amongst these, the "Great Gospel of John", dealing with the values of the Christian faith. Some notations from that book are presented herein, as they are so appropriate to our day, to day, lives; and to the discussions outlined in these chapters. On judging, and condemning, it has been written that, *"For, with whatever measure a person metes, with the same measure he will be rewarded in the other world"*. *"The bailiffs, and executioners, however, shall never see the countenance of God"*. Then, there was this, *"Justice that does not have its roots in love, is no justice, in the eyes of God"*. How relevant is any of that, to all the factions, no matter which religion they profess, who are involved in so many conflicts in our world of today- - - to Iraq, to the Middle East, the Sudan, and many other places; to the plight of the poor; to the reports of abuse, and torture, of detainees; to those who occupy our prisons; to the millions of people who feel marginalized, and abandoned; to so much injustice in our world? ***Should we consider all that, and much more, in relation to the above quotations?***

Then, we had this "- - -that, in whatever day you performed a good deed, that will be the right Sabbath, in the eyes of the Lord", an important reference to those, who, in the old days "wanted to erect so-called houses of God"; that "they should build hospitals, and homes to care for their poor brothers"! Yes, these were written hundreds of years ago, when society was indeed, extremely corrupt, and violent. *But, have we as a people, shed much of that stigma, or are we still at it, under different guises, of one form, or another -?*

On arrogance, it was stated that, some of the Pharisees of those days, claimed that they did not have to pay compensation for damage to forests, because the earth belonged to them 'to do with as they pleased'! Is it not amazing how, after so many hundreds of years, mankind still exhibits some of the same arrogance? There was another reference, this time, to materialism, *"But the time is not distant, when the gold, silver, and brass, will be governing people, and determining their value, before the world. And that will be a bad time; the light of faith will go out; and neighborly love will be as hard, and as cold, as ore"!* **Are such references not a good reflection of what still goes on, in too many countries, indeed, on planet earth?**

On other encounters with the Pharisees, we had this, "A man is not defiled by what goes into his mouth, but by what comes out of it"; and on the building of temples, the Lord had pointed out how the one in Jerusalem would be devastated, and heathenish temples would vanish. But, "instead of a few temples, many more would follow, because man would continue to build them, large, or small, to seek salvation within them; *but only few would be attempting to build God a living temple in their hearts"*. Then we were also reminded that, "If you praise someone, praise someone who has truly deserved praise". These writings also pointed out how the Lord always seeks the lowest, and most oppressed; *but all that is great, and highly respected, by the world, is an abomination in the eyes of God!*

Do most of us appear to act in contradiction to many of these precepts? *There, is some food for thought!* There remains a widening gap between the 'haves', and the 'have not', that must be resolved. Yet, there is great hope, and we must persevere. Throughout these pages certain topics have been repeated to some degree, both because of different news sources; **but also in the hope that, they will impress readers, and thus, foster within all of us, the will to change direction in our behavior patterns.**

There is little doubt that the teachings in the Good Book, often urge us that, when we are ready to criticize, condemn, and attack, others, we should be quick to scrutinize our own 'Mirror reflections'- - -yes, to attempt to constantly show love, and charity for others, *as Mother Theresa of Calcutta, and Pope John Paul II, often reminded us; and from these, would flow, quite readily, peace and justice for all, and solutions to many of the difficulties, besetting Planet Earth- - - - -!*

www.ingramcontent.com/pod-product-compliance
Lightning Source LLC
Chambersburg PA
CBHW080407290526
45791CB00008BA/2185